FOURTH EDITION

# The Curious Researcher

## A Guide to Writing Research Papers

**Bruce Ballenger**

*Boise State University*

D0124750

PEARSON

Longman

New York   San Francisco   Boston
London   Toronto   Sydney   Tokyo   Singapore   Madrid
Mexico City   Munich   Paris   Cape Town   Hong Kong   Montreal

*For Rebecca,*
*who reminds me to ask,*
Why?

---

*Senior Vice President and Publisher:* Joseph Opiela
*Executive Marketing Manager:* Ann Stypuloski
*Senior Supplements Editor:* Donna Campion
*Media Supplements Editor:* Nancy Garcia
*Senior Production Manager:* Valerie Zaborski
*Project Coordination, Text Design, and Electronic Page Makeup:* Elm Street Publishing Services
*Cover Design Manager:* Wendy Ann Fredericks
*Cover Designer:* Kay Petronio
*Cover Illustration:* ©Stanley Martucci/SIS, Inc.
*Manufacturing Buyer:* Al Dorsey
*Printer and Binder:* Courier Corporation-Westford
*Cover Printer:* Coral Graphic Services, Inc.

**Library of Congress Cataloging-in-Publication Data**
Ballenger, Bruce P.
    The curious researcher : a guide to writing research papers /
    Bruce Ballenger. — 4th ed.
        p.   cm.
    Includes index.
    ISBN 0-321-17521-2
        1. Report writing—Handbooks, manuals, etc.   2. Research—Handbooks,
    manuals, etc.   I. Title.
    LB2369.B246 2004
    808'.02—dc21                                                     2002043480

Please visit our website at http://www.ablongman.com/ballenger

ISBN 0-321-17521-2

    3  4  5  6  7  8  9  10—CRW—06  05  04

# Contents

# Chapter 1
# The First Week    25

## Chapter 2
## The Second Week 63

## Chapter 4
## The Fourth Week    173

## Chapter 5
## The Fifth Week        221

# Appendix B
# Guide to APA Style    313

# Appendix C
# Tips for Researching and Writing Papers on Literary Topics    353

# Index    369

# Contents by Subject

# Preface

## Placing Inquiry at the Heart of the Course

Several years ago, the Boyer Commission offered a national report on the state of undergraduate education in America's research universities. The report was sobering. Among other things, the commission complained that undergraduates, particularly first- and second-year students, experience a curriculum dominated by knowledge transmission—large lectures rather than seminars—and rarely get the chance to "enter a world of discovery in which they are active participants, not passive receivers." Commissioner members called for a "radical reconstruction" of undergraduate education. "The ecology of the university," they wrote, "depends on a deep and abiding understanding that inquiry, investigation, and discovery are the heart of the enterprise. . . . Everyone at a university should be a discoverer, a learner." The freshman year, in particular, should provide "new stimulation for intellectual growth and a firm grounding in inquiry-based learning."

*The Curious Researcher* answers that call. It is a sad fact that most students misunderstand formal academic research. Because it often reports conclusions—the *results* of the process of inquiry—students naturally assume that the research writer didn't engage in an act of inquiry in the first place. They assume that the academic writer always sets out *to prove* rather than *to find out,* that she scrupulously avoids ambiguity and is more concerned with answers than questions. The conventional research paper in the composition course—often students' first introduction to academic research—reinforces all of these mistaken assumptions about the nature of inquiry.

## Teaching the Spirit of Inquiry

While *The Curious Researcher* features plenty of material on the conventions of research writing—citation methods, approaches to organization, evaluating sources, how to avoid plagiarism, and so on—a major emphasis of the book is introducing students to *the spirit of inquiry.* The habits of mind that good research writers develop is something we can teach that is truly multidisciplinary. That spirit is charged with curiosity, of course—the itch to know and learn and discover. But it also involves the ability to ask researchable questions, the instinct to look in the right places for answers, a willingness to suspend judgment, and an openness to changing one's mind. Embracing the spirit of inquiry must begin with the belief that one *can* be an inquirer, a knower, an active agent in making knowledge.

I think this affective dimension of critical thinking is underrated, especially when it comes to writing research papers. That's why this book promotes the research *essay,* a potentially more subjective, less formal, often more exploratory mode than the formal argumentative research paper. The research essay is, I think, a much better *introduction* to research and research writing and excellent preparation for more conventional academic research because it places the writer in the center of the discourse. As a result, he cannot avoid his role as the main agent of the inquiry nor can he escape the question of his own authority in the conversation about what might be true. When it's a good experience, the writer of the research essay often adopts a new identity as a *knower.*

I am often amazed at what students do with this new freedom. I believe little is lost in not prescribing a formal research paper, particularly in an introductory composition course. As students move on from here to their declared majors, they will learn the scholarly conventions of their disciplines from those best equipped to teach them. In the meantime, students will master valuable library skills and learn many of the technical elements of the research paper, such as citation methods and evaluating sources. But most important, students will discover, often for the first time, what college research is really about: *using the ideas of others to shape ideas of their own.*

# Ways of Using This Book

Since procrastination ails many student researchers, this book is uniquely designed to move them through the research process, step-by-step and week-by-week, for five weeks, the typical period allotted for the assignment. The structure of the book is flexible, however; students should be encouraged to compress the sequence if their research assignment will take less time or ignore it altogether and use the book to help them solve specific problems as they arise. A "Contents by Subject" makes using the book as a reference much easier.

If you do encourage your students to follow the five-week sequence, I think you'll find that they'll like the way *The Curious Researcher* doesn't deluge them with information, as do so many other research paper texts, but doles it out, week-by-week, when the information is most needed.

The Introduction, "Rethinking the Research Paper," challenges students to reconceive the research paper assignment. For many of them, this will amount to a "declaration of independence." During "The First Week," students are encouraged to discover topics they're genuinely curious about and to learn to develop a "working knowledge" of their topics through library and Web research. This working will guide them as they decide on a tentative focus for their investigations. In "The Second Week," students develop and research strategy, hone their skills in evaluating sources, and then begin working to develop a "deep knowledge" of their topics by systematically searching for information in the library and on the Web. In "The Third Week," students learn notetaking techniques, the dangers of plagiarism, and tips on how to conduct a search that challenges them to dig more deeply for information. During "The Fourth Week," students begin writing their drafts; this chapter also gives tips on integrating sources, structure, voice, and beginnings. In "The Fifth Week," students are guided through the final revision.

In this edition of *The Curious Researcher,* the details about citation conventions and formats for both the Modern Language Association (MLA) and the American Psychological Association (APA) are in Appendixes A and B, respectively. This organization makes the information easier for students to find and use. Sample papers—one on some men's obsession with building muscle (in MLA format) and the other on racism in America (in APA format)—are included as well. I like these student essays not simply because they are effectively written. They also offer an interesting contrast between two approaches: One is more "essayistic" and openly subjective, and the other is a more conventional argumentative paper. While the author of the latter paper never uses the first-person singular or autobiographical anecdotes, she still registers a strong writerly presence. In this new edition, I hope to expand the notion of what it means *to get personal* in research writing.

Unlike other textbooks, which relegate exercises to the ends of chapters, *The Curious Researcher* makes them integral to the process of researching and writing the paper. Though techniques such as fastwriting and brainstorming—featured in some of the writing exercises—are now commonplace in many composition classes, they have rarely been applied to research writing and certainly not as extensively as they have been here. Fastwriting is an especially useful tool, not just for prewriting but for open-ended thinking throughout the process of researching and writing the paper. The exercises are also another antidote to procrastination, challenging students to stay involved in the process as well as providing instructors with a number of short assignments throughout the five weeks that will help them monitor students' progress.

## Features of the New Edition

Writing a textbook is like discovering an aunt you never knew you had. She arrives unexpectedly one summer and stands at your door beaming and expectant. Naturally, you welcome her in. How charming she is, and as you get to know your aunt you get to know yourself. This is her gift to you. At some point, many months later, you see her luggage by the door, and with a certain sadness you send her off. "Come again," you yell as she ambles off. "Come again anytime. I'll miss you!" And you do. Your fondness for this newly discovered relative grows as you learn that others, people who aren't even blood related, like her too.

Two years later, your aunt appears at your door again, and of course you're glad to see her. She inhabits your house for the summer, and, while she does get a bit demanding, that doesn't diminish your fondness for the old girl, at least not much. You've grown to know her well, and while familiarity doesn't breed contempt you do develop a slight weariness. You've heard all the same stories a few times, and her voice, well, her voice can get a bit irritating at times. This time when she leaves you confess that you're just a little bit relieved, happy to move on to other things.

But, bless her heart, your aunt has got something of a following and this has given her a new lease on life. It also seems she got a lease on *your* life, and once more she appears one summer day at the door expecting to stay until September or October. You do love her, but you wish she wouldn't visit so often, and though her stay is often pleasant, you feel compelled to remind her that she's getting older and maybe a bit out of fashion. You do what you can to remake her into someone you don't mind spending the summer with.

This is *The Curious Researcher's* fourth visit, and I do remain very fond of the old girl. I'm proud of her. But this visit has been a particularly rough one because I've had so many ideas about how to make the book better, a number of them suggested by reviewers, friends, and instructors who have used the book. The result is that

I've been a bit brutal to portions of the book, moving some sections, consolidating others, adding new material, and, of course, hacking away at the old. Several new concepts inform this edition:

■ I've paid too little attention to how researchers *read* source materials, and in this edition of *The Curious Researcher* I've included new exercises and other content that look at that process.

■ I've also introduced a new way of thinking about researching *strategically*. Borrowing from William Badke, I suggest that students develop competency to write about their topics by first developing "working knowledge," and later, "deep knowledge." Each of these involves using different kinds of references and searching techniques on the Web and in the library.

■ Along with developing working and deep knowledge, I've re-organized the old library and Web exercises under each of those categories. It's my sense that this makes the introductions to key references more useful and feels less like "busy work."

■ At the suggestion of reviewers, I've consolidated interview and survey techniques into a single chapter (Chapter 2) and expanded treatment of APA and MLA citation conventions.

■ I've expanded discussion of notetaking strategies beyond the double-entry journal technique in an effort to encourage "writing in the middle" but also to accommodate a wider range of personal preferences among student writers.

■ Plagiarism is a growing concern now that the Web figures as a source of information in most student papers. I've added new discussions and exercises concerning this important topic that should help students understand the problem and avoid it.

After this summer's visit, I send *The Curious Researcher* off to other destinations, confident that she'll be recognized and, with these changes, a better companion to students and instructors who have graciously adopted her. As always, let me know what you think.

# Acknowledgments

Teaching writing is often a deeply personal experience. Because students often write from their hearts as well as their minds, I've been privileged to read work that genuinely matters to them. More often than they realize, students teach the teacher, and they have especially tutored me in how to rethink the research paper.

Because students move so quickly in and out of my life, I rarely get the chance to acknowledge their lessons. I'd like to take that opportunity now. Jayne Wynters was a student of mine more than a decade ago, and she deserves much credit for challenging my ideas about the college research paper, which led to *The Curious Researcher.* Other students who either contributed directly to this text or helped me conceive it include Kim Armstrong, Christine Bergquist, Daniel Jaffurs, Heather Dunham, Candace Collins, Jason Pulsifer, Jennifer White, Karoline Ann Fox, Kazuko Kuramoto, André Sears, Christina Kerby, and Carolyn Nelson.

Many of my former colleagues at the University of New Hampshire were instrumental in the genesis of this book. I am especially grateful to three of them. Thomas Newkirk has been my mentor for some years now, and it was his belief that I had something useful to say about the freshman research paper that inspired me to write this text. Robert Connors was not only a preeminent composition scholar but a friend, and his early encouragement and advice were also extremely valuable. I know I'm not alone in feeling the field is not the same without him. And Donald Murray, my first writing teacher, continues to cast his long and welcome shadow on everything I do as a writer and teacher.

I have known Barry Lane for many years. He is a wonderful friend, writer, and teacher. In many ways, Barry is a co-author of everything I do. His praise of this book means a great deal to me, and our conversations about it continue to make it better. I look forward to more books, and more conversations about them, with this good friend.

I'm deeply indebted to my colleagues and students at Boise State, people who share their enthusiasm for this book, help me find time to revise it, and give me advice about how to make it better. Two students, in particular, made a significant contribution by allowing me to publish their essays in the fourth edition—Alex Siegwin and T. J. Fuller. I'm also grateful for Devan Cook's encouragement, a colleague who never hesitates to regale me with success stories about her students' experiences with *The Curious Researcher.* The failures she graciously keeps to herself.

Brock Dethier, now at Utah State University, is my good friend and hiking partner. Our discussions of teaching and writing while trudging up mountains in southern Idaho not only keep my mind off the burning in my legs but always inspire me to imagine new ways to help students learn. Brock and his wife Melody are both teachers who remind me of what's possible in the classroom.

It's impossible to imagine writing this book or any other without the counsel of my dear friend Michelle Payne, with whom I collaborated recently on *The Curious Reader*. She's made my professional and personal life immeasurably better through her thoughtfulness and love. Michelle's ideas about the importance of reading for research, among other things, profoundly influenced how this edition of the book handled that topic.

Other writers and writing teachers who have contributed directly to *The Curious Researcher* or given me valuable ideas include Teresa Dewey, Barbara Tindall, Nora and Tony Nevin, Stephanie Cox, Driek Zirinsky, Ann McNary, Sherry Gropp, Cheryl Johnson, Jane Harrigan, Greg Bowe, Bronwyn Williams, Lad Tobin, Karen Uehling, Patricia Sullivan, and Leaf Seligman.

I am also grateful to my editor at Longman Publishers, Joseph Opiela, who believed in this project from the very beginning, and also to his talented assistant, Julie Hallett.

I would like to thank those individuals who reviewed earlier versions of this book. Reviewers for the first edition included the following: Joseph T. Barwick, Central Piedmont Community College; Arnold J. Bradford, Northern Virginia Community College; Jack Branscomb, East Tennessee State University; Patricia E. Connors, Memphis State University; A. Cheryl Curtis, University of Hartford; John Fugate, J. Sargeant Reynolds Community College; Walter S. Minot, Gannon University; Michele Moragne e Silva, St. Edwards University; Al Starr, Essex Community College; Henrietta S. Twining, Alabama A&M; and Matthew Wilson, Rutgers University. Reviewers for the second edition included these individuals: Anne Maxham-Kastrinos, Washington State University; Martha W. Sipe, Boise State University; Sally Terrell, University of Hartford; and David Wasser, University of Hartford. The following reviewed the third edition: Rachel Edelson, Sacramento City College; Donald Jones, University of Hartford; Michael Morgan, Bemidji State University; Robert Pickford, Washington State University; Michael Robertson, The College of New Jersey; and Deborah Coxwell Teague, Florida State University. For the fourth edition, I extend my thanks to the following reviewers: Greg Bowe, Florida International University; Deborah Coxwell Teague, Florida State University; David Fenimare, University of Nevada, Reno; Michael Gurin, DeVry Institute of Technology (NY); Don Jones, University of Hartford; Michael C. Morgan, Bemidji State University; and Sundy Watanabe, Weber State University.

And finally, I am most indebted to my wife, Karen Kelley, who in the beginning helped me see this project through during a difficult time in our lives.

# The Curious Researcher

# Rethinking the Research Paper

Unlike most textbooks, this one begins with your writing, not mine. Find a fresh page in your notebook, grab a pen, and spend ten minutes doing the following exercise.

## Collecting Golf Balls on Driving Ranges and Other Reflections

Most of us were taught to think before we write, to have it all figured out in our heads before we pick up our pens. This exercise asks you to think *through* writing rather than *before,* letting the words on the page lead you to what you want to say. With practice, that's surprisingly easy using a technique called *fastwriting.* Basically, you just write down whatever comes into your head, not worrying about whether you're being eloquent, grammatical, or even very smart. It's remarkably like talking to a good friend, not trying to be brilliant and even blithering a bit, but along the way discovering what you think. If the writing stalls, write about that, or write about what you've already written until you find a new trail to follow. Just keep your pen moving.

**STEP 1:** Listed below is a series of sixteen statements about the research paper assignment. Check the five statements you think most students believe about the assignment. Then, in a five-minute fastwrite, explore whether *you* agree or disagree with one or more of the five statements you checked. Whenever possible, write about your own experiences (anecdotes, stories, scenes, moments, etc.) with

1

research and research papers as a means of thinking about what you believe to be true.

- It's okay to say things the instructor might disagree with.
- You need to follow a formal structure.
- You have to know your thesis before you start.
- You have to be objective.
- You can't use the pronoun *I*.
- You can use your own experiences and observations as evidence.
- The information should come mostly from books.
- You have to say something original.
- You're always supposed to make an argument.
- You can use your own writing voice.
- Summarizing what's known about the topic is most important.
- You're writing mostly for the instructor.
- You're supposed to use your own opinions.
- The paper won't be revised substantially.
- Form matters more than content.

**STEP 2:** Now, consider the truth of some other statements, listed below. These statements have less to do with research papers than with how you see facts, information, and knowledge and how they're created. Choose one of these statements* to launch a five-minute fastwrite. Don't worry if you end up thinking about more than one statement in your writing. Like before, start by writing about whether you agree or disagree with the statement, and then explore why. Continually look for concrete connections between what you think about these statements and what you've seen or experienced in your own life.

There is a big difference between facts and opinions.

Pretty much everything you read in textbooks is true.

People are entitled to their own opinions, and no one opinion is better than another.

There's a big difference between *a fact* in the sciences and *a fact* in the humanities.

How much I get out of school depends on the quality of my teachers.

When two experts disagree, one of them has to be wrong.

A story that doesn't have an ending isn't a very good story.

*Partial source for this list is Marlene Schommer, "Effects of Beliefs about the Nature of Knowledge," *Journal of Educational Psychology* 82 (1990): 498–504.

No matter how difficult they are, most problems have one solution that is better than the others.

Most words have one clearly defined meaning.

---

Very few of us recall the research papers we wrote in high school, and if we do, what we remember is not what we learned about our topics but what a bad experience writing them was. Joe was an exception. "I remember one assignment was to write a research paper on a problem in the world, such as acid rain, and then come up with your own solutions and discuss moral and ethical aspects of your solution, as well. It involved not just research but creativity and problem solving and other stuff."

For the life of me, I can't recall a single research paper I wrote in high school, but like Joe, I remember the one that I finally enjoyed doing a few years later in college. It was a paper on the whaling industry, and what I remember best was the introduction. I spent a lot of time on it, describing in great detail exactly what it was like to stand at the bow of a Japanese whaler, straddling an explosive harpoon gun, taking aim, and blowing a bloody hole in a humpback whale.

I obviously felt pretty strongly about the topic.

Unfortunately, many students feel most strongly about getting their research papers over with. So it's not surprising that when I tell my Freshman English students that one of their writing assignments will be an eight- to ten-page research paper, there is a collective sigh. They knew it was coming. For years, their high school teachers prepared them for the College Research Paper, and it loomed ahead of them as one of the torturous things you must do, a five-week sentence of hard labor in the library, picking away at cold, stony facts. Not surprisingly, students' eyes roll in disbelief when I add that many of them will end up liking their research papers better than anything they've written before.

I can understand why Joe was among the few in the class inclined to believe me. For many students, the library is an alien place, a wilderness to get lost in, a place to go only when forced. Others carry memories of research paper assignments that mostly involved taking copious notes on index cards, only to transfer pieces of information into the paper, sewn together like patches of a quilt. There seemed little purpose to it. "You weren't expected to learn anything about yourself with the high school research paper," wrote Jenn, now a college freshman. "The best ones seemed to be those with the most information. I always tried to find the most sources, as if somehow that would automatically make my paper better than the rest." For Jenn and others like her, research was a mechanical process and the researcher a lot like those machines that collect golf balls at driving ranges. You venture out to pick up information here and there, and then deposit it between the title page and the bibliography for your teacher to take a whack at.

# Learning and Unlearning

I have been playing the guitar ever since the Beatles' 1964 American tour. In those days, *everyone* had a guitar and played in a group. Unfortunately, I never took guitar lessons and have learned in recent years that I have much "unlearning" to do. Not long ago, I finally unlearned how to do something as simple as tying my strings to the tuning keys. I'd been doing it wrong (thinking I was doing it right) for about forty years.

Recent theories suggest that people who have developed a great deal of prior knowledge about a subject learn more about it when they reexamine the truth of those beliefs, many of which may no longer be valid or may simply be misconceptions. The research paper, perhaps more than any other school assignment, is laden with largely unexamined assumptions and beliefs. Perhaps some of the statements in the first part of Exercise 1 got you thinking about any assumtions you might have about writing academic research papers. Maybe you had a discussion in class about it. You may be interested to know that I presented that same list of statements to 250 first-year writing students, and the statements are listed in the order they were most often checked by students. In that case, however, students checked the statements they *agreed* with. For example, 85 percent of the students surveyed agreed that "it's okay to say things the instructor might disagree with," something I find encouraging. Sixty percent believed that they had to know their thesis before they began their papers. That bothers me.

The second part of Exercise 1 might have got you thinking about some beliefs and attitudes you haven't thought much about— what a "fact" is, the nature and value of "opinions," and how you view experts and authorities.

I hope that these beliefs about the assignment you are about to undertake and your perspectives on how knowledge is made and evaluated are views that you return to again and again as you work through this book. You may find that some of your existing beliefs are further reinforced, but I'd wager that you might find *you* have some unlearning to do, too.

# Using This Book

## The Exercises

Throughout *The Curious Researcher,* you'll be asked to do exercises that either help you prepare your research paper or actually help you write it. You'll need a research notebook in which you'll do the exercises and perhaps compile your notes for the paper. Any notebook will do, as long as there are sufficient pages and left margins. Your instructor may ask you to hand in the work you do in response to the exercises, so it would be useful to use a notebook with detachable pages.

Several of the exercises in this book ask that you use techniques such as fastwriting and brainstorming. This chapter began with one, so you've already had a little practice with the two methods. Both fastwriting and brainstorming ask that you suspend judgment until you see what you come up with. That's pretty hard for most of us because we are so quick to criticize ourselves, particularly about writing. But if you can learn to get comfortable with the sloppiness that comes with writing almost as fast as you think, not bothering about grammar or punctuation, then you will be rewarded with a new way to think, letting your own words lead you in sometimes surprising directions. Though these so-called creative techniques seem to have little to do with the serious business of research writing, they can actually be an enormous help throughout the process. Try to ignore that voice in your head that wants to convince you that you're wasting your time using fastwriting or brainstorming. When you do, they'll start to work for you.

## The Five-Week Plan

But more about creative techniques later. You have a research paper assignment to do. If you're excited about writing a research paper, that's great. You probably already know that it can be interesting work. But if you're dreading the work ahead of you, then your instinct might be to procrastinate, put it off until the week it's due. That would be a mistake, of course. If you try to rush through the research and the writing, you're absolutely guaranteed to hate the experience and add this assignment to the many research papers in the garbage dump of your memory. It's also much more likely that the paper won't be very good. Because procrastination is the enemy, this book was designed to help you budget your time and move through the research and writing process in five weeks. It may take you a little longer, or you may be able to finish your paper a little more quickly. But at least initially, use the book sequentially, unless your instructor gives you other advice.

This book can also be used as a reference to solve problems as they arise. For example, suppose you're having a hard time finding enough information on your topic or you want to know how to plan for an interview. Use the Table of Contents as a key to typical problems and where in the book you can find some practical help with them.

## Alternatives to the Five-Week Plan

Though *The Curious Researcher* is structured by weeks, you can easily ignore that plan and use the book to solve problems as they arise. The Contents by Subject in the front of the text is keyed to a range of typical problems that arise for researchers: how to find a topic, how to focus a paper, how to handle a thesis, how to search the Internet, how to organize the material, how to take useful notes, and so on. The overviews of Modern Language Association (MLA) and American Psychological Association (APA) research paper conventions in Appendixes A and B, respectively, provide complete guides to both formats and make it easier to find answers to your specific technical questions at any point in the process of writing your paper.

# The Research Paper and the Research Report

Anyone who spent a few years in high school clutching index cards and making a beeline for the *Encyclopaedia Britannica, Readers' Guide,* or Internet every time a research paper assignment was given will probably be glad that the college-level research paper will be a different experience. It's a little hard to get excited about paraphrasing an encyclopedia or the December issue of *Time* onto notecards and then inserting that information into the paper. But that's what seemed the logical thing to do when the assignment was to write a paper that reflects what's known about your topic. That's called a *research report,* and it's a fairly common assignment in the first few years of high school.

## Discovering Your Purpose

For the paper you're about to write, the information you collect must be used much more *purposefully* than simply reporting what's known about a particular topic. Most likely, you will define what that purpose is. For example, you may end up writing a paper whose purpose is to argue a point—say, eating meat is morally suspect because of the way stock animals are treated at slaughterhouses. Or your paper's purpose may be to reveal some less-known or surprising aspect of a topic—say, how the common housefly's eating habits are not unlike our own. Or your paper may set out to explore a thesis, or idea, that you have about your topic—for example, your topic is the cultural differences between men and women, and you suspect the way girls and boys play as children reflects the social differences evident between the genders in adults.

Whatever the purpose of your paper turns out to be, the process usually begins with something you've wondered about, some itchy question about an aspect of the world you'd love to know the answer to. It's the writer's curiosity—not the teacher's—that is at the heart of the college research paper.

In some ways, frankly, *research reports* are easier. You just go out and collect as much stuff as you can, write it down, organize it, and write it down again in the paper. Your job is largely mechanical and often deadening. In the *research paper,* you take a much more active role in *shaping and being shaped by* the information you encounter. That's harder because you must evaluate, judge, interpret, and analyze. But it's also much more satisfying because what you end up with says something about who you are and how you see things.

## How Formal Should It Be?

When I got a research paper assignment, it often felt as if I were being asked to change out of blue jeans and a wrinkled Oxford shirt and get into a stiff tuxedo. Tuxedos have their place, such as at the junior prom or the Grammy Awards, but they're just not me. When I first started writing research papers, I used to think that I *had* to be formal, that I needed to use big words like *myriad* and *ameliorate* and to use the pronoun *one* instead of *I.* I thought the paper absolutely needed to have an introduction, body, and conclusion—say what I was going to say, say it, and say what I said. It's no wonder that the first college research paper I had to write—on Plato's *Republic* for a philosophy class—seemed to me as though it were written by someone else. I felt at arm's length from the topic I was writing about.

You may be relieved to know that not all research papers are necessarily rigidly formal or dispassionate. Some are. Research

papers in the sciences, for example, often have very formal struc-
tures, and the writer seems more a reporter of results than someone
who is passionately engaged in making sense of them. This *formal
stance* puts the emphasis where it belongs: on the validity of the data
in proving or disproving something, rather than on the writer's individual way of seeing something. Some papers in the social sciences,
particularly scholarly papers, take a similarly formal stance, where
the writer not only seems invisible but also seems to have little relation to the subject. There are many reasons for this approach. One is
that *objectivity*—or as one philosopher put it, "the separation of the
perceiver from the thing perceived"—is traditionally a highly valued
principle among some scholars and researchers. For example, if I'm
writing a paper on the effectiveness of Alcoholics Anonymous (AA),
and I confess that my father—who attended AA—drank himself to
death, can I be trusted to see things clearly?

Yes, *if* my investigation of the topic seems thorough, balanced,
and informative. And I think it may be an even better paper because
my passion for the topic will encourage me to look at it more closely.
However, many scholars these days are openly skeptical about
claims of objectivity. Is it really possible to separate the perceiver
from the thing perceived? If nothing else, aren't our accounts of reality always mediated by the words we use to describe it? Can language ever be objective? Though the apparent impersonality of their
papers may suggest otherwise, most scholars are not nearly as dispassionate about their topics as they seem. They are driven by the
same thing that will send you to the library or the Web over the next
few weeks—their own curiosity—and most recognize that good
research often involves both objectivity and subjectivity. As the son
of an alcoholic, I am motivated to explore my own perceptions of his
experience in AA, yet I recognize the need to verify those against the
perceptions of others with perhaps more knowledge.

## When "Bad" Writing Is Good

You might find it tempting to simply dismiss formal academic
writing as "bad" writing, particularly after writing the less formal
research essay. But that would be a mistake. Some academic writing
only *seems* bad to you because you're not familiar with its conventions—the typical moves writers in that discipline make—nor are
you aware of the ongoing conversation in that field to which a particular academic article contributes. It's a little like stumbling into the
electricians' convention at the Hyatt while they're discussing new

regulations on properly grounding outlets. Unless you're an electrician, not a whole lot will make sense to you.

In a way, *The Curious Researcher* represents an apprenticeship in academic writing much like someone might apprentice to a master electrician. Among other things, you'll learn how to ground an outlet—learn some of the technical moves academic writers use, such as citation, incorporating source material, and using indexes—but even more important I hope you'll learn to *think* like an academic writer. Ironically, I think this is easier to practice by not necessarily writing formal academic research papers because they so often *conceal* the open-ended, even messy, process of inquiry. Less formal exploratory essays seem to make the process of inquiry more apparent.

## Thinking like an Academic Writer

What does it mean to *think* like an academic writer? Quite a few different things, of course, some of which vary from discipline to discipline. But there are a few habits of mind or perspectives that I think often shape academic inquiry no matter what the field. They are:

1. The understanding that inquiry is driven by questions, not answers.
2. The willingness to suspend judgment and to tolerate ambiguity.
3. The notion that new knowledge or perspectives are made through the back and forth of conversation in which the writer assumes at least two seemingly contrary roles: believer and doubter, generator and judge.
4. The writer's willingness to take responsibility for his or her ideas, accepting both the credit for and the consequences of putting forth those ideas for dialogue and debate.

Your instructor may want you to write a formal research paper. You should determine if a formal paper is required when you get the assignment. (See the box "Questions to Ask Your Instructor about the Research Assignment.") Also make sure that you understand what the word *formal* means. Your instructor may have a specific format you should follow or tone you should keep. But more likely, she is much more interested in your writing a paper that reflects some original thinking on your part and that is also lively and interesting to read. Though this book will help you write a formal research paper, it encourages what might be called a *research essay,* a paper that does not have a prescribed form though it is as carefully researched and documented as a more formal paper.

## Questions to Ask Your Instructor about the Research Assignment

It's easy to make assumptions about what your instructor expects for the research paper assignment. After all, you've probably written such a paper before and may have had the sense that the "rules" for doing so were handed down by God. Unfortunately, those assumptions may get in the way of writing a good paper, and sometimes they're dead wrong. If you got a handout describing the assignment, it may answer the questions below, but if not, make sure you raise them with your instructor when he gives the assignment.

- How would you describe the audience for this paper?
- Do you expect the paper to be in a particular form or organized in a special way? Or can I develop a form that suits the purpose of my paper?
- Do you have guidelines about format (margins, title page, outline, bibliography, citation method, etc.)?
- Can I use other visual devices (illustrations, subheadings, bulleted lists, etc.) to make my paper more readable?
- Can I use the pronoun *I* when appropriate?
- Can my own observations or experiences be included in the paper if relevant?
- Can I include people I interview as sources in my paper? Would you encourage me to use "live" sources as well as published ones?
- Should the paper *sound* a certain way, have a particular tone, or am I free to use a writing voice that suits my subject and purpose?

# "Essaying" or Arguing?

*Essay* is a term that is used so widely to describe school writing that it often doesn't seem to carry much particular meaning. But I have something particular in mind.

The term *essai* was coined by Michel Montaigne, a sixteenth-century Frenchman; in French, it means "to attempt" or "to try." For

Montaigne and the essayists who follow his tradition, the essay is less an opportunity *to prove* something than an attempt *to find out*. An essay is often exploratory rather than argumentative, testing the truth of an idea or attempting to discover what might be true. (Montaigne even once had coins minted that said *Que sais-je*—"What do I know?") The essay is often openly subjective and frequently takes a conversational, even intimate, form.

Now, this probably sounds nothing like any research paper you've ever written. Certainly, the dominant mode of the academic research paper is impersonal and argumentative. But if you consider writing a *research essay* instead of the usual *research paper,* four things might happen:

1. *You'll discover your choice of possible topics suddenly expands.* If you're not limited to arguing a position on a topic, then you can explore any topic that you find puzzling in interesting ways and you can risk asking questions that might complicate your point of view.

2. *You'll find that you'll approach your topics differently.* You'll be more open to conflicting points of view and perhaps more willing to change your mind about what you think. As one of my students once told me, this is a more honest kind of objectivity.

3. *You'll see a stronger connection between this assignment and the writing you've done all semester.* Research is something all writers do, not a separate activity or genre that exists only upon demand. You may discover that research can be a revision strategy for improving essays you wrote earlier in the semester.

4. *You'll find that you can't hide.* The research report often encourages the writer to play a passive role; the research essay doesn't easily tolerate Joe Fridays ("Just the facts, ma'am") easily. You'll probably find this both liberating and frustrating. While you may likely welcome the chance to incorporate your opinions, you may find it difficult to add your voice to those of your sources.

You may very well choose to write a paper that argues a point for this assignment (and, by the way, even an essay has a point). After all, the argumentative paper is the most familiar form of the academic research paper. In fact, a sample research paper that uses argument is featured in Appendix B. It's an interesting, well-researched piece in which the writer registers a strong and lively presence. But I hope you might also consider essaying your topic, an approach that encourages a kind of inquiry that may transform your attitudes about what it means to write research.

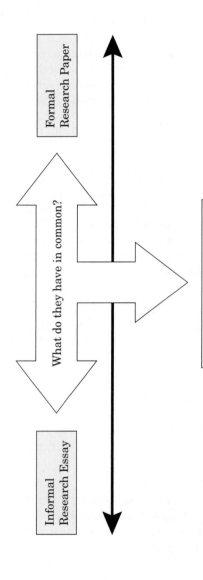

Informal
Research Essay

What do they have in common?

Formal
Research Paper

- Often explicitly subjective, using the first person
- Exploratory
- Written for an audience of nonexperts on the topic
- Few rules of evidence
- Thesis may be delayed rather than stated in introduction
- Writer may express tentativeness about conclusions
- Structure determined by purpose and subject
- *Process* of coming to know often included

- Motive is to answer a question or solve a problem
- Establish context of what has already been said about the question or problem
- Doubt and ambiguity natural part of process
- Have a thesis or tentative claim
- Use evidence/information to explore or prove claim

- Often avoids the first person
- Argumentative
- Written for other experts on the topic
- Established rules of evidence
- Thesis often stated in introduction
- Conclusions stated authoritatively
- Form usually prescribed
- Story of *how* conclusions were reached limited to methods

**FIGURE 1   Why Write Research Essays?**

# The Research Essay and Academic Writing

"If I'm going to have to write formal research papers in my other classes, why should I waste my time writing an informal research essay?" That's a fair question. In fact, the research essay you're about to write *is* different in some ways from the more formal academic scholarship you may be reading as you research your topic (see Figure 1, "Why Write Research Essays?"). And it's also a bit different from research papers you may write in other classes. But the *methods of thought*, what I called earlier the "habits of mind" behind academic inquiry, are fundamentally the same when writing the research essay and the formal research paper.

Because the research essay makes visible what is often invisible in formal academic writing—the process of coming to know what you've discovered about your topic—it's a great introduction to what academic research is all about. And because it removes what is often an artifice of objectivity in research papers, the research essay is like a hound flushing a grouse from the brush—writers can't hide under the cover of invisible authorship, concealing themselves in the safety of "one wonders" or "this paper will argue." *Writers* wonder and argue. *Your* questions, analysis, or assertions take center stage in the research essay as they do just as fundamentally, though less explicitly, in formal academic research. The research essay is good practice for this essential element of all academic inquiry: what you think and how you came to think it.

# Becoming an Authority by Using Authorities

Whether formal or less so, all research papers attempt to be *authoritative*. That is, they rely heavily on a variety of credible sources beyond the writer who helped shape the writer's point of view. Those sources are mostly already published material, but they can also be other people, usually experts in relevant fields whom you interview for their perspectives. Don't underestimate the value of "live" and other nonlibrary sources. Authorities don't just live in books. One might live in the office next door to your class or be easily accessible through the Internet.

Though in research papers the emphasis is on using credible outside sources, that doesn't mean that your own experiences or observations should necessarily be excluded from your paper when they're relevant. In fact, in some papers, they are essential. For example, if you decide to write a paper on Alice Walker's novel *The Color Purple,* your own reading of the book—what strikes you as important—should be at the heart of your essay. Information from literary critics you discover in your research will help you develop and support the assertions you're making about the novel. That support from people who are considered experts—that is, scholars, researchers, critics, and practitioners in the field you're researching—will rub off on you, making your assertions more convincing, or authoritative.

Reading and talking to these people will also change your thinking, which is part of the fun of research. You will actually learn something, rather than remain locked into preconceived notions.

### "It's Just My Opinion"

In the end, *you* will become an authority of sorts. I know that's hard to believe. One of the things my students often complain about is their struggle to put their opinions in their papers: "I've got all these facts, and sometimes I don't know what to say other than whether I disagree or agree with them." What these students often *seem* to say is that they don't really trust their own authority enough to do much more than state briefly what they feel: "Facts are facts. How can you argue with them?"

Step 2 of Exercise 1 that began this chapter may have started you thinking about these questions. I hope the research assignment you are about to start keeps you thinking about your beliefs about the nature of knowledge. Are facts unassailable? Or are they simply claims that can be evaluated like any others? Is the struggle to evaluate conflicting claims an obstacle to doing research, or the point of it? Are experts supposed to know all the answers? What makes one opinion more valid than another? What makes *your* opinion valid?

I hope you write a great essay in the next five or so weeks. But I also hope that the process you follow in doing so inspires you to reflect on how you—and perhaps all of us—come to know what seems to be true. I hope you find yourself doing something you may not have done much before: thinking about thinking.

## Facts Don't Kill

You probably think the words *research paper* and *interesting* are mutually exclusive. The prevalent belief among my students is that the minute you start having to use facts in your writing, then the prose wilts and dies like an unwatered begonia. It's an understandable attitude. There are many examples of informational writing that is dry and wooden, and among them, unfortunately, may be some textbooks you are asked to read for other classes.

But factual writing doesn't have to be dull. You may not consider the article "The Bothersome Beauty of Pigeons" (see the following exercise) a research paper. It may be unlike any research paper you've imagined. While the piece includes citations and a bibliography—two features of most research papers—it reads more like a personal essay, with narrative strands, personal experiences and observations, and a personal voice. "The Bothersome Beauty of Pigeons" is an essay like those I encourage you to write—it grows from an experience I had while traveling in Italy last year that quickly became a research project on pigeons. I knew little about them except that a pair insisted on roosting under the eaves of my Boise, Idaho, home, clucking and cooing at all hours and splattering the bedroom window with droppings. I was not amused. When in Italy I felt a bit differently about pigeons as I watched them sweep in and out of the piazzas in great flocks, feeding at the feet of tourists.

The essay you are about to read explores my ambivalence about the birds, a question that naturally led me to research their habits and behaviors, methods of controlling them, and even a bit of philosophy that speculates about animal consciousness. While "The Bothersome Beauty of Pigeons" is not a formal academic research paper (I write those, too), it does reflect many of the features of academic writing and especially academic inquiry. For example, the essay is driven by questions, works toward a controlling idea or thesis, involves my willingness to suspend judgment, and attempts to build on the ideas of others to extend my own thinking. While the essay is personal—growing from my experience—it attempts to say something larger; it is an effort to comment on "our" experience, and uses research to help enrich those understandings.

The purpose of research writing is not simply to show readers what you know. It is an effort to *extend a conversation about a topic* that is ongoing, a conversation that includes voices of people who have already spoken, often in different contexts and perhaps never together. The research writer begins with his own questions, and then finds the voices that speak to them. He then writes about what others have helped him to understand. As you read "The Bothersome Beauty of Pigeons," look for the traces of this process of inquiry. It may also inspire you to have a similar adventure.

## EXERCISE 2

### Reflecting on "The Bothersome Beauty of Pigeons"

Read my research essay first for pleasure and then reread it with the pen in your hand. Use two opposing pages of your notebook to explore your response to the piece. Begin on the left page by:

- Jotting down, in quotes, your favorite line or passage from the essay.
- Copying a passage—a few lines or paragraph—that uses outside research. Choose one that you particularly liked or didn't like, or both.
- Composing, in your own words, what you think is the main idea or thesis of the essay. Begin by speculating about exactly what central question seemed to be behind the essay. What do you think I was trying to understand? What is that that I *came* to understand by the end of the essay?

Shift across to the opposing, or right page of your notebook. Looking to the left at the notes you just took, begin a seven-minute fastwrite that explores your thinking in response to one or more of the following questions:

- When *you* write your research essay, what techniques or methods could you use to keep the essay interesting to readers even if it is fact-based?
- In what ways was "The Bothersome Beauty of Pigeons" *unlike* what you understood to be a research paper? Does it challenge those assumptions in ways that make you more interested in research? What questions does the essay raise about what you're supposed to do in your research assignment?
- Explore your thoughts about the contents of the essay. Did you find you could relate in some way to what the essay seemed to say? Did you learn anything about yourself, or about pigeons, or our relationships to nature that struck you in some way?

## The Bothersome Beauty of Pigeons

*By Bruce Ballenger*

The cardboard display tables of the mostly African vendors in Florence's largest piazzas are marvels of engineering. They are designed to be light and portable, and to fold in an instant without disrupting the orderly display of fashionable sunglasses, silver cigarette lighters, or art posters. I watch these street entrepreneurs from the steps of the city's great cathedral, Santa Maria della Fiore, as they work the roving bands of Italian schoolchildren on school holiday. It is a hard sell. The vendors line up side by side and though many sell exactly the same kinds of sunglasses or lighters or posters, they don't seem to aggressively compete with each other, in fact, they borrow money from each other to make change, and laugh together at quiet comments I can't hear.

For a few moments my attention to the scene strays, and when I look back the vendors and their cardboard displays have simply vanished. At first, I can't figure out a reason for the disappearing act. Nor can I explain the street vendors' sudden return minutes later, sweeping in like the flocks of pigeons that are everywhere in these squares. Then I see the small Renault of the Florence polizia driving slowly down an adjacent street, where two officers sit stiffly in their crisp blue uniforms and white leather belts; the police seem bored, indifferent, not even remotely interested in the sudden flight their slow passage through the square inspires.

The vendors are apparently unlicensed and the police routinely attempt to flush them out, but this is clearly a half-hearted campaign. Who can blame them? The vendors are everywhere, lingering at the edge of crowds, a fraternity of friendly bandits clutching their neatly folded cardboard tables, each equipped with a convenient handle of rope and duct tape. Within seconds of the officers' departure, the vendors descend on the square again, once again unfolding their tables to which the merchandise magically adhered.

I watch this flight and return again and again, and along with it I notice the pigeons, who participate in a similar performance of their own in these same squares. The birds are also everywhere, in bold flocks that peck at the heels of the sloppy eaters, each bird turning a greedy red eye up at the diner, the other eye fixed on the ground before it. It is impossible to ignore the pigeons, and tourists delight in tossing food and witnessing the free-for-all at their feet. I find myself looking for crumbs from the pannini I have just finished for lunch, wondering at my own impulse to feed a bird against which I had recently waged war.

Pigeons seem to inspire such paradoxical feelings. Pigeon racers in the Bronx tenderly kiss the beaks of their birds, finally home after flying 500 miles to their lofts after a remarkable feat of solar navigation (Blechman). Meanwhile, pigeon haters host Web sites like Pigeonsmakemesick.com and propose plans for ridding cities of the "vermin," including the tactical use of tennis rackets and loaves of bread (Thorne). Most of us, I think, can swing both ways in our feelings towards pigeons, an ambivalence that doesn't seem to apply to other "pests" because pigeons occupy an odd category of creatures that we can both love and hate, animals that are untidy and irritating yet, at times, utterly enchanting.

―――――――――

Florence does not feed a pigeon lover's longings nearly as well as Venice. In Florence's Piazza San Giovanni, where I sat, there were no seed sales, a business that thrives in Venice's St. Mark's square. For one euro, tourists there can buy a small bag of seeds to feed the pigeons, who respond to the encouragement by gathering in great flocks around the seed thrower. The birds lose their grace and shamelessly stumble over each other with eagerness, pecking wildly at the stone street and even eating out of the tourist's hand or perching on his head. This becomes a photographic occasion as tourists stand, arms outstretched before the great church, covered with pigeons.

One guidebook recommends that this feeding should be followed by throwing an article of clothing in the air, which like the police and the sunglass vendors, makes the pigeons take flight in a sudden pulse of wings, only to circle back in their greed and quickly land again at the tourists' feet (Steve 91). The same guidebook offers advice on dealing with pigeon droppings from one's hair—an obvious hazard for the pigeon lover and hater alike—suggesting that it's far better to wait until the stuff dries because it's easier to remove (85).

Such a thing goes completely against instinct. Among my most chilling childhood memories is politely heeding the patrol boy who commanded me to stop before I crossed the street in front of my home. He towered above me, no doubt growing some in memory, and I didn't see him gather the spit in his mouth to deposit on the top of my head. I ran home, heedless of traffic, my vision blurred by tears and my fingers wildly clawing at my fouled hair.

It is also, I think instinctual for human beings to respond warmly to many other animals, particularly those that we find attractive. Pigeons would seem to qualify. They are, after all, close relatives to doves—the lovely white birds of peace—and despite the unsettling red eyes, brown in the youngsters, most *Columbia livia* have smoothly sculpted bodies of blue-gray, and a certain grace when they're not pecking at the stale remnants of someone's lunch. While people rant online about the pestilence of pigeons, it's easy to find organizations of pigeon lovers all over the Web, including the many pigeon fanciers who race them from the rooftops of New York City and other urban areas around the world. Apparently, the fighter George Foreman and actor Paul Newman are among them. Others admire the pigeons' intelligence, something that has been demonstrated by behaviorists like B. F. Skinner who selected pigeons as their primary study subjects. "Pound for pound," gushes Pigeons.com, citing a University of Montana study, "[the pigeon] is one of the smartest, most physically adept creatures in the animal kingdom" ("Resources"). One recent study even demonstrated that pigeons could learn to distinguish between a Van Gogh and a Chagall (Watanabe 147).

It takes special skills to thrive in the world's cities, and pigeons, also called rock doves, are endowed with several ecological advantages that allow them to indulge in "high risk" behavior and escape unscathed. The birds, introduced to North America from Europe in the 1600s, possibly find in urban canyons the high cliffs of their wild ancestors ("FAQs"), and from their high perches they can live and breed and look down on the rest of us.

But they have other evolutionary advantages as well, some of which save them from the well-placed kicks of pigeon-haters or the tires of speeding taxis. For one thing, they "suck" puddle water rather than take it in their beaks and throw their heads back to swallow it, something like the difference between drinking a juice box and slinging back a shot of tequila. Sucking is quicker, apparently, and in very short order they get the water they need, 10 to 15 percent of their body weight daily. In addition, because they can store food in a crop, a pouch in the throat, pigeons can quickly gorge on bread crumbs and seed as the birds weave between the shuffling feet of busy urbanites and then fly to a safe roost to digest what they gathered (Wells and Wells 324).

It's hard not to admire these traits that give the birds such biological success, and yet somehow these evolutionary gifts seem unfair and unearned. I'm disappointed that, say, bluebirds weren't given these advantages, birds that would use them more graciously, judiciously. Pigeons are punks. Looking them in the eye, I'm sure they know this but they just don't care. Yet looking at pigeons also reminds me of my own arrogance, and I both hate them and love them for it.

---

"The problem with pigeons," said Lia Bartolomei, an Italian who led me through the churches of Lucca one day, "is that they turn marble to dust" (Bartolmei). She then pointed to the small statues and marble carving on the church that were pocked and disfigured. The blame seemed clear. Apparently marble is particularly vulnerable to the acid in pigeon droppings, an unintended consequence of the birds' passion to roost on high places as their ancestors did on cliffs.

This is made worse by the pigeon's social nature. Unlike most other birds, they apparently are not particularly territorial, something that is obvious watching pigeons stumble over each other pursuing breadcrumbs. In great concentrations, the birds produce especially damaging piles of droppings, stuff that not only turns marble to dust but can be

an ideal medium for fungus that can cause histoplasmosis and cryptococ-
cossis, both lung infections in humans ("Health Hazards"). It costs the
city of London $150,000 a year to clean up pigeon poop in Trafalgar
Square alone ("Proposed").

It's the decay of marble monuments, the caked pigeon poop on city
bridges, the messy nests on office buildings, and the health threats of
dung fungus that long ago thrust the pigeon into the category of "pest."
This is an undesirable label if you happen to be the plant or animal that
earned it because life for such things can suddenly become complicated.
The rock dove—cousin to the bird of peace, messenger for the Romans,
brave racer for the homing pigeon enthusiast—also earned the unlovely
name of "skyrat." Pigeon-haters find comrades on the Web and confer on
the most effective poisons. Their anthem is folksinger Tom Leher's tune
"Poisoning Pigeons in the Park," a macabre tune noting that *When they
see us coming, the birdies all try an' hide / But they still go for peanuts
when coated with cyanide* (Lehrer). But despite the rants of pigeon-
haters, (some of which are tongue-in-cheek) pigeons are not rats because
among other things they aren't ugly. "Pests" like these make things complicated for us, too.

———————

Like every urban area in the U.S., the pigeon thrives in Boise,
Idaho, where I live, and recently I went to war with a pair determined to
roost in the eaves of our turn-of-the century craftsman home. Let me be
clear about one thing: I am a lover of wild birds, even hooligan crows
who moodily gather in the neighborhood trees in late afternoon muttering curses. I never disliked pigeons, and even admired their success and
intelligence. But the white and green streaks on my windows, and the
pile of droppings at my back door turned me against them. The pigeons'
indifference to my shouts and shirt waving whenever I found them on
the eaves began to infuriate me.

It is human to rail against nature from time to time, and it may
even be human nature. It's true that one of the ecological lessons of our
time is that our determined efforts to dominate the natural world are
not, generally, successful or wise. Ecologically speaking, then, the belief
that we're apart from nature, that it can be easily "managed," doesn't
help ensure our survival as a species; in fact, our grand engineering
efforts often endanger our survival. But aren't these often matters of
scale? Pigeon wars, like the battle against dandelions in a suburban
lawn, may not matter as much in the ecological scheme of things, or at
least this is what we tell ourselves. Still, these campaigns against the
wild things that threaten our tidy world—bugs and weeds, rats and
pigeons—can say a great deal about the ecology of emotion that shapes
our response to nature.

Pigeons, unlike rats, aren't very good enemies. They *are* attractive, and the sweep of their flocks in and out of the squares and streets in Europe or America, expanding and contracting against the bright sky, can almost seem like breathing. Virginia Woolf compared the movement of the great flocks of starlings in the fall to the throwing of a net with "thousands of black knots" expanding and then contracting as the birds settle on the tops of trees (Woolf 266). From a distance, flocks of pigeons can seem like that, and unless you've imprinted images from Hitchcock's film *The Birds*, even the throbbing wings of dozens of the birds landing at your feet can be a little thrill.

Years ago, when I lived on the New England coast, I went on several whale watches to Stellwaggen Bank, an offshore area where there is an unusual concentrations of the animals, including some of the rarest like the Right Whale. On every one of these trips, I noticed that there was a longing not only to see these great animals but to *get close* to them. I sensed this desire had as much to do with the longing to make contact—to look in the eye of a whale, to feel a mutual presence between watcher and animal—as it did the desire to simply get a good look at something that large. I wonder if it's that same longing that feeds the pigeon watchers in St. Mark's square as they feed the pigeons? This might explain why there could be such an outcry when, several years ago, London's mayor proposed to end the long history of pigeon feeding in London's Trafalgar Square.

"People come from abroad just to do it," said one critic of the proposal. "For many children the pigeons are the first contact they have with animals. If a pigeon lands on a child's shoulder, it will paint a good picture in their mind and who then know that animals are worth caring for" ("Proposed"). I'm not sure what is behind this longing to get close. But perhaps it appeals to the biological memory, buried deep, that we are indeed a part of nature, not apart from it. Eye contact is the closest thing we get to a language of intimacy with wild things, though we won't look a rat in the eye. We don't want to get close to just anybody.

Yet these two feelings, our separation and connection to the natural world, are always in conflict, even among those who have tutored themselves to believe in one rather than the other. This seems especially true when confronted with creatures like pigeons, who aren't easy to hate and aren't easy to love, who both foul the nest and yet possess the beauty of a gray river stone, smoothed by the timeless movement of current. All of this was on my mind as I pounded small nails into my pigeons' favorite perches under the eaves and cut the tops off of them to make them sharp, one of the many methods recommended by experts for "controlling" pigeons. Another popular method that uses something called Avitrol, corn bait laced with toxic chemicals, might even mean killing them. The language of "pest control," like the language of warfare, is not immune to euphemism.

Most of the tactics recommended against pigeons, however, are intended to simply make life uncomfortable for them, methods that are more likely, as one combatant put it, to create "a good public relations image" (Loven 3): a perception problem, by the way, that campaigns against rats don't have. These more benign methods of pigeon combat include "porcupine wire," electric wires on roosting places, or chemical pastes that the birds find distasteful. Several cities are experimenting with pigeon contraceptives. Shouting, water pistols, and twirling T-shirts provide momentary satisfaction but are not considered effective. It was a plastic long-eared owl with a head that moves in the wind that finally scared my pigeons away. I moved the owl every two days, and found a strange satisfaction in bullying the birds with what I imagine is their worst nightmare. A big owl with a twirling head would scare the devil out of me if I were a pigeon.

My pigeons moved next door where an elderly couple feed them bird seed and have the time and the willingness to clean up after their new charges; so it seems, in this case, things worked out for everyone. But the large flocks still haunt the piazzas in Florence and Venice, the squares in London, and similar places in nearly every city across the globe. Despite their ability to distinguish between a Van Gogh and a Chagall, pigeons still deposit droppings that deface the great marble statues and facades— the works of art and architecture that are part of our human heritage— and yet people still buy bags of seed for about a dollar and pose for photographs, drenched in doves. Meanwhile, officials in these cities continue, sometimes quietly, to wage war against the birds.

Some historians believe that another war, this one in Viet Nam more than thirty years ago, was one that we could never win because politicians were unable to convince Americans to fully commit to it. That was a hard sell, too, because most Americans were smart enough to eventually realize that even with a full commitment the rewards of "winning" would not be worth the cost. We battle the birds with the same lack of conviction. Like Viet Nam, "pigeon control" is a war that we will never win because we also battle our own conflicting desires: the feeling that it is our obligation to protect and preserve humankind's great works and our hunger to coexist with at least the more appealing creatures with which we share space in our cities. We struggle, as we always have, with the sense that we are both a part of and apart from other species on the planet.

I've managed to scare the pigeons away from the eaves of my house. But it's not so easy to flush them from where they roost now in the back of my mind, cooing and clucking defiantly, daring me to hate them. I can't.

This aggravates me because I know that part of the reason is, quite simply, that pigeons are not rats. It seems unlikely that pigeons know this, though certain philosophers believe that some animals know what it's like to *be* that animal (Nagel 435–50). If this is true, I imagine pigeons may be aware that they're fouling the head of a human being when they roost on the copy of Michelangelo's *David* in Florence's Piazza della Signoria. It is part of the pigeon "experience" to sit confidently on marble heads, knowing that the unthinking stone beneath their feet is neither a source of food nor threat, just a benign roost from which they can turn their red eyes to the humans on the ground below. We look back at them with amusement and disgust, curiosity and contempt—the conflicting feelings and desires that bothersome beauty in nature often arouses. Meanwhile, pigeons hasten the mortality of marble, turning a dream to dust.

# Works Cited

Bartolomei, Lia Personal Interview. 15 April 2002.

Blechman, Andrew. "Flights of Fancy." *Smithsonian Magazine*. March 2002: 44–50.

"Frequently Asked Questions." Project Pigeon Watch. 5 May 2002 <http://birds.cornell.edu/ppw/faq.htm>.

"Health Hazards Associated with Bird and Bat Droppings." Illinois Department of Public Health—Health Beat. 2 May 2002 <http://www.idph.state.il.us/public/hb/hbb&bdrp.htm>.

Leher, Tom. "Poisoning Pigeons in the Park." 7 May 2002 <http://www.hyperborea.org/writing/pigeons.html>.

Loven, Judy. "Pigeons." Animal Damage Management: Purdue Cooperative Extension Service. April 2000. 4 pgs. 7 May 2002 <http://www.entm.purdue.edu/Entomology/ext/targets/ADM/index.htm>.

Nagel, Thomas. "What Is It Like to Be a Bat?" *Philosophical Review* 83 (1974): 435–50.

"Proposed Trafalgar Square Changes Ruffle Feathers." CNN.com. 15 November 2000. 2 May 2002 <www.cnn.com/2000/travel/news/11/15/Britain.trafalgar.ap/>.

"Resources: Interesting and Amazing Facts about Pigeons." Pigeons.com Resources. 2 May 2002 <http://www.pigeons.com/resources/facts.html>.

Steve, Rick. *Rick Steve's Italy, 2001*. Avalon, 2001.

Thorne, Jacob. "Jacob Rants Semicoherently about Pigeons." 18 November 2002. <http://www.angelfire.com/art/glorious/pigeons.html>.

Watanabe, Shigeru. "Van Gogh, Chagall, and Pigeons: Picture Discrimination in Pigeons and Humans " *Animal Cognition* 4 (2001): 147–151.

Wells, Jeffrey V. and Allison Childs Wells. "Pigeons and Doves." *The Sibley Guide to Bird Life and Behavior*. Illust. David Allen Sibley. New York: Knopf, 2001, 319–325.

Woolf, Virginia. "Death of a Moth." *Eight Modern Essayists*. Ed. William
    Smart. New York: St. Martin's Press.
Woolf, Virginia. "Death of a Moth." *The Art of the Personal Essay*. Ed. Philip
    Lopate. New York: Doubleday, 1994: 265–267.

## The Question Habit

The most uninspired research writing lumbers along from fact
to fact and quote to quote, saying "Look at what I know!"
*Demonstrating* knowledge is not nearly as impressive as *using* it
toward some end. And the best uses of research are to answer questions the writer is really interested in. In the next few days, your
challenge is to find those questions.

# The First Week

## The Importance of Getting Curious

A few years back, I wrote a book about lobsters. At first, I didn't intend it to be a book. I didn't think there was that much to say about lobsters. But the more I researched the subject, the more questions I had and the more places I found to look for answers. Pretty soon, I had 300 pages of manuscript.

My curiosity about lobsters began one year when the local newspaper printed an article about what terrible shape the New England lobster fishery was in. The catch was down 30 percent, and the old-timers were saying it was the worst year they'd seen since the thirties. Even though I grew up in landlocked Chicago, I'd always loved eating lobsters after being introduced to them at age eight at my family's annual Christmas party. Many years later, when I read the article in my local newspaper about the vanishing lobsters, I was alarmed. I wondered, Will lobster go the way of caviar and become too expensive for people like me?

That was the question that triggered my research, and it soon led to more questions. What kept me going was my own curiosity. If your research assignment is going to be successful, you need to get curious, too. If you're bored by your research topic, your paper will almost certainly be boring as well, and you'll end up hating writing research papers as much as ever.

## Learning to Wonder Again

Maybe you're naturally curious, a holdover from childhood when you were always asking, Why? Or maybe your curiosity paled as you got older, and you forgot that being curious is the best reason for wanting to learn things. Whatever condition it's in, your curiosity must be the driving force behind your research paper. It's the most essential ingredient. The important thing, then, is this: *Choose your research topic carefully. If you lose interest in it, change your topic to one that does interest you or find a different angle.*

In most cases, instructors give students great latitude in choosing their research topics. (Some instructors narrow the field, asking students to find a focus within some broad, assigned subject. When the subject has been assigned, it may be harder for you to discover what you are curious about, but it won't be impossible, as you'll see.) Some of the best research topics grow out of your own experience (though they certainly don't have to), as mine did when writing about lobster overfishing or pigeons. Begin searching for a topic by asking yourself this question: *What have I seen or experienced that raises questions that research can help answer?*

## Getting the Pot Boiling

A subject might bubble up immediately. For example, I had a student who was having a terrible time adjusting to her parents' divorce. Janabeth started out wanting to know about the impact of divorce on children and later focused her paper on how divorce affects father-daughter relationships.

Kim remembered spending a rainy week on Cape Cod with her father, wandering through old graveyards, looking for the family's ancestors. She noticed patterns on the stones and wondered what they meant. She found her ancestors as well as a great research topic.

Manuel was a divorced father of two, and both of his sons had recently been diagnosed with attention-deficit disorder (ADD). The boys' teachers strongly urged Manuel and his wife to arrange drug therapy for their sons, but they wondered whether there might be any alternatives. Manuel wrote a moving and informative research essay about his gradual acceptance of drug treatment as the best solution for his sons.

For years, Wendy loved J. D. Salinger's work but never had the chance to read some of his short stories. She jumped at the opportunity to spend five weeks reading and thinking about her favorite author. She later decided to focus her research paper on Salinger's notion of the misfit hero.

Accidental topics, ideas that you seem to stumble on when you aren't looking, are often successful topics. For example, Amy spent some time in an America Online chat room one night, and the conversation took an interesting turn. Participants began to discuss the theory that suggests a correlation between depression and heavy computer use. Could that be true? she wondered. She decided to write a paper to find out.

Sometimes, one topic triggers another. Chris, ambling by Thompson Hall, one of the oldest buildings on his campus, wondered about its history. After a little initial digging, he found some 1970s newsclips from the student newspaper describing a student strike that paralyzed the school. The controversy fascinated him more than the building did, and he pursued the topic. He wrote a great paper.

If you're still drawing a blank, try the following exercise in your notebook.

## EXERCISE 1.1

### Building an Interest Inventory

**STEP 1:** From time to time I'll hear a student say, "I'm just not interested in *anything* enough to write a paper about it." I don't believe it. Not for a second. The real problem is that the student simply hasn't taken the time to think about everything he knows and everything he might want to know. Try coaxing those things out of your head and onto paper by creating an "interest inventory."

Start with a blank journal page, or if you're using a word processor, define columns—say, three per page. Title the first column with one of the words below:

PLACES, TRENDS, THINGS, TECHNOLOGIES,

PEOPLE, CONTROVERSIES, HISTORY,

JOBS, HABITS, HOBBIES

Under the title, brainstorm a list of words (or phrases) that come to mind when you think about *what you know and what you might want to know* about the category. For example, under TRENDS you might be aware of the use of magnets for healing sore muscles, or you might know a lot about extreme sports. Put both down on the list. Don't censor yourself. Just write down whatever comes to mind, even if it makes sense only to you. This list is for your use only. You'll probably find that ideas come to you in waves—you'll jot down a few things and then draw a blank. Wait for the next wave to come and ride it. But if you're seriously becalmed, start a new column with a new word from the list above and brainstorm ideas in that category. Do this at least four times with different words. Feel free to return to any column to add new ideas as they come to you, and don't worry about repeated items. Some things simply straddle more than one category. For an idea of what this might look like, see what I did with this exercise (Figure 1.1, below).

Allot a total of twenty minutes to do this step: ten minutes to generate lists in four or more categories, a few minutes to walk away from it and think about something else, and the remaining time to return and add items to any column as they occur to you. (The exercise will also work well if you work on it over several days. You'd be amazed at how much information you can generate.)

**STEP 2:** Review your lists. Look for a single item in any column that seems promising. Ask yourself these questions: Is this something that raises questions that research can help answer? Are they potentially

| CONTROVERSIES | PEOPLE | PLACES |
|---|---|---|
| Pluto a planet? | Carmelita Pope | Great Lakes |
| "Johnny Can't Write?" | Sarah Orne Jewett | BWCA |
| Placement testing | Wallace Stegner | Sawtooths |
| Grizzly introduction | Leslie Marmon Silko | Boise River |
| Wolf introduction | John McPhee | Chicago |
| National Park funding | Joan Didion | Boston |
| Wilderness in Utah | Philip Lopate | Green Bay |
| Clinton impeachment | Richard Nixon | Midwestern upland |
| Falwell and | Tom Hayden | forest |
| Teletubbies | R. Jeffers | Aquarium |
| Microsoft antitrust | Aristotle | Wrigley Field |
| Grazing on federal | Montaigne | Fenway Park |
| lands | Bacon | Helena |
| Lobster harvest | A. S. Hill | Walden Pond |
| Effect of welfare reform | Martin Luther | Foothills |
| Internet privacy | King Jr. | St. John |
| Salmon recovery in | Richard Wright | High desert |
| Northwest | James Baldwin | Alpine ecology |
| AIDS in Africa | Alice Walker | Fire recovery in |
| Endangered Species | Toni Morrison | Yellowstone |
| Act | Rosa Parks | Ireland |
| Overfishing in | Shoeless Joe Jackson | Geology of northern |
| Third World | Quintillian | Rockies |
| Western water rights | Big Bill Heywood | Coral reef |
| Indian gambling | Frank Lloyd Wright | Italy |
| Tribal economies | | Alaska |
| Distance learning | | |
| Online university | | |

**FIGURE 1.1    Sample Interest Inventory**

interesting questions? Does this item get at something you've always wondered about? Might it open doors to knowledge you think is important, fascinating, or relevant to your own life?

Circle the item.

Many interesting things surfaced on my lists. My TRENDS list seemed the richest. For example, I recently finished Jon Krakauer's book *Into Thin Air,* a nonfiction account of a doomed Mt. Everest expedition. After reading the book, I was left wondering about the range of motivations that might account for the increasing popularity of that dangerous climb. On the same list I also wrote "decline of songbirds." I'm aware from personal experience and some limited reading that there has been a steady decline in songbird populations

| TRENDS | TECHNOLOGIES | HISTORY |
|---|---|---|
| Hiking | Computer | Vietnam |
| Cell phones | Palm Pilot/PDAs | Chicago fire |
| Coffeehouses | Children's software | Chicago River reversal |
| Barbies | Camcorder | Pioneer television |
| SUVs | WordPerfect | Sixties |
| Recycling | VCR | Earth Day, 1970 |
| Credit cards | DVD | Chinese in Boise |
| Debt | Bread maker | Native American |
| Malls | Metal detectors | literature |
| Decline of Main Street | Video/computer games | Watergate |
| Decline of songbirds | Cloning | Personal essay |
| Conservative talk radio | Genetic marking | Baseball |
| Fly-fishing | MP3 | Fly-fishing |
| ATMs | Web page design | College research paper |
| Internet real estate | | Serbian politics |
| Internet shopping | | Jazz |
| Antidepressants | | Guitar construction |
| Everest ascents | | Basque culture in |
| Reading books on | | Idaho |
| Internet | | Mining in Idaho City |
| Suburban sprawl | | or Owyhees |
| Suburban architecture | | Oregon Trail journals |
| Skateboarding | | History of trail |
| Snowboarding | | building |
| Magnetic treatments | | NRA |
| Beanie Babies | | Wilderness Act of 1964 |
| Voluntary simplicity | | |
| Decline of logging | | |
| industry | | |

in North America the last few decades. I spent many happy days watching warblers in the tree tops behind my suburban Chicago home as a kid, and it makes me sad that those trees in some future month of May might be more silent. What's going on? I wonder.

**STEP 3:** For the item you circled, generate a list of questions—as many as you can—that you'd love to explore about the subject. Here's what I did with my declining songbird topic:

> What role does habitat destruction play in the decline?
>
> Is this connected to rain forest destruction?
>
> Which kinds of birds are most affected?
>
> What has been the rate of decline? Will it get worse?
>
> What, if anything, are governments or other organizations doing to address the problem?
>
> Is there anyone who doesn't think this is a problem at all?
>
> What exactly might I notice if I returned home to Chicago and went back to the Skokie Lagoons to see the warblers in May? How would it compare to my experience twenty-five years ago?
>
> What are the impacts on other, less affected species of birds?
>
> Why, finally, does it matter that the warblers may be disappearing? What's at stake?

The kinds of questions I came up with on my tentative topic seem encouraging. Several already seem "researchable," and several remind me that I *feel* something about those missing warblers. I may not have developed a hunger to know more yet, but it has piqued my interest. Do you have an appetite for anything yet?

## Other Ways to Find a Topic

If you're still stumped about a tentative topic for your paper, consider the following:

■ *Surf the Net.* The Internet is like a crowded fair on the medieval village commons. It's filled with a range of characters—from the carnivalesque to the scholarly—all participating in a democratic exchange of ideas and information. There are promising research topics everywhere. Maybe begin with a site like *The Virtual Library* (http://www. vlib.org), which tries to organize Net resources by subject. Choose a subject that interests you, say, autos or cognitive science, and follow any number of trails that lead from there into cyberspace.

■ *Search an index.* Visit your library's Web site and check an online index or database in a subject area that interests you. For example, suppose you're a psychology major and would like to find a topic in the field. Try searching PyscINFO, a popular database of psychology articles. Most databases can be searched by author, subject, keyword, and so on. Think of a general area you're interested in—say, bipolar disorder—and do a subject or keyword search. That will produce a long list of articles, some of which may have abstracts or summaries that will pique your interest. Notice the "related subjects" button? Click that and see a long list of other areas in which you might branch off and find a great topic.

■ *Browse through an encyclopedia.* A general encyclopedia, such as the *World Book, Encyclopaedia Britannica,* or *Encarta,* can be fertile ground for topic ideas. Start with a broad subject (e.g., the Great Lakes) and read the entry, looking for an interesting angle that appeals to you, or just browse through several volumes, alert to interesting subjects.

■ *Consider essays you've already written.* Could the topics of any of these essays be further developed as research topics? For example, Diane wrote a personal essay about how she found the funeral of a classmate alienating, especially the wake. Her essay asked what purpose such a ritual could serve, a question, she decided, that would best be answered by research. Other students wrote essays on the difficulty of living with a depressed brother or an alcoholic parent, topics that yielded wonderful research papers. A class assignment to read Ken Kesey's *One Flew Over the Cuckoo's Nest* also inspired Li to research the author.

■ *Pay attention to what you've read recently.* What newspaper articles have sparked your curiosity and raised interesting questions? Rob, a hunter, encountered an article that reported the number of hunters was steadily declining in the United States. He wondered why. Karen read an account of a particularly violent professional hockey game. She decided to research the Boston Bruins, a team with a history of violent play, and examine how violence has affected the sport. Don't limit yourself to the newspaper. What else have you read recently—perhaps magazines or books—or seen on TV that has made you wonder?

■ *Consider practical topics.* Perhaps some questions about your career choice might lead to a promising topic. Maybe you're thinking about teaching but wonder about current trends in teachers' salaries. One student, Anthony, was being recruited by a college to play basketball and researched the tactics coaches use to lure players. What he learned helped prepare him to make a good choice.

■ *Think about issues, ideas, or materials you've encountered in other classes.* Have you come across anything that intrigued you, that you'd like to learn more about?

■ *Look close to home.* An interesting research topic may be right under your nose. Does your hometown (or your campus community) suffer from a particular problem or have an intriguing history that would be worth exploring? Jackson, tired of dragging himself from his dorm room at 3:00 A.M. for fire alarms that always proved false, researched the readiness of the local fire department to respond to such calls. Ellen, whose grandfather worked in the aging woolen mills in her hometown, researched a crippling strike that took place there sixty years ago. Her grandfather was an obvious source for an interview.

■ *Collaborate.* Work together in groups to come up with interesting topics. Try this idea: Organize the class into small groups of five. Give each group ten minutes to come up with specific questions about one general subject—for example, American families, recreation, media, race or gender, health, food, history of the local area, environment of the local area, education, and so forth. Post these questions on newsprint as each group comes up with them. Then rotate the groups so that each has a shot at generating questions for every subject. At the end of forty minutes, the class will have generated perhaps a hundred questions, some uninspired and some really interesting. Look for a question or topic you might like to research. Also look for opportunities to collaborate with others on a topic.

## What Is a Good Topic?

Most writing—be it a personal essay, a poem, or an instruction sheet for a swing set—is trying to answer questions. That's especially true of a research paper. The challenge in choosing the right topic is to find one that raises questions to which you'd really like to learn the answers. (See the box on page 33.) Later, the challenge will be limiting the number of questions your paper tries to answer. For now, look for a topic that makes you at least a little hungry to learn more.

Also consider the intellectual challenge your topic poses and where you will be able to find information about it. You might really want to answer the question, Is Elvis dead? It may be a burning question for you. But you will likely find that you must rely on

## Five Research Essays I'd Like to Read

- **The intelligence of crows.** What is up with these birds that seem to congregate like Hell's Angels in the large trees around my house?
- **The physiology of laughter.** Why does it sometimes feel so good? Is laughing really "good medicine"?
- **Democracy of the Internet.** It's common to say that the Internet is a democratic forum with equal access. But is that really true? What groups are excluded from the Internet revolution? Why?
- **Pro football players at fifty.** What does the knee or the spine that belongs to a man who has played football all his life look like? Is football worth the injuries?
- **AIDS and the plague.** How might the current AIDS epidemic in Africa be compared to the devastation of Europe by the bubonic plague in the fourteenth century?

sources like the *National Enquirer* or a book written by a controversial author who's a regular guest on *Oprah*. Neither source would carry much weight in a college paper. If you're considering several topic ideas, favor the one that might offer the most intellectual challenge and possibly the most information. At this point, you may not really know whether your tentative topic meets those criteria. The rest of this week, you'll take a preliminary look at some library sources to find out whether you have selected a workable topic.

### Checking Out Your Tentative Topic

Consider the potential of the tentative topic you've chosen by using this checklist:

- Does it raise questions I'd love to learn the answers to? Does it raise a lot of them?
- Do I feel strongly about it? Do I already have some ideas about the topic that I'd like to explore?
- Can I find authoritative information to answer my questions? Does the topic offer the possibility of interviews? An informal survey? Internet research?
- Will it be an intellectual challenge? Will it force me to reflect on what *I* think?

- Are a lot of people researching this topic or a similar one? Will I struggle to find sources in the library because other students have them?

Don't worry if you can't answer yes to all of these questions or if you can't answer any at all just yet. Being genuinely curious about your topic is the most important consideration.

## Making the Most of an Assigned Topic

If your instructor limits your choice of topics, then it might be a little harder to find one that piques your curiosity, but it will not be nearly as hard as it seems. It is possible to find an interesting angle on almost any subject, if you're open to the possibilities. If you're not convinced, try this exercise in class.

## EXERCISE 1.2

### The Myth of the Boring Topic

This exercise requires in-class collaboration. Your instructor will organize you into four or five small groups and give each group a commonplace object; it might be something as simple as a nail, an orange, a pencil, a can of dog food, or a piece of plywood. Whatever the object, it will not strike you as particularly interesting, at least not at first.

**STEP 1:** Each group's first task is to brainstorm a list of potentially interesting questions about its commonplace object. Choose a recorder who will post the questions as you think of them on a large piece of newsprint taped to the wall. Inevitably, some of these questions will be pretty goofy ("Is it true that no word rhymes with orange?"), but work toward questions that might address the *history* of the object, its *uses,* its possible *impact on people,* or *the processes* that led to its creation in the form in which you now see it.

**STEP 2:** After twenty minutes, each group will shift to the adjacent group's newsprint and study the object that inspired that group's questions. Spend five minutes thinking up more interesting questions about the object that didn't occur to the group before you. Add these to the list on the wall.

**STEP 3:** Stay where you are or return to your group's original object and questions. Review the list of questions, and choose *one* you find

## What Makes a Question "Researchable"?

- It's not too big or too small.
- The question focuses on some aspect of the topic about which something has been said.
- It interests the researcher.
- It potentially matters. The question has something to do with how we live or might live, what we care about, or what might be important for people to know.
- It implies an approach, or various means of answering the question.
- It raises more questions. The answer to the question might not be simple.

both interesting and most "researchable" (see the box above). In other words, if you were an editorial team assigned to propose a researched article for a general interest magazine that focused on their object, what might be the starting question for the investigation? The most interesting question and the most researchable question may or may not be the same.

In Idaho where I live there are stones called geodes. These are remarkably plain looking rocks on the outside, but with the rap of a hammer they easily break open to reveal glittering crystals in white and purple hues. The most commonplace subjects and objects are easy to ignore because we suspect there is nothing new to see or know about them. Sometimes it takes the sharp rap of a really good question to crack open even the most familiar subjects, and then suddenly we see that subject in a new light. What I'm saying is this: A good question is the tool that makes the world yield to wonder, and knowing this is the key to being a curious researcher. Any research topic—even if it's assigned by the instructor—can glitter for you if you discover the questions that make you wonder.

If all else fails, examine your assigned topic through the following "lenses." One might give you a view of your topic that seems interesting.

- *People*. Who has been influential in shaping the ideas in your topic area? Do any have views that are particularly intriguing to you? Could you profile that person and her contributions?

■ *Trends*. What are recent developments in this topic? Are any significant? Why?

■ *Controversies*. What do experts in the field argue about? What aspect of the topic seems to generate the most heat? Which is most interesting to you? Why?

■ *Impact*. What about your topic currently has the most effect on the most people? What may in the future? How? Why?

■ *Relationships*. Can you put one thing in relationship to another? If the required subject is Renaissance art might you ask, "What is the relationship between Renaissance art and the plague?"

Admittedly, it is harder to make an assigned topic your own. But you can still get curious if you approach the topic openly, willing to see the possibilities by finding the questions that bring it to life for you.

## Developing a Working Knowledge

If you have a tentative topic that makes you curious, then you're ready to do some preliminary research. At this stage in the process, it's fine to change your mind. As you begin to gently probe your subject, you may discover that there's another topic that interests you more, or perhaps a question that hadn't occurred to you. One of the advantages of developing a "working knowledge" of your topic at this stage is that these other possibilities may present themselves.

What's a working knowledge? William Badke, in an online version of his great book *Research Strategies* (http://www.acts.twu.ca/lbr/textbook.htm), calls a "working knowledge" of a topic the ability "to talk about it for one minute without repeating yourself." That's your challenge in Exercise 1.3. Another advantage to developing a working knowledge of your tentative topic at this point is that it will help you find a focus, the problem that vexes more research writers than any other. Aside from giving you something new to talk about when conversation lags at Thanksgiving dinner, a working knowledge helps you to understand:

1. How your topic fits into the *context* of other subjects.
2. Some of the areas of controversy, debate, questions, or unresolved problems that ripple through expert conversation about your topic.

Knowing both of these things really helps when you want to stake out your own small piece of the larger landscape, and it helps you find the question that will mark your location and drive your investigation.

There are at least three ways to develop a working knowledge of your topic: preliminary Web searches, some key library references, and interviews. In Exercise 1.3, we'll focus on the first two of these. The aim is not only to help you to find a focus but to introduce you to important reference sources and searching strategies on the Internet and in your campus library.

---

**Working Together**

In small groups, plan one-minute presentations of "working knowledge" you've developed on your topic doing Exercise 1.3. Following each presentation, ask group members to brainstorm a list of questions they have about your topic based on what you've said.

---

## EXERCISE 1 . 3

### Getting a Lay of the Land

In many ways, the Internet revolution has transformed the reference room. For one thing, you may not even have to step into it. Virtually all of the indexes that used to be available in bound versions or on CD at workstations in the library, you can now access through the Web from your dorm room, apartment, or home. Even certain basic references such as encyclopedias and almanacs are available electronically. I don't have anything against the library, but I have to admit that I love the convenience of this.

### *The Reference Librarian: A Living Source*

Alas, there are still reasons to visit the library. First and foremost is that the reference room is where reference librarians hang out, and these are people you should get to know. I recently told a reference librarian that I was having a hard time keeping up with the changes in library technology and she said that "things are changing so fast it even makes my head spin." Even blurred, the eyesight of reference librarians—people who know where to look and what to look for—is far, far better than ours. Reference specialists are invaluable to college researchers; without doubt they're the most important resource in the library.

## *The Library of Congress Subject Headings: Your Topic in the Larger Landscape*

Librarians will tell you that the reference room is the place to go to develop a working knowledge of your topic, something that can be done rather quickly if you know what you're doing. The most useful thing you can do to begin is to understand where your tentative topic fits into the organization of knowledge in the subject area. Now this sounds like a rather grand notion, but it isn't really; people who deal in library science have figured out ways to systematize the enormous riches of information they must handle and they've developed a language—certain ways of naming subjects—that will help you locate your topic in a larger context. Why does this matter? Because if you know the language that librarians use to describe what you're interested in, then you can find out where exactly they put the information you'll need to learn more about it. At this state in the research process, you might also see other trails and even other topics that might be even more interesting than the one you've tentatively chosen.

**STEP 1:** Describe your topic briefly in a phrase or a sentence.

---

---

---

**STEP 2:** In your reference room, find the book titled *Library of Congress Subject Headings (LCSH)*. It may be available at the reference desk. Otherwise, ask the reference librarian where it is shelved. The *LSCH* is a little appreciated but incredibly useful catalog of the standard headings used by most librarians to index information (see Figure 1.2). Locate your topic in the book. You might begin by imagining a subject within which your topic probably falls, looking up that subject in the *LSCH*, and then finding a good match among the many subheadings listed. Look for the abbreviation BT, or "broader term," to see if you might be redirected to a more appropriate subject heading. Look especially at the NT, or "narrower term" listing. That may lead you to an appropriate description of the topic you've chosen. Write several of these terms below:

---

---

---

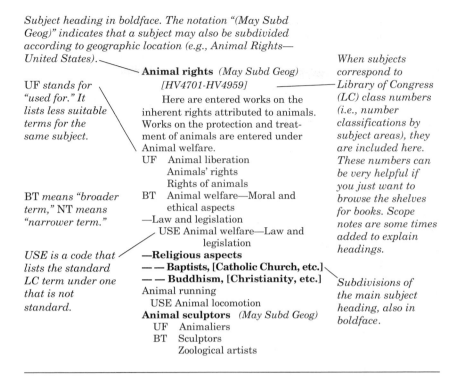

Subject heading in boldface. The notation "(May Subd Geog)" indicates that a subject may also be subdivided according to geographic location (e.g., Animal Rights—United States).

UF stands for "used for." It lists less suitable terms for the same subject.

BT means "broader term," NT means "narrower term."

USE is a code that lists the standard LC term under one that is not standard.

**Animal rights**  (May Subd Geog)
  [HV4701-HV4959]
      Here are entered works on the inherent rights attributed to animals. Works on the protection and treatment of animals are entered under Animal welfare.
      UF    Animal liberation
              Animals' rights
              Rights of animals
      BT    Animal welfare—Moral and
              ethical aspects
      —Law and legislation
          USE Animal welfare—Law and
              legislation
      **—Religious aspects**
      **— — Baptists, [Catholic Church, etc.]**
      **— — Buddhism, [Christianity, etc.]**
      Animal running
          USE Animal locomotion
      **Animal sculptors**  (May Subd Geog)
          UF    Animaliers
          BT    Sculptors
                  Zoological artists

When subjects correspond to Library of Congress (LC) class numbers (i.e., number classifications by subject areas), they are included here. These numbers can be very helpful if you just want to browse the shelves for books. Scope notes are some times added to explain headings.

Subdivisions of the main subject heading, also in boldface.

---

**FIGURE 1.2**    There's no need to guess what subject headings to use when searching on your topic. The *Library of Congress Subject Headings* will get you off to the right start. Here a student looking for sources on animal liberation will discover that "Animal rights" is the heading to use.

As you're perusing the *Library of Congress Subject Headings*, get a sense of how your subject area is broken down. What are some other topics or subtopics within the area of knowledge you're considering? Do any sound more interesting? Are there other trails you might want to follow?

You want to save these *LSCH* terms for your topic for later. These will help you know the words to use when you search the library's online book index and many of the library's periodical databases. Essentially, you've just had a language lesson that allows you to speak "libraryese"—the words that will help you find information more directly and quickly.

## Encyclopedias and Surveying the Landscape

There are two kinds of encyclopedias—general and specialized. You're familiar, no doubt, with the first. For many of us, the

*Encyclopaedia Britannica* marked our passage through junior high and high school. I spent many hours in the glass-walled reference room of the Highland Park public library making note cards from *Britannica* for stunning reports on China and pollution. While it is true that the general encyclopedia is not a particularly authoritative source for college writing, it remains a wonderful reference for acquiring some working knowledge of a subject. I know, of course, that there are electronic encyclopedias such as *Encarta*, and these are worth checking, too, but for my money nothing matches the more detailed treatments in the bound version of *Encyclopaedia Britannica*.

Begin by looking for your topic in the Macropaedia. That's a kind of index and abstract of subjects that will point you to sometimes longer treatments in the Micropaedia. Sometimes you will find information about your topic *within* articles about other topics, which is the real benefit of starting your search with the Macropaedia.

Alternatively, see if you can find a specialized encyclopedia in your topic's subject area. These are more focused encyclopedias, obviously, that often have a wealth of information on a topic lacking in a more general encyclopedia. These specialized references abound. (My personal favorite is the *Encyclopedia of Hell*). The accompanying list provides a sampling of specialized encyclopedias.

**SPECIALIZED ENCYCLOPEDIAS**

**HUMANITIES**

Encyclopedia of World Art
Encyclopedia of Religion
Encyclopedia of Philosophy
Encyclopedia of African-
    American Culture and
    History
Encyclopedia of America
    Social History

**SOCIAL SCIENCES**

Encyclopedia of Marriage
    and the Family
Encyclopedia of Psychology
The Blackwell Encyclopedia
    of Social Pyschology
Encyclopedia of Educational
Research
Encyclopedia of Sociology
Encyclopedia of Social Work
Encyclopedia of World Cultures
Encyclopedia of the
    Third World
Encyclopedia of Democracy
Guide to American Law:
    Everyone's Legal
    Encyclopedia

**SCIENCE**

Encyclopedia of the
   Environment
Concise Encyclopedia of
   Biology
Encyclopedia of Bioethics
Encyclopedia of Science
   and Technology
Macmillan Encyclopedias of
   Chemistry and Physics
Food and Nutrition
   Encyclopedia

**OTHER**

The Baseball Encyclopedia
Encyclopedia of Women and
   Sports
Encyclopedia of World Sport
The World Encyclopedia of
   Soccer
Worldmark Encyclopedia of
   the Nations

To find these and other specialized encyclopedias relevant to your topic, ask your reference librarian or search your campus library's online book index. Try searching using the subject area with the word "encyclopedia" (e.g., Internet and encyclopedia). The *Guide to Reference Books* (see next section) might also provide you with the names of specialized encyclopedias (or dictionaries) that you can use.

**STEP 3:** While you're in the library, search either a general and/or specialized encyclopedia for background information on your tentative topic. List which reference you used below:

_____

Then write three or four sentences to describe something interesting you found out about your topic from the encyclopedia.

_____

_____

_____

_____

In addition to providing useful background information, articles in encyclopedias often feature bibliographies, with citations to other articles and books that might prove useful as you dig more deeply into your topic. Check the bibliography of an encyclopedia article, and if there is a promising citation, write it below. Copy it carefully.

_____

_____

## The Guide to Reference Books: Closest Thing to One-Stop Shopping

There's one last reference you should know. Balay's *Guide to Reference Books* (in earlier editions, it was edited by Sheehy)* is as close as reference books get to being a sacred text. Now in its eleventh edition, the *Guide* indexes nearly 16,000 indexes, bibliographies, specialized encyclopedias, handbooks, almanacs, and other references that will directly provide information—or citations for other publications that will provide information—on thousands of topics (see Figure 1.3). The *Guide* will reveal to you—maybe for the first time—the incredible variety of references that are available these days, including some electronic texts. The book is organized by field of study (e.g., Humanities, Social and Behavioral Sciences, History, Science and Technology, etc.), but the index at the back is the place to start. The *Guide to Reference Books (GRB)* takes some getting used to, but once you know how to use it, you'll be amazed at how helpful it can be for any academic research project. It may even inspire prayer. . . .

Smaller libraries may not have Balay's book, but *Reference Sources for Small and Medium-Sized Libraries*** is a fine alternative to the heftier *Guide*.

**STEP 4:** Find the *Guide to Reference Books* (or Kennedy's *Reference Sources*) in the reference room of the library. Check the index in the back of the book, using the topic headings you found in the *LCSH* or any others you think might work. With luck, you'll find a subject area that encompasses your topic, as one student studying television violence did when he found a whole range of sources on radio and television. Sometimes, though, you won't find a relevant subject in the index; in that case, look in the front of the book at the more general subject headings. For example, I searched for "Internet addiction" in the index and couldn't even find the more general heading of "Internet." I flipped to general subject headings and found the pages for GENERAL WORKS under "Science, Technology, and Medicine." That took me to a great list of guides, indexes, and bibliographies, several of which would lead me to the best reference sources for research in computer technology. The GENERAL WORKS section begins each subject chapter, and it's a great place to begin if the index fails you. In particular, keep your eye out for guides aimed at researchers, including students, that introduce you not only to the key references in the subject

---

*Robert Balay, ed. *Guide to Reference Books*. 11th ed. (Chicago: ALA, 1996).
**Scott Kennedy, ed. *Reference Sources for Small and Medium-Sized Libraries*. 6th ed. (Chicago: ALA, 1999).

## RADIO AND TELEVISION

*See also* BG229–BG230, BG233.

## Guides

**Schreibman, Fay C.** Broadcast television: a research guide. Ed. by Peter J. Bukalski. Los Angeles, Calif., American Film Inst., Education Services, 1983. 62p. (Factfile, no. 15)

**BG290**

A useful guide for an area not well covered bibliographically.

## Bibliography

**McCavitt, William E.** Radio and television: a selected, annotated bibliography. Metuchen, N.J., Scarecrow Pr., 1978. 229p., Suppl. one, 1977–81. Metuchen, N.J., 1982. 155p.　**BG291**

For full information *see* CH503.

**NAB broadcasting bibliography:** a guide to the literature of radio & television. Comp. by the staff of the NAB Library and Information Center, Public Affairs Dept. 2d ed. Wash., Nat. Assoc. of Broadcasters, [1984]. 66p.　**BG292**

1st ed. 1982.

Lists 360 books, most of them published since 1975, under seven categories (with numerous subdivisions): fundamentals of broadcasting, the business of broadcasting, broadcasting and the law, the technology and technique of broadcasting, broadcasting and society, comparitive broadcasting, related technologies. Also includes a list of periodicals and a publishers directory. Author/title index.

## *Dissertations*

**Kittross, John M.** A bibliography of theses & dissertations in broadcasting, 1920–1973. Wash., Broadcast Education Assoc., 1978. [238]p.　**BG293**

An author listing of some 4,300 dissertations and master's theses completed at American universities, with keyword-in-title index plus an index by year of completion and another by broad topics.

**Sparks, Kenneth R.** A bibliography of doctoral dissertations in television and radio. [3d ed.] Syracuse, N.Y., School of Journalism, Syracuse Univ., [1971]. 119p.　**BG294**

A classified listing of some 900 dissertations completed through June 1970. Author index.　Z7221.S65

## Indexes

**International index to television periodicals;** an annotated guide. 1979/80– . London, Internat. Federation of Film Archives, [1983]– . Biennial.　**BG295**
　　Michael Moulds, ed.

---

**FIGURE 1.3**　A student researching violence on television in the *Guide to Reference Books* might check the index at the back of the book under "Television" and be referred to this page. Note the wide range of possible references that might be useful, especially the bibliographies. The student would then check to see which of the pertinent sources are in his library's collection.

*Source:* Reprinted with permission of ALA from *Guide to Reference Books,* 10th edition.

43

area but strategies for conducting research in related disciplines. Try to find *one* good entry in the *GRB* (see Figure 1.3 for example) that seems relevant to your project, and list the bibliographic information below. (Don't bother to try to find the reference in your library yet.)

*Type of Source (circle):*    Index    Almanac    Bibliography
     Dictionary    Encyclopedia    Directory    Handbook    Other

*Author:* _____

*Title:* _____

*Publication information:* _____

*Comment:* _____

## *Surveying the Electronic Landscape*

The World Wide Web is the elephant in the room. It just can't be ignored as an accessible, and for most of us, appealing source of research information. Later, we'll explore in more detail some of the advantages and disadvantages of Web searching and information, but for now I'm pretty sure that no matter what I say you'll do a Web search on your tentative topic. Rather than do an extensive search, however, at this point your goal is to develop enough working knowledge on your topic to talk for a minute about it without repeating yourself. The Web can be really useful for this. But where do you begin?

## *Subject Search*

You are probably itching to fire up a general search engine such as Google.com, type in a few keywords, and see what turns up. (See Figure 1.4.) Do that if you want. I can't stop you. But I'm pretty sure that you'll be overwhelmed (or possibly underwhelmed) by the results, and it will probably provide you with much more information than you need at the moment. Typically, keyword searches like the one I just described are the most common method of searching the Web, but don't overlook a subject search, particularly as you try to get a handle on your tentative topic or want to consider alternative topics.

As you probably know, information on the Web is horribly disorganized; it's a librarian's worst nightmare. But there are librarians and others who are knowledgeable about organizing information who have worked quietly for years trying to impose some order on the chaos. What they've done is created *subject directories* on the Web. Perhaps the most famous subject directory is Yahoo! (yahoo.com), but there are several other sites that feature directories that were specifically developed by library experts and educators, people who

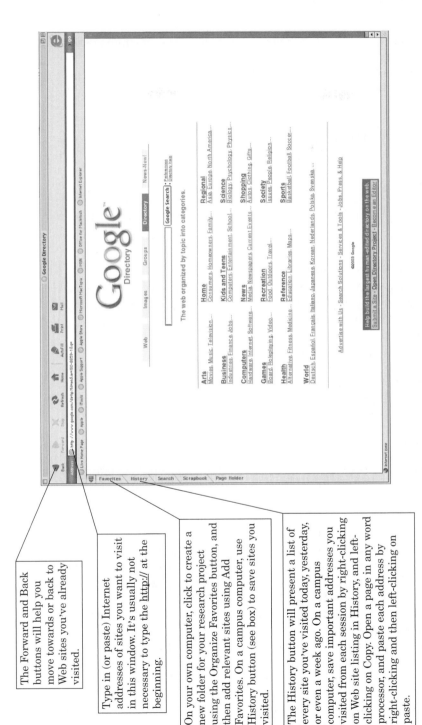

The Forward and Back buttons will help you move towards or back to Web sites you've already visited.

Type in (or paste) Internet addresses of sites you want to visit in this window. It's usually not necessary to type the http:// at the beginning.

On your own computer, click to create a new folder for your research project using the Organize Favorites button, and then add relevant sites using Add Favorites. On a campus computer, use History button (see box) to save sites you visited.

The History button will present a list of every site you've visited today, yesterday, or even a week ago. On a campus computer, save important addresses you visited from each session by right-clicking on Web site listing in History, and left-clicking on Copy. Open a page in any word processor, and paste each address by right-clicking and then left-clicking on paste.

**FIGURE 1.4** Microsoft's Internet Explorer is now the dominant Web browser for viewing documents on the Web. For a fuller treatment of how the browser works, click on "Help" on the toolbar at the top, and under "Contents" click on "Getting Started With Internet Explorer."

45

are concerned both with order and the value of information in cyberspace. As you try to develop working knowledge of your topic, these subject directories can do what the *LCSH* and encyclopedias do—help you understand your topic in context. You will be able to see how it relates to larger and smaller subject areas and possibly see an appealing focus for your essay.

One of the best subject directories is the Virtual Library (see Figure 1.5). It's not the largest, but it is managed by people—mostly volunteers—all over the world who are experts in the library's various subject areas, contributing and evaluating the best sites. There are other sites like the Virtual Library that are worth visiting as well. The accompanying list shows some of the best sites for academic research.

**ACADEMIC RESEARCH SITES**

The Argus Clearinghouse
  http://www.clearinghouse.net/
BUBL Link http://bubl.ac.uk/link/
Infomine http://infomine.ucr.edu/
Lii.org/The Librarians' Index to
  the Internet http://lii.org/
Best Information on the
  Net http://library.sau.
  edu/bestinfo/Default.htm

The Internet Public Library
  http://www.ipl.org/
Academic Net http://www.
  academicinfo.net/
Britannica Online
  http://britannica.com
Virtual Library
  http://vlib.org

**STEP 5:** For those who aren't experienced with Web searching, Figure 1.4 describes the basics of a browser window and how it works. In the address window of your browser, type in the address of the Virtual Library or one of the other subject directories listed above. (For most browsers, it's no longer necessary to type "http" at the beginning of an Internet address—*vlib.org* should be enough to get you there). Find the appropriate subject area and then slowly work your way down the subject hierarchy until you find a Web site that seems relevant. As you proceed, also pay attention to other angles on your topic—or even other topics—that are interesting to you. On a separate piece of paper, draw a navigation map of your journey from your initial subject choice to the Web page that was your final destination. Print out a copy of the document you found and hand it in with this exercise. See Figure 1.6 for an example of a navigation map done by a student interested in researching the bubonic plague.

Finally, conclude your subject search by collecting the basic bibliographic information about a Web document that you found

**FIGURE 1.5**
Managed by volunteers, the Virtual Library is one of the best subject directories on the Internet.

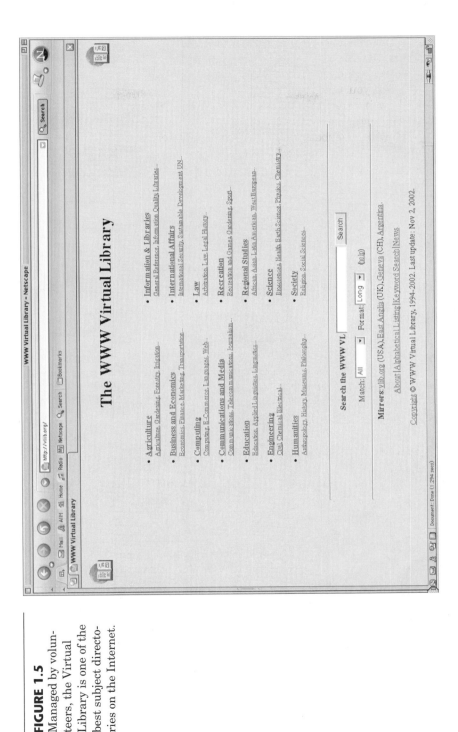

47

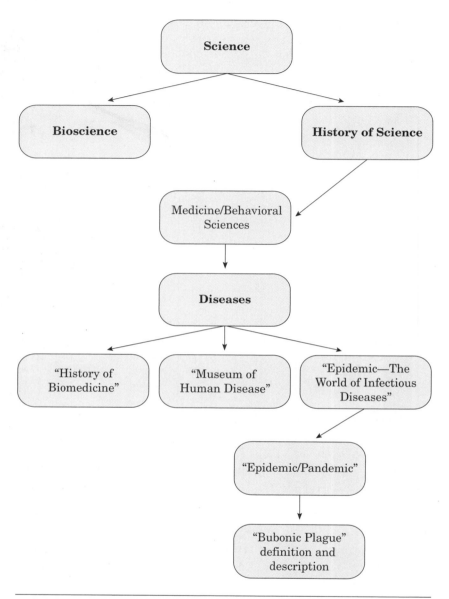

**FIGURE 1.6    Navigation Map of Subject Search**    A student interested
in the bubonic plague, a pandemic that wiped out nearly  a third of Europe's
population in the fourteenth century, began in the "Science" category at the
Virtual Library. She followed the most promising trail down through the
subject hierarchy (using the "back" button on her browser to get out of dead
ends when necessary), and ended finally at a Museum of Natural History
site with and interesting definition and description of the plague. On the
way, she began to think about AIDs and the plague. Might she explore the
connection between the two?

interesting and relevant to your tentative topic. Enter the information in the blanks below.

*Author (if any):* _____

*Title:* _____

*Publication name and date of print version (if any):* _____

_____

*Online publication name or database (e.g., Boston Globe Online,*

*Oxford Text Archives, Alzheimer's Disease Research Center, etc.):*

_____

*Publication information of online version (volume or issue, date,*

*page or paragraph numbers, or if none, n. pag.):* _____

*Date you accessed it (day, month, year):* _____

*Internet address:* _____

Also make sure to "Bookmark" the site.

## Narrowing the Subject

It never occurred to me that photography and writing had anything in common until I found myself wandering around a lonely beach one March afternoon with a camera around my neck. I had a fresh roll of film, and full of ambition, I set out to take beautiful pictures. Three hours later, I had taken only three shots, and I was definitely not having fun. Before quitting in disgust, I spent twenty minutes trying to take a single picture of a lighthouse. I stood there, feet planted in the sand, repeatedly bringing the camera to my face, but each time I looked through the viewfinder, I saw a picture I was sure I'd seen before, immortalized on a postcard in the gift shop down the road. Suddenly, photography lost its appeal.

A few months later, a student sat in my office complaining that he didn't have anything to write about. "I thought about writing an essay on what it was like going home for the first time last weekend," he said, "but I thought that everyone probably writes about that in Freshman English." I looked at him and thought about lighthouse pictures.

## Circling the Lighthouse

Almost every subject you will choose to write about for this class and for this research paper has been written about before. The challenge is not to find a unique topic (save that for your doctoral dissertation) but to find an angle on a familiar topic that helps readers to see what they probably haven't noticed before. In "The Bothersome Beauty of Pigeons," I took the most common of subjects—the urban pigeon—and took a close look at its habits and behaviors, finding in them an explanation for my conflicted feelings about "pests" that are inconveniently attractive.

I now know that I was mistaken to give up on the lighthouse. The problem with my lighthouse picture, as well as with my student's proposed essay on going home, was not the subject. It was that neither of us had yet found our own angle. I needed to keep looking, walking around the lighthouse, taking lots of shots until I found one that surprised me, that helped me see the lighthouse in a new way, in *my* way. Instead, I stayed put, stuck on the long shot and the belief that I couldn't do better than a postcard photograph.

It is generally true that when we first look at something, we mostly see its obvious features. That became apparent when I asked my Freshman English class one year to go out and take pictures of anything they wanted. Several students came back with single photographs of Thompson Hall, a beautiful brick building on campus. Coincidentally, all were taken from the same angle and distance— straight on and across the street—which is the same shot that appears in the college recruiting catalog. For the next assignment, I asked my students to take multiple shots of a single subject, varying angle and distance. Several students went back to Thompson Hall and discovered a building they'd never seen before, though they walk by it every day. Students took abstract shots of the pattern of brickwork, unsettling shots of the clock tower looming above, and arresting shots of wrought iron fire escapes, clinging in a tangle to the wall.

The closer students got to their subjects, the more they began to see what they had never noticed before. The same is true in writing. As you move in for a closer look at some aspect of a larger subject, you will begin to uncover information that you—and ultimately your readers—are likely to find less familiar and more interesting. One writing term for this is *focusing*. (The photographic equivalent would be *distance from the subject*.)

## From Landscape Shots to Close-Ups

When you wrote research reports in high school, you were a landscape photographer, trying to cram into one picture as much information as you could. A research report is a long shot. The college research essay is much more of a close-up, which means narrowing the boundaries of your topic as much as you can, always working for a more detailed look at some smaller part of the landscape.

Of course, you are not a photographer, and finding a narrow focus and fresh angle on your research topic is not nearly as simple as it might be if this were a photography exercise. But the idea is the same. You need to see your topic in as many ways as you can, hunting for the angle that most interests you; then go in for a closer look. One way to find your *focus* is to find your *questions*.

## E X E R C I S E   1 . 4

### Finding the Questions

Although you can do this exercise on your own, your instructor will likely ask that it be done in class this week. That way, students can help each other. (If you do try this on your own, only do Steps 3 and 4 in your research notebook.)

**STEP 1:** Take a piece of paper or a large piece of newsprint, and post it on the wall. At the very top of the paper, write the title of your tentative topic (e.g., *Internet Addiction*).

**STEP 2:** Take a few minutes to briefly describe why you chose the topic.

**STEP 3:** Spend five minutes or so and briefly list what you know about your topic already (e.g., any surprising facts or statistics, the extent of the problem, important people or institutions involved, key schools of thought, common misconceptions, observations you've made, important trends, major controversies, etc.).

**STEP 4:** Now spend fifteen or twenty minutes brainstorming a list of questions *about your topic* that you'd like to answer through your research. Make this list as long as you can; try to see your topic in as many ways as possible. Push yourself on this; it's the most important step.

**STEP 5:** As you look around the room, you'll see a gallery of topics and questions on the walls. At this point in the research process, almost everyone will be struggling to find her focus. You can help each other. Move around the room, reviewing the topics and questions other students have generated. For each topic posted on the wall, do two things: Add a question *you* would like answered about that topic that's not on the list, and check the *one* question on the list you find most interesting. (It may or may not be the one you added.)

If you do this exercise in class, when you return to your newsprint, note the question about your topic that garnered the most interest. This may not be the one that interests you the most, and you may choose to ignore it altogether. But it is helpful to get some idea of what typical readers might most want to know about your topic.

You also might be surprised by the rich variety of topics other students have tentatively chosen for their research projects. The last time I did this exercise, I had students propose papers on controversial issues such as the use of dolphins in warfare, homelessness, the controversy over abolishment of fraternities, the legalization of marijuana, and the censorship of music. Other students proposed somewhat more personal issues, such as growing up with an alcoholic father, date rape, women in abusive relationships, and the effects of divorce on children. Still other students wanted to learn about more historical subjects, including the role of Emperor Hirohito in World War II, the student movement in the 1960s, and the Lizzie Borden murder case. A few students chose topics that were local. For example, one student recently researched the plight of nineteenth-century Chinese miners digging for gold in the mountains just outside of Boise. Another did an investigation of skateboard culture in town, a project that involved field observation, interviews, as well as library research.

If the topic you've tentatively chosen is broad—such as abortion, whales, or child abuse—then Exercise 1.4 may help you discover the questions needed to narrow your topic into something more manageable. For example, if you're considering a paper on abortion, you'll quickly see how many angles there are on such a complicated subject: What is the history of abortion rights in the United States? How will the conservative majority on the Supreme Court influence *Roe* v. *Wade?* What is the impact of the abortion issue on local election campaigns? Each one of these questions could easily be answered in a ten-page paper, and most of these topics could likely be narrowed further.

Knowing the many questions your research project *could* answer is a start. But you obviously need to limit how many questions to ask, too. Once you've unleashed the many possibilities, you must harness a few in the service of your paper. If you need some help with that, try the next exercise.

## EXERCISE   1 . 5

### Finding the Focusing Question

Review the questions you or the rest of the class generated in Exercise 1.4, Steps 4 and 5, and ask yourself, Which questions on the list am I most interested in that could be the focus of my paper? Remember, you're not committing yourself yet.

**STEP 1:** Write the *one* question that you think would be the most interesting focus for your paper on the top of a fresh piece of newsprint or paper: This is your *focusing question.*

**STEP 2:** Now build a new list of questions under the first one. What else do you need to know to answer your focusing question? For example, suppose your focusing question is, *Why do some colleges use unethical means to recruit athletes?* To explore that focus, you might need to find out:

> Which colleges or universities have the worst records of unethical activities in recruiting?
>
> In which sports do these recruiting practices occur most often? Why?
>
> What are the NCAA rules about recruiting?
>
> What is considered an *unethical practice?*
>
> What efforts have been undertaken to curb bad practices?

Many of these questions may already appear on the lists you and the class generated, so keep them close at hand and mine them for ideas. Examine your tentative focusing question carefully for clues about what you might need to know. See also the box, "Focusing: A Case Study," which describes how one student completed this exercise.

## Choosing a Trailhead

The importance of finding a narrow focus early can't be overestimated. I asked a reference librarian recently what she thought was the most common problem with student research papers. "That's easy," she said. "Students haven't narrowed their topics sufficiently. They come to us and ask where to begin looking for information on air pollution, and I could send them to any one of a hundred places."

Your research will be much more efficient if you have a limited focus, allowing you to concentrate on perhaps five relevant articles rather than wading through fifty about the broader topic. And by taking a closer look at a smaller part of your subject, you're much more likely to encounter information that will surprise you and your readers.

Settling on *one* central question that your research paper will attempt to answer is key. I call this a *trailhead question,* or the one that provides a path into your subject. It is just one of many paths, but it's the one that—at least for now—you're most interested in following. As you follow it into the library or onto the Internet this week, you may encounter other questions and other trails that take you off in new directions. That's fine. But at least have an initial direction.

## Focusing: A Case Study

Al, a student working on the topic children of alcoholics, came up with the following questions from Exercise 1.5:

Which family members are most affected by the drinker?

What can they realistically do to encourage the drinker to stop?

How likely is it that I will drink because my father did?

How effective is AA? Al-Anon? ACOA?

What's the relationship among these organizations?

What do they mean by "tough love"?

Do teenage children of alcoholics have any special problems?

How do the reactions of children differ?

Does a family share any of the responsibility for the alcoholic's disease?

Does it matter whether the father or mother is the drinker, or are the problems for the family the same in both cases?

What do they mean by "adult child"?

Al, the son of an alcoholic, had plenty of good questions. He had already done some reading on the subject, which helped, but he wasn't quite sure what he wanted to focus on. One question intrigued him the most—*Do teenage children of alcoholics have any special problems?*—but he was afraid the focus was too narrow. Would he be able to find enough information? Al was also interested in the last question, the meaning of the term *adult child*. But was that subject too broad? He was aware that scores of books had been published on adult children of alcoholics in recent years and thought he might be swamped by information.

If you can, start with the narrower focus. As you immerse yourself in research, you can broaden it a bit if you're having difficulty finding information, or you may encounter some interesting material that encourages you to change the focus altogether. If you start with a closer look at some aspect of your subject, your research efforts will be more efficient and the information you unearth will more likely surprise you.

Al tentatively chose the narrower focusing question: *Do teenage children of alcoholics have any special problems?* Working from that main question, he generated an additional list of questions that he may need to explore:

> Does anything about being a teenager make alcoholism harder?
>
> What do I remember from my own experience with my father at that age?
>
> Do groups like Al-Anon and ACOA have special meetings for teens?
>
> How do teenagers with alcoholic parents deal with the pressures to drink themselves?

Armed with this focus and some ideas about what to look for, Al was ready to begin his research in earnest.

### Finding the Relationship:
### An Alternative Way of Focusing

My friend and colleague Nancy DeJoy at Milliken University asks her students to develop a narrow focus by asking them at the outset to research a relationship. She asks, What might be the relationship between your topic and something else? For example, if the topic is learning disabilities, might the focus be learning disabilities and self-esteem? Or perhaps the topic is the federal Endangered Species Act. A focus might be, *What is the relationship between the Endangered Species Act and the survival of small ranching operations in the Northern Rockies?*

## What's Your Purpose?

Sometimes with high school research reports, it didn't seem to matter what you thought about the subject you were writing about. It seemed that what really mattered was whether you followed the proper format, cited sources correctly, and had a long bibliography. Though following the technical conventions is important in the college research paper, what matters even more is what you do with the information you find. Your paper must have a *purpose.*

### Do You Have a Thesis?

In a broad sense, the purpose of your paper might be *to persuade, to analyze, to describe,* or *to explain* some aspect of your subject. Your purpose might even be a combination of all four. More specifically, your purpose in writing this paper is to find out *what you want to say* about your topic—in other words, finding your *thesis,* or your main idea—and then using persuasion, analysis, description, narration, or exposition to make that idea convincing to someone else. You may have learned that you need to define your thesis before you begin the research. That might be appropriate if you already know what you think. Last semester, I had a student, Kate, who believed strongly in the legalization of marijuana; she wanted to write a persuasive paper arguing that limited legalization was workable. Kate started with a thesis and went from there.

You might have a more tentative notion of what your paper's point will be, based on your current understanding of the topic. For example, Al, the student investigating children of alcoholics, believed that the answer to his focusing question—*Do teenage children of alcoholics have any special problems?*—might be that they do. That's what his own experience seemed to tell him. It's possible that the research will convince Al otherwise, or finding new information may help him make his thesis more specific. Perhaps the controlling idea of Al's paper might later become the assertion that teenage children of alcoholics have particular difficulty maintaining relationships later in life.

You may have chosen your topic precisely because *you don't know what you think.* So how do you know what you want to say until you've learned what others have said and had the chance to explore your topic? What I love about research is that it is a process of discovery. That demands an openness to what you'll find and a willingness to change your mind.

If, at this point, you can state your thesis, it would be useful to do so. But don't be inflexible. As with my students and their pictures of Thompson Hall, the more you look, the more you'll see. Be open to surprise.

If you can't state your thesis yet, don't worry. You can nail that down later, after you've done some digging. (See Exercise 4.2, "Reclaiming Your Topic," in Chapter 4.) But as you begin to mine your topic for information this week, always keep two questions in mind: What do I think? and What do I want to say?

## EXERCISE 1 . 6

### Charting Your Course

You're now standing at the trailhead, ready to begin the journey into researching your topic. Before you do, in your research notebook, jot down the answers to the following questions. They'll help you get your bearings. Your instructor may ask you to bring this information to class or conference this week.

- What is my tentative focusing question?
- What other questions might help me explore that focus?
- What is my tentative thesis?

# Reading for Research

## EXERCISE 1 . 7

### Ways of Reading to Write

1. Complete the following sentence in your journal or notebook:

   *The most important thing about **reading** for a research paper is*

   _____.

2. The following passage is from the opening chapter of John Yount's wonderful novel, *Trapper's Last Shot*. It's a pretty startling scene, powerfully narrated. Read the excerpt, and then in your journal compose an explanation of how you interpret the purpose of this scene as an opening to the novel. What themes and feelings does it seem to introduce that you predict might be central to the rest of the story? Don't forget to use specific passages from the excerpt to support your assertions.

## *Chapter One*

The summer of 1960 was hot and dry in Cocke County, Georgia. No rain fell from the second week in June through the entire month of July. The loblolly pines turned yellow in the drought. The grass scorched and withered in the fields, and bare patches of red clay earth began to appear and to crack and cake in the sun like the bottoms of dried up lakes. The first day of August some clouds drifted in from the mountains in Tennessee and the Carolinas, and the air grew still and heavy, and for a while a thin rain fell as warm as sweat. But before the rain had quite stopped, the sun came out again, and steam began to rise from the fields and woods, from the dirt roads and concrete slab highways, and the countryside cooked like so many vegetables in a pot.

The next day five boys started out to go swimming in the south fork of the Harpeth river. Except for a thin crust like a pastry shell over the pink dust, there was no evidence of the rain. As they walked toward the river, the heat droned and shimmered in the fields, and locusts sprang up before them to chitter away and drop down and then spring up again as they came on. When they got among the trees on the river bank, the oldest of them, who was fourteen, shucked quickly out of his britches and ran down the bank and out on a low sycamore limb and, without breaking stride, tucked up his legs and did a cannonball into the water. The surface all around, even to the farthest edge, roiled when he hit as if the pool were alive, but they didn't see the snakes at first. The boy's face was white as bleached bone when he came up. "God," he said to them, "don't come in!" And though it was no more than a whisper, they all heard. He seemed to struggle and wallow and make pitifully small headway though he was a strong swimmer. When he got in waist deep water, they could see the snakes hanging on him, dozens of them, biting and holding on. He was already staggering and crying in a thin, wheezy voice, and he brushed and slapped at the snakes trying to knock them off. He got almost to the bank before he fell, and though they wanted to help him, they couldn't keep from backing away. But he didn't need them then. He tried only a little while to get up before the movement of his arms and legs lost purpose, and he began to shudder and then to stiffen and settle out. One moccasin, pinned under his chest, struck his cheek again and again, but they could see he didn't know it, for there was only the unresponsive bounce of flesh.

From the novel *Trapper's Last Shot* by John Yount.

———————————

3. The following is an excerpt from an academic article on how college students think about their own masculinity. Obviously, this differs in many ways from the piece you just read. Your aim here

is to carefully read the passage and write a summary of the author's main idea(s) based on your understanding of the text. A summary, you'll recall, is a brief capsulation of the important ideas in a much longer text. Write this summary in your journal and be prepared to share it with others in the class.

> Researchers' understanding of identity formation is commonly attributed to Erikson's (1968) developmental theory. According to Erikson, individuals gain a sense of who they are by confronting a universal sequence of challenges or crises (e.g., trust, intimacy, etc.) throughout their lives. Marcia (1966) operationalized Erikson's original theory and similarly suggested that identity formation is the most important goal of adolescence. Marcia viewed identity development as a process of experiencing a series of crises with one's ascribed childhood identity and subsequently emerging with new commitments. That is, as individuals consider new ideas that are in conflict with earlier conceptions, they weigh possibilities, potentially experiment with alternatives, and eventually choose commitments that become the core of a newly wrought identity. Individuals avoiding the process altogether, neither experiencing crises nor making commitments, are in a state of identity diffusion. Individuals may also be somewhere between these two possibilities by either simply maintaining a parentally derived ideology (foreclosed) or actively by experimenting with and resolving identity-related questions prior to commitment (moratorium).*

4. After you've completed the preceding three steps, spend some time fastwriting in your journal your responses to some of the following questions. These will also be discussed in class.

- Did your approach to reading the two excerpts differ? How?
- What are your "typical" reading strategies. Did you use them here?
- What are your typical reading "behaviors," things such as underlining highlighting, marginal notes, rereadings, and so on? Would they vary with each excerpt?
- To what extent did you take your own advice in your answer to Step 1 of this exercise,

The most important thing about reading for a research paper is

_____?

*T. L. Davis, "Voices of Gender Role Conflict: The Social Construction of College Men's Masculinity," *Journal of College Student Development 43*: 508–21.

- The two excerpts are clearly different kinds of writing—one is literary and the other academic. They're also different *forms* of writing. What are the key differences between them?
- What problems did you encounter when you read these excerpts? How did you solve them?

## Reading Rhetorically

We all learned to read in school but we never really learned how to read *rhetorically*. That means that there are particular reading strategies that are most effective in certain situations and for certain purposes. In high school, much of the writing about reading you may have done was in English class, writing critical essays about novels, poems, or a short stories. In many ways, reading to write about novel or a short story is quite different from reading to write research essays, something you may have discovered in Exercise 1.7. For one thing, there are very basic differences between a literary text and a research article. In a short story, the author's purpose may be *implicit*; you have to "read into" the evidence provided in a narrative to make some interpretation about its meaning. An academic article, on the other hand, is *explicit*. The author states his or her conclusions rather than inviting the reader to make a reasoned interpretation. In addition, academic writing like the second excerpt in Exercise 1.7 uses specialized language and conventions—terms, references, evidence, and organizing principles that the people for whom the article was intended (usually other experts in the field) can understand. Stories have their own internal logic and language, but that is usually accessible to most readers even if the meaning is not.

Finally, we usually enjoy the *experience* of reading a story, or at least feel something in response to a good one, but we usually read articles with a much more practical purpose in mind: to acquire information.

Shouldn't the fundamental differences between these types of texts mean that the *way* we read them is also different? I think so. But we rarely think about our reading strategies, pretty much resorting to reading the way we always have in school. Maybe you never highlight, or the pages you read are fields plowed with yellow rows. Maybe you make marginal notes when you read, or never write a thing. Maybe you always read everything just once, or read a text many times to make sure you understand it. Maybe you always read every word, or you skim like a flat rock on smooth water. Whatever your reading practices, become aware of them as a first step to reading strategically.

## Reading like an Outsider

Why spend precious time thinking about your reading process? For the same reason this course focuses on the writing process: By becoming aware of *how* you do things that have become habits, you exercise more control over them. In many ways, this book is about challenging old habits and assumptions about research, and this includes approaches to reading when you have to write a research essay. For example, consider what's unique about this situation:

- In a general sense, you're just reading to collect information. But researchers use what they read in some particular ways: to provide support for their ideas, to create a context for the questions they're asking, and to complicate or extend their thinking.
- College research often requires students to read the specialized discourses of fields they're not familiar with. That means they must struggle with jargon and conventions that make reading particularly difficult.
- Typically, the purpose of the research paper is not to report, but to explore or argue. Information is in the service of the writer's own ideas about a topic.
- In some classes (though probably not this one), the main audience for the research essay is an expert in the subject the writer is exploring.

In a way, the student researcher has to read like an outsider— or as essayist Scott Russell Sanders put it, "an amateur's raid in a world of specialists." What does this suggest about your reading strategy? First, it makes sense to develop a working knowledge of your topic *before* you tackle the more scholarly stuff. Research in reading suggests that knowledge of a subject makes a big difference in comprehension and retention of information. Second, your own purposes should firmly guide what you read and how you read it. Mentally juggle at least the three purposes I mentioned earlier— reading for example, for context, and for challenge. Third, anticipate your own resistance to

---

**Reading Strategies for Research Writers**

- First develop a working knowledge
- Let your own purposes guide: example, context, challenge
- Anticipate your own resistance
- Learn the organizing principles of articles
- Read with a pen in your hand

the scholarly writing that seems "boring." It's boring because you're an outsider and haven't broken the code. The more you read in your subject area, the more you'll understand; the learning curve is steep. Fourth, in scholarly writing especially, quickly learn the organizing principles of the articles. For example, in the social sciences, articles often have *abstracts, introductions, methods*, and *discussion* sections. Each provides particular kinds of information that might be useful to you. It often isn't necessary to read an academic article from beginning to end. And finally, the most important thing: read with a pen in your hand. In the next chapter, I'll introduce you to some notetaking strategies that encourage you to use writing to think about what you're reading *as* you're reading it. Write-to-learn activities such as fastwriting can help you take possession of information and help you write a stronger paper.

CHAPTER **2**

# The Second Week

## Developing a Research Strategy

A few years ago, I wanted a pair of good birding binoculars for my birthday. I thought of the local store that seemed to carry the largest selection of binoculars, went down there, and within twenty minutes or so spent about three hundred bucks on some Swift binoculars, a brand that is highly regarded by wildlife watchers. Did you ever notice that is often *after* your purchase when you're most motivated to seek out information that reinforces your decision to buy something? Within days of buying the Swifts, I searched the Internet just to make certain that the model I bought was the one recommended by most birders. Sure enough, that seemed to be the case. Then I casually checked the prices on the binoculars, quite certain that I made a fairly good deal on them. To my horror I discovered that I had paid about $100 more than I had to.

Sometimes having no research strategy costs more than time.

A research essay is time-consuming, and while you aren't risking money the quality of your paper may make a big difference in your final grade—two reasons that it pays to be thoughtful about *how* you approach gathering and using information. A typical "strategy" is something like this: (1) get the assignment, (2) choose a topic, (3) wait until a few days before the paper is due, (4) madly search the Internet, (5) write the paper the night before you have to hand it in, (5) pray.

In fact, you've already approached this paper more strategically. In the last chapter, you spent time exploring possible topics, narrowing your focus, and developing research questions that will help guide your search for information. This will make a big difference in the efficiency of your research in the library and the Web. But what do experienced researchers know that will help you find what you're looking for fast, and use what you find effectively?

Here's what you will learn this week:

1.  A chronology for the search.
2.  How to control the language of your searches to get the best results.
3.  Advanced searching techniques for the library and the Web, and other sources of information including surveys and interviews.
4.  Evaluating what you find.
5.  Notetaking methods that will help you to begin writing your essay even before you begin the draft.

## The Internet Itch: Should You Scratch It First?

The first thing you want to do is begin your research on the Internet. I don't really blame you. It's fun (at least at first), and you may even be able to do the work from home. But is this the place to begin? It depends.

1.  How much do you already know about your topic? Do you know enough to invent fairly specific keywords that will produce useful information fairly quickly? Or is your project mostly exploratory? Did you choose your topic largely because you wanted to learn more about it? If you consider yourself a novice on your topic, it's likely that you'll initially waste a lot of time on the Web trying to find relevant and reliable information that will provide basic knowledge. The library is a far better place to find this information efficiently.
2.  Have you had enough experience with Web sources to evaluate them critically? As you know, cyberspace is cluttered with information, much of it pretty questionable for academic research. The main advantage of the campus library when you're starting out is that the materials in it were selected by librarians, chosen because those materials are useful for college research.
3.  Got time to kill? Then by all means go online—whether you're knowledgeable about your topic or not, or even inexperienced with Web searching—and watch the time fly!

Most searches, however, should begin in the campus library. Library research is time-consuming, too, but you'll be amazed at how much you can get done this week by developing a thoughtful research strategy.

## Library Research Strategy

If you're finding questions about your topic that light small fires under you, then you may feel ready to plunge headlong into research this week. Before you do, plan your attack. At this point, you will likely return to the library with a stronger sense of what you want to know than you had last week, when you worked through the library exercise. But keep in mind that you still have many trails to follow and a formidable mass of information to consider. Where should you begin? How do you know where to go from there?

## Moving from General to Specific

Often, researchers move from general sources to those that give topics more specific treatment. Look at it this way: You're not likely much of an authority on your topic yet, but by the time you write the final draft of your paper, you will be. What you have going for you at this point is your own curiosity. You're going to teach yourself about child abuse or the effects of caffeine, starting with the general knowledge you can find in the *New York Times* or *Redbook* and moving toward more specialized sources, such as the *Journal of Counseling Psychology* and the *New England Journal of Medicine*. Plan to begin with the general sources, as you did in Week 1 when you surveyed the landscape of your subject with the general encyclopedia and the *Readers' Guide.* Then move to progressively more specialized indexes and materials, digging more deeply as you become more and more of an expert in your own right.

Visualize books and articles—and the indexes that will help you find them—as occupying some spot on an inverted pyramid. Those sources toward the top are often written by nonexperts for a general audience. Those sources toward the bottom are more likely written by experts in the field for a more knowledgeable audience. An inverted pyramid of sources is shown in Figure 2.1.

Consider beginning with these generalized references, which will lead you to sources intended for a popular audience:

- General encyclopedias, almanacs, and dictionaries (e.g., *Encyclopaedia Britannica, Webster's Dictionary*)
- Indexes to popular periodicals and newspapers (e.g., *Readers' Guide,* InfoTrac, Newsbank)
- Card catalog (for popular books)

After consulting these sources, move to more specialized references, which will often lead you to books and articles written by experts on your topic for a more knowledgeable audience:

- Specialized encyclopedias and dictionaries (e.g., *Encyclopedia of Religion and Ethics, Dictionary of Philosophy and Psychology*— see "Second-Level Searching," Chapter 3)

*General knowledge*                                    *Less authoritative*

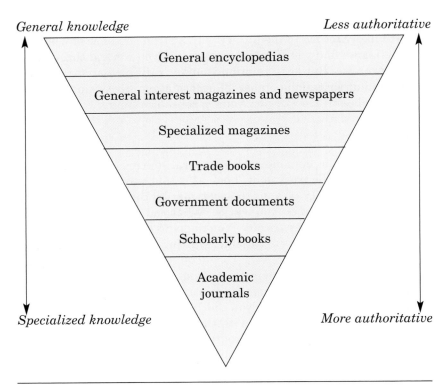

General encyclopedias

General interest magazines and newspapers

Specialized magazines

Trade books

Government documents

Scholarly books

Academic
journals

*Specialized knowledge*                                 *More authoritative*

**FIGURE 2.1**   **Pyramid of Library Sources**

- Specialized fact books (e.g., *Statistical Abstract of the United States, Facts on File*—see "Finding Quick Facts," Chapter 5)
- Academic indexes (e.g., the *Humanities* and *Social Science Citation Indexes,* ERIC, Psyclit, and other CD databases)
- Card catalog (for more authoritative books on your topic)
- Government documents
- Biographical indexes
- Bibliographic indexes (see "Third-Level Searching," Chapter 3)
- Dissertation abstracts (see "Third-Level Searching," Chapter 3)

You may find as you work that this progression from the more general to the more specialized treatment of your topic occurs quite naturally. You'll quickly find that articles in popular magazines, newspapers, and books tell you what you already know. Your hunger to unearth new information will inevitably lead you to more specialized indexes, and you'll be able to read the articles they lead you to with more understanding as you become more of an authority on your topic.

## *Evaluating Library Sources*

The aim of your research strategy is not only to find interesting information on your topic but also to find it in *authoritative* sources. What are authoritative sources? In most cases, they are the most current sources. (The exception may be sources on historical subjects.) Authoritative sources are also those types found on the bottom of the pyramid (see Figure 2.1).

In part, the kinds of sources you rely on in preparing your paper depend on your topic. Sandra has chosen as her tentative focusing question, *How has the Kosovo conflict influenced the way war crimes are prosecuted?* Because Sandra's topic addresses public policy and current events, she'll likely find a wealth of information in newspapers and magazines but not much in books. She certainly should check the academic indexes on this topic—a database called *PAIS,* or Public Affairs Information System, would be a good bet—because it's likely that political scientists have something to say on the subject.

**Why Journal Articles Are Better than Magazine Articles.** If your topic has been covered by academic journal articles, rely heavily on these sources. I've already mentioned that an article on, say, suicide among college students in a magazine like *Time* is less valuable than one in the *American Journal of Psychology.* Granted, the latter may be harder to read. But you're much more likely to learn something from a journal article because it's written by an expert and is usually narrowly focused. Also, because academic articles are carefully documented, you may be able to mine bibliographies for additional sources. And finally, scholarly work, such as that published in academic journals and books (usually published by university presses), is especially authoritative because it's subject to peer review. That means that every manuscript submitted for publication is reviewed by other authorities in the field, who scrutinize the author's evidence, methods, and arguments. Those articles that end up being published have truly passed muster.

**Look for Often-Cited Authors.** As you make your way through information on your topic, pay attention to names of authors whose work you often encounter or who are frequently mentioned in bibliographies. These individuals are often the best scholars in the field, and it will be useful to become familiar with their work and use it, if possible, in your paper. If an author's name keeps turning up, use it as another term for searching the card catalog and the indexes. Doing so might yield new sources you wouldn't necessarily encounter using subject headings. A specialized index—such as the *Social Science* and *Humanities Citation Indexes*—will help you search for articles both by a particular author and by other authors who cite a particular author in their articles. (For more information on how to use the citation indexes, see "Using Citation Indexes" in Chapter 3.)

**Primary over Secondary Sources.**   Another way of looking at information is to determine whether it's a *primary* or a *secondary* source. A primary source presents the original words of a writer—his speech, poem, eyewitness account, letter, interview, autobiography. A secondary source presents somebody else's work. Whenever possible, choose a primary source over a secondary one, since the primary source is likely to be more accurate and authoritative.

The subject you research will determine the kinds of primary sources you encounter. For example, if you're writing a paper on a novelist, then his novels, stories, letters, and interviews are primary sources. A topic on the engineering of the Chicago River in 1900, a partly historical subject, might lead to a government report on the project or a firsthand account of its construction in a Chicago newspaper. Primary sources for a paper in the sciences might be findings from an experiment or observations, and for a paper in business, marketing information or technical studies.

**Not All Books Are Alike.**   When writing my high school research reports, I thought that a book was always the best source because, well, books are thick, and anyone who could write that much on any one subject probably knows what she's talking about. Naive, I know.

One of the things college teaches is *critical thinking*—the instinct to pause and consider before rushing to judgment. I've learned not to automatically believe in the validity of what an author is saying (as you shouldn't for this author), even if he did write a thick book about it.

If your topic lends itself to using primarily books as sources, then evaluate the authority of each before deciding to use it in your paper. This is especially important if your paper relies heavily on one particular book. Consider the following:

- Is the book written for a general audience or more knowledgeable readers?
- Is the author an acknowledged expert in the field?
- Is there a bibliography? Is the information carefully documented?
- How was the book received by critics? To find out, consider checking the following indexes, which may feature summaries of reviews or refer you to articles reviewing the book

in magazines and journals. Entries are usually listed by author, title, or reviewer.

> *Book Review Digest.* New York: Wilson, 1905–date. Provides summaries and quotations from reviews.
>
> *Current Book Review Citations.* New York: Wilson. Indexes reviews in more than one thousand periodicals.

## Internet Research Strategy

The Internet is an information resource that acts like I did when I was thirteen: at times, forthcoming, amiable, and responsible, and at other times, rebellious, disorganized, and unreliable. Despite this schizophrenic character—or perhaps because of it—the Net can inspire among its users an obsessive relationship that rivals anything you experienced in the eighth grade: The Internet can drive you crazy, yet you can't seem to get enough of it. I have frequently seen my students spend hours browsing the Net for information, wandering from one end of cyberspace to the other, when they could walk across the quad to the library and find what they needed in less than thirty minutes.

## Three Drawbacks of Internet Research

For all its promise as an information source for the researcher—and the Internet's potential is really quite stunning—know that, for now at least, its drawbacks are worth considering. Let me mention a few:

1. *Information on the Internet is disorganized.* While search tools such as Alta Vista and Yahoo! and indexes such as the Virtual Library are beginning to fence off some of cyberspace and organize some of the information that rushes helter-skelter into that virtual village commons every day, there is no limited set of comprehensive reference sources. This means you cannot be certain that a single search, using one of the many so-called search engines like Yahoo!, will ever offer adequate coverage on what might be available on your topic. To research effectively on the Internet, then, you have to be extra resourceful. You have to learn how to launch multiple searches that will explore as much of that commons as possible.

2. *Information on the Internet is unreliable.* The free-for-all atmosphere of the Internet makes it a surprisingly democratic forum for ideas, debate, and dialogue. As a participant, I find that enormously appealing, but as a researcher, the openness of the Internet makes me nervous. How reliable is the information I find there? Will it still be there tomorrow? And how can I establish the authority of Internet

sources, especially since so much information is authored anonymously? For the moment, the Internet is not nearly as good a source for scholarly information as the library. Peer-reviewed journals—publications that will only print an article after it has been scrutinized by other experts in the discipline—are the most authoritative sources for college research papers, and some of these journals are available online, though not nearly as many as are in the library. Moreover, some information on the Internet is downright wacky. So, while there *is* useful material to be found online, the researcher must, as Ernest Hemingway put it somewhat more graphically, always keep her "crap detector" on.

3. *It's easy to go nowhere very slowly*. Navigating the Internet can be like driving in Boston: You're constantly confronted by no street signs and complex intersections that seem to end up in rotaries. In fact, moving around in cyberspace, looking for information, is a lot like that: tentatively trying one street, then returning to try another—moving forward, then back, then forward, then back—until you find your way to a useful destination. Then, there are the breakdowns. *Servers*—the software programs that make information available to other computers on the Net—are sometimes fickle things. They can crash at the most inconvenient times.

Internet forays require patience, so if you're easily discouraged, online research may drive you batty. To avoid that, do what I did in Boston: First, learn to drive to Fenway Park without getting lost. There are a number of Internet sites that are fairly easy to find and frequently rewarding sources for college researchers; many of them are listed in this book. Learn to find and use these sites first; then, when you're more confident, you can try to find the Internet equivalent of the underground parking garage at Boston Common.

## Three Reasons to Use the Internet for Research

Now that I've sobered you up about the drawbacks of online research, consider its unique advantages:

1. *The Internet is a marvelous source for topical information*. Do you want to read the March 23 *New York Times* article on the relationship between writing and Alzheimer's? Check the *New York Times Online*. Want to read the text of the president's most recent speech on funding student loans for higher education? Search *Fedworld*'s Web site for an FTP file of the president's speeches. If it's

current information you're after, the Internet offers fast access to it through online newspapers and periodicals, commercial information services, and government sources. And the Internet is a particularly good resource for timely information on things to do with computer technology and the Net.

2. *The Internet is most useful when you're after something specific.* Say you want some information on how the population of Bosnia-Herzogovinia breaks down according to religious affiliation. Or perhaps you need an electronic version of the Bill of Rights, or you're interested in getting more information from Alcoholics Anonymous (AA). You will likely find all of this kind of specific information much more quickly on the Net than at the library. If you're not exactly sure what you're looking for or have only a broad notion of what it might be, the Internet can be a swamp. That's why so-called keyword searches, if they're carefully expressed, can produce useful information much more quickly than broader subject searches. (As you'll see, working your way through a subject search *can* be quite useful. But you can't be in a hurry.)

3. *Online documents can be easy to transport.* Downloading files or printing documents from the Net is easy, particularly with current Web browsers, such as Netscape. And once downloaded into your computer or onto a floppy disk, these documents are in an electronic format, which makes it easy to move the information into your own document. Suppose you need a passage from *The Adventures of Huckleberry Finn,* or a quote from the president's latest speech on health care, or a table on high school students' drug use. Using the "Edit" and "Move" or "Cut" and "Paste" features of your word-processing program, you can drop the passages or tables into your paper (assuming the texts are compatible or can be converted by your program). However, the ease of transporting online documents should make you extra vigilant about avoiding plagiarism. Carefully cite and attribute any material in your own paper that is not your own.

## The Invisible Web

There are really two Webs (see Figure 2.2). One contains documents indexed by various popular search engines such as Northern Light or Yahoo! The other Web—often described by Internet experts as the "Invisible Web"—is a frontier that is difficult to access the usual ways. The Invisible Web is largely composed of massive databases that often defy attempts by search engines to describe their contents. As one commentator put it, "when [search engine spiders]

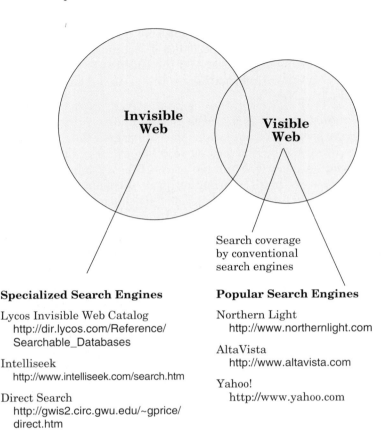

**FIGURE 2.2**    The range, variety, and amount of information you'll find on the Internet may be much greater if you search both the visible and Invisible Web; each is accessible using different kinds of search engines. Remember to launch multiple searches. Don't rely on any one tool.

come across a database . . . it's as if they've run smack into the entrance of a massive library with securely bolted doors. Spiders can record the library's address, but can tell you nothing about the books, magazines, or other documents it contains." Fortunately, there are ways to reach this information. But more about that later.

The purpose of a successful Internet search strategy is to be as comprehensive as possible—no small task since less than half of the Web is currently indexed, and even the best search engines can access about 16 percent of that material. However, a strategy that recognizes the two Webs—one mapped and the other a largely uncharted frontier—and is designed to explore both is likely to be as comprehensive as any Internet search can be. In other words, if the basic library research strategy is to move down the pyramid of sources, from the more general to the more specific, then the basic Internet strategy is simply to cover as much ground as possible.

Start with the visible Web using conventional search engines, and then check the Invisible Web using specialized search engines designed to unlock those bolted doors that conceal information in databases.

## Evaluating Online Sources

Any sound Internet search strategy for an academic essay will focus on discovering not only relevant but *authoritative* information on your topic. In general, this isn't necessarily hard to figure out. Some of the same standards for a print source apply to an online source. Is it current? Is the author a recognized expert? Is the material well documented? What is the *context* of the information—is it included in a reputable publication, or is it presented on behalf of some commercial or other special interest? But pretty quickly, evaluating online sources can become tricky. Many Web documents have no author. Sometimes it's hard to determine when they were published and how often they've been updated. It can even be a challenge to figure out the author's affiliation or the organization—if any—that published the material on the Internet.

Here are some general guidelines to follow, and then I'll suggest a more vigorous approach for evaluating online sources:

■ *Always keep your purpose in mind.* For example, if you're exploring the lobbying methods of the National Rifle Association, then you will want to hear, and see, what they have to say and do on their Web site, knowing full well that this is not an unbiased source. The NRA Web pages are, however, both relevant and authoritative in this instance. After all, who knows more about the NRA than the NRA?

■ *Favor governmental and educational sources over commercial ones.* There are plenty of exceptions to this (like the one mentioned above), but in general you're wise to rely more heavily on material sponsored by groups without a commercial stake in your topic. How can you tell the institutional affiliation of a source? Sometimes it's obvious. They tell you. But when it's not obvious, the *domain name* provides a clue. The *.com* that follows a server name signifies a commercial site, while *.edu, .org,* or *.gov* usually signals an educational, nonprofit group, or governmental. The absence of ads on a Web site also implies a site that is noncommercial.

■ *Favor authored documents over those without authors.* There's a simple reason for this: You can check the credentials of an author. You can do this by sending an e-mail message to him or her, a convenience often available as a link on a Web page, or you can do a quick search with the name on library indexes to see if that author has published other books or articles on your topic.

■ *Favor documents that are also available in print over those only available online.* These might be articles that have appeared in magazines or newspapers or even journals. They might be conference reports or studies or even books. Sources that are published in more than one medium may be more credible because they undergo more scrutiny.

■ *Favor Web pages that were recently updated over those that haven't been changed in a year or more.* Frequently at the bottom of a Web page there is a line indicating when the information was posted to the Internet and/or when it was last updated. Look for it.

■ *Favor Web sources that document their claims over those that don't.* Most Web documents won't feature a bibliography. That doesn't mean that they're useless to you, but be suspicious of a Web author who makes factual assertions without supporting evidence.

**Key to Evaluating Internet Sources.**    As an undergraduate, I was a botany major. Among other things, I was drawn to plant taxonomy because the step-by-step taxonomic keys for discovering the names of unfamiliar plants gave the vegetative chaos of a Wisconsin meadow or upland forest a beautiful kind of logic and order. The key that follows is modeled after the ones I used in field taxonomy, but this one is a modest attempt to make some sense of the chaos on the Web for the academic researcher, particularly when the usual approaches for establishing the authority of traditional scholarship and publications fail. For one thing, many Internet documents are anonymous, and the date of publication isn't always clear. In some cases, even if there is an author of an online document, his or her affiliation or credentials may not be apparent.

If you're not sure whether a particular Web document will give your essay credibility, see Figure 2.3 and work through the following steps:

1. Does the document have an author or authors? If yes, go to step 2. If no, go to step 10.

2. Does the document appear in an online journal or magazine that is "refereed"? In other words, is there any indication that every

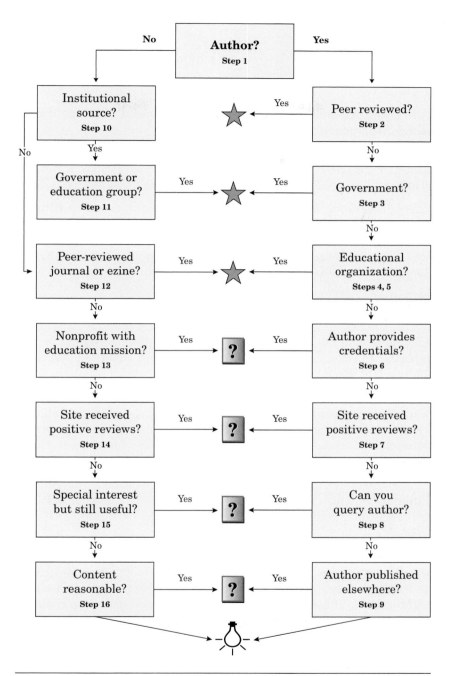

**FIGURE 2.3**   Follow the flowchart for a rigorous review of a Web document or page, beginning with whether the author is obvious or not. Sites that earn stars are generally more trustworthy. Those with question marks still may be useful, depending on the situation. Be particularly wary of information on commercial or special interest sites.

article submitted must be reviewed by other scholars in the field before it is accepted for publication? If so, you've found a good source. If not (or you're unsure), go to step 3.

3. Is the document from a government source? If yes, then it may be a good source. If not, go to step 4.

4. Does the document appear in an online publication affiliated with a reputable educational institution or organization? If not, go to step 5.

5. Is *the author* affiliated with a reputable educational institution or organization? (For example, is he or she connected with a large university or a national nonprofit organization? Individuals associated with businesses or special interest groups may be reliable, though researchers should be vigilant about whether they have axes to grind and qualify the information to make that clear.) If so, be encouraged. If not, move on to step 6.

6. If the author isn't clearly affiliated with a reputable institution, does he or she offer any credentials that help establish his or her expertise to write on the topic? (For example, an advanced degree in the relevant discipline is encouraging.) If not, go to step 7.

7. Did you find the document in a Web site that has earned high marks from scholarly reviewers and others interested in the reliability of Internet information? (See "Other Ways to Avoid Disinformation on the Internet " in the section that follows for ways to check this.) Yes? Great. No? Move on to step 8.

8. Does the author include an e-mail address link on the online document so that you can write to inquire about affiliations or professional credentials or other publications on the topic? If not, go to step 9.

9. Has the author published elsewhere on the topic in reputable journals or other publications? Check this at the library by searching under the author's name in the electronic catalog or appropriate CD-ROM indexes. If not, reconsider the value of the source. You could be dealing with a lone ranger who has no expertise on your topic and no relevant affiliations.

10. If the online document has no author, is it from an institutional source like a university, the state or federal government, or a non-profit organization? If yes, go to step 11. If no, go to step 14.

11. Is the material from the federal or state government? If so, that's encouraging. If not, go to step 12.

12. Is the anonymous document published in an online journal or magazine? Is it refereed? (See step 2 above.) If so, it's likely a good source. If not, go to step 13.

13. Is the document part of a publication or Web page from a non-government source whose mission is described in the document, and does it suggest that the organization's goals include research and education? Is there a board of directors, and does it include professionals and academics who are respected in the field? If not, go to step 14.

14. Does the Web site in which the document is located get high marks from scholarly or other reviewers interested in the reliability of Internet information? (See "Other Ways to Avoid Disinformation on the Internet" in the section that follows for ways to check this.) If not, start to wonder whether you should use this source. Go to step 15 before giving up on it.

15. Even if the organization offering the information represents a special interest group or business with an axe to grind (e.g., the Forest Products Association or Microsoft Corporation), the information may be useful as a means of presenting their point of view. Make sure, if you use it, that the information is qualified to make that obvious.

16. Do any of the usual criteria for evaluating a source apply to this anonymous document? Does it have a citations page, and do the citations check out? Was it published on the Internet recently? Does the argument the writer is making seem sound? Do the facts check out? If the answer is no to all of the above, then don't trust the document. If you can answer yes to more than one of these questions, the material probably has marginal value in a college paper, though there might be exceptions.

## Other Ways to Avoid Disinformation on the Internet

Not surprisingly, scholars, librarians, and others share the concern about the reliability of the Internet for research. To address the problem, a growing number of Web sites—usually sponsored by universities—are devoted to reviewing Internet information and offering researchers links to authoritative online scholarship. The following are just a few of these sites that I've found useful:

*Infomine: Scholarly Internet Resource Collections*
http://lib-www.ucr.edu/

Sponsored by the University of California, this site offers more than 9,500 links to Web sites and databases useful to college researchers. The material is indexed under subject headings such as "Biological, Agricultural, and Medical Sources" and "Social Sciences and the Humanities." *Infomine* also offers a search feature that allows the user to look with keywords, as well as subject and title.

*Britannica Internet Guide*

http://www.britannica.com

This site is the *Encyclopaedia Britannica*'s contribution to sorting the wheat from the chaff on the Internet. Editors review millions of Web sites for reliability, including checking the credentials of authors or organizations, the usefulness of the information, and the frequency of updates. Currently, only 75,000 sites have passed muster. But the list includes sites in fourteen categories. The service is free.

*Internet Scout Project*

http://wwwscout.cs.wisc.edu/scout/index.html

Every week, this site publishes the *Scout Report,* which describes Internet resources that have managed to survive the "highly selective" review of the librarians and scholars who contribute to the project. Perhaps the most useful feature is the *Scout Report Signpost*, a page that allows the user to search three years' worth of *Scout Report*-approved sites in a range of fields. What you get is a summary of the Internet resource and a link to retrieve it.

A good researcher always takes a skeptical view of claims made in print; she should be even more wary of claims made in Internet documents. And while these approaches for evaluating online sources should help, it still can be pretty tricky deciding whom to take seriously in cyberspace. So to sort it all out, always ask yourself these questions: How important is this Internet document to my research? Do I really need it? Might there be a more reliable print version?

## EXERCISE 2.1

### Net-Casting: Evaluating the Catch

In the abstract, evaluating Web sources seems fairly straightforward. See if you find that remains true by offering your evaluation of the following two Web pages.

First, let me establish a context for the exercise. Assume that you've chosen the following as your research question: "Has the Endangered Species Act (ESA) been effective in the recovery of endangered animals?" Your instructor will organize your class into three groups: One group is assigned to argue that the ESA has been *ineffective* in protecting endangered animals and believes the act is flawed; another group will argue that the act has been *effective* in recovering species and doesn't need reform; and the third group will pursue an *exploratory* project, withholding judgment on the question.

An initial Internet search produces the following documents: A page from the Web site of the National Endangered Species Act Reform Coalition—a lobby group—and a news release from the federal U.S. Fish and Wildlife Service on the removal of the bald eagle from the list of endangered species.

In ten minutes or so each group must answer the following questions (based only on the information provided in Figures 2.4 and 2.5) and prepare to present their conclusions to the rest of the class.

1. Would your group use *both* these sources in drafting a research essay on the effectiveness of the ESA? If yes, answer the questions below. If no, go on to question 2.
   - If someone questioned your use of the sources, how would you defend your decision to use them? How might you handle the information in the essay to blunt some of this criticism? Do you need to know anything more to offer a convincing defense?
   - *How* might you use these sources in the essay? As evidence? As examples? As a means of raising a question or idea or qualifying a claim?

2. Might your group choose to use *one* of the two Web documents? If yes, answer the questions below. If no, go on to question 3.
   - Why would you use this document and not the other?
   - *How* might you use it in your group's essay?

3. On what basis would you reject *both* of these Web documents?

This exercise will not only challenge you to consider how to critically evaluate the credibility and relevance of a Web site, it might also remind you of how important it is to link that evaluation to your own particular purposes in using a source. The same principle, by

# What is the ESA?

Simply stated, the Endangered Species Act is the most powerful environmental law ever enacted.

Originally adopted in 1973, the Act's framers envisioned a law which would protect species believed to be on the brink of extinction. When the law was enacted, there were 109 species listed for protection. Today (January 2000), there are 1,210 on the list, with 241 species considered as "Candidates" for listing, and nearly 4,000 species designated as "Species of Concern".

**Is it true that the ESA has expired?** The authorization for funding under the ESA expired on October 1, 1992, though Congress has appropriated funds in each succeeding fiscal year to keep the program running.

**Have any species ever been delisted?** Unfortunately, the ESA has failed at recovering and delisting species since its inception. Only 29 species have been "delisted" or removed from the species list since 1973—seven due to extinction and nine due to "data error" (read: "never should have been listed in the first place"). The remaining species are either located outside the United States (and therefore receive no protection from the ESA) or were beneficiaries of other activities such as the banning of DDT.

**How can the ESA be improved?** NESARC has long championed making constructive changes to the Act which will allow it to work better both for the people who have to work with the law and the species who depend upon it. NESARC is recommending that changes be made in seven broad areas of the law.

**Who administers the ESA?** The Endangered Species Act is administered primarily by the Fish and Wildlife Service, but the National Marine Fisheries Service has responsibility for protecting certain marine and anadromous fish species.

**What is the difference between an endangered species and a threatened species?** Under the ESA, certain species of plants and animals (both vertebrate and invertebrate) are listed as either "endangered" or "threatened" according to assessments of the risk of their extinction. Once a species is listed, powerful legal tools are brought to bear to enforce the recovery of the species and protection of its habitat. A species may be classified for protection as "endangered" when it is in danger of extinction within the foreseeable future throughout all or a significant portion of its range. A "threatened" classification is provided to those animals and plants likely to become endangered within the foreseeable future throughout all or a significant portion of their ranges.

**FIGURE 2.4**    Frequently asked question (FAQ) pages, like this one from the National Endangered Species Act Reform Coalition, can be a useful source of information for the Internet researcher since they often raise—and answer— questions the researcher is posing. How credible are the answers? That depends . . . on what?

*Source:* NESARC Web page. Reprinted by permission of Jack Mingus.

**What is a species?** A species includes any species or subspecies of fish, wildlife, or plant; any variety of plant; and any distinct population segment of any vertebrate species that interbreeds when mature. Excluded is any species of the Class Insecta determined by the Secretary to constitute a pest whose protection under the provisions of the Act would present an overwhelming and overriding risk to man.

**How does a species get listed?** The government relies largely upon petitions, surveys conducted by the Fish and Wildlife Service and other agencies' surveys, and other substantiated reports on field studies. Anyone may petition the Service to have a species listed or reclassified as endangered or threatened, or removed from the list. Findings are required before any proposal is published in the *Federal Register.*

- Within 90 days of receiving a petition, the Service must make a finding as to whether the petition presents substantial information that the listing may be warranted.
- Within 1 year of receipt, a finding is required that the listing is either *warranted or not warranted.*
- A finding of *warranted* must lead directly to an immediate (less than 30 days) proposed listing, *or* the Service can find that such an immediate proposal is precluded by other listing activities such that the proposal may not be made for several additional weeks, months or even years. In order to make this secondary finding of *warranted but precluded* the Service must also be making expeditious progress in its overall listing program (e.g., candidates of higher priority are taken first).
- Any warranted but precluded finding must be re-examined on each successive anniversary of the petition's receipt until the listing is either proposed or the petition is turned down as not warranted.

**What is the criteria for listing?** A species is only determined to be an endangered species or a threatened species because of any one or more of the following factors (economics or others not listed here are not permissible under the Act):

- the present or threatened destruction, modification, or curtailment of its habitat or range;
- overutilization for commercial, recreational, scientific, or educational purposes;
- disease or predation;
- the inadequacy of existing regulatory mechanisms; or
- other natural or man-made factors affecting its continued existence.

**Can I see a copy of the ESA on-line?** Yes. The Fish and Wildlife Service has provided this copy of the Endangered Species Act to on-line visitors.

**What if I have more questions?** Feel free to contact NESARC via e-mail or call us at 202-333-7481.

http://www.nsearc.org/actmain.htm          02/25/2000

**FIGURE 2.4**   (Continued)

National News Release: U.S. Fish and Wildlife Service    http://www.fws.gov/r9extaff/eaglejuly2.html

U. S. Fish and Wildlife Service

# News Release

Office of Public Affairs
1849 C Street NW
Washington, DC 20240
202/208-5634 Fax:
202/219-2428

Contact: Cindy Hoffman
202/208-3008
202/208-5634

## The Bald Eagle Is Back!
## President Clinton Announces Proposal to Remove Our National Symbol From Endangered Species List

As a symbol of freedom, strength, and courage, the bald eagle represents the best of what America has to offer. On the eve of Independence Day weekend, President Clinton marked the culmination of a three-decade effort to protect and recover this majestic bird by announcing a proposal to remove it from the list of threatened and endangered species.

"The American bald eagle is now back from the brink of extinction, thriving in virtually every state of the union, " President Clinton said. "I can think of no better way to honor the birth of our nation than by celebrating the rebirth of our proudest living symbol."

The bald eagle once ranged throughout every state in the Union except Hawaii. When America adopted the bird as its national symbol in 1782, as many as 100,000 nesting bald eagles lived in the continental United States, excluding Alaska. By 1963, only 417 nesting pairs were found in the lower 48.

Today, due to recovery efforts by the Interior Department's U.S. Fish and Wildlife Service in partnership with other federal agencies, tribes, state and local governments, conservation organizations, universities, corporations and thousands of individual Americans, this number has risen to an estimated 5,748 nesting pairs. As a result, biologists believe it may no longer require the special protection of the Endangered Species Act.

"America was the first nation on earth to pass a comprehensive law protecting endangered species, the Endangered Species Act, and once again we have shown that this landmark law works," Interior Department Secretary Bruce Babbitt said. "Today the American bald eagle is back. The bald eagle joins a growing list of other once-imperilled species that are on the road to recovery, including the peregrine falcon and the Columbian white-tailed deer."

**FIGURE 2.5**    The news release is a specialized genre widely available from both noncommercial and commercial sites on the World Wide Web. A surprisingly large number of stories in print sources, such as newspapers, originate as news releases written by public relations people.

The bald eagle is a large, powerful, brown bird with a white head and tail. Females generally weigh up to 14 pounds and have a wingspan up to 8 feet. Males are smaller, weighing 7 to 10 pounds with a wingspan of 6-1/2 feet. Young bald eagles are mostly dark brown until they reach four to six years of age and may be confused with the golden eagle. The bird's life span in the wild can reach 30 years.

Bald eagles mate for life and build huge nests in the tops of large trees near rivers, lakes, and marshes. Nests, which are usually re-used and enlarged every year, can reach 20 feet across and weigh up to 4,000 pounds. The birds travel over great distances, but normally return to nest within 100 miles of where they were originally raised.

Bald eagles historically ranged throughout North America except extreme northern Alaska and Canada and central and southern Mexico. They nested on both coasts from Florida to Baja California in the south, and from Labrador to the western Aleutian Islands, Alaska, in the north. The raptors' habitat includes estuaries, large lakes, reservoirs, major rivers, and some seacoast areas. These areas, however, must have an adequate food base, perching areas, and nesting sites in order to support the species. In winter, bald eagles often congregate at specific wintering sites that are generally close to open water and offer good perch trees and night roosts.

When Europeans first arrived on the North American continent, there were an estimated one-quarter to one-half million bald eagles. The first major decline in the bald eagle population probably began in the mid to late 1800's. It coincided with declines in numbers of waterfowl and shorebirds and other major prey species. Many eagles were killed by humans. Coupled with loss of nesting habitat, these factors reduced bald eagle populations until the 1940's.

In 1940, Congress passed the Bald Eagle Protection Act, prohibiting killing or selling of bald eagles. The Act increased public awareness of the bald eagle, and populations stabilized or increased in most areas of the country.

Shortly after World War II, however, the use of DDT and other organochlorine pesticides became widespread. Initially, DDT was sprayed extensively along coastal and other wetland areas to control mosquitos. Later it was used as a general insecticide. Eagles ingested DDT by eating contaminated fish. The pesticide caused the shells of the bird's eggs to thin and resulted in nesting failures. Loss of nesting habitat also contributed to the population decline.

In 1967, the Secretary of the Interior listed bald eagles south of the 40th parallel as endangered under the Endangered Species Preservation Act of 1966. In 1972, the Environmental Protection Agency took the historic and, at the time, controversial step of banning the use of DDT in the United States. This was the first step on the road to recovery for the bald eagle.

Following enactment of the Endangered Species Act of 1973, the U.S. Fish and Wildlife Service listed the species as endangered throughout the lower 48 states, except in Michigan, Minnesota, Oregon, Washington, and Wisconsin where it was designated as threatened.

**FIGURE 2.5**   (Continued)

The species was never listed as threatened or endangered in Alaska or Canada because populations there have always been healthy.

The listing of the species as endangered provided the springboard for the U.S. Fish and Wildlife Service and its partners to accelerate the pace of recovery through captive breeding programs, reintroduction efforts, law enforcement, and the protection of nest sites during the breeding season.

"It is fitting that we close out this century with such a great tribute to America's commitment to conserving our natural heritage," Babbitt said. "Generations to come will not just see bald eagles on our coins, stamps and flag poles; they will be able to look up in the sky and see our national symbol flying overhead."

Even if the U.S. Fish and Wildlife Service removes the bald eagle from the list of threatened and endangered species, the bird would still be protected by the Migratory Bird Treaty Act and the Bald and Golden Eagle Protection Act. The MBTA prohibits the taking, killing, possession, transportation, and importation of migratory birds, their eggs, parts, and nests except when specifically authorized by the Department of the Interior. The Bald and Golden Eagle Protection Act, the successor to the Bald Eagle Protection Act, prohibits, except under certain specified conditions, the taking, possession, transportation, export or import, barter, or offer to sell, purchase, or barter a bald or golden eagle, alive or dead, or any part, nest, or eagle egg.

If the bald eagle is delisted, the Service also would work with state wildlife agencies to monitor the status of the species for a minimum of five years, as required by the Endangered Species Act. At any time it becomes evident that the bird again needs the Act's protection, the Service would relist the species. The Service's proposal to delist the bald eagle will be published in the Federal Register on July 6, 1999. The public may comment on the proposal in writing until (October 5, 1999). Comments should be sent to Jody Millar at 4469 48th Avenue Court, Rock Island, IL 61201 or through the U.S. Fish and Wildlife Service website at www.fws.gov. A final decision is expected in July 2000.

The U.S. Fish and Wildlife Service is the principal federal agency responsible for conserving, protecting, and enhancing fish and wildlife and their habitats for the continuing benefit of the American people. The Service manages the 93-million-acre National Wildlife Refuge System comprised of more than 500 national wildlife refuges, thousands of small wetlands, and other special management areas. It also operates 66 national fish hatcheries and 78 Ecological Services field stations. The agency enforces Federal wildlife laws, administers the Endangered Species Act, manages migratory bird populations, restores nationally significant fisheries, conserves and restores wildlife habitat such as wetlands, and helps foreign governments with their conservation efforts. It also oversees the Federal Aid program that distributes hundreds of millions of dollars in excise taxes on fishing and hunting equipment to state fish and wildlife agencies.

-FWS-

**Editors' note: **Press materials are available on the Service'swebsite at www.fws.gov.** B-roll and still photographs of bald eagles are available. A satellite feed of the b-roll footage will run from 12:30 - 12:45 eastern time on Friday, July 2 on C-Band, Galaxy 6, Transponder 9, Downlink Frequency 3882 Horizontal, Audio Frequency 6.2-6.8. Interviews with Service employees and other leaders involved in the recovery of the bald eagle are also available.

Comments, questions? See our Frequently Asked Questions (FAQ's), or contact Mitch Snow at mitch_snow@fws.gov

Visit the U. S. Fish and Wildlife Service Home Page

Privacy/Disclaimer Statements

---

**FIGURE 2.5**    (Continued)

the way, applies to using print sources. Also, make sure you discuss some of the things that would be helpful to know about these Web sources that may not be evident from looking at the documents. Finally, spend some time talking about which of the three groups, if any, is most likely to consider the evidence presented in the most fair and balanced way. Why is that?

# Search Languages: Words that Open Doors

Around our house, the Harry Potter phenomenon has everyone muttering magic words. "Flipendo," says Julia, trying to turn the dog into a gerbil. "Wingardium leviosa" says Becca, who is determined to elevate her little sister six feet off the ground. Chopsticks substitute for magic wands. I know this because we suddenly have too few when the take-out Chinese meal arrives; that's the only part of this magical revival sweeping the household that I don't much like.

Some writers foolishly think that there's magic involved in getting good words to the page when it's really much more simple and not at all mysterious: You have to have your seat in the chair and your fingers on the keyboard or curled around a pen. But there is a kind of magic you can perform as a researcher, and it also involves the right words uttered in the right order. *How* you phrase your search of a library database or the World Wide Web makes an enormous difference in the results. I've come to believe that this ability, almost more than any other, is the researcher's most important skill.

## Controlled Language Searches

One of the things that is so good about libraries compared to the Web is that information there is organized. That's the good news. The bad news is that there is so much information to organize that librarians had to develop a special language for searching it. It's not alien language—the words are familiar—but it is a language that requires that certain words be used in the combinations that librarians use to organize information. These are *controlled language searches*, and they are much more common in the library than on the Web.

This sounds far more complicated than it is. In fact, you already know something about controlled language searches because in the last chapter you practiced with the book that is a kind of dictionary of them: the *Library of Congress Subject Headings*. This underused reference is an essential guide to knowing what words you should use to find information on your topic in database searches. Get to know it well, and use it religiously.

## Boolean Searching

Frequently, you'll be searching using a *combination* of keywords. For example, searching for books using the word "Wildfires" will produce an avalanche that will quickly bury you. Efficient research requires that you maximize the number of relevant results and minimize the number of irrelevant ones. That's where searches that use careful combinations of keywords are so important. Many libraries use something called "Boolean" connectors to help you do this when you search databases. A guy named George Boole, a British logician, invented the system more than a hundred years ago, and it still dominates library searching (it's somewhat less widespread on the Web).

The system essentially requires the use of the words AND, OR, and NOT between the search terms or keywords. The word AND, say, between the "Animal" and "Rights" will search a database for documents that include *both* of those terms.

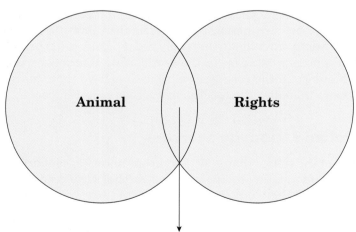

Using AND as a connector between "Animal" and "Rights" will find documents that contain *both* terms.

The use of the connector OR between search terms, obviously, will produce a list of documents that contain either of the terms. That can be a lot of results. Sometimes by simply putting two words together,

"Animal Rights," the OR is implied and you'll get the same results as if you used the word. This is often true when using a Web search engine.

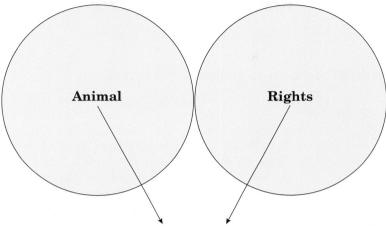

The connector OR will generate documents that contain either word. Depending on the level of generality of the words you use, this can trigger an avalanche.

The NOT connector is less frequently used but really can be quite helpful if you want to *exclude* certain documents. Suppose, for example, you were interested in researching the problem of homelessness in Washington State, where you live. To avoid getting information on Washington DC, where it's also a problem, use the connector NOT.

## Homeless AND Washington NOT D.C.

As you can see from the example above, it's possible to use the connectors between a number of terms, not just two. In fact, the art of creating keyword searches is using both the right words (those used by librarians) in the right combination (those that in combination sufficiently narrow your search and give you the best results).

One final search technique that can be very useful, especially in library searches, is something called "nesting." This involves the use of parentheses around two or more terms in a phrase. This prompts the computer to look for those terms first. For example, suppose you were searching for articles on the ethics of animal rights, but you were particularly interested in information in two states, Idaho and Montana. You might construct a search phrase like this one:

> **(Montana OR Idaho) AND animal AND rights AND ethics**

## Magic Words on the World Wide Web

In the last chapter, you did a subject search on the Web, using popular sites such as Virtual Library that specialize in those kinds of searches. Far more common are searches that use so-called "search engines" such as Google. As you probably know, these are really quite remarkable software programs that in a split second "crawl" the Web, searching for documents that contain the keywords you type in. Lately, the magic of these search engines has been tarnished a bit by commercialism, allowing advertisers to purchase priority listings in search engine results and not always making that fact obvious to the searcher. But these search engines are still essential and getting better all the time.

Keyword searches are the most common methods of searching the Web. Unfortunately, there isn't consistency in search languages used by the many search engines available for scouring the Web. Some permit Boolean searching. More use a variation on Boolean that involves symbols rather than words. The most common symbols are the following:

> **+ is the same as AND**          **" "surrounds a phrase**
>
> **– is the same as NOT    Leaving no punctuation between terms is the same as OR**

The smartest approach to understanding how to construct keyword searches is to read the help file for your favorite search engines and find out what commands they prefer. For example, the most popular search engine, Google, can handle all the Boolean commands mentioned earlier as well as the symbolic substitutes, +, – , " "and so on.

Because of the mind-boggling amount of information on the Web, careful keyword searches are critical. More online time is wasted either not finding what is wanted or sifting through layers and layers of irrelevant documents because of thoughtless keyword searches. For example, notice in Figure 2.6 how the search on the ethics of animal rights can be dramatically changed by adding terms and using search language symbols. An initial search on Google

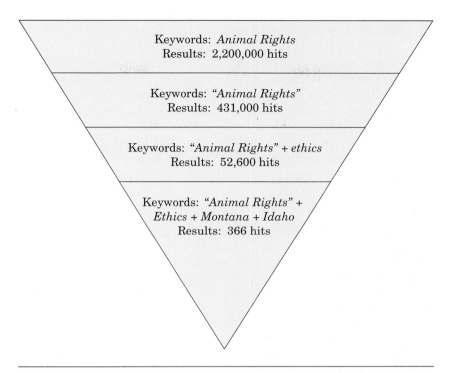

**FIGURE 2.6** **Effects of Keyword Elaboration** A search on Google offers dramatically different numbers of results as the keywords are refined and elaborated on. Whenever possible use three or more terms to narrow your results.

simply using the broad keywords "animal rights" produced 2.2 million documents. The use of a phrase, along with three additional terms winnowed those results to 366 hits, many of which will be relevant.

# Developing Deep Knowledge

If working knowledge equips you to sustain a one-minute dinner conversation on your topic, then deep knowledge is enough for you to make a fifteen-or twenty-minute presentation to the rest of the class. You'll probably be able to answer all their questions, too. (See suggestions for class presentations on page 90 in the box, "Working Together: Could You Clarify, Mr. Ziegler?"). You'll hardly be an expert, but you'll know a lot more about your topic than any of your peers.

Deep knowledge is the product of smart research this week and the next, refining your search terms, knowing where to look for the

## Working Together: "Could You Clarify, Mr. Ziegler?"

By the end of this week, you should be ready to make a presentation to your class on your topic. Imagine that it's a press conference similar to the ones shown on television. You will give a fifteen-minute talk on your topic to your classmates, who will later, like veteran newspaper reporters, follow up with questions. Your presentation will be carefully timed. It shouldn't be any longer than the allotted time limit; any less than the allotted time suggests that you haven't yet developed a deeper knowledge of your topic.

Plan your presentation with the following things in mind:

- *Rather than simply report everything you've learned about your topic, try to give your talk some emphasis.* For example, focus on what you've learned so far that most surprised you and why. Or present the most common misconceptions about your topic and why they miss the mark. Or provide some background about why the question you're exploring is important and share some of the answers you've discovered so far. If your topic has a personal dimension, tell the story, and share how your research has helped you understand your experience differently.
- *Don't read a speech.* It's fine to have notes with you—in fact, it's a good idea—but try to avoid reading them. Make your presentation as interesting as you can. After all, this is a chance to discover what other people think about your topic— what interests them about it and what doesn't. This talk is a great chance to try out some approaches to your topic that you may later use to make your essay more compelling.
- *Consider visuals.* Itching to try out PowerPoint? Here's your chance. Also think about photographs, graphs, charts, and other visual ways to present your information.
- *Begin by stating your focusing question.* Every presentation should start by establishing what question is driving your investigation. You might even put this on the board when you begin.

While you listen to your peers' presentations, think about what questions they raise that interest you. These might be questions of clarification, questions about an assertion the presenters or one of their sources made, or areas that the speakers didn't cover but that you wonder about. Imagine that you're a hard-nosed reporter anxious to get the story right.

most useful information, and using your time efficiently. As you'll see later in this section, deeper knowledge also depends on what you *do* with what you find. Are you able to not only collect information on your topic but think about its significance to your project? Remember that you'll be reading with at least three questions in mind:

1. Does this information help create a *context* for the question I'm posing?
   - Can it provide background on what has already been said about it, and who has said it?
   - Or what is already known and when?
   - Or possibly why this is a question worth asking?

2. Does the information *support* or *develop* an idea or claim I'm making?
   - Is it evidence that what I'm saying might be true?
   - Does it help refine or qualify an idea I have my topic?

3. Does this information *challenge* or *complicate* what I've been thinking about my topic?
   - Does it raise new questions I hadn't thought of?
   - Is it a point of view that is opposed to mine? If so, what do I think about it?
   - Does this change my thinking in some way?

With these three questions in mind—and a number of others that interest you—you'll be implementing your research strategy this week and next, looking at sources in the library and on the Web. The exercises that follow will help guide these searches, making sure that you don't overlook some key source or reference. Your instructor may ask you to hand in a photocopy of the exercise as a record of your journey.

# Library Research Techniques

Despite the appeal of the Web, the campus library remains your most important source of information for academic research. Sure, it can be aggravating. There's that missing book that was supposed to be there, or that magazine with the pages ripped out. You needed that article. Most of all, there's the sense of helplessness you might feel as a relative novice using a reference system that is bigger and more complicated than the library back home.

In the last chapter, you were introduced to basic library search strategies, knowledge that will help give you some mastery over the university library. In the exercise that follows, you'll expand on that knowledge, and at the same time you'll move from a "working knowledge" of your topic to a deeper understanding, one that will crystallize by reading and writing about what you find.

## Finding Books

In the years since I wrote the first edition of *The Curious Researcher*, the old card catalog has completely disappeared. In its place is an electronic catalog, usually Web-based, that allows researchers to search for books even from home. This is a wonderful advance, one of the many ways technology has made researching easier, faster, and more efficient. But not everything has changed. Cataloging and indexing books is still done the old-fashioned way, and it helps to know how librarians do organize books in the university library.

There are two systems for classifying books: the *Dewey Decimal* and the *Library of Congress* systems. Each is quite different. The Dewey system, reportedly conceived in 1873 by an Amherst College undergraduate while daydreaming in church, is numerical, dividing all knowledge into ten broad areas and further subdividing each of these into one hundred additional classifications. Adding decimal points allows librarians to subdivide things even further. Just knowing the *call number* of a book will tell you its subject.

The *Library of Congress* system, which uses both letters and numbers, is much more common in college libraries. This is the system with which you should become most familiar. Each call number begins with one or two letters, signifying a category of knowledge, which is followed by a whole number between 1 and 9,999. A decimal and one or more Cutter numbers sometimes follow. The Library of Congress system is pretty complex, but it's not hard to use. As you get deeper in your research, you'll begin to recognize call numbers that consistently yield useful books. It is sometimes helpful to simply browse those shelves for other possibilities.

## Understanding Call Numbers*

The call number, that strange code on the spine of a library book, is something most of us want to understand just well enough to find that book on the shelf. How much do you need to know? First, you should know that there is more than the alphabet at work in

---

*"Understanding Call Numbers" is adapted from the Web site of the Hawaii Community College library and used here with their permission.

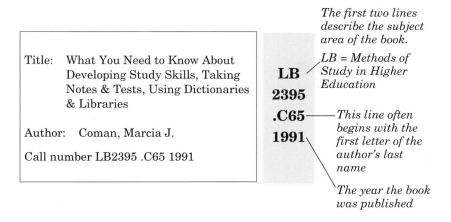

Title:   What You Need to Know About
        Developing Study Skills, Taking
        Notes & Tests, Using Dictionaries
        & Libraries

Author:   Coman, Marcia J.

Call number LB2395 .C65 1991

**LB**
**2395**
**.C65**
**1991**

*The first two lines describe the subject area of the book.*

*LB = Methods of Study in Higher Education*

*This line often begins with the first letter of the author's last name*

*The year the book was published*

**FIGURE 2.7    Deciphering the Call Number Code**

arranging books by their call numbers, and that call numbers tell you more than merely where books are shelved.

For example, the call number shown in Figure 2.7 tells you the subject area of the book, a little something about its author, and when the book was published. This is useful to know not only because it will help you find the book, but it might prompt you to find other, possibly more recent books on the same subject on a nearby shelf.

Figure 2.8 shows you how to read call numbers. Read them from top to bottom (or left to right if displayed horizontally). While alphabetical and numerical order are key to understanding the sequencing

Read call numbers line by line:

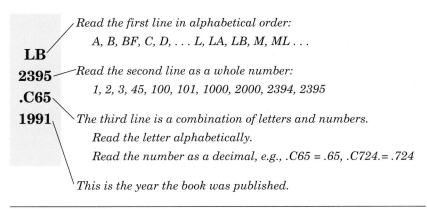

**LB**
**2395**
**.C65**
**1991**

*Read the first line in alphabetical order:*
   *A, B, BF, C, D, . . . L, LA, LB, M, ML . . .*

*Read the second line as a whole number:*
   *1, 2, 3, 45, 100, 101, 1000, 2000, 2394, 2395*

*The third line is a combination of letters and numbers.*
   *Read the letter alphabetically.*
   *Read the number as a decimal, e.g., .C65 = .65, .C724.= .724*

*This is the year the book was published.*

**FIGURE 2.8    Reading Call Numbers**

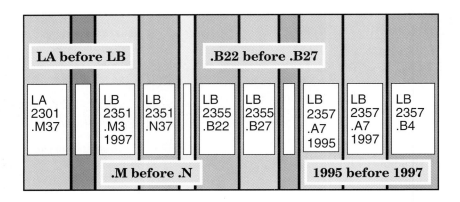

**FIGURE 2.9**    **How Books Are Arranged on the Library Shelf**

of books in the library, the third line of a call number is a weird combination of letters and decimals. This always mystifies me.

In Figure 2.9, you can see how Library of Congress call numbers determine the arrangement of books on the shelf. The only

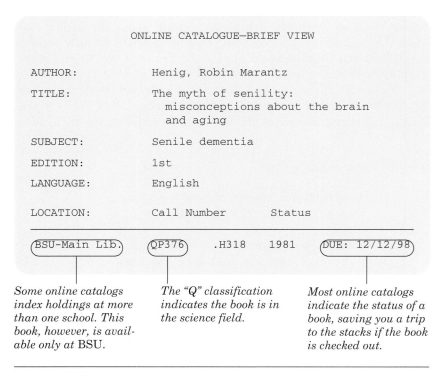

*Some online catalogs index holdings at more than one school. This book, however, is available only at* BSU.

*The "Q" classification indicates the book is in the science field.*

*Most online catalogs indicate the status of a book, saving you a trip to the stacks if the book is checked out.*

**FIGURE 2.10**    A typical screen of an online catalog. This one shows a brief display; a full display would include more bibliographic information on the book.

tricky part is that odd letter and decimal combination in the third line of the call number. Note that the small decimal number (.B22) precedes a larger one (.B27). The year a book was published also determines its position on the shelf.

It's likely your college library, like mine, has retired its 3″ × 5″ cards and replaced them with an *online card catalog.* This online system uses a computer to do the same thing that you used to do, thumbing through the card catalog. And of course, the computer is much faster. Search on a subject, author, or title, or on *keywords* that explain the topic you want to find. Figure 2.10 shows what a typical screen of an online catalog looks like.

## EXERCISE 2.2

### Library Investigations

**STEP 1:** It's the rare topic that isn't covered, in some way, in a book or part of one. Subject headings on your topic that you gleaned from the *Library of Congress Subject Headings* really pay off when you use the electronic index to launch a search for relevant books. Begin with those, manipulating search terms on the search page of your online book index. Try several until you begin to see book titles that look promising. Figure 2.11 shows a sample search page.

Sort your results in a list from most promising to least promising on a separate piece of paper. This is the beginning of your working bibliography, and will be part of your progress report to your instructor this week. Use the following format for each entry. (It's based on the MLA method of listing citations, something you'll learn more about later).

*Call number:* _____

*Author(s):* _____

*Title:* _____

*Place of publication:* _____

*Date of publication:* _____

*Two- or three-sentence summary of what seems relevant about each*

*text to your project:* _____

_____

_____

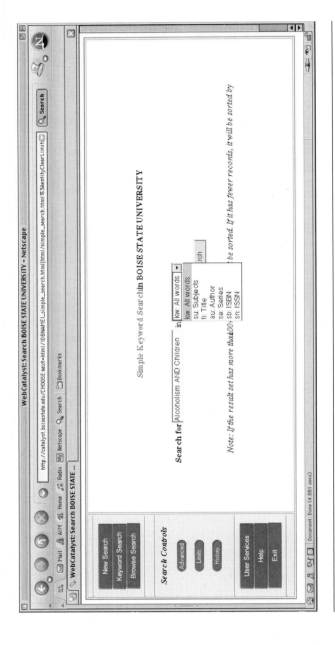

**FIGURE 2.11  Search Page of Web-Based Book Catalog**   The search page of WebCatalyst, the online book index at Boise State University, is fairly typical. Notice that you can search by subject, keyword, title, or author. Searches can also use Boolean terms.

## Coming Up Empty-Handed?

In the unlikely event that you can't find any books by searching directly using the online catalog, there's another reference you can check that will help locate relevant articles and essays that are *a part* of a book whose title may otherwise seem unpromising. Check to see if your library has a database called the *Essay and General Literature Index.* Search that database with your keywords or subject and see if that produces something useful. List the relevant results as instructed above.

## Checking Bibliographies

One tactic that might lead to a mother lode of sources for your essay is to look at the bibliographies at the back of (mostly) scholarly books (and articles). Don't ever set aside a promising book until you've checked the bibliography! Jot down complete bibliographic information from citations you want to check out later. Keep a running list of these in your research notebook.

## Interlibrary Loan

If your library doesn't have the book (or article) you really want, don't despair. Most college libraries have a wonderful low- or no-cost service to students called interlibrary loan. The library will search the collections of other libraries to find what you're looking for and have it sent, sometimes within a week or less. Use the service by checking with the reference desk or your library's Web site.

## Finding Magazine and Journal Articles

It used to be that those green, well-thumbed volumes of the *Readers' Guide to Periodical Literature* were the only game in town if you were after an article published in a general interest magazine. However, now online databases have largely replaced the old *Readers' Guide*. While the *Guide* is still invaluable for finding articles published before 1990 (and as early as 1890) that may not be included in the new databases, the online indexes are much easier to use. See Figure 2.12. But perhaps the real weakness of the *Readers' Guide,* particularly for academic research, is that it's mostly an index of nonscholarly sources such as *Time, Redbook,* and *Sports Illustrated.* There's nothing wrong with these publications. In fact, you may end up using a few in your essay. But as you dig more deeply into your subject, you may find that the information in popular periodicals will often begin to tell you what you already know.

Many of the electronic databases include popular magazines, but they also index some scholarly journals as well. That's another reason they're so useful. For example, EBSCO MasterFILE indexes

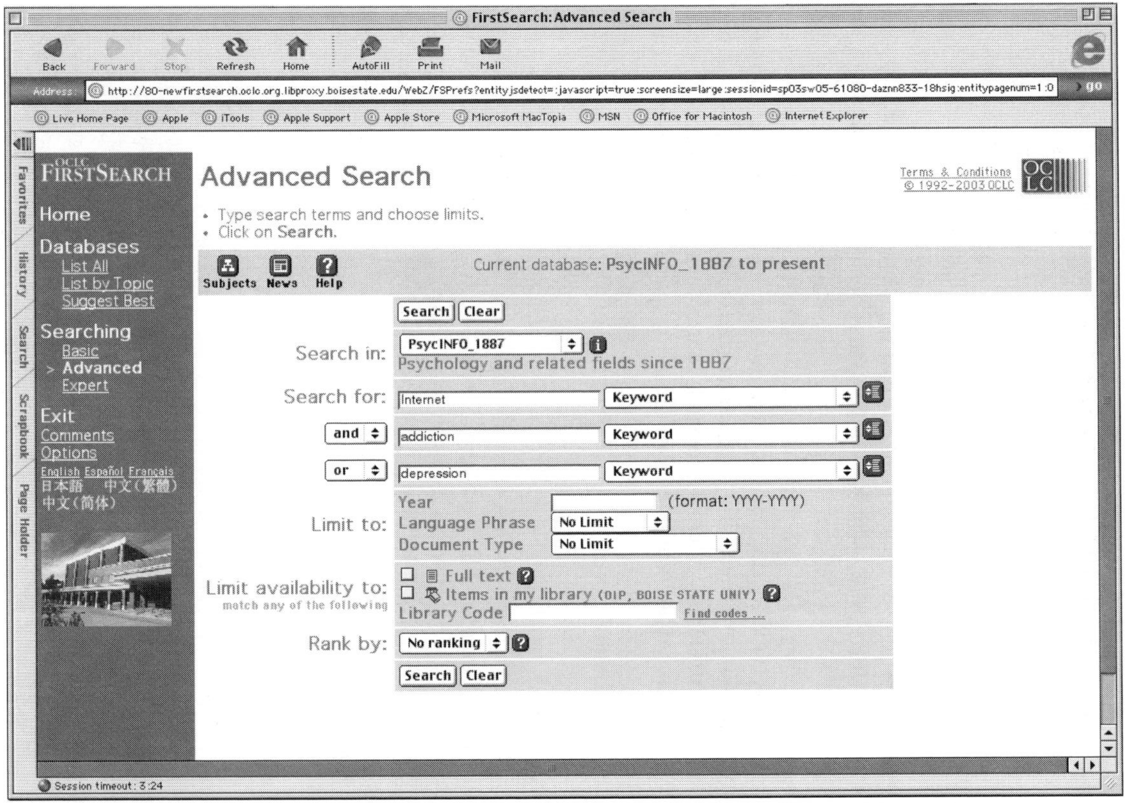

## FIGURE 2.12
## Search Form for
## Periodical Database

PsycINFO is a popular online database for scholarly articles in psychology. But this search page is fairly typical for a number of indexes to other subjects. Notice how the Boolean connectors AND and OR are provided by drop-down menus between the keywords. You can also search by subject and author.

nearly 3,000 journals and magazines and even provides full-text arti-cles—rather than simply citations—from more than 1,800 periodi-cals. Another online index, UnCover, has a database of more than 18,000 magazines and journals and claims to describe nearly nine million articles.

**STEP 2:** Visit your library's Web page that lists all of the available periodical databases. Depending on the size of your campus library, the list of databases might be really long. Which should you use? In some cases, you'll know immediately which are relevant to your research topic just by the name. Some indexes, usually for scholarly sources, are very subject specific. Some of the more common periodical databases at university libraries are shown in the accompanying list.

### COMMON PERIODICAL DATABASES

| Humanities | Science and Technology | Social Sciences |
|---|---|---|
| America, History and Life | Applied Science & Technology Index | Anthropological Index |
| Arts and Humanities Search | CINAHL (Nursing) | ComAbstracts (Communication) |
| Art Index | Biological Abstracts | PsychINFO |
| MLA Bibliography (Literature and composition) | GeoRef (Geology) | Social Work Abstracts |
| Historical Abstracts | MathSciNet | Sociological Abstracts |
| Literary Index | Medline (Medicine) | Worldwide Political Science Abstracts |
| Music Index | Computer Literature Index | PAIS (Public Affairs) |
| Philosopher's Index | Health Reference Center | Criminal Justice Abstracts |
| Humanities Index | AGRICOLA (Agriculture) | Contemporary Women's Issues |
| Religion Index | General Science Index | Social Sciences Index |

| **Business** | **Education** |
|---|---|
| ABI/Inform | ERIC |
| FreeEDGAR | Education Index |
| Business Source Elite | Education Full Text |

In addition to these more specialized databases, there are a number of online indexes that provide more general subject coverage. In some cases, the database mixes both popular periodicals such as *Time* or *Psychology Today* with more academic journals. In other cases, a general database might include full-text versions as well as citations of articles. There are really too many of these more general reference indexes to provide a complete list, but some of the more common on university campuses are shown in the accompanying list.

**GENERAL SUBJECT DATABASES**

Article First

MasterFile Premier

InfoTrac One File

General Reference Center Gold

MasterFILE Premier

Readers' Guide Abstracts

UnCover (fee for article)

Expanded Academic ASAP

Academic Research Library

Proquest Direct

Lexis-Nexis Academic Universe

Ebsco

Begin your search with a general subject database, and then move, if possible, to a more subject-specific one. That way, you can start finding *both* more popular and scholarly articles on your topic, and then focus on the more challenging scholarly material that is often unearthed using the more focused databases. As always, keep using different combinations of search terms until you start getting useful results.

On a separate piece of paper, begin a page of promising periodical articles to create a working bibliography like the one you created for books in Step 1 of this exercise. For each listing, provide the following information:

*Author:* _____

*Title:* _____

*Title of periodical:* _____

*Volume or issue number and date:* _____

*Pages covered by the article:* _____

*Two or three sentence comment about what information you hope to get from the article or what questions you hope it answers:*

_____

_____

## Newspaper Articles

If your topic is local, current, or controversial, then it's likely that newspapers will be an important source of information for your essay. You'll rarely get much in-depth information or analysis from newspapers, but they can often provide good quotes, anecdotes, and case studies as well as the most current printed information on your topic. Newspapers are also sometimes considered primary sources because they provide firsthand accounts of things that have happened.

**STEP 3:** Guess what? There are databases of newspaper articles, too. See the accompanying list. They don't index the hometown paper but they do provide citations to the so-called "national newspapers" such as the *New York Times, Washington Post, Los Angeles Times, Wall Street Journal,* and *Christian Science Monitor.* Bound indexes of several of these papers are in your university library, but nobody ever uses them anymore. What's good about the national newspapers is that they're among the most authoritative journalistic sources; in other words, because of their large and experienced staffs, the information they provide is more trustworthy.

**NEWSPAPER DATABASES**

National Newspaper Index

Proquest National Newspapers

Newspaper Source

Lexis-Nexis Academic Universe

Newspaper Abstracts

The larger local and statewide papers also are on the Web, and their sites often provide search windows for their archives where it's sometimes possible to retrieve full-text articles. Occasionally, the local papers are also indexed online by the university library, and copies are available on microfilm.

Search for newspaper articles on your topic. Begin with one of the larger databases such as the *National Newspaper Index,* and then, depending on your topic, search the archives or online indexes of your local newspapers. If you find a promising full-text article on the Web, print it out. Also try to find a citation for a promising article on one of the databases and go to the microfilm room of your campus library, find the article, and copy it. If your topic just doesn't lend itself to a newspaper search, then go to the microfilm room and find the *New York Times* for the date and year of your birthday; then print a copy of the front page. Your instructor will ask you to hand in this material along with your bibliographies.

A word about the microfilm room: It's the room with those odd machines that read microfilm—reels of film in little boxes—or microfiche, which is a small rectangular film. These machines are easy to use for everybody except me. I need a lesson every time I go in there from the pleasant reference librarian who both knows my face and my problems. If your library is like mine, several of the microfilm machines are set up to make photocopies. These are the ones you want to use for printing the articles for this step of the exercise. Ask for help if you need it. The machines usually make embarrassing sounds when you do something wrong.

# Internet Research Techniques

I love the word "portal." It summons images of a little window on some vast space ship that frames the face an open-mouthed observer looking in wonder at the vast reaches of the universe beyond. Researching on the Internet is a lot like peeping out that window. There is just so much out there, billions of documents, gazillions of words, each a fragment of electronic data floating in cyberspace like dust motes is some vast sunbeam. Earlier in this chapter, you were reminded that this universe, while tantalizing, is also a librarian's nightmare. There's useful knowledge for academic writing out there, but it's hard to find and it's easy to get lost.

You're already better prepared for the search than most. Earlier you learned how to evaluate Web sources and design keyword searches. This is crucial knowledge. In Exercise 1.3 you also used some of the Web's key subject directories, several of which are maintained by librarians, actual human beings who sift and sort Internet materials and list those that are worthy. However, the more common method of searching the Web doesn't use a human being at all but a piece of software that electronically crawls the Web creating massive indexes of documents that respond to your keyword searches.

## Types of Search Engines

The most popular search engine at the moment is Google, a search engine with an enormous database that is relatively simply to use. There are many other search engines like Google, including Northernlight, AltaVista, MSN Search, Yahoo!, Hotbot, LookSmart, and others. For current reviews and ratings of each of these, as well as research on what particular search engines do well and not so well, visit Search Engine Watch (http://searchenginewatch.com/). Google and the others are really quite amazing, but they do have limitations. For one thing, they only index pages on the Web that have hyperlinks pointing to them elsewhere, or whose creators have requested they be indexed by a particular search tool. In addition, these databases may not be current.

Search tools such as MSN Search or Google aren't the only vehicles for scouring the Web. There are also specialized search engines that focus on particular subjects such as education, politics, and psychology, as well as search engines that specialize in going where conventional Web crawlers like Google do not go—the vast "Invisible Web," containing the types of documents that Google and other search engines cannot find or will not find. No one knows the size of the Invisible Web, but it's probably much larger than the visible one.

Finally, there are so-called "metasearch" tools such as MetaCrawler (www.metacrawler.com) that are able to deploy multiple individual search engines in the service of a single search. These are very useful, particularly at the beginning of an Internet search on your topic. However, metasearch engines aren't quite as good as they sound because they skim off the top results from each individual search tool so you won't see the range of results you would get if you focus on one of search engine with its own large database.

What's the key to maximizing the efficiency of your Internet research?

1. Maximize your coverage by using multiple search engines, not just your favorite one.
2. If possible, exploit subject directories put together by people, not software, concerned with quality content.
3. Be thoughtful about what and how many keywords you use to search. Generally, the more words—and especially phrases—you use, the more likely you are to generate relevant hits.

## E X E R C I S E   2 . 3

### Investigating the Internet

**STEP 1:** Using some of the keyword combinations you developed for your topic, launch a search on one or more of the metasearch engines shown in the accompanying list. These tools are a good place to begin because of their breadth—you can quickly see the more popular sites on your topics, and the various contexts in which information about it might be found.

> **METASEARCH ENGINES**
>
> MetaCrawler (<u>www.metacrawler.com</u>)
>
> Dogpile (<u>www.dogpile.com</u>)
>
> Mamma (<u>www.mamma.com</u>)
>
> Search.com (<u>www.search.com</u>)
>
> Profusion (<u>www.profusion.com</u>)

Remember to play around with keywords, and don't forget the search language you learned earlier in this chapter. The "Help" button on whatever metasearch tool you use will give you the specifics on what connectors, Boolean or others, that search engine accepts.

Develop a "working bibliography" of Web pages (see Figure 2.13) that seem promising and print copies of them for notetaking. For each page include the following information if available:

> Author (if any).
>
> Title of page.
>
> Publication name and date of print version (if any).
>
> Name of online publication or database.
>
> Online publication (volume or issue, date, page or paragraph numbers).
>
> Date you accessed the page.
>
> Full Internet address.

Also include a brief summary of what you found particularly promising or interesting about the site.

To make assembling this information easier, open a blank page in Word or some other word-processing program in another window while you search the Web. When you find a page you want to keep, highlight the address in your browser's address window, right-click

**Internet Research**
**Topic:** The Intelligence of Crows
**Focusing Question:** Do crows exhibit unusual intelligence when compared with similar birds?

### Working Bibliography

1. Hutchins, Lisa. "The Intelligence of Crows." Pica Productions. March 99. 2 July 2002 <http://www.users.qwest.net/~lhutchins/intelli_crows.htm>. Article reviews crow's problem-solving abilities and specific social behaviors like "mobbing."
2. "ASCAR's Frequently Asked Questions About Crows and Ravens." American Society of Crows and Ravens. ASCAR Online. 3 July 2002 <http://www.ascaronline.org/crowfaq.html>. FAQ page that includes some useful but limited information about crow behavior and common myths about the bird.
3. "Crow Family." Crow City. 3 July 2002 <http://website.lineone.net/~crowseed/crowcity/info/family.html>. British-based site discusses crow species in England with especially useful information on crows in Celtic mythology. Seems like a personal site.
4. Davies, Garweth Huw. "Bird Brains." PBS Online. 3 July 2002 <http://www.pbs.org/lifeofbirds/brain/index.html>. Page tells story of crows in Japan that use cars at intersections to open nuts. Also examines intelligence of other bird species. Linked to David Attenborough PBS program "The Life of Birds."

**FIGURE 2.13**  A sample working bibliography of Web sites related to topic on the intelligence of crows.

to copy, go to your open page in Word, and right-click to paste. Because it's so important to get Internet addresses right, this copy and paste function can be very helpful.

**STEP 2:** Select *at least* two other single search engines (see list) for a keyword search on your topic. Add what you find useful for your project to the working bibliography you started in Step 1. Though it's a bit of a pain, this working bibliography will be enormously useful later as you assemble the final draft of your essay.

In the searches you conduct for both steps of the exercise, you'll likely find links to pages that didn't appear in response to your original query. Follow these, too. The Web is aptly named since it presents knowledge through hyperlinks as multidisciplinary and interconnected.

**POPULAR SINGLE SEARCH ENGINES**

Google www.google.com

MSN Search search.msn.com

AltaVista www.altavista.com

Yahoo! www.yahoo.com

Hotbot www.hotbot.com

Search.com www.search.com

AllTheWeb.com www.alltheweb.com

Ask Jeeves www.askjeeves.com

By now you're well on your way to developing deeper knowledge of your topic. If you've successfully completed Exercises 2.2 and 2.3 you will have

1. A working bibliography, annotated with your initial comments, of books, periodicals, and Web pages relevant to your topic. This will be invaluable later as you develop the bibliography for your essay.
2. Copies of promising articles or Web documents for notetaking.

# Living Sources: Interviews and Surveys

## Arranging Interviews

A few years ago, I researched a local turn-of-the-century writer named Sarah Orne Jewett for a magazine article. I dutifully read much of her work, studied critical articles and books on her writing, and visited her childhood home, which is open to the public in South Berwick, Maine. My research was going fairly well, but when I sat down to begin writing the draft, the material seemed flat and lifeless. A few days later, the curator of the Jewett house mentioned that there was an eighty-eight-year-old local woman, Elizabeth Goodwin, who had known the writer when she was alive. "As far as I know, she's the last living person who knew Sarah Orne Jewett," the curator told me. "And she lives just down the street."

The next week, I spent three hours with Elizabeth Goodwin, who told me of coming for breakfast with the famous author and eating strawberry jam and muffins. Elizabeth told me that many years after Jewett's death, the house seemed haunted by her friendly presence. One time, when Elizabeth lived in the Jewett house as a curator, some unseen hands pulled her back as she teetered at the top of the steep stairs in the back of the house. She likes to believe it was the author's ghost.

This interview transformed the piece by bringing the subject to life—first, for me as the writer, and then later, for my readers. Ultimately, what makes almost any topic compelling is discovering why it matters to *people*—how it affects their lives. Doing interviews with people close to the subject, both experts and nonexperts, is often the best way to find that out.

If you'd like to do some interviews, now is the time to begin arranging them.

## Finding Experts

You may be hesitant to consider finding authorities on your topic to talk to because, after all, you're just a lowly student who knows next to nothing. How could you possibly impose on that sociology professor who published the book on anti-Semitism you found in the library? If that's how you feel, keep this in mind: *Most people, no matter who they are, love the attention of an interviewer, no matter who she is, particularly if what's being discussed fascinates them both.* Time and again, I've found my own shyness creep up on me when I pick up the telephone to arrange an interview. But almost invariably, when I get there and start talking with my interview subject, the experience is great for us both.

How do you find experts to interview?

■ *Check your sources.* As you begin to collect books, articles, and Internet documents, note their authors and affiliations. I get calls from time to time from writers who came across my book on lobsters in the course of their research and discovered that I was at Boise State University. Sometimes the caller will arrange a phone interview or, if he lives within driving distance, a personal interview.

■ *Check the phone book.* The familiar Yellow Pages can be a gold mine. Carin, who was writing a paper on solar energy, merely looked under that heading and found a local dealer who sold solar systems to homeowners. Mark, who was investigating the effects of sexual abuse on children, found a counselor who specialized in treating abuse victims.

■ *Ask your friends and your instructors.* Your roommate's boyfriend's father may be a criminal attorney who has lots to say about the insanity defense for your paper on that topic. Your best friend may be taking a photography course with a professor who would be a great interview for your paper on the work of Edward Weston. One of your instructors may know other faculty working in your subject area who would do an interview.

■ *Check the faculty directory.* Many universities publish an annual directory of faculty and their research interests. On my campus, it's called the *Directory of Research and Scholarly Activities*. From it, I know, for example, that two professors at my university have expertise in eating disorders, a popular topic with student researchers.

■ *Check the* Encyclopedia of Associations. This is a wonderful reference book that lists organizations with interests ranging from promoting tofu to preventing acid rain. Each listing includes the name of the group, its address and phone number, a list of its publications, and a short description of its purpose. Sometimes, these organizations can direct you to experts in your area who are available for live interviews or to spokespeople who are happy to provide phone interviews.

■ *Check the Internet.* You can find the e-mail addresses and phone numbers of many scholars and researchers on the Internet, including those affiliated with your own and nearby universities. Often, these experts are listed in online directories for their colleges or universities. Sometimes, you can find knowledgeable people by subscribing to a listserv or Internet discussion group on your topic. Occasionally, an expert will have her own Web page, and her e-mail address will provide a hypertext link. (For more details, see "Finding People on the Internet," later in this chapter.)

## Finding Nonexperts Affected by Your Topic

The distinction between *expert* and *nonexpert* is tricky. For example, someone who lived through twelve months of combat in Vietnam certainly has direct knowledge of the subject, though probably he hasn't published an article about the war in *Foreign Affairs*. Similarly, a friend who experienced an abusive relationship with her boyfriend or overcame a drug addiction is, at least in a sense, an authority on abuse or addiction. Both individuals would likely be invaluable interviews for papers on those topics. The voices and the stories of people who are affected by the topic you're writing about can do more than anything else to make the information come to life, even if they don't have Ph.D.'s.

You may already know people you can interview about your topic. Last semester, Amanda researched how mother-daughter relationships change when a daughter goes to college. She had no problem finding other women anxious to talk about how they get along with their mothers. A few years ago, Dan researched steroid use by student athletes. He discreetly asked his friends if they knew anyone who had taken the drugs. It turned out that an acquaintance of Dan's had used the drugs regularly and was happy to talk about his experience.

If you don't know people to interview, try posting notices on campus kiosks or bulletin boards. For example, "I'm doing a research project and interested in talking to people who grew up in single-parent households. Please call 555-9000." Also poll other students in your class for ideas about people you might interview for your paper. Help each other out.

## *Making Contact*

By the end of this week, you should have some people to contact for interviews. First, consider whether to ask for a personal, telephone, or e-mail interview or perhaps, as a last resort, to simply correspond by mail. The personal interview is almost always preferable; you cannot only listen but watch, observing your subject's gestures and the setting, both of which can be revealing. When I'm interviewing someone in her office or home, for example, one of the first things I may jot down are the titles of books on the bookshelf. Sometimes, details about gestures and settings can be worked into your paper. Most of all, the personal interview is preferable because it's more natural, more like a conversation.

Be prepared. You may have no choice in the type of interview. If your subject is off campus or out of state, your only options may be the telephone, e-mail, or regular mail.

When contacting a subject for an interview, first state your name and then briefly explain your research project. If you were referred to the subject by someone she may know, mention that. A comment like "I think you could be extremely helpful to me" or "I'm familiar with your work, and I'm anxious to talk to you about it" works well. That's called *flattery,* and as long as it isn't excessive or insincere, we're all vulnerable to it.

It is gracious to ask your prospective subject what time and place for an interview may be convenient for her. Nonetheless, be prepared to suggest some specific times and places to meet or talk. When thinking about when to propose the interview with an expert on your topic, consider arranging it *after* you've done some research. You will not only be more informed, but you will have a clearer sense of what you want to know and what questions to ask.

## Conducting Interviews

You've already thought about whether interviews might contribute to your paper. Build a list of possible interview subjects and contact several of them. By the end of this week, you should begin interviewing.

I know. You wouldn't mind putting it off. But once you start, it will get easier and easier. I should know. I used to dread interviewing strangers, but after making the first phone call, I got some momentum going, and I began to enjoy it. It's decidedly easier to interview friends, family, and acquaintances, but that's the wrong reason to limit yourself to people you know.

**Whom to Interview?**   Interview people who can provide you with what you want to know. And that may change as your research develops. In your reading, you might have encountered the names of experts you'd like to contact, or you may have decided that what you really need is some anecdotal material from someone with experience in your topic. It's still not too late to contact interview subjects who didn't occur to you earlier. But do so immediately.

**What Questions to Ask?**   The first step in preparing for an interview is to ask yourself, What's the purpose of this interview? In your research notebook, make a list of *specific questions* for each person you're going to interview. Often, these questions are raised by your reading or other interviews. What theories or ideas encountered in your reading would you like to ask your subject about? What specific facts have you been unable to uncover that your interview subject may provide? What don't you understand that he could explain? Would you like to test one of your own impressions or ideas on your subject? What about the subject's work or experience would you like to learn? Interviews are wonderful tools for clearing up your own confusion and getting specific information that is unavailable anywhere else.

Now make a list of more *open-ended questions* you might ask each or all of the people you're going to talk to. Frankly, these questions are a lot more fun to ask because you're more likely to be surprised by the answers. For example:

- In all your experience with _____, what has most surprised you?
- What has been the most difficult aspect of your work?

- If you had the chance to change something about how you approached _____, what would it be?
- Can you remember a significant moment in your work on _____? Is there an experience with _____ that stands out in your mind?
- What do you think is the most common misconception about _____? Why?
- What are significant current trends in _____?
- Who or what has most influenced you? Who are your heroes?
- If you had to summarize the most important thing you've learned about _____, what would it be? What is the most important thing other people should know or understand?

As you develop both specific and open-ended questions, keep in mind what you know about each person—his work in the field and personal experience with your topic. You may end up asking a lot of the same questions of everybody you interview, but try to familiarize yourself with any special qualifications a subject may have or experiences he may have had. That knowledge might come from your reading, from what other people tell you about your subject, or from your initial telephone call to set up the interview.

Also keep in mind the *kinds* of information an interview can provide better than other sources: anecdotes, strong quotes, and sometimes descriptive material. If you ask the right questions, a live subject can paint a picture of his experience with your topic, and you can capture that picture in your paper.

**During the Interview.**   Once you've built a list of questions, be prepared to ignore it. Interviews are conversations, not surveys. They are about human interaction between two people who are both interested in the same thing.

I remember interviewing a lobsterman, Edward Heaphy, on his boat. I had a long list of questions in my notebook, which I dutifully asked, one after the other. My questions were mechanical, and so were his answers. I finally stopped, put my notebook down, and talked informally with Edward for a few minutes. Offhandedly, I asked, "Would you want your sons or daughter to get in the business?" It was a totally unplanned question. Edward was silent for a moment, staring at his hands. I knew he was about to say something important because, for the first time, I was attentive to him, not my notepad. "Too much work for what they get out of it," he said quietly. It was a surprising remark after hearing for the last hour how much Edward loved lobstering. What's more, I felt I had broken through. The rest of the interview went much better.

Much of how to conduct an interview is common sense. At the outset, clarify the nature of your project—what your paper is on and where you're at with it. Briefly explain again why you thought this individual would be the perfect person to talk to about it. I find it often helps to begin with a specific question that I'm pretty sure my subject can help with. But there's no formula. Simply be a good conversationalist: Listen attentively, ask questions that your subject seems to find provocative, and enjoy with your subject sharing an interest in the same thing. Also don't be afraid to ask what you fear are obvious questions. Demonstrate to the subject that you *really* want to understand.

Always end an interview by making sure you have accurate background information on your subject: name (spelled correctly), position, affiliation, age (if applicable), phone number. Ask if you can call him with follow-up questions, should you have any. And always ask your subject if he can recommend any additional reading or other people you should talk to. Of course, mention that you're appreciative of the time he has spent with you.

**Notetaking.**    There are basically three ways to take notes during an interview: Use a tape recorder, a notepad, or both. I adhere to the third method, but it's a very individual choice. I like tape recorders because I don't panic during an interview that I'm losing information or quoting inaccurately, but I don't want to spend hours transcribing the tapes. So I also take notes on the information I think I want to use, and if I miss anything, I consult the recording later. It's a backup. Sometimes, I find that there is no recording—the machine decided not to participate in the interview—and at least I have my notes. Again, a backup.

Get some practice developing your own notetaking technique by interviewing your roommate or taking notes on the television news. Devise ways to shorten often-used words (e.g., *t* for *the, imp* for *important,* and *w/o* for *without*).

## The E-Mail Interview

The Internet opens up new possibilities for interviews; increasingly, experts (as well as nonexperts interested in certain subjects) are accessible through e-mail and newsgroups. While electronic communication doesn't quite approach the conversational quality of the conventional face-to-face interview, the spontaneous nature of e-mail exchanges can come pretty close. It's possible to send a message, get a response, respond to the response, and get a further response—all in a single day. And for shy interviewers and interviewees, an e-mail conversation is an attractive alternative.

**Finding People on the Internet.**   Finding people on the Internet doesn't have to involve a needle and hay if you have some information on whom you're looking for. If you know an expert's name, his organizational affiliation, and his geographical location, several search tools may help you track down his e-mail address, if he has one. But perhaps the easiest way to use the Net to find someone to interview is through a Web document on your topic. For example, when researching this new edition of this book, I encountered an online version of the Alliance for Computers and Writing's proposals for MLA-style electronic citations, authored by Janice Walker. Walker's e-mail address was a hyperlink in that document, so had I wanted to ask her some questions, all I would have had to do was click on her name. Authors of Web pages frequently provide their addresses as links, inviting comments about their texts and the like. Thus, it seems safe to assume that they are probably willing to entertain questions from researchers, too.

Plucking an e-mail address from a Web page is the easiest way to find an interview subject. But what if you just have someone's name and organizational affiliation? There are a multitude of search tools for finding e-mail (and snail mail) addresses on the Internet. Among the most useful are Yahoo! People Search (http://people.yahoo.com) and Bigfoot (http://bigfoot.com). These programs search USENET postings, listservs, and Web pages for addresses as well as inviting people to register their Internet addresses with their search service.

Unfortunately, these search tools are not always productive for academic projects because they tend not to cull e-mail addresses from universities, where you're most likely to find experts useful for a research essay. The best way I've found to track down the addresses of academics is to visit the Web sites of the universities or colleges where they teach and use the online faculty/staff directories to find their addresses. Obviously, this won't work if you don't know the name of the institutions with which a scholar is affiliated, but this is often listed on an academic's articles, books, or Web page. To find the home pages of hundreds of American universities and colleges, visit the following site:

*The University Pages*

http://isl-garnet.uah.edu/Universities_g/

Lists the home pages of universities and colleges by state. A really useful place to begin a search for interview subjects who are scholars on your topic.

**Making Contact by E-Mail.**   Once you find the e-mail address of someone who seems a likely interview subject, proceed courteously and cautiously. One of the Internet's haunting issues is its potential to violate privacy. Be especially careful if you've gone to great lengths in hunting down the e-mail address of someone involved with your research topic; she may not be keen on receiving unsolicited e-mail messages from strangers. It would be courteous to approach any potential interview subject with a short message that asks permission for an online interview. To do so, briefly describe your project and why you thought this individual might be a good source for you. As always, you will be much more likely to get an enthusiastic response from someone if you can demonstrate your knowledge of her work on or experience with your topic.

Let's assume your initial contact has been successful and your subject has agreed to answer your questions. Your follow-up message should ask a *limited* number of questions—say, four or five—that are thoughtful and, if possible, specific. Keep in mind that while the e-mail interview is conducted in writing rather than through talking, many of the methods for handling conventional interviews still apply.

**Finding People on Listservs and Newsgroups.**   Another way to find interview or survey subjects on the Internet is through *listservs* and *Usenet newsgroups.* These are electronic discussion groups, both academic and nonacademic, that people subscribe to when they share an interest in something; topics run well into the thousands, from mountain biking to medieval music to David Barry. I belong to several listservs, including one called *Writing Program Administrators,* or *WPA-L.* Subscribers determine the topics of discussion by sending e-mail messages to the list, which often prompt responses from others.

Anyone can post a question to an e-mail discussion group if he subscribes to the list, and in most cases, that's easy to do (see the box "How to Subscribe to an Internet Discussion Group"). Posting a message to a Usenet group is even easier—you don't have to subscribe if you use the Deja.com's posting service. All you have to do is find a relevant Usenet group using the search tool and follow the online directions to post a message to that group.

Since you're querying people who already know something about your topic, you're likely to get good information and quotable comments. You will, that is, if you ask good questions that demonstrate you've already done some thinking about your topic.

*Querying a discussion group is not something to do to collect general or background information.* People subscribe to these lists because they're anxious to participate in a stimulating conversation with others knowledgeable about the topic. While they often welcome research questions from students and others, subscribers may have little patience for questions that imply the researcher doesn't know

## How to Subscribe to an Internet Discussion Group

To get on a listserv, you'll obviously need to have your own e-mail address, to which posts will be sent. You'll also need a browser (or other program) that can both read and send e-mail messages.

Every e-mail discussion list has two addresses: (1) the list address to which you send messages to other subscribers, and (2) the listserv address from which you send requests to subscribe and unsubscribe. The distinction between these two addresses is important.

- *Subscribing*—To subscribe to a list, send an e-mail message with the following line:

  SUB listname yourname

For example, to subscribe to *Studies in Antiquities and Mormonism,* or *SAMU-L,* I'd send a message to LISTSERV@BINGVMB.CC.BINGHAMTON.EDU that would simply say:

  SUB SAMU-L Bruce Ballenger

- *Unsubscribing*—To unsubscribe to a list, send an e-mail message to the listserv address with this line:

  SIGNOFF listname

If I tired of antiquities and Mormonism, I'd send the following message to the listserv address:

  SIGNOFF SAMU-L

- *Posting*—If I wanted to send a message to all the members of a list, I'd send it to the list address *rather* than the listserv address. For example, to send a question to the antiquities and Mormonism list, I'd send an e-mail to:

  SAMU-L@BINGVMB.CC.BINGHAMTON.EDU

the field or know what he's after. For example, several members of an environmental listserv complained that the list was "flooded" with "ill-expressed" questions from students, asking obvious and general questions such as "What is hazardous waste?" This example should not discourage you from posting research questions to a discussion group, but do so only when you're ready to pose questions that have grown out of your reading on the topic.

**The Chat Room Interview.**   In addition to surveying particular groups of people through listservs, e-mail discussion groups, and Usenet, so-called real-time communication tools such as IRCs (Internet Relay Chat) are particularly promising new ways to conduct online surveys (or interviews). "Real-time" simply means that it is possible to have a live conversation with people online. Such "chat rooms" are a permanent feature of commercial Internet service providers such as America Online, but there are also thousands of IRC "channels" that conduct live discussions on topics ranging from depression to dreams. Some of these channels can theoretically allow as many as a thousand people to be part of an online conversation, though usually there are fewer than ten people participating at one time. What is particularly appealing about real-time communication on the Internet for the interviewer is the possibility of posing questions and then immediately following up on the answers.

How do you find IRCs on the Internet? Unfortunately, currently there isn't a single comprehensive chat directory. Several of the directories listed below, like Topica, that will help you find discussion groups will also help you locate chat channels related to your topic. In order to participate in real-time communication you'll need software such as America Online's Instant Messenger, which is available free. This is one of those Internet technologies that is just becoming useful for academic researchers—and it still has a ways to go. But it promises to be an exciting new avenue for Internet interviews.

**Deciding What to Ask.**   Another way to get some help with knowing what to ask—and what not to—is to spend some time following the discussion of list participants before you jump in yourself. You might find, for example, that it would be far better to interview one participant with interesting views rather than to post questions to the whole list.

But if you do want to query the whole listserv or newsgroup, avoid posting a question that may have already received substantial attention from participants. You can find out what's been covered by consulting the list's *FAQs (frequently asked questions)*. The issue you're interested in may be there, along with a range of responses from list participants, which will spare you the need to ask the question at all. FAQs are often available through the discussion group at an FTP (File Transfer Protocol) site, but one Web site that archives FAQs from most of the Usenet groups is located at http://www.cis.ohio-state.edu/hyptertext/faq/usenet/FAQ-List.html. I found, for example, a wonderfully informative collection of FAQs on acquired immune deficiency syndrome (AIDS), archived by the newsgroup sci.med.aids. Its FAQs would be a great place to start a research project on this topic.

**Finding a Group on Your Topic.** With thousands of discussion groups on every imaginable topic, how do you find one on your topic? You can use a number of Web search engines to retrieve articles from Usenet groups, but you should try some searchable indexes to Usenet and listservs. Here are several of the more popular discussion group directories:

> **Google Groups** http://groups.google.com/
>
> **Publicly Accessible Mailing Lists** http://www.paml.net/
>
> **Cata-List** http://www.lsoft.com/lists/listref.html
>
> **Directory of Scholarly and Professional E-Conferences** http://www.kovacs.com/directory.html
>
> **Liszt (Topica)** http://www.listz.com

## Planning Informal Surveys

Christine was interested in dream interpretation, especially exploring the significance of symbols or images that recur in many people's dreams. She could have simply examined her own dreams, but she thought it might be more interesting to survey a group of fellow students, asking how often they dream and what they remember about it. An informal survey, in which she would ask each person several standard questions, seemed worth trying.

You might consider it, too, if the responses of a group of people to some aspect of your topic would reveal a pattern of behavior, attitudes, or experiences worth analyzing. Informal surveys are decidedly unscientific. You probably won't get a large enough sample size, nor do you likely have the skills to design a poll that would produce statistically reliable results. But you probably won't actually base your paper on the survey results, anyway. Rather, you'll present specific, concrete information that *suggests* some patterns in your survey group, or at the very least, some of your own findings will help support your assertions.

## Defining Goals and Audience

Begin planning your informal survey by defining what you want to know and whom you want to know it from. Christine suspected that many students have dreams related to stress. She wondered if there were any similarities among students' dreams. She was also curious about how many people remember their dreams, and how often, and if that might be related to gender. Finally, Christine wanted to find out whether people have recurring dreams and, if so, what those were about. There were other things she wanted to know, too. But she knew she had to keep the survey short, probably no more than seven questions.

If you're considering a survey, make a list in your research notebook of things you might want to find out and specify the group of people you plan to talk to. College students? Female college students? Attorneys? Guidance counselors? Be as specific as you can about your target group.

## Types of Questions

Next, consider what approach you will take. Will you ask *open-ended questions,* which give respondents plenty of room to invent their own answers? For example, Christine might ask, *Have you ever had any dreams that seem related to stress?* The payoff for an open-ended question is that sometimes you get surprising answers. The danger, which seems real with Christine's question, is that you'll get no answer at all. A more *directed question* might be, *Have you ever dreamed that you showed up for class and didn't know that there was a major exam that day?* Christine will get an answer to this question—yes or no—but it doesn't promise much information. A third possibility is the *multiple-choice question.* It ensures an answer and is likely to produce useful information. For example:

```
Have you ever had any dreams similar to these?

   a. You showed up for a class and didn't know

      there was a major exam.

   b. You registered for a class but forgot to

      attend.

   c. You're late for a class or an exam but can't

      seem to move fast enough to get there on

      time.
```

```
    d. You were to give a presentation but forgot
       all about it.
    e. None of the above.*
```

Ultimately, Christine decided to combine the open-ended question about stress and the multiple-choice approach, hoping that if one didn't produce interesting information, the other would (see Figure 2.14). She also wisely decided to avoid asking more than seven questions, allowing her subjects to respond to her survey in minutes.

## Survey Design

A survey shouldn't be too long (probably no more than six or seven questions), it shouldn't be biased (asking questions that will skew the answers), it should be easy to score and tabulate results (especially if you hope to survey a relatively large number of people), it should ask clear questions, and it should give clear instructions for how to answer.

As a rule, informal surveys should begin as polls often do: by getting vital information about the respondent. Christine's survey began with questions about the gender, age, and major of each respondent (see Figure 2.14). Depending on the purpose of your survey, you might also want to know things such as whether respondents are registered to vote, whether they have political affiliations, what year of school they're in, or any number of other factors. Ask for information that provides different ways of breaking down your target group.

**Avoid Loaded Questions.**   Question design is tricky business. An obviously biased question—*Do you think it's morally wrong to kill unborn babies through abortion?*—is easy to alter by removing the charged and presumptuous language. (It is unlikely that all respondents believe that abortion is killing.) One revision might be, *Do you support or oppose providing women the option to abort a pregnancy during the first twenty weeks?* This is a direct and specific question, neutrally stated, that calls for a yes or no answer. The question would be better if it were even more specific.

Controversial topics, like abortion, are most vulnerable to biased survey questions. If your topic is controversial, take great care to eliminate bias by avoiding charged language, especially if you have strong feelings yourself.

*Reprinted with permission of Christine Bergquist.

The following survey contains questions about dreaming and dream content. The findings gathered from this survey will be incorporated into a research paper on the function of dreaming and what, if anything, we can learn from it. I'd appreciate your honest answers to the questions. Thank you for your time!

### General Subject Information

Gender:    ☐ Male    ☐ Female

Age: _____

Major: _____

### Survey Questions
*(circle all letters that apply)*

1. How often do you remember your dreams?
   A. Almost every night
   B. About once a week
   C. Every few weeks
   D. Practically never

2. Have you ever dreamt that you were:
   A. Falling?
   B. Flying?

3. Have you ever dreamt of:
   A. Your death?
   B. The death of someone close to you?

4. Have you ever had a recurring dream?
   A. Yes
   B. No
   If yes,    How often? _____
             What period of your life? _____
             Do you still have it? _____

5. Have you ever had any dreams similar to these?
   A. You showed up for a class and didn't know there was a major exam.
   B. You're late for a class or an exam but can't seem to move fast enough to get there.
   C. You were to give a presentation but forgot all about it.

6. Do you feel your dreams:
   A. Hold some deep, hidden meanings about yourself or your life?
   B. Are meaningless?

7. Please briefly describe the dream you best remember or one that sticks out in your mind. (Use the back of this survey.)

**FIGURE 2.14    Sample Informal Survey**

*Source:* Reprinted with permission of Christine Bergquist.

**Avoid Vague Questions.**   Another trap is vague questions: *Do you support or oppose the university's alcohol policy?* In this case, don't assume that respondents know what the policy is unless you explain it. Since the campus alcohol policy has many elements, this question might be redesigned to ask about one of them: *The university recently established a policy that states that underage students caught drinking in campus dormitories are subject to eviction. Do you support or oppose this policy?* Other equally specific questions might ask about other parts of the policy.

**Drawbacks of Open-Ended Questions.**   Open-ended questions often produce fascinating answers, but they can be difficult to tabulate. Christine's survey asked, *Please briefly describe the one dream you best remember or one that sticks out in your mind.* She got a wide range of answers—or sometimes no answer at all—but it was hard to quantify the results. Almost everyone had different dreams, which made it difficult to discern much of a pattern. She was still able to use some of the material as anecdotes in her paper, so it turned out to be a question worth asking.

**Designing Your Multiple-Choice Questions.**   The multiple-choice question is an alternative to the open-ended question, leaving room for a number of *limited* responses, which are easier to quantify. Christine's survey had a number of multiple-choice questions.

The challenge in designing multiple-choice questions is to provide choices that will likely produce results. From her reading and talking to friends, Christine came up with what she thought were three stress-related dreams college students often experience (see question 5, Figure 2.14). The results were interesting (45 percent circled "B") but unreliable, since respondents did not have a "None of the above" option. How many respondents felt forced to choose one of the dreams listed because there was no other choice? Design choices you think your audience will respond to, but give them room to say your choices weren't theirs.

**Continuum Questions.**   Question 6 (see Figure 2.14) has a similar choice problem in that it asks a direct either/or question: *Do you feel your dreams: (A) Hold some deep, hidden meanings about yourself or your life?* or *(B) Are meaningless?* Phrased this way, the question forces the respondent into one of two extreme positions. People are more likely to place themselves somewhere in between.

A variation on the multiple-choice question is the *continuum,* where respondents indicate how they feel by marking the appropriate place along a scale. Christine's question 6 could be presented as a continuum:

> How do you evaluate the significance of your dreams? Place an "X" on the continuum in the place that most closely reflects your view.

My dreams
always hold
some meaning

My dreams
are meaningless

Though it is a bit more difficult to tabulate results of a continuum, this method often produces reliable answers if the instructions are clear.

## Planning for Distribution

Surveys can be administered in person or by phone, with the surveyor asking each respondent the questions and recording the answers, or by letting respondents fill out the surveys themselves. Although there are some real advantages to administering the survey yourself (or lining up friends to help you do it), reflect on how much time you want to devote to gathering the information. How important will the survey be to your paper? Are the results crucial to your argument? If not, consider doing what Christine did: Print several hundred survey forms that are easy for respondents to fill out themselves, and distribute them with some help from your instructor or friends.

## Conducting Surveys

Last week, you considered whether your topic lends itself to an informal survey. If so, you generated three types of questions you might ask: *open-ended, multiple choice,* and *directed* (see "Survey Design" in Chapter 2). After all the reading you did this week, you likely have some fresh ideas of questions you might ask. Finalize the questions, and begin distributing the survey to the target group you defined earlier.

**Distribution.**    Surveys administered by telephone have some advantages. People are more likely to be direct and honest over the phone, since they are relatively anonymous. Surveys are also more likely to be completed correctly, since the answers are recorded by the survey giver. However, making multiple phone calls can be tedious and expensive, if your target group goes beyond the toll-free calling area. But you may have no choice, especially if the target group for your survey isn't exclusively on campus.

The alternative to conducting a telephone survey is to distribute the survey yourself. The university community, where large numbers of people are available in a confined area, lends itself to administering surveys this way, if there's a university audience you're interested in polling. A survey can be distributed in dormitories, dining halls, classes, or anywhere else the people you want to talk to gather. You can stand outside the student union and stop people as they come and go, or you can hand out your survey to groups of people and collect them when the participants have finished. Your instructor may be able to help distribute your survey to classes. I asked a number of my colleagues to distribute Christine's survey (see Figure 2.14) in their Freshman English classes, a required course representing a relatively random sample of freshmen. Since the survey only took five minutes to fill out, other instructors were glad to help, and in one day, Christine was able to sample more than ninety students.

The campus and its activities often self-select the group you want to survey. Anna, writing a paper on date rape, surveyed exclusively women on campus, many of whom she found in women's dormitories. For his paper on the future of the fraternity system, David surveyed local "Greeks" at their annual awards banquet.

How large a sample should you shoot for? Since yours won't be a scientific survey, don't bother worrying about statistical reliability; just try to survey as many people as you can. Certainly, a large (say, more than one hundred) and representative sample will lend more credence to your claims about any patterns observed in the results.

## The Internet Survey

Usenet newsgroups, e-mail discussion groups, and even real-time communication tools such as IRCs, or MOOs, all organize people with similar interests—and in some cases similar demographics. This makes cyberspace a potentially appealing place to conduct survey work. Consider, for example, posting three or four questions on your topic to a relevant discussion group or to a group that may reach an audience you'd like to survey. For example, Marty was working on an essay that explored the extent to which college students felt a generational identity. A search on *Deja.com* produced a Usenet group, *alt.society.generation-x*, that proved an ideal forum to respond to her questions.

Another possibility that has yet to be exploited by any of my students is posting a survey form on a personal Web page. The challenge would be to attract respondents. This might work well in conjunction with a conventional survey—in this case, however, subjects would be responding to an electronic survey rather than to a paper one. It might also be effective to send a short message to a range of appropriate newsgroups or e-mail discussion lists to invite people to respond to your online survey. This may, however, be viewed by some as "spamming," or sending irrelevant messages to multiple e-mail lists or newsgroups. Net-savvy students who know how to design Web pages to ensure maximum hits by search engines might also be able to generate traffic for an online poll, particularly if the search terms that attracted respondents to the site might produce a suitable audience—with suitable interests—for the survey.

## CHAPTER 3

# The Third Week

## Writing in the Middle

I was never crazy about taking notes for a research paper. Notetaking seemed so tedious. Instead, I developed a love affair with the photocopier and walked around sounding like a slot machine, my pockets full of change, ready to bolt to the nearest copier whenever I encountered a promising article. I collected these articles to read later. I also checked out scores of books that seemed useful, rather than taking the time to skim them in the library and jot down notes on what seemed important. I was quite a sight at the end of the day, walking back to my dormitory or apartment, reeling under the weight of a mound of books and articles, all precariously balanced, defying natural laws.

When the time came to begin writing my paper, the work seemed agonizingly slow. I would consult my meager notes, thumb through two or three books from the stack, reread a dog-eared copy of an article, stop and think, write a line or two, stop and go back to a book, and then maybe write another line or two. I was always a _low_ writer, but I now realize that one major reason I got bogged _wn_ writing my research paper drafts was my inattention to note-_ng_. I paid the price for doing so little writing before I had to do _riting_.

_now_ believe that the writing that takes place in the _middle_ of _rch_ process—the notetaking stage—may be as important, if _o_, than the writing that takes place at the end—composing _Vriting_ in the middle helps you take possession of your _establish_ your presence in the draft. It sharpens your _t_ your topic. And it is the best cure for unintentional

_nave_ a sales job to do on this. Writing in the middle, _ou've_ been weaned on notecards, feels like busy-_n_ the way of doing the research," one student told me. "I just want to collect as much stuff as I can, as quickly as I can. Notetaking slows me down." Though it may seem inefficient, writing as you read may actually make your research *more* efficient. Skeptical? Read on.

## Becoming an Activist Notetaker

Notetaking can and probably should begin the process of writing your paper. Notetaking is not simply a mechanical process of vacuuming up as much information as you can and depositing it on notecards or in a notebook with little thought. Your notes from sources are your first chance to *make sense* of the information you encounter, to make it your own. You do need more time to take thoughtful notes, but doing so pays off in writing a draft more quickly and in producing a paper that reflects your point of view much more strongly.

I'll show you what I mean. Here's a passage from the essay "How the Web Destroys the Quality of Students' Research Papers" by David Rothenberg, an essay you will read later in this chapter.

> But too much of what passes for information these days [on the Web] is simply *advertising* for information. Screen after screen shows you where you can find out more, how you can connect to this place or that. The acts of linking and networking and randomly jumping from here to there become as exciting or rewarding as actually finding anything of intellectual value.

As part of a conference presentation, I decided to write an essay that explores some of the issues raised in the article. I wondered, "Is David Rothenberg right when he argues that so far Web research has had a mostly negative impact on student writing?" The passage above struck me, and I wrote it down—word for word—on the left page of my journal. On the opposing page I began an open-ended fastwrite, exploring my reaction to Rothenberg's claim.

Here's what I found myself saying about four minutes into the fastwriting:

*It strikes me that the real virtue of the Web might be its central weakness: Because so much of the Web is, as Rothenberg claims, insubstantial and unreliable, we have a wonderful opportunity to get students to*

*consider that distinction between information and
knowledge, between legitimate and specious claims to
authority . . . Where Rothenberg sees pitfalls, I see
opportunities, I guess.*

And here's what I ended up writing in my own essay, "A Net
Full of Nothing?":

> I don't think most of my students think that the Internet
> makes research easier. It makes research more *convenient,* and
> that's why students' first instinct these days is to pull up a
> chair in front of a monitor rather than to journey into the
> stacks. For the foreseeable future, the campus library will
> remain the best place to cast a net for term papers, but I'm
> coming around to seeing that the Web may be an even better
> place for students to practice how to evaluate their catch. *Can
> the Internet's weakness as a source of knowledge tutor students
> in the opportunities for knowlege-making?* I'm not sure yet.

It's quite possible, of course, that I could have used some
other way to come up with the idea that the Web's weaknesses as
an information source might be one of its virtues. But time and
again I've seen in my own writing—and in my students'—that this
kind of open-ended, often messy writing *as I'm reading* a book or
article produces suprises: new ways of seeing things, and sometimes even new ways of saying things. It is also a great way to talk
to, with, and sometimes against the published author. Talking
freely to yourself in writing about what you're reading, how you
understand it, and how it relates to what you already think (or
may have never thought of) is one of the best ways to make outside sources your own. Such writing to yourself also allows you to
indulge in "the gift of perhaps," trying out ideas and posing questions you wouldn't dare to do in a draft because it would complicate things.

Try the following exercise to discover how well you can hold up
your end of a conversation with Mark Edmundson, a college professor
who raises serious questions about the state of universities and their
students these days. Among other things, Edmundson compares the
college culture with Club Med, asserting that recruiting students and
keeping them happy requires that the university cater to their leisure
interests.

## EXERCISE 3 . 1

### Getting a Word in Edgewise

To get into the spirit of conversation, image this scenario: You've been invited to lunch by a fellow named Mark Edmundson. Seems like a nice guy, so you accept. After you both order, Edmundson suddenly blurts out, "There's something on my mind and I really want to know what you, as a college student, think about it."

"Shoot," you say.

And then Edmundson says this:

Whether the students are sorority/fraternity types, grunge afficionados, piercer/tattooers, black or white, rich or middle class . . . they are, nearly across the board, very, very, self-contained. On good days they display a light, appealing glow; on bad days, shuffling disgruntlement. But there's little fire, little passion to be found.*

**STEP 1:** Begin a five-minute fastwrite in which you respond to Edmundson's comment. Try to hold up your end of the conversation. Whenever the writing stalls, return to the passage above and find something else to respond to—ask questions, react, present your own ideas, try to restate what you think Edmundson seems to be saying.

Lunch continues. Edmundson seems genuinely interested in your response to his ideas. He sets his glass of water down after a sip, looks you in the eye, and says, "Okay, what do you think of this?":

Before they arrive, we ply students with luscious ads, guaranteeing them a cross between summer camp and lotusland. When they are here, flattery and nonstop entertainment are available, if that's what they want. . . . Is it a surprise, then, that this generation of students—steeped in consumer culture before going off to school, treated as potent customers by the university well before their date of arrival, then pandered to from day one . . . are inclined to see the books they read as a string of entertainments to be placidly enjoyed or languidly cast down?

**STEP 2:** Begin another five-minute fastwrite in your notebook in which you respond to this latest proposition by your luncheon partner. Again, try to preserve the relatively informal, conversational quality of the situation.

*Mark Edmundson, "On the Uses of Illiberal Education: As Lite Entertainment for Bored College Students," *Harper's,* September 1997: 34–49.

Lunch is nearly over, and Edmundson seems finished talking. You're wondering about who will pick up the check. Suddenly, Edmundson says, "Sorry. There's just one more thing I'd like to say. Will you hear me out?"

Your pen is at the ready.

He says:

> Perhaps it would be a good idea to try firing the counselors and sending half the deans back into their classrooms, dismantling the football team and making the stadium into a playground for local kids, emptying the fraternities, and boarding up the student-activities office. Such measures would convey the message that American colleges are not northern outposts of Club Med.

**STEP 3:** You graciously respond to Edmundson once more in a five-minute fastwrite.

---

Your instructor may have you read the full text of Edmundson's article and ask you to compose an essay that grows out of this written conversation. What I most want you to notice at this point, however, is whether this dialog with a published author has anything in common with conventional notetaking. If not, what are the differences? Later in this chapter, I suggest an approach to notetaking that combines conventional quotation, summary, and paraphrase with the kind of open-ended writing you accomplished here. It's a process that encourages the kind of *dialectical* thinking that is at the heart of inquiry, the movement back and forth between your observations and your ideas about them, between generating and judging, and collecting evidence and developing theories about what it might mean.

> **A Variation in Responding: Believing and Doubting**
>
> In each fastwrite response to Edmundson, consider spending the first two minutes playing "the believing game" and the next two minutes "the doubting game." In other words, begin by thinking through writing about why Edmundson might see things the way he does. What can you *understand* about his point of view? What might you agree with? Then shift your stance, and critically examine his claims. What is he ignoring? What fault do you find with his reasoning? How does your own experience offer contrary evidence?

Most *good* conversations make demands on both speakers. The most important of these is simply to listen carefully to what the other person is saying, even (and perhaps especially) if you don't agree. In couples therapy there's a method to help this along called "say back"—each partner has to listen first and then repeat what he or she heard the other say. Response or reaction comes later. Researchers entering into a conversation with their sources need to engage in the same practice: Listen or read carefully, first making an effort to understand a subject or author's arguments or ideas, and then exploring your response to them, as you did in the preceding exercise.

The academic equivalent of "say back" is paraphrasing or summarizing. Both are undervalued skills, I think, that require practice. Try your hand at it in the following exercise.

## EXERCISE   3 . 2

### "Say Back" to a Source

The following passage is from an article by linguist Deborah Tannen on the complexity of communication within families.

> Through talk, we create and shape our relationships. Through talk, we are comforted; through talk we are hurt. We look to family members for come-as-you-are-acceptance, but instead of an intimate ally, we sometimes find an intimate critic. A small remark can spark a big conflict because with the family, no utterance stands alone. Every remark draws meaning from innumerable conversations that came before.*

In your notebook, rewrite the passage in your own words in roughly the same length—a *paraphrase*. You'll find it's easier to do if you first focus on understanding what Tannen is trying to say and then write without looking much at the passage, if possible. If this is an in-class exercise, exchange your rewrite with a partner. Then read the following section on plagiarism.

## Recognizing Plagiarism

Simply put, *plagiarism* is using others' ideas *or* words as if they were your own. The most egregious case is handing in someone else's

---

*Deborah Tannen, "I Heard What You Didn't Say," *The Washington Post* 13 May 2001: B1.

work with your name on it. Some schools also consider using one paper to meet the requirements of two classes to be a grave offense. But most plagiarism is unintentional. I remember being guilty of plagiarism when writing a philosophy paper my freshman year in college. I committed the offense largely because I didn't know what plagiarism was and I hadn't been adequately schooled in good scholarship (which is no excuse).

## I Read What You Said and Borrowed It, Okay?

Here's another passage from the same article by Deborah Tannen. In this excerpt she is talking about a situation with which we're all familiar. We're talking with a loved one and they make a comment that seems innocuous—"I'll put the dishes in the dishwasher because I can pack more in"—but the comment is heard as a larger criticism: "You're not good at housework." There are what seem to be simple messages with equally simple motives, and then there are "metamessages" that we sometimes hear instead of the simple ones. What follows is Tannen's original passage, and what seems like a pretty good paraphrase.

## What Is Plagiarism?

Each college or university has a statement in the student handbook that offers a local definition. But that statement probably includes most or all of the following forms of plagiarism.

1. Handing in someone else's work—a downloaded paper from the Internet or one borrowed from a friend—and claiming that it's your own.
2. Using information or ideas that are not common knowledge from any source and failing to acknowledge that source.
3. Handing in the same paper for two different classes.
4. Using the exact language or expressions of a source and not indicating through quotation marks and citation that the language is borrowed.
5. Rewriting a passage from a source by minor substitutions of different words but retaining the same syntax and structure of the original.

**Original passage:** *Distinguishing the message from the metamessage (terms I have adopted from anthropologist Gregory Bateson) is necessary to ensure that family members work things out rather than working each other over. It's frustrating to have the same arguments again and again. But some arguments can be constructive—if family members use them to articulate and understand the metamessages they are intending and hearing.*

**Paraphrase:** Sometimes family members can have the same argument over and over and not realize that they're arguing about two different things. Linguist Deborah Tannen writes that it's important to distinguish between the message and the metamessages; a message may have a simple intention but it is heard as something quite different, something the speaker didn't intend at all. By articulating what was said and what was heard, arguments can be constructive rather than frustrating.

There are a couple of problems with this paraphrase but they might, at first, seem pretty subtle. Notice that the first line uses the phrase "have the same argument over and over" which, though worded slightly different, copies the pattern of Tannen's original "have the same arguments again and again." That won't do.

Worse, the paraphrase fails to include quotation marks around the borrowed phrase "the message and the metamessage." It also lifts "constructive" from the original without quotation marks and uses the word "articulating" in the paraphrase, without quotation marks, which also is uncomfortably close to Tannen's "articulate." But the bigger problem is not one I would expect you to notice yet. Even though the paraphrase uses an attribution tag—"Linguist Deborah Tannen writes . . . "—the paraphrase doesn't include a parenthetical citation, something like (Tannen 2) indicating the page number from which the passage was borrowed. We'll talk later about citation, but here's the key thing to remember: *Whenever you quote, paraphrase, or summarize a source, it must always be cited, even if you mention the author's name.*

**Corrected paraphrase:** Old family arguments may not really be about what family members have always thought they were about. Linguist Deborah Tannen writes that it's important to distinguish between "**the message and the metamessage**"; a message may have a simple intention but is heard as something quite different, something the speaker didn't intend at all. Even old family arguments can be "**constructive**," says Tannen, if family members are careful to talk openly about this difference (**Tannen 2**).

Here are some simple tactics for avoiding plagiarism:

- It's fine to borrow distinctive terms or phrases from a source, but also signal that you've done so with quotation marks.
- Make a habit of using attribution tags, signaling to your reader who is the source of the idea, quotation, or fact. These tags include things such as, *Tannen argues, Tannen writes, According to Tannen,* etc. For a lengthy list of these tags, see the box, "Active Verbs for Discussing Ideas," in Chapter 5.
- *Always* cite borrowed material (more about how to do that later).

As a follow up to Exercise 3.2, return to the paraphrase you composed of the Tannen passage on talk within families. Do you need to edit or alter the paraphrase you wrote to avoid possible plagiarism problems? If you're in class, your instructor may ask you to work in pairs on this. What are the common plagiarism mistakes—almost always unintentional—that students in the class made when they paraphrased the passage in Exercise 3.2?

## Why Plagiarism Matters

It may seem that all the fuss over plagiarism is just another example of English teachers' obsession with rules. In fact, the saddest days I've ever had as a writing teacher have always been when I've talked with a student about a paper she downloaded from the Internet or borrowed from her roommate. Most instructors hate dealing with plagiarism. It is, of course, a moral issue, but the motive to be careful about distinguishing what is yours and what you've borrowed isn't just a matter of "being good." It's really a gesture of gratitude. Research is always built on the work that came before it,

---

### The Common Knowledge Exception

While you always have to tell readers what information you have borrowed and where it came from, things that are "common knowledge" are excluded from this. Everyone knows, for example, that John Kennedy died in Dallas in November 1963. These and other widely known facts need not be cited. Neither do observations that anyone could make, or common sayings such as "home is where the heart is."

## Why Cite?

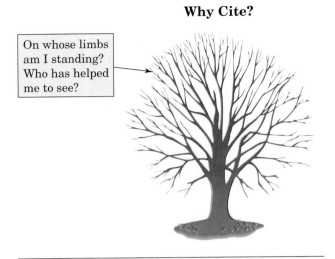

**FIGURE 3.1**    Like a tree, knowledge in a discipline is a living thing, from time to time losing and adding branches, growing in new directions.

and as you read and write about your topic, I hope that you come to appreciate the thoughtful writing and thinking of people before you who may have given you a new way of seeing or thinking.

Knowledge is a living thing (see Figure 3.1), growing like a great tree in multiple directions, adding and losing branches which keep reaching higher toward new understandings and truths. As researchers we are tree climbers, ascending the branches in an effort to see better. It's only natural that as we make this climb, we feel grateful for the strength of certain limbs under our feet. Citing and acknowledging sources is a way of expressing this gratitude.

## Sources Are from Mars, Notetakers Are from Venus

I have got to admit I never read John Gray's bestseller about the complexity of communication between men and women, *Men Are from Mars, Women Are from Venus,* but I like the metaphor that sometimes it seems as if men and women are from different planets; I think the metaphor applies to notetaking, too. Consider how awkward it is to read someone else's words, make a concerted effort to understand what they mean, and then find your own words to restate the ideas. What's worse is that sometimes the authors are experts who use language you may not easily grasp or use reasoning in ways you can't easily follow. And then there are those authors who write so beautifully, you wonder how you could possibly say it better. Finally, there might be the fear that somehow you will goof and plagiarize the source's ideas or words.

For all of these reasons, the relationship between a source and a research writer is often complex. Both might as well be on different planets.

## Paraphrasing

In the last exercise, you practiced "say back," a technique that helps many married couples who are headed for divorce. As I mentioned, *paraphrase* is the academic equivalent of this therapeutic method for getting people to listen to each other. Try to say in your own words—and in about the same length as the author said it— what you understand that author to mean. This is hard, at first, because instead of just mindlessly quoting—a favorite alternative for many students—you have to *think*. Paraphrasing demands that you make your own sense of something. The time is well worth it. Why? Because not only are you lowering the risk of unintentional plagiarism and being fair to the source's ideas, *you are essentially writing a fragment of your draft.*

This returns me to my original argument: Thoughtful notetaking pays off in the long run because you're essentially writing your essay in the middle of the process. Imagine what an advantage you'll have over those who wait until the night before the paper is due. Rather than pages of journal notes ripe for the picking, the night-before-it's-due clan is looking at bare branches. In a few pages, I'll suggest several notetaking methods that I think will give you the most to harvest; one of these, the double-entry journal, is a method that combines both the kind of listening that paraphrase demands and the open-ended exploratory thinking that you enjoyed in Exercise 3.1, the conversation with Edmundson. But first, let's review another listening technique useful for academic writers: summary.

## Summarizing

I heard recently that in order to sell a movie to Hollywood, a screenwriter should be able to summarize what it's about in a sentence. "*The Big Chill* is a film about six friends from the sixties who reunite some years later and are suddenly confronted with reconciling past and present." That statement hardly does justice to the film—which is about so much more than that—but I think it basically captures the story and its central theme.

Obviously, that's what a *summary* is: a reduction of longer material into some brief statement that captures a basic idea, argument, or theme from the original. Like paraphrasing, summarizing often requires careful thought, since you're the one doing the distilling, especially if you're trying to capture the essence of a whole movie, article, or chapter that's fairly complex.

But many times, summarizing involves simply boiling down a passage—not the entire work—to its basic idea. Mark, who researched patterns of alcohol abuse among college students, found an article from the *Journal of Studies on Alcoholism* that surveyed college students on situations in which they might choose to intervene—or not to intervene—to help a fellow student with a drinking problem. Much of the article discussed methodology, which wasn't very useful to Mark's essay, but one passage had some interesting facts:

> Decisions not to intervene were reported less often by the respondents. In the drunk-driving situation, only 26% of the respondents in the sample (30% of the men and 24% of the women) indicated that, at least once, they both saw someone who was too drunk to drive and chose not to do or say anything. . . . Students indicated they chose not to intervene because they did not know the person well enough (24%) or that they were too drunk themselves to be of any help (24%). However, additional reasons for nonintervention in the drunk-driving situation included the anticipated response (17%) of the target (no matter what the intervener did, the behavior of the target could not be changed); the degree to which intervention would result in the intervener's negative self-image (16%) (fear of looking foolish in front of others present); [and] misperceptions (13%) of the situation (unsure how drunk the target was). . . . Interestingly, men (23%) more frequently cited concern about creating a negative self-image than did women (11%), while women (20%) more frequently identified the anticipated response of the target as a reason for nonintervention than did men (14%).*

There's nothing particularly distinctive about how this information is presented (in fact, it's pretty dry), so there's nothing particularly quotable. And paraphrasing the whole passage seems unnecessary, since not all the information is important for Mark's purposes. But embedded in this passage is some pretty interesting stuff, especially given Mark's project: to explore how students' personal relationships influence their drinking habits.

*Richard W. Thomas and David R. Siebold, "College Students' Decisions to Intervene in Alcohol-Related Situations," *Journal of Studies on Alcohol* 56.5 (1995): 580–88.

A simple summary might be something like this:

```
According to Thomas and Siebold, most college
students say they would try to stop a drunk
student from getting into his car and driving
away. Roughly one-quarter of the students
surveyed, however, wouldn't intervene, and 24
percent of those said it was because they were
"too drunk themselves."
```

This summary helps Mark emphasize only the information from this source that's important to his essay. He uses that information selectively and powerfully by putting it in his own words.

A summary such as this one, where you distill only part of a larger source, is selective. You choose to emphasize some key part of a source because it fits your paper's purpose. But the same warning applies to selective summarizing as was given earlier about paraphrasing: Don't misrepresent the general thrust of the author's ideas. Ask yourself, Does my selective use of this source seem to give it a spin the author didn't intend? Most of the time, I think you will discover the answer is no.

## Quoting

The quotation mark may be the student researcher's best friend, at least as demonstrated by how often papers are peppered by long quotes!

As a general rule, the college research paper should contain no more than 10 or 20 percent quoted material, but it's an easy rule to ignore. For one thing, quoting sources at the notetaking and drafting stages is quicker than restating material in your own words. When you quote, you don't have to think much about what you're reading; you just jot it down the way you see it and, if you have to, think about it later. That's the real problem with verbatim copying of source material: There isn't much thinking involved. As a result, the writer doesn't take possession of the information, shape it, and allow herself to be shaped by it.

That's not to say that you should completely avoid quoting sources directly as a method of notetaking. If you're writing on a literary topic, for example, you may quote fairly extensively from the novel or poem you're examining. Or if your paper relies heavily on interviews, you'll want to bring in the voices of your subjects, verbatim.

**When to Quote.**   As a rule, jot down a quote when someone says or writes something that is distinctive in a certain way and when restating it in your own words wouldn't possibly do the thought justice. I'll never forget a scene from the documentary *Shoah,* an eleven-hour film about the Holocaust, which presented an interview with the Polish engineer of one of the trains that took thousands of Jews to their deaths. Now an old man and still operating the same train, he was asked how he felt now about his role in World War II. He said quietly, "If you could lick my heart, it would poison you."

It would be difficult to restate the Polish engineer's comment in your own words. But more important, it would be stupid even to try. Some of the pain and regret and horror of that time in history is embedded in that one man's words. You may not come across such a distinctive quote as you read your sources this week, but be alert to *how* authors (and those quoted by authors) say things. Is the prose unusual, surprising, or memorable? Does the writer make a point in an interesting way? If so, jot it down.

Heidi, in a paper on the children's television program *Sesame Street,* began by quoting a eulogy for Muppets creator Jim Henson. The quote is both memorable and touching. Heidi made an appropriate choice, establishing a tone that is consistent with her purpose: to respond to certain critics of the program. The fact that a quote sounds good isn't reason enough to use it. Like anything else, quotes should be used deliberately, with purpose.

There are several other reasons to quote a source as you're notetaking. Sometimes, it's desirable to quote an expert on your topic who is widely recognized in the field. Used to support or develop your own assertions, the voice of an authority can lend credit to your argument and demonstrate your effort to bring recognized voices into the discussion.

Another reason to quote a source is that his explanation of a process or idea is especially clear. Such quotes often feature metaphors. Robert Bly's *Iron John,* a book that looks at American men and their difficult journey into manhood, is filled with clear and compelling explanations of that process. As a son of an alcoholic father, I found Bly's discussion often hit home. Here, using a metaphor, he explains in a simple but compelling way how children in troubled homes become emotionally unprotected, something that often haunts them the rest of their lives:

> When a boy grows up in a "dysfunctional" family (perhaps there
> is no other kind of family), his interior warriors will be killed
> off early. Warriors, mythologically, lift their swords to defend
> the king. The King in a child stands for and stands up for the

child's mood. But when we are children our mood gets easily overrun and swept over in the messed-up family by the more powerful, more dominant, more terrifying mood of the parent. We can say that when the warriors inside cannot protect our mood from being disintegrated, or defend our body from invasion, the warriors collapse, go into a trance, or die.*

I'm sure there's a more technical explanation for the ways parents in dysfunctional families can dominate the emotional lives of their children. But the warrior metaphor is so simple; and that is, partly, its power. As you read or take notes during an interview, be alert to sources or subjects who say something that gets right to the heart of an important idea. Listen for it.

If your paper is on a literary topic—involving novels, stories, poems, and other works—then purposeful and selective quoting is especially important and appropriate. The texts and the actual language the writers use in them are often central to the argument you're making. If you're writing about the misfit hero in J. D. Salinger's novels, asserting that he embodies the author's own character, then you'll have to dip freely into his books, quoting passages that illustrate that idea. (See Appendix C for an essay on literary topics that use quotes effectively.)

**Quoting Fairly.**   If you do choose to quote from a source, be careful to do three things: (1) Quote accurately, (2) make sure it's clear in your notes that what you're jotting down is quoted material, and (3) beware of distorting a quote by using it out of context. The first two guidelines protect you from plagiarism, and the last ensures that you're fair to your sources.

To guarantee the accuracy of a quote, you may want to photocopy the page or article with the borrowed material. A tape recorder can help in an interview, and so can asking your subject to repeat something that seems especially important. To alert yourself to which part of your notes is a quote of the source's words, try using oversized quotation marks around the passage so that it can't be missed.

Guarding against out-of-context quotations can be a little more difficult. After all, an isolated quote has already been removed from the context of the many other things a subject has said. That shouldn't be a problem if you have represented her ideas accurately. However, sometimes a quote can misrepresent a source by what is omitted. Simply be fair to the author by noting any important qualifications she may make to something said or written, and render her ideas as completely as possible in your paper.

*Robert Bly, *Iron John: A Book about Men* (Reading, MA: Addison-Wesley, 1990), 147.

## E X E R C I S E     3 . 3

### Your Words, His Words

Get some practice with purposeful notetaking with the article "How the Web Destroys the Quality of Students' Research Papers," which follows. First, read it carefully, simply to absorb the author's argument. Underline passages you think are important to your understanding. Reread it quickly and do the following in your research notebook:

1. Summarize the article in a sentence or two. Try to do this without looking at the article. Trust that you'll remember what's important.

2. Select at least two passages that seem quotable to you, and carefully jot them down.

3. Below your summary and quotations, begin a five-minute fast-write in which you explore your reaction to the article. How do the author's observations of student use of the Web compare with your own experiences? What did you find most convincing about Rothenberg's argument? What seemed least convincing? What other ideas or questions does the article inspire you to consider? What is your own opinion about using the Internet for research papers?

4. Now take ten minutes a compose a single paragraph that brings summary, quotation, and, perhaps, paraphrase together with your own ideas about whether "the Web destroys the quality of students' research papers." Obviously, take care to avoid any plagiarism by using your own voice, by citing the source, and by using quotation marks to signal borrowed material. Use the article, but make it your own.

## *How the Web Destroys the Quality of Students' Research Papers*
*by David Rothenberg*

SOMETIMES I LOOK forward to the end-of-semester rush, when students' final papers come streaming into my office and mailbox. I could have hundreds of pages of original thought to read and evaluate. Once in a while, it *is* truly exciting, and brilliant words are typed across a page in response to a question I've asked the class to discuss.

But this past semester was different. I noticed a disturbing decline in both the quality of the writing and the originality of the thoughts expressed. What had happened since last fall? Did I ask worse questions? Were my students unusually lazy? No. My class had fallen victim to the latest easy way of writing a paper: doing their research on the World Wide Web.

It's easy to spot a research paper that is based primarily on information collected from the Web. First, the bibliography cites no books, just articles or pointers to places in that virtual land somewhere off any map: http://www.etc. Then a strange preponderance of material in the bibliography is curiously out of date. A lot of stuff on the Web that is advertised as timely is actually at least a few years old. (One student submitted a research paper last semester in which all of his sources were articles published between September and December 1995; that was probably the time span of the Web page on which he found them.)

Another clue is the beautiful pictures and graphs that are inserted neatly into the body of the student's text. They look impressive, as though they were the result of careful work and analysis, but actually they often bear little relation to the precise subject of the paper. Cut and pasted from the vast realm of what's out there for the taking, they masquerade as original work.

Accompanying them are unattributed quotes (in which one can't tell who made the statement or in what context) and curiously detailed references to the kinds of things that are easy to find on the Web (pages and pages of federal documents, corporate propaganda, or snippets of commentary by people whose credibility is difficult to assess). Sadly, one finds few references to careful, in-depth commentaries on the subject of the paper, the kind of analysis that requires a book, rather than an article, for its full development.

Don't get me wrong, I'm no neo-Luddite. I am as enchanted as anyone else by the potential of this new technology to provide instant information. But too much of what passes for information these days is simply *advertising* for information. Screen after screen shows you where you can find out more, how you can connect to this place or that. The acts of linking and networking and randomly jumping from here to there become as exciting or rewarding as actually finding anything of intellectual value.

Search engines, with their half-baked algorithms, are closer to slot machines than to library catalogues. You throw your query to the wind, and who knows what will come back to you? You may get

234,468 supposed references to whatever you want to know. Perhaps one in a thousand might actually help you. But it's easy to be sidetracked or frustrated as you try to go through those Web pages one by one. Unfortunately, they're not arranged in order of importance.

What I'm describing is the hunt-and-peck method of writing a paper. We all know that word processing makes many first drafts look far more polished than they are. If the paper doesn't reach the assigned five pages, readjust the margin, change the font size, and . . . *voila!* Of course, those machinations take up time that the student could have spent revising the paper. With programs to check one's spelling and grammar now standard features on most computers, one wonders why students make any mistakes at all. But errors are as prevalent as ever, no matter how crisp the typeface. Instead of becoming perfectionists, too many students have become slackers, preferring to let the machine do their work for them.

What the Web adds to the shortcuts made possible by word processing is to make research look too easy. You toss a query to the machine, wait a few minutes, and suddenly a lot of possible sources of information appear on your screen. Instead of books that you have to check out of the library, read carefully, understand, synthesize, and then tactfully excerpt, these sources are quips, blips, pictures, and short summaries that may be downloaded magically to the dorm room computer screen. Fabulous! How simple! The only problem is that a paper consisting of summaries is bound to be fragmented and superficial, and to demonstrate more of a random montage than an ability to sustain an argument through 10 to 15 double-spaced pages.

Of course, you can't blame the students for ignoring books. When college libraries are diverting funds from books to computer technology that will be obsolete in two years at most, they send a clear message to students: Don't read, just connect. Surf. Download. Cut and paste. Originality becomes hard to separate from plagiarism if no author is cited on a Web page. Clearly, the words are up for grabs, and students much prefer the fabulous jumble to the hard work of stopping to think and make sense of what they've read.

Libraries used to be repositories of words and ideas. Now they are seen as centers for the retrieval of information. Some of this information comes from other, bigger libraries, in the form of books that can take time to obtain through interlibrary loan. What happens to the many students (some things never change) who scramble to write a paper the night before it's due? The computer screen, the gateway to the world sitting right on their desks, promises instant access—but actually offers only a pale, two-dimensional version of a real library.

But it's also my fault. I take much of the blame for the decline in the quality of student research in my classes. I need to teach students how to read, to take time with language and ideas, to work through arguments, to synthesize disparate sources to come up with original thought. I need to help my students understand how to assess sources to determine their credibility, as well as to trust their own ideas more than snippets of thought that materialize on a screen. The placelessness of the Web leads to an ethereal randomness of thought. Gone are the pathways of logic and passion, the sense of the progress of an argument. Chance holds sway, and it more often misses than hits. Judgment must be taught, as well as the methods of exploration.

I'm seeing my students' attention spans wane and their ability to reason for themselves decline. I wish that the university's computer system would crash for a day, so that I could encourage them to go outside, sit under a tree, and read a really good book—from start to finish. I'd like them to sit for a while and ponder what it means to live in a world where some things get easier and easier so rapidly that we can hardly keep track of how easy they're getting, while other tasks remain as hard as ever—such as doing research and writing a good paper that teaches the writer something in the process. Knowledge does not emerge in a vacuum, but we do need silence and space for sustained thought. Next semester, I'm going to urge my students to turn off their glowing boxes and think, if only once in a while.

---

## A Loop, an Inverted Pyramid, and a Diamond: Three Ways to Use a Source

I'm going to guess that your instincts in the last exercise were to decide whether you agreed or disagreed with the article "How the Web Destroys the Quality of Students' Research Papers." If so, you probably used the article—perhaps a quotation or phrase or summary of an idea—to explain why you took a particular position. Nothing wrong with that.

But I'd like you to consider other ways of using source material in your writing. Here are my attempts at the final step of Exercise 3.4. I tried to write each paragraph differently to illustrate a range of ways a writer might use an outside source in his or her work.

### AS MEANS TO EXTEND YOUR THINKING

David Rothenberg may be quite right that "the Web destroys the quality of students' research papers" because it lures them away from books, deceives them into thinking that form is a substitute for substance, and encourages a "randomness of thought" inspired by the fragmented nature of Internet information. But his description of the "fabulous jumble" of words on the Web, words that "are up for grabs" because they are so easy to cut and to paste, makes me consider what that might mean for our understanding of knowledge. On the Web, knowledge is moveable—it can be updated, anyone can contribute to it, and anyone can claim it. Is this a good thing because it democratizes knowledge— inviting us all to contribute—and shows the incremental nature of knowing as well? What might have happened if Einstein had had a Web page?

Note here that I ignore the supposed need to take sides in response to the Rothenberg article. Instead, his ideas—which I initially summarize—push me tentatively in new directions and toward new ideas. The article becomes a launching place for my own thinking rather than an argument for or against the author's position. I see a loop when I write like this, one that begins with the source but arcs away for a while (and maybe for good) before arcing back.

### AS EVIDENCE OR EXAMPLE

The campus library, once the hub of learning at most American universities, is now in danger of becoming like the bank ATM: no need to actually talk with a human being to get what you need, or even to walk in the building. Just put your debit card in the ATM slot and get your money and leave. While they once used to be "repositories of words and ideas," libraries are now merely "centers for retrieval of information," according to David Rothenberg, in "How the Web Destroys the Quality of Students' Research Papers." Much of this information can now be obtained through the library's Web site or by simply surfing the Web itself, turning the reference librarian into the equivalent of the Maytag washing machine man—a very lonely person.

Here Rothenberg's essay offers a view that conveniently supports my assertion that campus libraries, and especially librarians, are becoming less relevant because of the Internet revolution. Again, I'm not necessarily taking sides on the argument that the Web is destroying student research papers but using Rothenberg's piece as evidence for another argument I want to make. I visualize this approach as an inverted pyramid. It often starts with some larger claim or idea or observation that rests on the specific evidence drawn from sources.

### AS OPPORTUNITY FOR ANALYSIS OR INTERPRETATION

 When David Rothenberg writes that the "placelessness of the Web leads [student research writers] to an ethereal randomness of thought," I wonder whether at the heart of his complaint is the odd habit of linking pages on the Web, each link taking the reader to another site that contains supposedly relevant information. These links can radiate outward in all directions from the original Web page, making it impossible to follow the "progress of an argument," and making writers rely too heavily on the hope that each link will add something new and useful. As Rothenberg observes, "Chance holds sway, and it more often misses than hits."

Sometimes the best use of a source is to locate an interesting point or piece of information and then to try to "unpack" it, raising questions about the meaning or significance of what the author is saying or reporting. I see a diamond here. The analysis begins with some specific idea or fact from the source, which is then drawn out and examined and commented on, which then allows the writer to return once again to a specific part of the author's text with new understanding.

# Notetaking Techniques

In the first edition of *The Curious Researcher,* I confessed to a dislike of notecards. Apparently, I'm not the only one. Mention notecards, and students often tell horror stories. It's a little like talking about who has the most horrendous scar, a discussion that can prompt participants to expose knees and bare abdomens in public places. One student even mailed me her notecards—fifty bibliography cards and fifty-three notecards, all bound by a metal ring and color coded. She assured me that she didn't want them back—ever. Another student told me she was required to write twenty notecards a day: "If you spelled something wrong or if you put your name on the left side of the notecard rather than the right, your notecards were torn up and you had to do them over."

It is true, of course, that some students find recording information on notecards an enormously useful way of organizing information. And some teachers have realized that it's pretty silly to turn notetaking into a form that must be done "correctly" or not at all. For these reasons, I included suggestions about how to use notecards effectively in the first edition of this text. But in good conscience, I can't do it anymore. I no longer believe that 3" × 5" or 4" × 6" cards are large enough to accommodate the frequently messy and occasionally extended writing that often characterizes genuinely useful notes. Little cards get in the way of having a good conversation with your sources.

If conventional notecards encourage a monologue, then what method will encourage dialogue? Basically any notetaking strategy that encourages the two things that you've practiced so far in this chapter: listening and responding, collecting and evaluating. It's that movement back and forth between information and what you think of that information, between your observations of things and your ideas about them, between what you once understood and what you *now* understand, that will involve you in the process of *knowledge-making*, rather than simply information retrieval and reporting. Now this probably sounds pretty grandiose. Your research essay will probably not earn space in an academic journal. But as you begin to understand the difference between knowledge and information, you will earn yourself a place in an academic community that values people with their own ideas. Isn't that inviting?

I'm convinced that something as seemingly mundane as notetaking can be a key part of becoming a knower rather than a parrot. One method, in particular, seems especially effective at encouraging dialogue between the researcher and his sources: the double-entry journal.

## The Double-Entry Journal

The double-entry approach (see Figure 3.2) is basically this: Divide each page of your research notebook into two columns (or use opposing pages). On each left side, compile your notes from a source—paraphrases, summaries, quotes—and on each right side, comment on them. Imagine that line down the middle of the page—or that spiral binder that divides opposing pages—as the lunch table at which you sat with Mark Edmundson in the opening exercise of this chapter. On the left sits the published author. You sit on the right. Take care to listen to what the author said through paraphrase, summary, and quotation on the left, and then on the right respond with your own commentary, questions, interpretations, clarifications, or even feelings about what you heard. Your commentary can be pretty open ended: What strikes you? What was confusing? What was surprising? How does the information stand up to your own experiences and observations? Does it support or contradict your thesis (if you have one at this point)? How might you use the information in your paper? What purpose might it serve? What do you think of the source? What further questions does the information raise that might be worth investigating? How does the information connect to other sources you've read?

**Notes from Source**

- In this column, collect direct quotations, paraphrases, and summaries of key ideas that you cull from your source.

- Collect material that's relevant to your project, but also write down passages, facts, and claims from the source that you find surprising or puzzling or that generate some kind of emotional response in you.

- Make sure you write down this material carefully and accurately.

- Don't forget to include the page number from the source to the left of the borrowed material or idea.

**Fastwrite Response**

- In this column, think through writing about some of the information you collected in the other column. This will likely be a messy fastwrite but a focused one.

- Try shifting between two stances: believing and doubting. Spend a few minutes writing about the possible merits of an author's ideas, assertions, or study. Then spend a few minutes writing about questions, doubts, or counterclaims you would raise.

- Whenever your writing dies, skip a space, look to the left, and find something else to respond to.

- Some questions to ponder as you're writing might include:
  1. What strikes me about this?
  2. What are my first thoughts when I consider this? And then what? And then? And then?
  3. What exactly does this make me think of or remember?
  4. How would I qualify or challenge this author's claim? In what ways do I agree with it?
  5. What else have I read that connects with this?
  6. How do I feel about this?

**FIGURE 3.2    Double-Entry Journal Method**

There are a variety of ways to approach the double-entry journal. If you're taking notes on a photocopied article or a book you own, try reading the material first and underlining passages that seem important. Then, when you're done, transfer some of that underlined material—quotes, summaries, or paraphrases—into the left column of your journal. Otherwise, take notes in the left column *as* you read.

While you take notes, or after you've finished, do some exploratory writing in the right column. This territory belongs to you.

Ehrenstein, David. "Film in the Age of Video." *Film Quarterly* 49.3 (1996): 38-42.

38 ". . . today the once distinct spheres of theatrical and home exhibition have been radically conflated."

Let's see. So the "spheres" of showing films in theaters and in home video have been "conflated." What I think he means is that movies are now produced with both means of showing them in mind, which would seem to have implications for <u>how</u> they're made these days. E. talks later in the article about this, I think, when he mentions how only the dimension of sound has been preserved from the old days of big screens in dark theaters. The "big image" is lost. I'm not sure what this means, exactly.

39 <u>That's Entertainment 3</u>, which started as video, is "less a spectacular to be enjoyed in a darkened theater than a work of historical and cultural research that invites detailed analysis—a mode of consumption that home video, by its very nature, encourages."

I like this phrase that home video represents a particular "mode of consumption" for film. You may see more than one film at a sitting, in a lighted room, and you can rewind and reexamine favorite scenes and images. There is something about sitting in the dark, too, watching a big screen with a few hundred other people. It's like you experience nothing but image because there's nothing else to see. And somehow the act of watching with strangers, instead of in your living room by yourself or with friends, creates a kind of community. But E. talks here about how even the theater experience is no longer "distinctive." But he doesn't really say why. What exactly was lost with the

40 "There are any number of (video) sets devoted to films, old and new, that enable the average everyday consumer to examine cinema now as never before."

"The illusion of depth" is destroyed on home video.

---

**FIGURE 3.3   Sample Double-Entry Journal.** Here, the writer concentrates on collecting and responding to quoted material from the source.

41 "To remember the movie palaces, with enormous images floating in a velvety darkness, framed by curtains that never seemed to close on an ever-shifting program (features, cartoons, shorts, news, coming attractions) is not to indulge in nostalgia but rather to note how radically cinematic object relations have changed. There's nothing in any way distinctive about the modern theatrical movie-going experience, save the sound.

42 "We have entered an era of lowered cinematic expectations."

Jacque Rivette: "The cinema is necessarily fascination and rape, that is how it acts on people; it is something pretty unclear, something one sees shrouded in darkness."

disappearance of the "movie palace?" Size, for one thing. Maybe that's one way that home video and movies in theater have been "conflated." Because, as E. says, films are now made for both video and theaters, and the "illusion of depth" as well as size of the image is destroyed by home video, then there's really no need for the really big screen of the "movie palace." Instead, we now have theaters divided and subdivided into eight theaters. Screens have shrunk, rooms have shrunk, and the theater experience begins to approximate home video. That leads to this "era of lowered cinematic expectations."

I don't get this quote at all. How can Rivette compare the experience of watching a film as both "fascination and rape?" Does he mean that film does violence in the dark to viewers in the same way a rapist would?

Check Rivette cite.

**FIGURE 3.3**  (Continued)

Here, through language, your mind and heart assert themselves over the source material. Use your notes in the left column as a trigger for writing in the right. Whenever your writing stalls, look to the left. The process is a little like watching tennis—look left, then right, then left, then right. Direct your attention to what the source says and then to what *you* have to say about the source. Keep up a dialogue.

Figures 3.3, 3.4, and 3.5 illustrate how the double-entry journal works in practice. Note these features:

■ Bibliographic information is recorded at the top of the page. Do that first, and make sure it's complete.

Fredrick, Christina M. and Virginia M. Grow. "A Mediational Model of Autonomy, Self-Esteem, and Eating Disordered Attitudes and Behaviors." *Psychology of Women Quarterly* 20 (1996): 217-228.

218 Study begins by reviewing evidence that eating disorders and "autonomy" are closely related. "Wagner et al. found . . . that eating disordered individuals not only perceive themselves as lacking independence, but that this lack of self-determination extends into social situations, such as dating and attending parties.

At first the whole premise of this study seemed totally obvious. Of course women who have low self-esteem and don't feel independent are going to be at risk for eating disorders and maybe any number of other problems. But then I began to see what they were getting at: that there might be some kind of "developmental" thing going on here. That lack of autonomy might lead to low self-esteem and that might lead to eating disorders. Give girls a strong feeling of independence then and you're likely to help them avoid eating disorder.

Low self-esteem has also been shown to be linked to eating disorders.

219 Authors believe that autonomy and self-esteem may have a relationship to each other: "We would predict that by the time people reach adulthood, they would have internalized messages from their environment pertaining to their needs for autonomy with ramifications for their self-esteem. . . . For women in Western societies, one way to cope with intrapsyhic distress from unfulfilled needs for autonomy and resulting low self-esteem may be to focus on body-related issues."

Why would "body-related issues" naturally develop from lack of autonomy and low self-esteem? The key, I think, is that autonomy is all about control. The one thing an anorexic or bulimic thinks she can control is her body.

---

**FIGURE 3.4    Sample Double-Entry Journal.** This writer, taking notes on an article from a scholarly journal, collects and responds to summaries, quotes, and paraphrases from the source.

220 Authors describe a developmental pathway: lack of autonomy leads to low self-esteem leads to eating disorders.

Studied 71 women in an undergrad psych class at Univ. of Rochester.

224 "... autonomy provides a fundamental foundation for true self-esteem and the development of other healthy personality characteristics."

This seems like a really important idea.

"... a young woman who grows up in an environment that fails to support her needs for autonomy may learn to shift her focus from satisfying her own needs to satisfying the needs of others. Thus, she may believe that she is valued not as a separate worthwhile individual but rather for what she does to make others happy. ... By learning to be 'perfect' and seemingly in control, the girl subsequently fails to develop a separate sense of self-esteem because her feelings of worth are contingent on pleasing others."

The connection I can't quite see here is why unfulfilled needs for autonomy would lead someone to focus on pleasing others. What the authors seem to be missing here is the connection between autonomy and control and eating disorders. Like what I was saying earlier: If you don't feel you have control over your life, you can exert control over your body (or so you think). "The effort to be perfect" is a set-up for failure, and this leads to low self-esteem. But I'm still not sure this low self-esteem is because she failed others. It's because she failed herself. That's my experience with it.

Study concludes that there is a "statistically suggestive ... developmental pattern" of lack of autonomy leading to low self-esteem leading to eating disorders. Treatment strategy? Deal with lack of autonomy.

**FIGURE 3.4**   (Continued)

Oppenhiemer, Todd. "The Computer Delusion." _Atlantic Monthly_ (July 1997). <http://www.theatlantic.com/issues/97jul/computer.htm>.

4   Alan Lesgood, director of Learning and Development Center at U of Pitt: The computer is an "amplifier," involves both sound "study practices and thoughtless ones." Which of the two will predominate?

5   Are computers "the filmstrips of the 90s"? Clifford Stoll, author of _Silicon Snake Oil:_ "We loved them (filmstrips) because we didn't have to think for an hour, teachers loved them because they didn't have to teach and parents loved them because it showed their schools are high tech. But no learning happened."

8   Children with disabilities show most evidence of improvement with computer use.

10  A number of experts argue that visual learning produces much less than sensory learning.

    ". . . the senses have little status after kindergarten."

The article upended some of my thinking about the virtues of computer technology. What was most helpful for my project, though, were the comments about the need for learners to engage in sensory activity, and the idea that computers do not seem to encourage creativity. I'm not sure that the analysis holds for the activity of research, which unlike some of the examples—mostly high school and elementary—seem directed towards a whole range of teacher guided instruction. The task of collecting research off the Web seems more directed and purposeful. But maybe not.

One quote that really stands out: "School is not about information, it's about _using_ information." And here this seems relevant. The Web offers the student the illusion she's getting somewhere if she simply collects information, something that is easy to do surfing the Web. Like the photocopying machine, the Web will help the student research accumulated material but at what point will she think about it? How much does the student, for example, have to reflect before she decides to click the printer icon? At least with the photocopy machine, it costs money to print a copy, an incentive to think about whether the material is _worth_ copying; this incentive is missing on the Web.

---

**FIGURE 3.5**   Here's one of my double-entry scribbles. I was researching how students use the Web for research and found a related article in the _Atlantic Monthly_ titled "The Computer Delusion." In the right-hand column, I found myself taking off on a quotation: "Schooling is not about information, it's about using information."

■ Page numbers are included in the far-left margin, right next to the information that was taken from that page. Make sure you keep up with this as you write.

■ While the material from the source in the left column may be quite formal or technical—as it is in Figure 3.4—the response in the right column should be informal, conversational. Try to write in your own voice. Find your own way to say things. And don't hesitate to use the first person: *I*.

■ As you read the writers' responses to their sources in Figures 3.3 and 3.4, notice how often the writers use their own writing to try to question a source's claim or understand better what that claim might be (e.g., "What the authors seem to be missing here . . ." and "I don't get this quote at all . . .").

■ Seize a phrase from your source, and play out its implications; think about how it pushes your own thinking or relates to your thesis. For example, the student writing about the rise of home video (Figure 3.3) plays with the phrase "mode of consumption"—a particular way of using film that the author believes home video encourages—and she really takes off on it. It leads her to a meditation on what it's like to see movies in theaters and what might be lost in the transition to home viewing.

■ Use questions to keep you writing and thinking. In both Figure 3.3 and 3.4, the writers frequently pause to ask themselves questions—not only about what the authors of the original sources might be saying but what the writers are saying to themselves as they write.

What I like about the double-entry journal system (see Figure 3.5) is that it turns me into a really active reader as I'm taking notes for my essay. That blank column on the right, like the whirring of my computer right now, impatiently urges me to figure out what I think through writing. All along, I've said the key to writing a strong research paper is *making the information your own*. Developing your own thinking about the information you collect, as you go along, is one way to do that. Thoughtful notes are so easy to neglect in your mad rush to simply take down a lot of information. The double-entry journal won't let you neglect your own thinking, or at least, it will remind you when you do.

The double-entry system does have a drawback. Unlike index card systems, double-entry journals don't organize your information particularly well. A lot of page flipping is involved to find pieces of information as you draft your paper. But I find I often remember which sources have what information, partly because I thought about what might be important as I read and took notes on each source.

# Other Notetaking Techniques

## The Research Log: A Jay Leno Approach

The research log is an alternative to the double-entry journal that promotes a similar "conversation" between writer and source, but with a few differences. One is that, like Jay Leno, the researcher starts with a monologue and always gets the last word. Another difference is that the research log may be more adaptable than the double-entry journal for researchers who prefer to write on computers. The standard format of the research log can serve as a template, which can be retrieved whenever you're ready to take notes on another source. Those notes can then be easily dropped into the draft as needed, using the "Cut and Paste" feature of your word-processing program. Obviously, the research log format works just as well in a paper notebook.

The basic approach is this:

1. Take down the full bibliographic information on the source (see Figure 3.6). Then read the article, book chapter, Web page, or whatever first, marking up your personal copy in the usual fashion by underlining, making marginal notes, and so on.
2. Your first entry will be a fastwrite that is an *open-ended response* to the reading under the heading, "What Strikes Me Most." You could take the following stances or pose the following questions to guide this writing:
   - Begin by playing the "believing game," exploring how the author's ideas, arguments, or findings are sensible. Then shift to the "doubting game," looking for gaps, questions, and doubts you have about what the source says.
   - What strikes you as the most important thing the author was trying to say?
   - What surprised you most?
   - What do you remember best?
   - What seemed most convincing? Least convincing?
   - How has it changed your thinking on the topic?
   - How does it compare to other things you've read?
   - What other research possibilities does it suggest?
3. Next, mine the source for nuggets. Take notes under the heading "Source Notes." These are quotations, summaries, paraphrases, or key facts you collect from the reading. They are probably some of the things you marked as you read the source initially.
4. Finally, follow up with one more fastwrite under the heading "The Source Reconsidered." This is a second, *more focused* look at the source in which you fastwrite about what stands out in

**Project:** The Disappearing Frog

**Citation:** Petit, Charles. "Disappearance of toads, frogs has some scientists worried." <u>San Francisco Chronicle</u> 20 April 1992: 3 pgs. <u>NEWS WEEK2</u>. Online. Prodigy. 12 August 1996. Available HTTP:
http://www.cs.yale.edu/homes/sj1/froggy/
frogs disappear.txt

**Date:** 8/12/02

**What Strikes Me Most:**
I was relieved to read in this article that at least a few biologists believe that the trend of frog disappearance around the world may not be terribly unusual but rather a natural cycle of growth and decline in numbers. But clearly that one expert from Rutgers that made that claim in this article was in the minority. I need to follow up and find if he has said more in any other articles. The key thing in this article is the point that the frog decline appears to be worldwide, so the cause is probably global. The article cited at least three possiblities: UV light from the ozone layer depletion, toxic substances, and one other that I can't remember. It mentioned a five-year study to determine which might be the cause. Another thing that struck me was the tone of some of the biologists' comments about the problem. One called the situation a "catastrophe" already. If he's right, then a five-year study may simply confirm that. It might be too late to do anything about it. I keep thinking as I read an article like this of the pond at the Wisconsin farm I spent time at as a child going silent.

**Source Notes:**
Article attributes decline to three possible causes:
1. acid rain
2. "thinning ozone layer"
3. wind-blown toxics (2)

Peter Morin, Rutgers University, called disappearance of amphibians "a phenomenon with much empirical support, not much data." Predicts that if researchers looked hard enough, they just might find that "there are places right around the corner that are full of frogs." (2)

---

**FIGURE 3.6** Sample Research Log

"These are not just declines but appear to be absolute
losses," said John Wright, who curates herpetology at the
Los Angeles Museum of Natural History. "They are not just
dropping down, they are in catastrophe." (3)

Study of back country in Cascades looked at 50 areas,
including ponds where frogs typically found. "We found two,"
said Gary Fellers, a biologist. "Not frogs in two places.
Two frogs total." (1)

"Scientists are hard pressed to understand how a diverse
order of animals that has been on Earth for 200 million
years should be highly vulnerable to an environmental chaos
so subtle that experts cannot agree what it is." (2)

**The Source Reconsidered:**
I'm a little mystified by that last quote. Why is it
surprising that even a creature that is a 200-million-year
survivor should be vulnerable to subtle enviornmental
changes, particularly if historically they're relatively
recent human-induced changes? I wonder if there are certain
qualities of so-called indicator species that the frog
doesn't meet. Is that why scientists would be surprised by
how easily frogs are affected by environmental change? Need
to talk to somebody about that. My reconsideration of the
article has deepened my sense that, notwithstanding the
statement of the Rutgers guy, it's highly likely that the
disappearance globally of amphibians is not part of a natural vairation in numbers of the creatures. The Cascades
study was alarming. If, as Morin suggests, they look hard
enough they might "find places full of frogs," doesn't it
seem odd that a look in 50 places only produced 2?

---

**FIGURE 3.6**   (Continued)

the notes you took. Which facts, findings, claims, or arguments
that you jotted down shape your thinking now? If the writing
stalls, skip a line, take another look at your source notes, and
seize on something else to write about.

## Narrative Notetaking

Narrative notetaking (see Figure 3.7) is an episodic approach to
reading for research. It documents the writer's narrative of thought

*Focusing Question:* What's the relationship between the conflict in my family and the how we talk to each other?

*Source:* Tannen, Deborah. "I Heard What You Didn't Say." The Washington Post 13 May 2001: B1.

## Layer 1: Story the Source

The article begins with a general discussion about family, and how it can be a source of support and love, yet at the same time a source of great hurt. That obvious idea is then followed up by a focus on family talk, and how it is a double-edged sword. We benefit from the trust and intimacy of talking with other family members, but all of that talk has a history that creates unspoken meanings for each participant. Tannen then talks about this as "messages" and "metamessages" and uses an example about a guy and his wife talking about recycling. She tells him that a cardboard thing is recyclable, he says he knows it, and feels criticized. She was just trying to be helpful—message and metamessage. The piece then goes on to use more examples that lead up to a discussion of what Tannen calls "alignment," a concept that I think means how family members' allegiances are perceived. The example I remember is Tannen's own confession that her mother once hassled Tannen about her unmarried status, then stopped. Tannen later learned that her sister and mother had talked about it, a fact that the sister shared with Tannen in an attempt to be supportive. This bothered Tannen because she hated being talked about by them, in essence being excluded. The piece ends with a

**FIGURE 3.7**　**Sample of Narrative Notetaking**

discussion about how family talk that is hurtful can be unraveled by exposing these sometimes hidden meanings. People aren't always hearing the same things. She also gives an example of a mother that shows "dual allegiances" that make her husband and daughter feel supported at the same time.

## Layer 2: Rapid Summary

Tannen's discussion of messages and metamessages seems most important to me. She argues that in families especially, "no utterance stands alone"; the fact is that much talk between family members occurs in the context of other discussions about the same things, and all the feelings these arouse that may have nothing to do with the literal topic under discussion. This seems really relevant to my question because it offers an explanation for the story I want to tell about my difficult relationship with my mom when I told her I was getting married. When she was trying to give me advice, I heard judgment. It was the "metamessage" that I was hearing.

## Layer 3: Narrative of Thought

Before I read this Tannen article, I thought that the best explanation for the fact that I cry after almost every phone conversation with my mom is that we are just totally different people, with different values, and the gap is so wide that communication is pretty impossible. I also thought our conflict was because she hadn't ever gotten to know me or appreciate who I had become, a

---

**FIGURE 3.7**  (Continued)

*person different from the person she wanted me to become. But now I think that those difficult conversations could be avoided if we stop being so literal in our understandings of what the other said. I know that I often hear judgment when she's just trying to help. I need to tell her that is the "metamessage" I hear. I should also ask her the same thing. When I tell her that I want a different life from her, what "metamessage" does she hear? That I don't think her choices were good?*

**FIGURE 3.7**   (Continued)

about a source, developing several "layers" of response with each reading and rereading; in that sense, it's a bit like the research log. Narrative notetaking essentially turns the double-entry journal on its side, creating layers of thought and information rather than columns, each layer building on the other; yet it also preserves the contrary thinking that makes the double-entry journal so valuable. The number of layers the writer makes depends on the value of the source to his or her project.

**First Layer: Story the Source.**   Read the source carefully from beginning to end, marking up your personal copy with underlining, marginal notes, highlighter, or whatever you use to signal important passages. Then in your notebook (or on your computer) quickly tell the story of the text and how it developed from beginning to end. This should be a rough chronological account or the source's chain of reasoning or development.

- How did the piece begin?
- And then where did it go from there?
- And then?
- How did it end?

When finished, draw a line under your entry.

**Second Layer: Rapid Summary.**   This step involves a rereading, but a selective one. Review the text, including your underlining and other marks to find ideas, concepts, or claims that seem to be *repeated* or that seem to be important assertions, claims, or findings. Circle or mark with Post-its the lines or passages that seem most important to your understanding of the source's argument or findings, or that seem most relevant to your project. Now, *in your own words,* compose a few sentences that summarize your understanding of what the source is saying about your topic. Remember that a summary doesn't simply state the topic of the passage, but what the reading *says* about the topic.

Draw another line under this entry.

**Third Layer: Narrative of Thought.**   Now push the text aside for a moment and reflect on how it has contributed to your thinking about the topic. Begin a fastwrite that tells the story of your thinking since reading and writing about this source. Start with this "seed" sentences or ones like it:

> *Before I started reading this article / book / Web document / etc., I*
>
> *thought _____, but now I understand that _____.*
>
> *That makes me think _____.*

These three layers certainly don't have to be the end of the writing you do about a source, and you may find that one or more of the layers command most of your attention, perhaps generating much longer entries than those in the model, Figure 3.7. Customize this approach to make it most productive for you. For example, you might find that the third layer, "Narrative of Thought," might be more useful as an initial step, or you might find that the second layer of notes is a collection of quotes, summaries, or paraphrases from the source, rather than the rapid summary. Experiment and make narrative notetaking work for you. The most important thing with all of these notetaking techniques—the double-entry journal, the research log, or narrative notetaking—is that you're using writing to think *when you're in the middle,* engaging with the voices, views, and findings of the people you're reading.

# Digging Deeper for Information: Advanced Searching Techniques

## First-Level Searching

At the end of the third week of the research assignment last semester, Laura showed up at my office, looking pale.

"I spent all night at the library, and I couldn't find much on my topic," she said. "What I *could* find, the library didn't have—it was missing, or checked out, or wasn't even part of the collection. I may have to change my topic."

"I hate libraries!" she said, the color returning to her face.

Laura's complaint is one that I hear often at this point in the research process, especially from students who have dutifully tried to find a narrow focus for their papers, only to realize—they think— that there isn't enough information to make the topic work. They have tried the online catalog, periodical databases, and the Internet (see Figure 3.8). The students found a few articles but not enough for a ten-page paper. Like Laura, they may decide to broaden their focus or bail out on their topic altogether, even though they're still interested in it.

I always give these frustrated students the same advice: Don't despair yet. And don't give up on your narrow focus or your topic until you've dug more deeply for information. There are still some more specialized indexes to try and some nonlibrary sources to consider. You are, in a sense, like the archaeologist who carefully removes the dirt from each layer of a dig site, looking to see what it might reveal. If little turns up, the next layer is systematically explored and then the next, until the archaeologist is convinced she's digging in the wrong place. Student researchers too often give up the dig before they've removed enough dirt, believing too quickly there's nothing there.

If you're still curious about your topic and your tentative focus but you're not finding much information, work through the three levels of the search before you decide to explore different ground. It might also be productive to expand the site of your search; you might basically be looking in the right place but not ranging far enough, perhaps limiting yourself to looking at books and articles when the real riches are in less conventional sources, possibly outside the library. See Figure 3.9.

## Second-Level Searching

By the time you reach this level in your dig, you will have at least consulted the major general indexes on your topic. If you're swamped with information at this point, it means one of two things: You're a thorough researcher, or your focus is too broad. You decide which it is, though I strongly encourage you to consider tightening your focus and resuming the dig. You're likely to find even more interesting stuff that will contribute to a paper that will probably surprise both you and your readers.

## FIRST-LEVEL SEARCHING

### Library Resources
1. Check all bibliographies in relevant books and articles for useful citations.
2. Check *Guide to Reference Books* for additional references you might have missed.
3. Check government documents if topic relates to public policy.
4. Check additional library databases, particularly subject specific ones.

### Internet Research

1. Try using multiple search engines to maximize coverage.

### Search Language

1. Use alternative subject headings (check *LCSH*).
2. In Web searches, use phrase searches related to topic.

## SECOND-LEVEL SEARCHING

### Library Resources
1. Check the *Essay and General Literature Index* for articles in books.
2. Check citation indexes for articles by often mentioned authors.
3. Check bibliographies on subject.
4. Check *Dissertation Index.*

### Internet Research
1. Search the invisible Web.
2. Search using subject specific search engine.

### Search Language
1. Search by author rather than topic.

## THIRD-LEVEL SEARCHING

### Library Resources
1. Search current and unbound periodicals on topic.
2. Check library's audiovisual catalog for film or audio information.
3. Check whether your library's special collections has relevant material.
4. Use interlibrary loan to get materials unavailable at your library.
5. Search other local libraries for unavailable sources.

### Nonlibrary Sources
1. Check local and online bookstores for newer materials on your topic.
2. Write for information from organizations.
3. Attend campus lectures if related to subject.
4. Search for relevant TV and radio programs.

### Internet Research
1 Search for archived radio and TV programs on topic.
2. Search for relevant images.

**FIGURE 3.8    Levels of Research**

**FIGURE 3.9**   FirstGov is a useful starting point for a search of government documents on your topic.

If you're still coming up empty handed and not finding much information after completing the first-level search, obviously, proceed with the second level.

## Essays and Articles Buried in Books

Somewhere, there may be an article or essay that's perfect for your paper, but you'll never find it because it's buried in a book about a related subject or the book's title doesn't sound promising when you come across it in the card catalog. How do you dig out this hidden gem? Check the following index:

> *Essay and General Literature Index.* New York: Wilson, 1900–33, supplements 1934–date.

This index, also available as an online database, covers the humanities and the social sciences and is easy to use. Search by subject or author.

**Using Citation Indexes.**   Three bound citation indexes may also prove valuable when you have authors' names to work with: They may also be available online at your campus library.

> *Arts and Humanities Citation Index.* Philadelphia: Institute for Scientific Information, 1977–date.
> *Science Citation Index.* Philadelphia: Institute for Scientific Information, 1961–date.
> *Social Science Citation Index.* Philadelphia: Institute for Scientific Information, 1966–date.

Each of these indexes has three separate but related volumes: the *Source Index,* the *Citation Index,* and the *Permuterm Subject Index.*

Among other things, these indexes identify when the authors were cited *by other writers* in their own work, which may be relevant to your work. For example, when researching the purpose of dreaming, Christine came across an influential theory and book, *The Dreaming Brain,* by J. Allan Hobson,* that she wanted to discuss in her paper. The *Social Science Citation Index* helped her find other authors who mentioned Hobson in their articles, including a review of *The Dreaming Brain* (see Figure 3.10). By looking under "Hobson" in the *Source Index,* Christine was also able to find articles Hobson had written in a given year and a complete bibliography for each (see Figure 3.11).

The *Permuterm Subject Index* is the place to check if you don't have a specific author in mind. It will refer you to authors in the *Source Index.* The citation indexes take a little getting used to, but they're often full of helpful leads. This index, published annually, is organized by subject and lists books and journals published on that subject that feature bibliographies, including the pages where they can be found.

## Bibliographies

Another kind of specialized reference book available in most disciplines is the bibliographic index. Don't confuse this type of source with the bibliographic citations at the end of a book or article. That's a bibliography, too—a list of materials used by the author. A bibliographic index also lists books and articles but for a particular

---

*J. Allan Hobson, *The Dreaming Brain* (New York: Basic Books, 1988).

*Author*

*Reference year (\*means undated); title of Hobson's book*

| | | | | | |
|---|---|---|---|---|---|
| **HOBSON ES** | | | | | |
| 78 CONTRASTS BEHAVIOR A | | 219 | | | |
| CALDWELL JP | COPEIA | | 938 | 89 | |
| **HOBSON EW** | | | | | |
| 14 J NAPIER INVENTION L | | | | | |
| BRYDEN DJ | ANN SCI | 47 | 445 | 90 | |
| **HOBSON GN** | | | | | |
| 69 J EXP PSYCHOL 80 386 | | | | | |
| HEDLUND MA | J ANXIETY D | 4 | 221 | 90 | |
| **HOBSON J** | | | | | |
| 02 IMPERIALISM STUDY | | | | | |
| SHAPIRO H | WORLD DEV | 18 | 861 | 90 | |
| 52 BRIT J ADDICT 49 5 | | | | | |
| BERRIDGE V | BR J ADDICT | 85 | 983 | 90 | R |
| 77 AM J PSYCHIAT 134 | | 97 | | | |
| MOFFIT A | PSYCHIAT J | 15 | 66 | 90 | |
| **HOBSON JA** | | | | | |
| \*\* DREAMING BRAIN | | | | | |
| TURNEY J | NEW STATE S | 3 | 35 | 90 | B |
| 1894 EVOLUTION MODERN CAP | | | | | |
| 1894 MODERN CAPITALISM ST | | | | | |
| HOVENKAM H | STANF LAW R | 42 | 993 | 90 | |
| 00 EC DISTRIBUTION | | | | | |
| ( ANON ) | J ECON STUD | 17 | 18 | 90 | |
| 00 WAR S AFRICA | | 233 | | | |
| PORTER A | J AFR HIST | 31 | 43 | 90 | |
| 01 SOCIAL PROBLEM 87 | | | | | |
| FREEDEN M | ETHICS | 100 | 489 | 90 | |
| 02 IMPERIALISM STUDY | | | | | |
| DUSSEL E | LAT AM PERS | 17 | 62 | 90 | |
| 09 CRISIS LIBERALISM | | | | | |
| BEETHAM D | ARCH EUR SO | 30 | 311 | 89 | N |
| 11 SCI WEALTH | | | | | |
| HAINES WW | INT J SOC E | 17 | 17 | 90 | |
| 12 CHARACTER LIFE | | 94 | | | |
| FREEDEN M | ETHICS | 100 | 489 | 90 | |
| 26 EVOLUTION MODERN CAP | | | | | |
| INIKORI JE | SOC SCI HIS | 13 | 343 | 89 | |
| 29 EC ETHICS STUDY SOCI | | | | | |
| HOVENKAM H | STANF LAW R | 42 | 993 | 90 | |
| 30 RATIONALISATION UNEM | | | | | |
| HOWARD MC | HIST POLIT | 22 | 81 | 90 | |
| 31 LT HOBHOUSE HIS LIFE | | | | | |
| HELMESHA R | CAN R SOC A | 27 | 357 | 90 | |
| 56 PHYSL IND | | | | | |
| SALTER J | HIST POLIT | 22 | 65 | 90 | |
| 63 ANN INTERN MED 58 | | 324 | | | |
| SEE SCI FOR 1 ADDITIONAL CITATION | | | | | |
| DELVA NJ | BR J PSYCHI | 157 | 703 | 90 | |
| GLUSAC E | CAN J PSY | 35 | 268 | 90 N | |
| 65 EVOLUTION MODERN CAP | | | | | |
| KUHN R | AUST ECON H | 26 | 53 | 88 | |
| 65 J PSYCHIAT RES | | 79 | | | |
| ARANTES JM | ARQ BRAS P | 41 | 77 | 89 | |
| 71 IMPERIALISM | | | | | |

*J. Turney cites Hobson's book in review in journal New State S, vol. 3, p. 35, 1990. Code letter at end for type of source (e.g., B—Book reviews, M—Meeting abstracts); if no code, source is article or report*

**FIGURE 3.10**    Entry in the *Social Science Citation Index* for author J. A. Hobson, listing works that cited him in 1990.

*Source:* From Social Science Citation Index®. Copied with the permission of the Institute for Scientific Information®, 1992.

field of study, broken down according to various areas of interest. For example, the student working on the paper mentioned earlier about special problems faced by teenage children of alcoholics could look in the index at the back of the *Guide to Reference Books* under "Alcoholism" and find the page number for bibliographies on the subject. There's quite a list, including a bibliography of books and articles on alcohol and reproduction, another on alcohol education materials published in the United States, and many other lists of sources on areas of interest in the study of alcoholism. One bibliography seems

| | | | | |
|---|---|---|---|---|
| **TURNER Y** | | | | |
| **CLARKSCH.K—DYNAMIC CORPORATE TRAINING FOR WOMEN - A CREATIVE ARTS THERAPIES APPROACH** | | | | |
| *ART PSYCH* | *17(3):217–222* | *90* | *9R* | DXO53 |
| HAHREMANN UNIV, PHILADELPHIA, PA 19102, USA | | | | |
| BRONDOLILLO D | 89 HARVARD BUSINESS MAY | | | |
| CLANCE PR | 85 IMPOSTER PHENOMENON | | | |
| GRANT J | 86 ORG DYNAMICS | | | |
| JOSSELSON R | 87 FINDING HERSELF PATH | | | |
| MADDEN TR | 87 WOMEN WOMEN | | | |
| MILLER JB | 76 NEW PSYCHOL WOMEN | | | |
| PIERCE C | 88 MALE FEMALE CONTINUU | | | |
| SCHEFLEN AE | 72 BODY LANGUAGE SOCIAL | | | |
| SCHWARTZ FN | 89 HARVARD BUSINESS JAN | | | |
| **TURNBARRY MM** | | | | |
| see PONCHILL.SV | J VIS IMP B | 84 | 364 | 90 |
| **TURNEY J** | | | | |
| **QED - THE STRANGE THEORY OF LIGHT AND MATTER-FEYNMANN,R ➤ BOOK REVIEW** | | | | |
| *NEW STATE S* | *3(103):35–36* | *90* | *1R* | DG586 |
| **WHAT MAD PURSUIT - CRICK,F ➤ BOOK REVIEW** | | | | |
| *NEW STATE S* | *3(103):35–36* | *90* | *1R* | DG586 |
| **THE DREAMING BRAIN - HOBSON,JA ➤ BOOK REVIEW** | | | | |
| *NEW STATE S* | *3(103):35–36* | *90* | *1R* | DG586 |
| **THE WORLD WITHIN THE WORLD - BARROW,J ➤ BOOK REVIEW** | | | | |
| *NEW STATE S* | *3(103):35–36* | *90* | *1R* | DG586 |
| **END - COSMIC CATASTROPHE AND THE FATE OF THE UNIVERSE - CLOSE,F ➤ BOOK REVIEW** | | | | |
| *NEW STATE S* | *3(103):35–36* | *90* | *1R* | DG586 |
| **TURNEY P** | | | | |

*Author of source in citation index*

*Citation of Hobson book*

**FIGURE 3.11** The *Source Index* will provide a fuller description of a source mentioned in the citation index, including the bibliography (if any) of the article. (Turney's book review had no bibliography.)

*Source:* From Social Science Citation Index®. Copied with the permission of the Institute for Scientific Information®, 1992.

particularly promising: *Alcoholism and Youth: A Comprehensive Bibliography,* by Grace Barnes.*

A good bibliography can save you a lot of work. Someone else has gone to the trouble of surveying the literature for you, and you can pick and choose what seems useful. One disadvantage is that often bibliographies do not include recent material. Obviously, check when the reference was published, and decide how far back you want to go.

## Unpublished Scholarly Papers

A vast amount of scholarly research is generated each year by graduate students working on advanced degrees. Much of this material

*Grace Barnes, *Alcoholism and Youth: A Comprehensive Bibliography* (Westport, CT: Greenwood, 1982).

is unpublished and therefore uncataloged in the usual indexes. But there's an index to these sources, too. The bound index is

> *Dissertation Abstracts International.* Ann Arbor, MI: University Micro-films, 1970–date (from 1938–51, titled *Microfilm Abstracts,* and from 1952–69, *Dissertation Abstracts*).

This index is also widely available as an online database. When I was writing my book on lobsters, I found a wonderful doctoral dissertation on a Maine island lobstering community that proved fascinating and useful.

First look for the subject/author index in a given year, which will then direct you to the *abstract,* or summary, of the paper in which you're interested. The abstract may be enough. If you want the entire paper, you can order it by mail through University Microfilms, Inc., Ann Arbor, MI 48106. (Copies, however, are costly: about $36.)

## Searching the Invisible Web

The majority of the Web, perhaps as much as 60 percent of it, is unreachable using popular search engines, and much of this "invisible Web" contains useful databases for academic researchers. If Yahoo! won't get you there, what will? The following specialized search engines are designed to send their tendrils out into this vast, frequently unexplored territory of cyberspace.

> Lycos Invisible Web Catalog
> http://dir.lycos.com/Reference/Searchable_Databases
>
> Intelliseek
> http://www.intelliseek.com/search.htm
>
> InvisibleWeb.com
> http://www.invisibleweb.com
>
> Librarians Index to the Internet
> http://www.lii.org
>
> Profusion
> http://www.profusion.com
>
> Infomine
> http://infomine.ucr.edu/search.phtml

## Using Specialized Search Engines

So-called "focused crawlers" work a lot like general coverage search engines, but they concentrate their efforts on certain subject or topic databases. This means they are more thorough than Google, and many are updated more frequently. There are quite a few of these, and the best place to find one in your topic's subject area is on sites that actually index these search tools. Here are some of the sites:

Fossick.com: Web Search Alliance
http://www.fossick.com/

SearchIQ: A Directory of Specialty Engines
http://www.zdnet.com/searchiq/subjects/

Beaucoup
http://www.beaucoup.com/

A Collection of Specialized Search Engines
http://www.leidenuniv.nl/ub/biv/specials.htm#Par62

## Search by Author

Typically, most searching is done by subject, but you may suddenly open up new doors if you begin using particular authors' names as keywords. Look for authors' names that repeatedly appear in bibliographies from articles and books you've found on your topic. These people are likely important authorities in the field and may have much more to say about your topic. Also note the names of authors whose work you particularly like or who seem influential. Use the online card catalog and periodical indexes to see what else these authors have written. Is any of this information relevant?

## Library Sources

Sometimes, you're digging in the right place, but the site needs to be expanded. Students rarely take advantage of the enormous resources of their campus libraries. Most stick to the online card catalog or the periodical indexes. But libraries contain some unusual sources of information, such as special collections and media departments, that can produce useful material on your topic.

**Current Periodicals.**   The indexing of periodicals in databases naturally lags behind the actual publication of the journals and magazines. Indexes may be up to eight months to a year behind depending on the periodical. That means you may be missing key articles on your topic because they're simply not appearing when you search a database. However, most campus libraries have a *current periodicals section* for recent and unbound copies of journals and articles. If there is a particular magazine or journal that is relevant to your topic, it might be worth spending some time browsing through the current issues. It's a bit hit-or-miss, but it also doesn't take long to skim the table of contents of a periodical.

**Audiovisual Departments.**  Audiovisual materials (films, DVDs, records, tapes, slides, videocasettes, etc.) are available in separate departments in many libraries and are often cataloged separately. You may find some surprisingly useful sources on your topic in this catalog, such as a taped lecture by an authority who spoke on your campus or a film that offers some useful case studies.

**Special Collections.**   Many university libraries are homes to unusual collections of material—historical documents, personal papers of prominent people, and the like—and may even be designated archives for significant works. Often, this material is cataloged separately. If your library has a special collection, consult the staff there about whether it may contain any useful material on your topic.

**Interlibrary Loan.**   If you have a little time—say, several weeks—before you essay is due, don't ignore your library's interlibrary loan service to get that book or article that is unavailable locally. Many universities provide this service at no or low cost to their students. Increasingly, interlibrary loan is a Web-based service, which makes it even easier to use. All you need is the complete citation for the book or article; in most cases your library will find it and have it sent where you can pick it up. The loan on books is often brief, but you will receive a photocopy of that article you need to keep through interlibrary loan services.

**Other Libraries.**   Your hometown library will likely not have a good collection of scholarly journals and books, but it may contain some useful sources that were perhaps missing or checked out from your university library's collection. Other public libraries in the area might be worth checking, too. Also remember that you can probably make use of interlibrary loan to get materials, given enough lead time. See Chapter 2, "Interlibrary Loan."

Libraries and library resources across the United States and around the world are also accessible through the Internet. Hundreds of library catalogs, for example, are available using the Telnet protocol, but an increasing number of library resources can be reached through the Web, too. One site (and there are many) that offers convenient links to Web-based library materials is Libraries on the Internet, with lines to more than 2,300 libraries in 70 countries:

http://sunsite.berkeley.edu/LibWeb

Also consider other specialized libraries. Most museums have their own collections, which they often make available to college researchers. Historical societies and many large corporations have libraries, as well.

## Nonlibrary Sources

It's so easy to forget that research doesn't begin and end at the library's front door. Be creative about other places to look!

**Bookstores.** Your campus library may not have recently published books on your topic (titles published in the last year), but your campus or local bookstore might. First, to find out what books seem promising that may not be listed in your library's catalog, check one or more of the bibliographies of these trade books:

> *Books in Print.* New York: Bowker, 1948–date. Lists books by title and
> author.
> *Paperbound Books in Print.* New York: Bowker, 1955–date. Lists only
> paperbacks.
> *Subject Guide to Books in Print.* New York: Bowker, 1957–date. As the
> title implies, organized by subject.

One of the easiest ways to find new books on your topic is to do a search at one of the online bookstores, such as Amazon.com. Try a keyword search.

If you find a promising title, check local bookstores or online to find out if the book is in stock. If a book is not available and you have a week or ten days, you can order the book. The obvious drawback to ordering through the bookstore or online is that you have to buy the book. Doing so may very well be worth it, however, for a book that seems especially useful.

**Writing Letters.**   There are people and organizations out there with exactly what you need. If you have enough lead time, you can write or call and have them send along some information. How do you find out who these people and organizations are and how you can contact them?

First, ask people you know for information: your instructor, your friends, the people you interview for your paper. Also pay attention to the names of groups that crop up in your reading as well as the names of experts and the institutions they're associated with. Several reference sources can also help:

> *Encyclopedia of Associations.* 32nd ed. Edited by Sandra Jaszczak.
> Detroit, MI: Gale Research, 1997. Three parts; the last is a name
> and keyword index. Also available online.

> *Research Centers Directory.* 22nd ed. Edited by Anthony Gerring. Detroit, MI: Gale Research, 1997. Two volumes; covers 12,000 nonprofit and university-related research organizations.

Both books will give you addresses and phone numbers of a variety of institutions and groups and, in many cases, names and phone numbers of key contact people.

E-mail also opens up new possibilities for reaching people and organizations. A growing number of groups have their own Web pages, which feature links to the e-mail addresses of information officers, authors of online documents, and other informed individuals. You can also sometimes unearth the e-mail addresses of experts on your topic using search tools designed for that purpose. For tips on how to do this, check out "Finding People on the Internet" in Chapter 2.

**Lectures.**   Every week on my campus, there are ten or more public lectures on a variety of subjects, ranging from the biodynamics of the rain forest to the dangers of date rape. A lecture on your topic—or a closely related one—could be a boon to your research, providing not only fresh material that often has a local angle but also a live person to quote and interview. Going to lectures in the hope of finding useful information is a hit-or-miss approach. Nonetheless, keep your eye on the listings of public lectures in your campus newspaper.

**TV and Radio.**   Most people in the United States get most of their information about public issues from television. That doesn't mean TV is the best source of information, but it is certainly an influential one. Television and radio news, public affairs programs, and even talk shows can be useful sources of information. *TV Guide* can be a useful reference, and so can the local newspaper, which may list the topics discussed on various television talk shows that day.

Web-based archives of TV and radio have grown by leaps and bounds in recent years, and increasingly researchers find them useful. One that I particularly recommend for academic research projects is the online National Public Radio (NPR) archive (see Figure 3.12), which you can search by keyword or subject. You don't even have to know which program to search. Since NPR covers a wide range of subjects, you might very well find an audio of a program relevant to your topic. The Web address is http://npr.org.

**Image Searches.**   Another source of material you may not have thought of is images available on the Internet. A photograph of an African AIDS victim, for example, will do much to dramatize that tragedy. Or an historical essay on lynching in the South might be

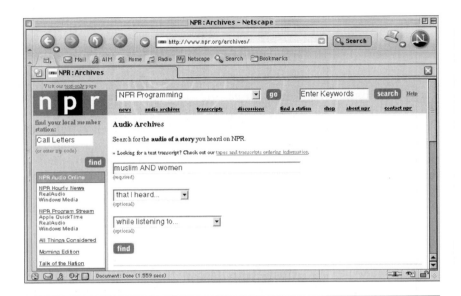

**FIGURE 3.12**    **Searching the Archives at National Public Radio**

more powerful with a picture of a murder from the Library of Congress archives. Some search engines, such as Google, offer image searches. For historical photographs (and even some audio), the Library of Congress is a rich resource. You can find it at www.loc.gov.

# CHAPTER 4

# The Fourth Week

## Getting to the Draft

It is *not* 2 A.M. Your paper is *not* due in twelve hours but in one or two weeks. For some students, beginning to write a research paper this early—weeks before it's due—will be a totally new experience. An early start may also, for the first time, make the experience a positive one. I know that starting early will help ensure writing a better paper.

Still, there are those students who say they thrive on a looming deadline, who love working in its shadow, flirting with failure. "I work best that way," they say, and they wait until the last minute and race to the deadline in a burst of writing, often sustained by cigarettes and strong doses of caffeine. It works for some students. Panic is a pretty strong motivator. But I think most who defend this habit confuse their relief at successfully pulling off the assignment once again with a belief that the paper itself is successful.

Papers done under such pressure often aren't successful, and that is particularly true of the last-minute research paper, where procrastination is especially deadly. Research writing is recursive. You often have to circle back to where you've already been, discovering holes in your research or looking at your subject from new angles. It's hard to fit in a trip back to the library the night before the paper is due, when you've just started the draft and need to check some information. This book is designed to defeat procrastination, and if, in the past few weeks, you've done the exercises, taken thoughtful notes, and attempted a thorough search for information, you probably have the urge to begin writing.

On the other hand, you may feel as if you don't know enough yet about your topic to have anything to say. Or you may be swamped with information, and your head may be spinning. What do you do with it all?

When Christy came to my office, she was three weeks into her research on a paper that asked, Why do diets fail? She really wanted to know, since she was having such a hard time with her own diet. Though she'd really done a good job collecting information, she was exasperated.

"I found a whole bunch of articles on how heredity affects obesity," she said, "and all this stuff on how people's upbringing determines how they eat. I also found some articles that said our bodies *want* to be certain weights."

It sounded pretty interesting to me.

"I've got all this information, but I'm worried that I'll lose my focus," she said. "*And so much of it seems contradictory.* I don't know what to think."

## When the Experts Disagree

Christy was pretty sure she was in trouble because her sources sometimes didn't agree on the same things. I thought she was right where she should be: standing on the curb at a busy intersection, watching the experts on her topic collide and then go off in different directions. Knowledge in any field—nutrition, literature, or entomology—is not static. It is contested—pushed, pulled, probed, and even sometimes turned over completely to see what is underneath. Scholars and experts devote their lifetimes to disagreeing with each other, not because they enjoy being disagreeable but because when knowledge is contested, it is advanced.

When I researched lobsters, I discovered a fascinating scientific mystery: More than 90 percent of the lobsters that grow to the minimum legal size every year end up on someone's dinner table. At that size, most lobsters haven't even had a chance to breed. How is it possible, asked the scientists, that there are any lobsters left at that rate of exploitation? I discovered several explanations. Some people argued that the millions of lobster traps—each of which is designed to allow undersize lobsters to escape—serve as a kind of giant soup kitchen, providing extra food to lobsters. That, some experts said, accounted for lobsters' resilience. Other experts believed that laws protecting females carrying eggs have worked remarkably well. Still others believed that lobsters migrate into areas depleted by overfishing. Recently, another idea won favor with scientists. They suggested that large lobsters at the edge of the continental shelf are the "parental stock" for coastal lobsters, sending their larval offspring inshore on tides and currents.

## Evaluating Conflicting Claims

As a writer—and in this case, a nonexpert—I had to sort through these conflicting opinions and decide which I thought were most convincing. I had to claim my point of view and later make it convincing to my own readers.

That was Christy's challenge, and it's your challenge, too. When you're thorough in your research, you're bound to find sources that square off against each other or come at your subject from different directions. What do you make of these competing claims and differing perspectives?

## EXERCISE   4 . 1

### Grade Inflation: Myth or Reality?

Few topics about higher education have generated more heat in the last few years than grade inflation. There is widespread public agreement that rigorous standards for grading have withered in American high schools and universities, and that getting a "B" or higher is a breeze. One Harvard professor is so fed up with grade inflation at the Ivy League school that he now gives his students two grades—one "official" grade for their transcripts, duly inflated, and the other a private grade that he says is more honest.

Search the Web for documents on grade inflation, and you'll see pages and pages of articles that briefly begin with the assumption that grade inflation is a serious national problem, and then explore its causes at length. Many public debates are like this; they begin by assuming something "everyone knows is true" and then proceed from there. But is the premise that grade inflation is a serious problem true?

In this exercise, you'll confront a situation common to academic researchers: You have two credible sources of information that seem to be saying totally opposed things. One, a study by professors Henry Rosovsky and Matthew Hartley for the American Academy of Arts and Sciences, claims that the "available evidence" suggests that "grading has become more lenient" since the 1960s. The other study, by the think tank Rand Corporation, disputes this, arguing that there was "no substantial grade inflation between 1982 and 1992," the period the research focused on.

The analysis of the evidence of grade inflation from the Academy study and the summary from the Rand investigation follow. You must answer this simple question: *Which of these opposing claims about the evidence for grade inflation is more believable to you and why?*

## Working Together:
## Questions for Discussion

- On what basis does one source seem more credible than the other?
- What *don't* you know that you would like to know to make a judgment on the credibility of each claim?
- In what ways are the studies comparable? In what ways don't they compare?
- What kinds of evidence are more persuasive? Why?
- Were there areas of agreement between the two studies?
- Might it be possible to reconcile *both* claims?

Your instructor may ask you to write a brief response that develops your answer to this question, or ask you to work in groups in class to develop your response.

### First Claim: Grading Has Become More Lenient

**Excerpt from Analysis of Academy Study[1]**

Grade inflation can be defined as an upward shift in the grade point average (GPA) of students over an extended period of time without a corresponding increase in student achievement.[2] Unlike price inflation, where dollar values can—at least in theory—rise indefinitely, the upper boundary of grade inflation is constrained by not being able to rise above an A or a 100. The consequence is grade "compression" at the upper end.

We will begin by reviewing grading trends as described in the literature, but will confine our sample to undergraduates. The situation in professional and graduate schools requires separate analysis . . .

Most investigators agree that grade inflation began in the 1960s[3] and continued through, at least, the mid-1990s. Several studies have examined the phenomenon over time, as illustrated in the following table:

[1]Henry Rosovsky and Matthew Hartley, "Evaluation and the Academcy: Are We Doing the Right Thing?" Cambridge, MA: American Academy of Arts and Sciences, 2002: 4–7.

[2]Goldman, "The Betrayal of the Gatekeepers: Grade Inflation," 1985.

[3]Juola, "Grade Inflation in Higher Education: What Can or Should We Do?" 1976.

## Grade Inflation from 1960 to 1997

| Author(s) and years studied | Sample size | Findings |
| --- | --- | --- |
| Arvo E. Juola 1960–1978[a] | 180 colleges (with graduate programs) | From 1960 to 1974 the average GPA increased half a grade point (0.432). From 1974 to 1978, a leveling of grade inflation was detected. |
| Arthur Levine and Jeanette S. Cureton 1967, 1976, 1993[b] | Data from survey of 4,900 under-graduates at all institutional types | Grades of A– or higher grew from 7 to 26 percent. Grades of C or below fell from 25 to 9 percent. |
| George Kuh and Shouping Hu 1984–1987; 1995–1997[c] | 52,256 student surveys from the Colleges Student Experiences Questionaire (CSEQ) at all institutional types | College grades increased over time in every institutional type on the average from 3.07 to 3.343. |

[a] Arvo E. Juola, "Grade Inflation in Higher Education—1979. Is It Over?" ED189129 (March 1980).

[b] Arthur Levine and Jeanette S. Cureton, *When Hope and Fear Collide: A Portrait of Today's College Student* (San Francisco: Jossey-Bass, 1998).

[c] George Kuh and Shouping Hu, "Unraveling the Complexity of the Increase in College Grades from the Mid-1980s to the Mid-1990s," *Educational Evaluation and Policy Analysis* (Fall 1999): 297–320.

Arvo Juola from Michigan State University was one of the earliest researchers to raise concerns about grade inflation.[4] His surveys of colleges and universities found that grade inflation continued unabated between 1960 and 1977.[5] From 1960–1974 the average GPA increased nearly half a letter grade (0.432) with the greatest annual increases occurring between 1968 and 1972.[6] Arthur Levine and Jeanette Cureton compared data from under-graduate surveys of 4,900 college students from all types

[4] Ibid.

[5] Juola, "Grade Inflation in Higher Education—1979. Is It Over?" 1980.

[6] Ibid.

of institutions in 1969, 1976 and 1993. Their research found that the number of A's increased nearly four fold during that time (from 7 percent in 1969 to 26 percent in 1993) and the number of C's declined by 66 percent (from 25 percent in 1969 to 9 percent in 1993).[7] Different estimates suggest that across all institutional types GPA's rose approximately 15–20 percent from the mid-1960s through the mid-1990s.[8] A recent study by George Kuh and Shouping Hu comparing the GPA's of 52,000 students—approximately half from the mid-1980s and half from the mid-1990s—found that student grades had risen from 3.07 in the mid-1980s to 3.34 in the mid-1990s.[9] By the mid-1990s, the average grade (formerly a C) resided in the B− to B range.[10] More recent research across all types of schools shows that only between 10 percent and 20 percent of students receive grades lower than a B−.[11]

Grade inflation moderated by the second half of the 1990s; its rate of growth has declined from the highs of the 1960s and 1970s. This result is to be expected because—as noted earlier—unlike price inflation, grade inflation is constrained by an immovable ceiling. An A is the upper limit, and, therefore, the recent decline in the growth rate is not an unambiguous indication of changed standards. Indeed, the seemingly mild degree of inflation in the table is, over time, very much magnified by compression at the top, which inexorably lessens the possibility of meaningful gradations.

Patterns of grading show inflation to be more prevalent in selected disciplines. Grades tend to be higher in the humanities than in the natural sciences, where objective standards of measurement are enforced more easily.[12] This was probably always true, but the differences by discipline appear

---

[7]Levine and Cureton, *When Hope and Fear Collide: A Portrait of Today's College Student,* 1998.

[8]Basinger, "Fighting Grade Inflation: A Misguided Effort?" 1997; Stone, "Inflated Grades, Inflated Enrollment, and Inflated Budgets: An Analysis and Call for Review at the State Level," 1996.

[9]Kuh and Hu, "Unraveling the Complexity of the Increase in College Grades from the Mid-1980's to the Mid-1990's," 1999.

[10]Weller, "Attitude Toward Grade Inflation: A Random Survey of American Colleges of Arts and Sciences and Colleges of Education," 1986; Reibstein, "Give Me an A, or Give Me Death," 1994; Landrum, "Student Expectations of Grade Inflation," 1999.

[11]Farley, "A Is for Average: The Grading Crisis in Today's Colleges," 1995.

[12]Wilson, "The Phenomenon of Grade Inflation in Higher Education," 1999.

to have increased over time. It is not surprising that the "softer" subjects exhibit the severest grade inflation.

Although higher grades appear in all types of institutions, grade inflation appears to have been especially noticeable in the Ivy League. In 1966, 22 percent of all grades given to Harvard undergraduates were in the A range. By 1996 that percentage had risen to 46 percent and in that same year 82 percent of Harvard seniors graduated with academic honors.[13] In 1973, 30.7 percent of all grades at Princeton were in the A range and by 1997 that percentage had risen to 42.5 percent. In 1997, only 11.6 percent of all grades fell below the B range.[14] Similarly, at Dartmouth, in 1994, 44 percent of all grades given were in the A range.

When considered alongside indexes of student achievement, these increases in grades do not appear to be warranted. During the time period in which grades increased dramatically, the average combined score on the Scholastic Achievement Test (SAT) actually declined by 5 percent (1969–1993).[15] Since the SAT's recentering in 1995 (when the mean was reset to a midpoint of 500 in a range of 200 to 800) scores increased only slightly—the average combined score in 1995 was 1,010 and in 2000 it was 1,019.

By one estimate, one third of all college and university students were forced to take remedial education courses, and the need for remediation has increased over time. One study found that between 1987 and 1997, 73 percent of all institutions reported an increase in the proportion of students requiring remedial education.[16] Further, from 1990 to 1995, 39 percent of institutions indicated that their enrollments in remedial courses had increased.[17] Currently, higher education devotes $2 billion a year to remedial offerings,[18] and faculty have noticed a shift in student ability and preparation. In 1991, a survey conducted by the

[13]Lambert, "Desperately Seeking Summa," 1993.

[14]Report of the faculty committee on examinations and standings on grading patterns at Princeton, 5 February 1998.

[15]The College Board; Levine and Cureton, *When Hope and Fear Collide: A Portrait of Today's College Student,* 1998; Schackner in Nagle, "A Proposal for Dealing with Grade Inflation: The Relative Performance Index," 1998.

[16]Levine, "How the Academic Profession Is Changing," 1997.

[17]National Center for Education Statistics, "Remedial Education at Higher Education Institutions, Fall 1995–October 1996," NCES-97-584.

[18]Schmidt, "Colleges Are Starting to Become Involved in High-School Testing Policies," 2000.

Higher Education Research Institute found that only 25 percent of faculty felt their students were "well-prepared academically."[19]

Discussions that led to standards-based reform also show that systems' administrators, regents, and state boards of education felt a growing unease about the competence of their students. Eighteen states have currently implemented competency tests that all high school graduates must pass. Similar testing programs are being considered in several states for institutions of higher learning. The University of Texas System, Utah's State Board of Regents, and the sixty-four campus SUNY system are all considering implementing competency tests.[20]

Measures of average achievement are far from perfect, but the available evidence does support the proposition that grading has become more lenient since the 1960s. Higher average grades unaccompanied by proportionate increases in average levels of achievement defines grade inflation.

We have already mentioned that increases in average grades appear to have been especially noticeable in the Ivy League. Because admission into these institutions became increasingly competitive since the 1960s, it might be possible to argue that higher average grades merely reflected a more academically talented student body. There is some evidence for higher quality, but the magnitude of grade increases in Ivy League institutions seems to indicate inflationary pressures as well.[21]

## Opposing Claim: No Substantial Grade Inflation

### Excerpt from Summary of Rand Study[1]

In recent years, many observers have maintained that grades in secondary and postsecondary institutions have become inflated. Anecdotal reports of grade inflation, in some instances seemingly egregious, are common, but few studies have attempted to evaluate systematically changes in grading standards over time.

[19]Dey, Astin, and Korn, "The American Freshman: Twenty-Five Year Trends, 1966–1990," 1991.

[20]Schmidt, "Faculty Outcry Greets Proposal of Competency Tests at U. of Texas," 2000.

[21]This is verified by data provided by C. Anthony Broh, director of research for COFHE.

[1]Daniel M. Koretz and Mark Berends. "Changes in High School Grading Standards in Mathematics, 1982–1992." Summary. Rand's Publication Database. 2001: 3 pgs. 4 July 2002 <http://www.rand.org/publications/MR/MR1445>.

This study explores changes in high school grading standards by comparing the senior cohorts of 1982 and 1992. The data used are nationally representative surveys, the High School and Beyond study (HSB, for the 1982 cohort) and the National Education Longitudinal Study of 1988 (NELS-88, for the 1992 cohort). The study explores how the distribution of grades changed over that time, how those changes varied across types of students and schools, whether the relationship between tested achievement and grades changed between 1982 and 1992, how grades changed when changes in tested proficiency and course-taking were taken into account, and whether the predictors of grades changed over that decade. Descriptive analyses were carried out for overall high school grade point average (GPA) and for academic GPA in several subject areas. Multivariate analyses were restricted to mathematics because the surveys provided equatable tests only in that subject, making it impossible to control for changes in proficiency in the other subject areas. Efforts were made to use Scholastic Aptitude Test (SAT) and American College Test (ACT) scores as surrogates in other subjects, but that approach was abandoned after analyses showed substantial changes in the self-selection of the tested subsamples between 1982 and 1992.

The term "grade inflation" typically refers to an increase in the average grades attained by students with a given level of proficiency in the material grades are supposed to represent. This change in grading standards, however, which is called "mean shift" inflation in this report, is not the only way in which grades might become inflated. Another form of possible inflation is labeled "decreased correlation." This refers to a weakening of the relationship between proficiency and grades, such that low achievers are penalized less and high achievers rewarded less by the grading system. This report examined both of these possible changes in grading standards.

Despite the widespread discussion of grade inflation, these analyses did not show substantial grade inflation between 1982 and 1992. Indeed, they suggested that if changes in tested proficiency are taken into account, grades were deflated over the period, at least in academic mathematics courses. Simple descriptive analyses showed an increase in mean grades and in the percentage of grades above a grade of B or better, but these increases were mostly very small. For example, overall academic GPA increased by only 0.07 on a sclae of 0 (F) to 4.3 (A+)—that is on a scale in which the change from a B− to a B would be 0.30. The frequency of grades of B or better increased by 3.1 percentage points. Overall changes in specific subject areas were similarly small. However, the increase was considerably larger among high-income students and in urban schools: Overall mean grades increased by 0.21 for the former group and by 0.22 in the latter.

During the same period, however, performance on the mathematics tests included in the HSB and NELS surveys, which were linked to be on the same scale, increased by about one-third of a standard deviation.[2] At the same time, the relationship between performance on the test and academic mathematics GPA *increased*. After disattenuating for unreliability (which was greater in HSB than in NELS), the correlation increased from 0.47 to 0.58. When the increase in tested proficiency was controlled, mean grades actually *declined* for all but high-scoring students. Because of the increase in the correlation between test scores and GPA from 1982 to 1992, this decrease in adjusted GPA was larger among lower-scoring students; it was 0.16 for students whose scores were at the mean and 0.35 for students whose scores were a standard deviation below the mean. Between 1982 and 1992, the number of mathematics courses taken by the average student increased markedly, as did enrollment in some courses traditionally considered college preparatory. To the extent that the data allow adjustment for these trends in course-taking, however, they appeard to have had little effect on changes in grades. Controlling for changes in both course-taking and tested proficiency again showed deflation of mathematics grades, albeit slightly less substantial than appeared when only test scores were controlled. A multivariate analysis of the prediction of academic mathematics GPA by student- and school-level variables found only modest changes from 1982 to 1992.

---

[2]Throughout this report, we maintain a distinction between "linking" and "equating" as methods of placing scores from two different tests, or two different forms of the same test, on the same scale. In modern usage, "linkage" is a more general term that refers to a range of statistical techniques that place the scores from two tests on a single scale. Linkage does not necessarily make tests functionally equivalent; for example, linked tests may contain somewhat different content, so that it is not a matter of indifference to some individuals which test they take. In contrast, "equating" refers to methods that endeavor to make tests as nearly equivalent as is practical. For example, successive forms of the SAT are equated, so it is not a matter of importance to students which form they take. The NELS and HSB tests were not constructed to be equivalent and, therefore, a linkage of the two cannot be considered an equating. The implications of this for our findings are discussed below where pertinent.

The analyses reported here have several important limitations. The test scores used to adjust for changes in proficiency were not ideal. Although the NELS and HSB mathematics tests had sufficient similarity and overlap to permit use of a conventional equating method, they were not equivalent, and differences between them may have contributed to the findings, e.g., the stronger relationship between grades and scores found in NELS. More important, the HSB and NELS tests were general-purpose survey tests and do not provide a measure of mastery of the specific content pertinent to grades in each course. Coursework variables were also limited in important ways. Courses with similar titles may vary markedly in content, for example, and the mix of content subsumed by any given course title might have changed between 1982 and 1992, perhaps as a result of the large increases in course-taking. Thus, analyses using better variables might have produced somewhat different results, but given the pattern of results reported here, it seems unlikely that they would have shown score inflation.

What accounts for the inconsistency between this study, which found no evidence of overall grade inflation between 1982 and 1992, and the widespread reports of high school grade inflation? There are at least three possibilities. One is that inflation has occurred but not during the decade examined here. A second possibility is that increases in grades in some schools, such as schools serving high-income families, may have attracted attention and may have been misconstrued as an indication of more widespread grading changes. Yet another possibility is that grading standards were not as harsh in the past as some observers believe and that examples of overly lenient grading would not be restricted to the present, if similar information were available about earlier cohorts.

Grading standards warrant further research, not only because of their importance to selective postsecondary institutions but also because of the centrality of standards to the current reform movement in K–12 education. It would be important to explore, for example, whether grades were inflated during other time periods, and the incidence and distribution of overly lenient grading would be an important issue regardless of trends over time. Further research should not be restricted to the use of large survey databases, which are a good tool for providing a first look at issues of this sort but lack the detail needed to explore them in depth.

**Follow-Up Discussion.**    Careful researchers are systematic in their evaluation of competing claims. After reading these two excerpts, can you imagine a series of questions you might ask to help you determine whom to believe when faced with this situation in the future? In groups on a piece of newsprint, brainstorm such a list of questions. Do these fall into any categories?

Finally, on a fresh piece of newsprint, refine your list. Which questions and in what order might you ask yourself when trying to decide between conflicting claims? Discuss these lists in class.

## EXERCISE 4 . 2

### Reclaiming Your Topic

More than two weeks ago, you began researching a topic that you may have known little about. But you were curious enough to dive in and immerse yourself in the research, listening to the voices of people who know more than you. You may feel, as Christy did, that your paper is beginning to slip away from you; there is just too much information, or the contradictions can't possibly be sorted out. It might seem presumptuous to think that your ideas matter. You may feel as if you're in over your head. After all, you're not an expert.

If you're not at all confused at this stage in the research process, that's great. Now is the time, through writing, to tighten your grasp on the material. But if you're feeling overwhelmed, writing now can help you get a grip. Try this exercise, which will take about forty minutes.

**STEP 1:** Spend ten or fifteen minutes reviewing all of the notes you've taken so far and skimming key articles or passages from books. Glance at your most important sources. Let your head swim with information.

**STEP 2:** Now clear your desk of everything but your research notebook. Remove all your notes and all your sources. You won't use them while doing the rest of this exercise. Trust that you'll remember what's important.

**STEP 3:** Now fastwrite about your topic for eight minutes. Tell the story of how your own thinking about your topic has evolved. When you began the project, what did you think? Then what happened, and what happened after that? What were your preconceptions about your topic? How have they changed? This is an open-ended fastwrite. Don't let the writing stall out. If you run out of things to say, talk to yourself through writing about your research, thinking about other trails you might follow. Time yourself.

**STEP 4:** Skip a few lines in your notebook. Write "Moments, Stories, People, and Scenes." Now fastwrite for another ten minutes, this time focusing on more specific case studies, situations, people, experiences, observations, and so on that stand out in your mind from the research done so far or perhaps from your own experience with the topic. Keep your pen moving for a full ten minutes. Time yourself.

**STEP 5:** Skip a few more lines. For ten minutes, quickly write a dialogue between you and someone else about your topic. You choose whom to converse with—a friend, your instructor. Don't plan the dialogue. Just begin with the question most commonly asked about your topic, and take the conversation from there, writing both parts of the dialogue.

**STEP 6:** Finally, skip a few more lines and write these two words in your notebook: "So What?" Now spend a few minutes trying to summarize the most important thing *you* think people should understand about your topic based on what you've learned so far. Distill these comments down to a sentence or two. This may be hard, but it's important. Remember, you can change your mind later.

## An Application Example

What did doing Exercise 4.2 accomplish, besides giving you a cramp in your writing hand? If the exercise worked, you probably already know. By freeing yourself from the chorus of expert voices in your sources and thinking to yourself about what the ideas you've collected mean, you've taken possession of the information again. You may have reaffirmed your purpose in writing the paper.

It may help you grasp the meaning of this exercise—and what completing it can do for you—by looking at how another student, Candy,* found her purpose in writing. After reviewing her notes

*The following excerpts are reprinted with permission of Candyce C. Collins.

and materials (Step 1) and then putting them away in preparation to write (Step 2), Candy was ready for Step 3, the first fastwrite. She told the story of finding her focus—how child abuse affects language development—by noting things that struck her as she went along:

**STEP 3**

*Well, let's see, in the beginning, I was going to do the effects in general of child abuse. As I was researching this, I discovered that I would have to narrow it down because there was so much information on the general effects of child abuse. Initially, when I came across the idea that child abuse creates an impairment in speech and language development, I almost just threw it out. But, I went ahead and read the article. It was very interesting and I was able to relate to it. I have taken a course in linguistics, so I was able to relate to how this could be possible. So, I looked further into the topic of the effects that child abuse has on the language development of children and found quite a bit of information. It became more and more interesting to me as I read the information and all the tests that have been run to prove this idea. Before I began research, I never thought that this could be a possible effect of child abuse. But, after researching and thinking more and more about it, I find it quite logical.*

By focusing on specifics in Step 4, the second fastwrite, you should discover some ways to anchor your ideas about the topic to particular people, situations, and case studies you discovered in your reading or from your own experience. Making these connections will not only strengthen your own thinking; case studies and personal accounts often make compelling examples, important to your paper.

In doing Step 4, Candy recalled the story of Genie, a girl who was confined to a closet by an abusive parent until she was thirteen. Genie later became a case used at the beginning and ending of Candy's paper. Here's Candy's second fastwrite:

**STEP 4**

*One case study that stands out is a story about Genie. This little girl had an extreme case of child abuse and neglect when she was a child up until she was 13 when she was found. At 13, she spoke nothing. Now, this is a severe case of language deficiency as a result of child abuse but it goes on to show that it happens. She was locked away in her room, tied to her crib. Her father would beat her whenever she made a noise, so as she got older, she feared to say or utter a sound, so she didn't. As a result, she was unable to talk. She was never brought out in the world, never watched TV or heard the radio.*

*Other studies have been done on groups of abused, neglected, and both abused and neglected children. The tests prove that all three groups showed signs of slower language development when compared to nonabused children. The highest results were found in the neglected only children, then the both neglected and abused and lastly the abused only children. This is due to the fact that the two groups of children that were abused had some stimulation in their lives even though it might not have been pleasant.*

Step 5, the dialogue writing activity, invites someone else to the discussion of your topic, challenging you to consider an audience. What might most people want to know about your topic? How might you explain the answers? These questions may later shape how you organize your paper.

Candy's dialogue started with the question that began her research—What are some of the effects of child abuse?—and then went from there, getting more and more specific. Can you visualize the inverted pyramid progression of her questions and answers? Candy later used this form in part of her paper.

It actually might be more productive to construct a more free-wheeling dialogue than Candy's. Have a real conversation with an imagined reader. Push yourself with questions that really get you thinking about your topic and that might help you see it in a fresh way.

Here's Candy's dialogue:

**STEP 5**

*What are some of the effects that children suffer from as a result of child abuse?*

*Well, there's lots of them. One in particular that most don't think of is that child abuse can cause language development problems in children.*

*What kind of language problems do they have?*

*Primarily, they lack the ability to communicate as well with others as do the nonabused children. Studies show that they have a distinct style of communication. One that is more aggressive and hostile and they try to avoid any true contact through conversations. In extreme cases, like one girl named Genie whose dad beat her whenever she made a sound, couldn't speak at all by the age of 13.*

*What causes this development problem with language?*

*When it comes down to it, the main reason is that these children are lacking the normal stimulation that they should receive. They're not exposed to the experiences that would be necessary to learn new words. Also, they are deprived of the parent-child relationship that is an important part of the language acquisition process.*

*What types of abuse are you talking of? Is it all kinds?*

*No, it's not all kinds of abuse that cause this. It is limited to those children who were either neglected, physically abused or both. Primarily, those that were solely neglected suffer the most. It has been proven that sexual abuse doesn't have an adverse effect on language but in fact these children seem more mature as far as language goes. But, I didn't research into that.*

Finally, asking "So What?" in Step 6 should help you redefine your thesis, or the controlling idea of your paper. In fact, your thesis may change. But for now, you need some brief statement—a sentence or two—that summarizes the most important thing you want your readers to understand.

Candy's answer to the "So What?" question later became the main point of her paper:

**STEP 6**

*"So What?"*

*Child abuse has a negative effect on the language development of a child. This is a result of the child's lack of stimulation, interaction, experiences, and parent-child relationships, which are all essential to the proper development of language.*

If you're not happy with your answer to "So What?" spend some more time thinking about it. Don't proceed too much further with writing until you have some kind of tentative thesis statement to keep in mind. Put your thesis on an index card or piece of paper, and post it over your desk as a reminder. Pull it down and revise it, if necessary, as you continue with research and writing.

But keep that thesis up there on the wall, at least while you're writing the first draft.

If Exercise 4.2 didn't work for you, you may need to collect more information. Consider circling back to some of the suggestions made in the third week in "Digging Deeper for Information" (see Chapter 3). But if you feel ready to begin writing a draft, read on.

## Deciding Whether to Say *I*

I'm a writer who seems unable to stop talking about myself. As a reader of this textbook, that should be apparent to you by now. I share anecdotes about my photography failures, my high school girl-friend, and my predilection for lobsters. I've chosen to do this, though I know that getting personal in a piece of writing is some-what risky business. If it's excessive, self-disclosure can seem ego-tistical or narcissistic. Constant self-reference—"I believe that . . . " or "I always wondered about . . . " or "I feel that . . . "—is usually unnecessary. (After all, if you simply make the assertion without the attribution, it's pretty obvious that you believe it or feel it.) The overuse of *I* can also seem to get in the way of the real subject, which may not be you. The personal profile is one genre of nonfiction writing that often suffers from explicit authorial intrusion. And teachers of research papers, as you know, often seem downright hostile to the intruding *I*.

By now, you know I don't agree with the view that all research writing should be objective (as if such a thing were possible). And in the research *essay* that you are about to draft this week, I certainly invite you to consider using the first person, presenting your own observations and experiences as evidence (if they're relevant) and yes, even talking about yourself.

There are many reasons this might be a good idea. First, by sig-naling our personal experiences and prejudices about a topic, we make explicit not only our particular purposes in exploring it but also why we might have a reason for (or even a vested interest in) seeing it a certain way. Readers like to know a writer's motivation for writing about something and appreciate knowing how her experi-ences might influence her ways of seeing. But maybe even more important, when a writer stops pretending that the *text* talks instead of the *author* (e.g., "This paper will argue that . . .") and actually enters into her text, she is much more likely to initiate a genuine conversation with her readers *and* with her sources. This dialogue might very well lead to some new ways of seeing her topic—that is, after all, the purpose of inquiry.

## *Getting Personal without Being Personal*

Conversation takes place between people, and in writing that embodies conversation, readers sense what Gordon Harvey* called *presence*—an awareness that a writer is making sense of things in his own particular ways, that he has a personal stake in what is being said. This is most easily achieved when the writer *gets* personal by using the first person, sharing personal experiences and perspectives. I hope that you sense my presence in *The Curious Researcher* through my willingness to do such things.

But I also want you to see, as Harvey observes, that presence in writing can be registered in ways other than simply talking about yourself. That is, you can write a research essay this week that *doesn't* use the first person or isn't autobiographical and still provides your readers with a strong sense of your presence as an individual writer and thinker. This presence may be much more subtle when it's not carried on the first-person singular's sturdy back. But it still makes writing come to life.

Before you begin drafting your essay this week, you'll have to decide how you'd prefer to get personal—explicitly or implicitly. For some of you, the choices may be limited. For instance, if your essay is on the causes of World War I, then integrating your own personal experience with the subject is obviously not an option. Most topics, however, offer the possibility of self-disclosure, and unless your instructor advises otherwise, almost all can accommodate *I*. But when you choose not to get personal in direct ways, you can still establish a strong presence in your essay.

## Beginning at the Beginning

John McPhee, a staff writer for *The New Yorker* magazine and one of the masters of writing the research-based essay, gave a talk some years back about beginnings, which vex many writers.

> The first part—the lead, the beginning—is the hardest part of all to write. I've often heard writers say that if you have written your lead you have written 90 percent of the story. You have tens of thousands of words to choose from, after all, and only one can start the story, then one after that, and so forth. And your material, at this point, is all fresh and unused, so you don't have the advantage of being in the middle of things. You could start

---

*Gordon Harvey, "Presence in the Essay," *College English* 56 (1994): 642–54.

in any of many places. What will you choose?* Leads must be sound. They should never promise what does not follow. Leads, like titles, are flashlights that shine down into the story.

## Flashlights or Floodlights?

I love this: *"Leads . . . are flashlights that shine down into the story."* An introduction, at least the kind I was taught to write in high school, is more like a sodium vapor lamp that lights up the whole neighborhood. I remember writing introductions to research papers that sounded like this:

```
There are many critical problems that face society
today. One of these critical problems is environmen-
tal protection, and especially the conservation of
marine resources. This paper will explore one of
these resources--the whale--and the myriad ways in
which the whale-watching industry now poses a new
threat to this species' survival. It will look at
what is happening today and what some people con-
cerned with the problem hope will happen tomorrow. It
will argue that new regulations need to be put into
effect to reduce boat traffic around our remaining
whales, a national treasure that needs protection.
```

This introduction isn't that bad. It does offer a statement of purpose, and it explains the thesis. But the window it opens on the paper is so broad—listing everything the paper will try to do—that readers see a bland, general landscape. What's to discover? The old writing formula for structuring some papers—"Say what you're going to say, say it, and then say what you said"—breeds this kind of introduction. It also gets the writer started on a paper that often turns out as bland as the beginning.

Consider this alternative opening for the same paper:

```
Scott Mercer, owner of the whale-watching vessel
Cetecea, tells the story of a man and his son who
```

*John McPhee, University of New Hampshire, 1977.

decide that watching the whales from inside their small motorboat isn't close enough. They want to swim with them. As Mercer and his passengers watch, the man sends his son overboard with snorkel and fins, and the boy promptly swims towards a "bubble cloud," a mass of air exhaled by a feeding humpback whale below the surface. What the swimmer doesn't know is that, directly below that bubble cloud, the creature is on its way up, mouth gaping. They are both in for a surprise. "I got on the P.A. system and told my passengers, just loud enough for the guy in the boat to hear me, that either that swimmer was going to end up as whale food or he was going to get slapped with a $10,000 fine. He got out of the water pretty fast."

I think this lead accomplishes nearly as much as the bland version but in a more compelling way. It suggests the purpose of the paper—to explore conflicts between whale lovers and whales—and even implies the thesis—that human activity around whales needs more regulation. This lead is more like McPhee's "flashlight," pointing to the direction of the paper without attempting to illuminate the entire subject in a paragraph. An interesting beginning will also help launch the writer into a more interesting paper, for both reader and writer.

It's probably obvious that your opening is your first chance to capture your reader's attention. But how you begin your research paper will also have a subtle yet significant impact on the rest of it. The lead starts the paper going in a particular direction; it also establishes the *tone,* or writing voice, and the writer's relationships to the subject and the reader. Most writers at least intuitively know this, which is why beginnings are so hard to write.

## Writing Multiple Leads
One thing that will make it easier to get started is to write three leads to your paper, instead of agonizing over one that must be perfect. Each different opening you write should point the "flashlight" in

a different direction, suggesting different trails the draft might follow. After composing several leads, you can choose the one that you—
and ultimately, your readers—find most promising.

Writing multiple openings to your paper might sound hard, but
consider all the ways to begin:

■ *Anecdote.* Think of a little story that nicely frames what your
paper is about, as does the lead about the man and his son who
almost became whale food.

■ *Scene.* Begin by giving your readers a look at some revealing
aspect of your topic. A paper on the destruction of tropical rain
forests might begin with a description of what the land looks like
after loggers have left it.

■ *Profile.* Try a lead that introduces someone who is important to
your topic. Candy's lead, using a case study on Genie, the abused
thirteen-year-old, is a good example. So is Christina's profile later in
this chapter of her own struggle to emote on stage in an essay on
method acting.

■ *Background.* Maybe you could begin by providing important
and possibly surprising background information on your topic. A
paper on steroid use might start by citing the explosive growth in use
by high school athletes in the last ten years. A paper on a novel or an
author might begin with a review of what critics have had to say.

■ *Quotation.* Sometimes, you encounter a great quote that beautifully captures the question your paper will explore or the direction
it will take. Heidi's paper on whether *Sesame Street* provides children with a good education began by quoting a tribute from *U.S.
News and World Report* to Jim Henson after his sudden death.

■ *Dialogue.* Open with dialogue between people involved in your
topic. Dan's paper on the connection between spouse abuse and alcoholism began with a conversation between himself and a woman who
had been abused by her husband.

■ *Question.* Pointedly ask your readers the questions you asked
that launched your research or the questions your readers might raise
about your topic. Here's how Kim began her paper on adoption: "Could
you imagine going through life not knowing your true identity?"

■ *Contrast.* Try a lead that compares two apparently unlike
things that highlight the problem or dilemma the paper will explore.
Dusty's paper "Myth of the Superwoman" began with a comparison

between her friend Susan, who married at twenty-one and grew up believing in Snow White and Cinderella, and herself, who never believed in princes or white horses and was advised by her mother that it was risky to depend on a man.

■ *Announcement.* Sometimes the most appropriate beginning *is* one like the first lead on whales and whale-watchers mentioned earlier, which announces what the paper is about. Though such openings are sometimes not particularly compelling, they are direct. A paper with a complex topic or focus may be well served by simply stating in the beginning the main idea you'll explore and what plan you'll follow.

## EXERCISE 4.3

### Three Ways In

**STEP 1:** Compose three different beginnings, or leads, to your research paper. Each should be one or two paragraphs (or perhaps more, depending on what type of lead you've chosen and on the length of your paper). Think about the many different ways to begin, as mentioned earlier, and experiment (see Figure 4.1). Your instructor may ask you to write the three leads in your research notebook or type them on a separate piece of paper and bring them to class.

**STEP 2:** Get some help deciding which opening is strongest. Circulate your leads in class, or show them to friends. Ask each person to check the one lead he likes best, that most makes him want to read on.

**STEP 3:** Choose the lead you like (even if no one else does). To determine how well it prepares your readers for what follows, ask a friend or classmate to answer these questions: Based on reading only the opening of the paper: (a) What do you predict this paper is about? What might be its focus? (b) Can you guess what central question I'm trying to answer? (c) Can you predict what my thesis might be? (d) How would you characterize the tone of the paper?

It's easy to choose an opening that's catchy. But the beginning of your paper must also help establish your purpose in writing it, frame your focus, and perhaps even suggest your main point, or thesis. The lead will also establish the voice, or tone, the paper will adopt (see the following section). That's a big order for one or two paragraphs, and you may find that more than a couple of paragraphs are needed to do it.

David Hancock
Brock Dethier
English 201
12 March 1998

### Leaping Dog Awakens Locals' Curiosity

LOGAN, UT—A dog with seemingly supernatural abilities astounded observers on the Quad at Utah State University Friday when it leaped nearly twenty feet high while trying to catch a frisbee.

The owner of the dog, Sam McDougle, aroused the suspicions of local residents when he suggested Logan water as a possible cause. "Don't feed him no special vitamins or nuthin', just dog food and tap water," McDougle said.

"I'm a little scared," commented Ruth Parkins about questionable elements in the water, "and I don't know that I'd want my kids turning into freaks." Authorities downplayed rumors of steroids and hormone stimulants contaminating the water source. "I wasn't there, but I'd say Mr. McDougle is quite a charlatan," said Doug Thompson, mayor of Logan.

According to witnesses, McDougle repeatedly tossed a frisbee high into the air, and the dog launched after it "like a Patriot Missile taking out some Scuds," said Air Force Lieutenant John Richards. "When I first saw him do it, I thought, 'well, ain't that neat,'" said McDougle. "But now I'm gonna need a lot bigger fence."

---

**FIGURE 4.1**    Here's the opening to a paper that doesn't fit neatly into any category. David's essay begins with a photograph of a dog jumping an unreasonable height and a mock newspaper article on the feat. His next page unravels the mystery—the photograph was doctored using a software program—and then the essay goes on to explore the dangers of digitally altered images. David asks, "Can we even trust photographs anymore?"

*Source:* Reprinted by permission of David Hancock.

Tentatively select the one opening (or a combination of several) from this exercise that does those things best. I think you'll find that none of the leads you composed will be wasted; there will be a place for the ones you don't use somewhere else in the paper. Keep them handy.

## Deciding on a Voice

How you begin has another subtle influence on your draft: It establishes the tone, or writing voice, you will adopt in your paper. Though you may think *writing voice* is not something you've considered much before, you probably paid a lot of attention to it when writing the essay that accompanied your college applications. Does this *sound* right? you wondered, considering whether what you wrote would impress the admissions officer. Did you sound like college material? You also know how to *change* your writing voice. For example, next time you get a speeding ticket and write home to ask for money to pay for it, notice the voice you adopt. And then, when you write your best friend a letter about the same incident, notice how your voice changes.

Of all the writing assignments you've done over the years, the research paper is probably the one in which you paid the most attention to writing voice. Research papers are supposed to sound a certain way, right? They're supposed to be peppered with words such as *myriad* and *thus* and *facilitate*. They're supposed to sound like, well, nobody you know—detached, mechanical, and ponderous.

These are understandable assumptions. So many of the sources you've read in the past weeks have sounded that way. It's also difficult to avoid sounding detached when you're writing about a topic that holds little interest for you. But the writing voice you choose for this or any other paper you write *is* a choice. Don't assume that all research papers are supposed to sound a certain way and that you must mindlessly conform to that voice.

### Considering Purpose, Audience, Subject, and Who You Are

How do you choose a writing voice for a research paper? Follow the same approach you would use when writing a letter to your parents, asking for money. Consider your *purpose,* your *audience,* and your *subject*. Most important, though, remember that, fundamentally, your writing voice is a reflection of *who you are*. Your natural writing voice is different from mine, just as your spoken voice is. You can change your spoken voice, something you're probably pretty experienced at already. But you may need to learn to know and appreciate your writing voice—the voice that sounds like you. It might even be appropriate for this paper.

I faced a difficult decision about voice in writing this text. My purpose was to instruct students in research skills as well as to motivate them to find some enthusiasm for the assignment. In order to motivate my readers, I wanted to present the research paper in a new way. That purpose would not be served, I thought, by writing in the detached, impersonal voice most people associate with textbooks (and research papers). I chose to sound like *me,* hoping that when explained in my voice, the subject would seem more accessible and my own enthusiasm for research would come through.

**The Differing Voices of Research.**   The voice in a piece of writing often comes through in the very first line. In case you still think all research papers sound alike, listen to these first lines from student papers:

> Ernst Pawel has said that "The Metamorphosis"
> by Franz Kafka "transcends the standard categories
> of literary criticism; it is a poisoned fairy
> tale about the magic of hate and the power of
> hypocrisy . . . charting the transmogrification of
> a lost soul in a dead bug" (279).
>
> *—From a paper on how Kafka writes the story to deal with*
> *his own childhood demons*

> As a waiter in a classy restaurant, I observe con-
> siderable variation in the way people dine, both in
> their treatment of other people and their skill at
> getting food and drink gracefully into their mouths.
>
> *—From an essay on the history of table manners*

> Even the sound of the word is vulgar.
>
> *—From a paper on ticks*

> Living during a period of war was something I had
> never experienced until the escalation of the
> recent Gulf crisis.
>
> *—From a paper on Igor Stravinsky's "The Soldier's Tale"*

```
I have often worried in the past months if there
was either something wrong with or missing from my
brain.
```

*—From a paper on dream interpretation*

```
No more fat jokes.
```

*—From a paper on a daughter coming to terms*
*with her mother's cancer*

These *are* different beginnings. But notice something all these beginnings share: They are concrete. None begins with a bland, broad stroke—some sweeping generalization or obvious statement (e.g., "War is an unhappy reality in today's society" or "Richard Wright's *Native Son* is about the African-American experience in America"). Rather, each gives the reader a specific handle on the topic. In some cases, the reader is given not only a concrete point of view but also, through a distinctive voice, an individual writer, as well.

The voices in the previous examples could be considered along a continuum, beginning with the more formal and moving to the much less formal, ranging from the impersonal to the personal, from a less visible writer to one who steps forward immediately. Any one of these voices might be appropriate for your paper, depending on your subject, purpose, and audience, and on who you are.

Generally, as the treatment of a topic becomes more technical and its audience more knowledgeable, the individual voice of the writer becomes less important. The writing often has less life, but then, it's not meant to entertain.

If you're writing a research paper that's intended to report the results of an experiment, you may choose a more impersonal writing voice. In such a case, it doesn't matter who you are, so don't draw attention to it. What does matter is communicating the results, simply and clearly, in a style that doesn't draw attention to itself in any way. You will find that academic writing in some disciplines is expected to assume an impersonal tone and in fact has its own language (though you may not have to strictly conform to it in this research paper).

But it's likely that, at this stage, you're not writing a technical paper for an audience of experts. And though your primary purpose is not to entertain your readers, you *are* trying to make your material as interesting to others as it is to you. As suggested earlier in this book, ask your instructor if you have some latitude in choosing a voice for your paper. (See "Things to Ask Your Instructor" in the Introduction.)

If so, review the lead you tentatively chose in Exercise 4.3. Does it establish a voice that's appropriate, given your topic, purpose, and audience? Do you like the way it sounds? Should you change it? Would another lead sound better? If so, write a new lead or choose another from the several leads you wrote earlier.

## Writing for Reader Interest

You've tentatively chosen a lead for your paper. You've selected it based on how well you think it frames your tentative purpose, establishes an appropriate tone or voice, and captures your readers' attention. Before you begin writing your draft, consider these other strategies for writing a lively, interesting paper that will help keep readers turning pages.

### *Working the Common Ground*

Here's how David Quammen, a nature writer, begins an essay on the sexual strategy of Canada geese:

> Listen: *uh-whongk, uh-whongk, uh-whongk, uh-whongk,* and then you are wide awake, and you smile up at the ceiling as the calls fade off to the north and already they are gone. Silence again, 3 A.M., the hiss of March winds. A thought crosses your mind before you roll over and, contentedly, resume sleeping. The thought is: "Thank God I live here, right here exactly, in their path. Thank God for those birds." The honk of wild Canada geese passing overhead in the night is a sound to freshen the human soul. The question is why.*

If you live in Puerto Rico or anywhere beyond the late-night call of geese flying overhead, this lead paragraph may not draw you into Quammen's article on the birds' sexual habits. But for the many of us who know the muttering of geese overhead, suddenly the writer's question—why this is a sound "to freshen the human soul"—becomes our question, too. *We want to know what he knows because he starts with what we both know already:* the haunting sound of geese in flight.

David Quammen understands the importance of working the common ground between his topic and his readers. In "The Miracle of Geese," he begins with an experience that many of us know, and once he establishes that common ground, he takes us into the less familiar territory he encountered while researching Canada geese.

*David Quammen, *The Flight of the Iguana* (New York: Delacorte, 1988), 233.

And we willingly go. Quammen gives us a foothold on his topic that comes from our own experience with it.

One of my interests in writing an essay about pigeons is the conviction that I'm not alone in feeling ambivalent about the birds. Though "The Bothersome Beauty of Pigeons" doesn't begin, as David Quammen's essay does, by establishing this common ground, on several occasions I try to exploit moments I think readers will find familiar, including the anecdote about the war I waged on pigeons roosting under the eaves of my house. In smaller ways, I work common ground by using it in explanations, particularly when I'm trying to bring research information to life. For example, here's how I described the drinking habits of pigeons in the essay:

```
[Pigeons]have other evolutionary advantages as well,

some of which save them from the well-placed kicks

of pigeon-haters or the tires of speeding taxis. For

one thing, they "suck" puddle water rather than take

it in their beaks and throw their heads back to

swallow it, something like the difference between

drinking a juice box and slinging back a shot of

tequila. Sucking is quicker, apparently, . . .
```

In an earlier draft, I had merely described the water sucking habits of pigeons, but I sensed that the information would be far more interesting and understandable if I exploited a comparison that readers would find familiar: drinking juice boxes and taking shots of tequila.

As you draft your research paper, look for ways to work the common ground between your topic and your readers: What typically is their relationship to what you're writing about? What might they know about the topic but not have noticed? How does it touch their world? What would they want to know from their own experiences with your topic?

Steve, writing a paper about the town fire department that services the university, began by describing a frequent event in his dormitory: a false alarm. He then went on to explore why many alarms are not really so false after all. He hooked his readers by drawing on their common experience with his topic.

Some topics, like geese and divorce and alcoholism, may have very real connections to the lives of your readers. Many people have heard geese overhead, seen families broken apart, or watched parents or friends destroy themselves with booze. As you revise your paper, look for opportunities to encourage readers to take a closer look at something about your topic they may have seen before.

**Topics in Which Common Ground Is Hard to Find.**    Some topics don't yield common ground so directly. They may be outside the direct experiences of your readers. For example, Margaret was a history major, and, thankfully, she had never had the bubonic plague. Neither have the rest of us. But she was interested in writing a research essay on the impact of the fourteenth century epidemic on the lives of European women. This is an age, and a disaster that in some ways is beyond the imagining of modern readers, though a skillful writer will look to highlight some of the similarities between our lives and those of the people she's writing about. One of these connections might be the modern AIDS epidemic in Africa, a disaster of truly epic proportions though it seems largely ignored by many Americans. Margaret might begin her essay with a brief glimpse at the devastation of families in South Africa today as a way of establishing the relevance of her 500-year-old topic.

Literary topics may also present a challenge in establishing common ground with readers, unless the author or work is familiar. But there are ways. When I was writing a paper on notions of manhood in Wallace Stegner's novels *The Big Rock Candy Mountain* and *Recapitulation,* I brought the idea of manhood home to my readers by describing my relationship with my own father and then comparing it to the relationship of two key characters in the books. Comparison to other more popular works that readers may know is often a way to establish some common ground.

Though it's unlikely that any of your classmates served on the ground in the recent Afghan war, images of that conflict—the debris-laden streets of Kabul, and the emergence of women in their burkas following the fall of the Taliban—are familiar to most of us through TV. This familiarity with such a distant place and culture might be a great way to establish the common ground with readers if, say, you were writing about the resurgence of female participation in the affairs of that nation.

In writing your paper, imagine the ways in which your topic intersects with the life of a typical reader, and in that way, bring the information to life.

## Putting People on the Page

Essayist E. B. White once advised that when you want to write about humankind, you should write about a human. The advice to look at the *small* to understand the *large* applies to most writing, not just the research paper.

Ideas come alive when we see how they operate in the world we live in. Beware, then, of long paragraphs with sentences that begin with phrases such as *in today's society,* where you wax on with generalization after generalization about your topic. Unless your ideas are anchored to specific cases, observations, experiences, statistics, and, especially, people, they will be reduced to abstractions and lose their power for your reader.

**Using Case Studies.**    Strangely, research papers are often people-less landscapes, which is one of the things that can make them so lifeless to read. Lisa wrote about theories of child development, citing studies and schools of thought about the topic yet never applying that information to a real child, her own daughter, two-year-old Rebecca. In his paper decrying the deforestation of the Amazon rain forest, Marty never gave his readers the chance to hear the voices of the Indians whose way of life is threatened.

*Ultimately, what makes almost any topic matter to the writer or the reader is what difference it makes to people.*

Candy's paper on child abuse and its effect on language development, for example, opened with the tragic story of Genie, who, for nearly thirteen years, was bound in her room by her father and beaten whenever she made a sound. When Genie was finally rescued, she could not speak at all. This sad story about a real girl makes the idea that child abuse affects how one speaks (the paper's thesis) anything but abstract. Candy gave her readers reason to care about what she learned about the problem by personalizing it.

Sometimes, the best personal experience to share is your own. Have you been touched by the topic? Kim's paper about the special problems of women alcoholics included anecdotes about several women gleaned from her reading, but the paper was most compelling when she talked about her own experiences with her mother's alcoholism.

**Using Interviews.**    Interviews are another way to bring people to the page. In "Why God Created Flies," Richard Conniff brought in the voice of a bug expert, Vincent Dethier, who not only had interesting things to say about flies but who also spoke with humor and enthusiasm. Heidi's paper on *Sesame Street* featured the voice of a school principal, a woman who echoed the point the paper made about the value of the program. Such research essays are filled not just with information about the topic but with people who are touched by it in some way.

As you write your paper, look for opportunities to bring people to the page. Hunt for case studies, anecdotes, and good quotes that will help your readers see how your topic affects how people think and live their lives.

## Writing a Strong Ending

Readers remember beginnings and endings. We already explored what makes a strong beginning: It engages the reader's interest, it's more often specific than general, and it frames the purpose of the paper, defining for the reader where it is headed. A beginning for a research paper should also state or imply its thesis, or controlling idea.

We haven't said anything about endings yet, or "conclusions," as they are traditionally described. What's a strong ending? That depends. If you're writing a formal research paper (in some disciplines), the purpose of the conclusion is straightforward: It should summarize major findings. But if you're writing a less formal research essay, the nature of the conclusion is less prescribed. It could summarize major findings, but it could also suggest new directions worth exploring, highlight an especially important aspect of the topic, offer a rethinking of the thesis, or end the story of the search. The conclusion could be general, or it could be specific.

**Endings to Avoid.**   The ending of your research paper could be a lot of things, and in a way, it's easier to say what it should *not* be:

■ Avoid conclusions that simply restate what you've already said. This is the "kick the dead horse" conclusion some of us were taught to write in school on the assumption that our readers probably aren't smart enough to get our point, so we'd better repeat it. This approach annoys most readers who *are* smart enough to know the horse is dead.

■ Avoid endings that begin with *in conclusion* or *thus*. Words such as these also signal to your reader what she already knows: that you're ending. Language such as this often begins a very general summary, which gets you into a conclusion such as the one mentioned above: dead.

■ Avoid endings that don't feel like endings—that trail off onto other topics, are abrupt, or don't seem connected to what came before them. Prompting your readers to think is one thing; leaving them hanging is quite another.

In some ways, the conclusion of your research paper is the last stop on your journey; the reader has traveled far with you to get there. The most important quality of a good ending is that it should add something to the paper. If it doesn't, cut it and write a new one.

What can the ending add? It can add a further elaboration of your thesis that grows from the evidence you've presented, a discussion of solutions to a problem that has arisen from the information you've uncovered, or perhaps a final illustration or piece of evidence that drives home your point.

Student Christina Kerby's research essay on method acting explores the controversy over whether this approach is selfish, subverting the playwright's intentions about a character's identity and replacing it with the actor's focus on her own feelings and identity. Christina's ending, however, first transcends the debate by putting method acting in context: It is one of several tools an actor can use to tap her emotions for a role. But then Christina humorously raises the nagging question about selfishness once more: Can we accept that Juliet is not thinking about the fallen Romeo as she weeps by his side but about her dead cat Fluffy? Here's Christina's ending:

Acting is no longer about poise, voice quality, and diction. It is also about feeling the part, about understanding the emotions that go into playing the part, and about possessing the skill necessary to bring those emotions to life within the character. . . . Whether an actor uses Stanislavski's method of physical actions to unlock the door to her subconscious or whether she attempts to stir up emotions from deep within herself using Strasberg's method, the actor's goal is to create a portrayal that is truthful. It is possible to pick out a bad actor from a mile away, one who does not understand the role because she does not understand the emotions necessary to create it. Or perhaps she simply lacks the means of tapping into them.

If genuine emotion is what the masses want, method acting may be just what every star-struck

```
actress needs. Real tears? No problem. The
audience will never know that Juliet was not
lamenting the loss of her true love Romeo but
invoking the memory of her favorite cat Fluffy,
who died tragically in her arms.*
```

An ending, in many ways, can be approached similarly to a lead. You can conclude with an anecdote, a quotation, a description, a summary, or a profile. Go back to the discussion earlier in this chapter of types of leads for ideas about types of conclusions. The same basic guidelines apply.

One of the easiest ways to solve the problem of finding a strong ending is to have the snake bite its tail. In other words, find some way in the end of your essay to return to where the piece began. For example, if your research essay began with an anecdote that dramatized a problem—say, the destruction of old growth forests in Washington—you might return to that opening anecdote, suggesting how the solutions you explored in your essay might have changed the outcome. If you pose a question in the first few paragraphs, return to the question in the last few. If you begin with a profile of someone relevant to your topic, return to him or her in the end, perhaps amplifying on some part of your picture of the person. Although this approach is formulaic, it often works well because it gives a piece of writing a sense of unity.

### Using Surprise

The research process—like the writing process—can be filled with discovery for the writer if he approaches the topic with curiosity and openness. When I began researching the *Lobster Almanac*, I was constantly surprised by things I didn't know: Lobsters are bugs; it takes eight years for a lobster in Maine to grow to the familiar one-pound size; the largest lobster ever caught weighed about forty pounds and lived in a tank at a restaurant for a year, developing a fondness for the owner's wife. I could go on and on. And I did in the book, sharing unusual information with my readers on the assumption that if it surprised me, it would surprise them, too.

As you write your draft, reflect on the surprising things you discovered about your topic during your research and look for ways

---

*Reprinted with permission of Christina B. Kerby.

to weave that information into the rewrite. Later, after you have written your draft, share it with a reader and ask for his ideas about what is particularly interesting and should be further developed. For now, think about unusual specifics you may have left out.

However, don't include information, no matter how surprising or interesting, that doesn't serve your purpose. Christine's survey on the dreams of college freshmen had some fascinating findings, including some accounts of recurring dreams that really surprised her. She reluctantly decided not to say much about them, however, because they didn't really further the purpose of her paper, which was to discover what function dreams serve. On the other hand, Bob was surprised to find that some politically conservative politicians and judges actually supported decriminalization of marijuana. He decided to include more information about who they were and what they said in his revision, believing it would surprise his readers and strengthen his argument.

## Considering Methods of Development

If you feel you have plenty of information and you're itching to get started writing the draft, maybe you should just follow your lead and see where it goes. Some of the best research papers I've read—and virtually all the research essays I've written—have grown organically from strong beginnings. When I write, I don't know what's going to happen until I see what I say.

Many people are not comfortable with such a free-fall approach to writing, including many professional writers. John McPhee is almost obsessed with the structure of his long research essays. He spends hours positioning and repositioning index cards of information from his research on a corkboard, looking for the right way to organize his material. He does all this before he writes a word of the draft.

If you're more of a planner than a leaper, then one option is to develop an outline, a map that will guide you from the opening to the ending of your paper. (In fact, your instructor may require that an outline be submitted with the final paper.) I've always resisted outlines, largely because they seem to take the surprise out of writing the first draft for me. But many people are uncomfortable without having a sense of where they're going before they get there. And if the outline isn't rigid, it doesn't have to preclude productive surprises.

There are a variety of ways to approach an outline. It can be a short list of things you want to cover, each summarized in a few words or phrases. It can be a list of headings that neatly break down your topic. It can be a list of questions the paper will try to answer, in the order you suspect readers may ask them. Or it can be a list of topic sentences that may even begin paragraphs or sections in the draft. You decide how detailed the outline needs to be at this point.

But before you tackle an outline, it might be helpful first to decide on the basic design of the paper. The following sections review some very general methods of development that can be used alone or in combination, as they serve your purpose.

## Narrative

Tell a story. It can be the story of someone who is affected by your topic, or it can be the story of what you've learned and how you learned it, a kind of narrative of thought that chronologically tells how your thinking about your topic evolved. Dan's research paper explored the connection between spouse abuse and alcoholism, beginning with the story of Louise, a woman who sought help from Dan while he was working at a counseling center. The paper continued using the narrative throughout, while Dan weaved in explanations gleaned from his research. Jessica began her research paper with a question about the meaning of a dream she had one night and then chronicled what she discovered about it and dream interpretation through her research and interviews.

Narratives often take a chronological structure (though not always), which makes them in some ways the easiest papers to organize. Can you build your paper around some story you can tell?

## Problem-to-Solution

Begin by framing the problem the paper will explore, and then focus on one or more solutions that seem promising or intriguing. For example, Anne Marie's paper on acquaintance rape first set out to establish the severity of the problem and then focused on student education programs at several colleges that have met with some success in heightening student awareness of this kind of assault. Bob's paper posed the dilemma of widespread marijuana use and then developed legalization as a possible solution.

Papers that examine problems need not always provide solutions, however.

## Cause-to-Effect or Effect-to-Cause

Causality, a primary interest of scientific researchers, can also be used to develop a research essay. Organize your paper around a cause of a problem, and then look at some effects, or vice versa. Consider beginning, for example, with a discussion of the dire effects of the removal of rain forests in Brazil, and then examine one cause—perhaps economic or political—that contributes to that problem. The key here is to avoid the temptation to examine *all* the causes and effects of a particular problem without ignoring its *complexity*. Things are seldom simple, and they are often interrelated. But pairing a cause and effect and building your paper around that can be illuminating. If your topic explores a problem, this may be a useful way to focus and organize your material.

### Question-to-Answer

As mentioned earlier, all writing answers questions. You've been asked to identify the focusing question that your paper attempts to answer. Design the paper around that question and your exploration of the answers. Anne began her research paper with a question about the absence of preschool in her education. Is preschool necessary, she asked, and does it contribute to later academic success? The rest of Anne's paper explored the answer, culled from both research and interviews.

Carolyn's research essay on the Endangered Species Act began by asking three questions: (1) Does the act benefit animals over humans? (2) Does it save creatures that have marginal value at the expense of the economy? and (3) Does it subvert property rights? Answering these questions became the organizing principle of her essay, as she examined each one in turn.

Question-to-answer is a quite natural method of development and can be combined with a narrative approach. How did you discover the answer to the question you pose? Be aware that this approach does not imply that you must find *the* answer. Again, things are rarely that simple or that neat. You may even note at the end of your paper that you asked the wrong question, a point that may be especially illuminating.

### Known-to-Unknown or Unknown-to-Known

Chris investigated a mysterious murder that took place on the Isle of Shoals, a tiny cluster of islands off New Hampshire's coast, one hundred years ago. Based on documents he collected, he first examined what was known about the case, but the bulk of his paper discussed what remained a mystery.

You might also examine what is known and unknown about your topic, especially if it's a source of controversy. What do authorities on your topic seem to agree and disagree on? Where does controversy lie?

## Simple-to-Complex

In a way, the simple-to-complex method of development is a variation of known-to-unknown. What is apparent about your topic? What is less obvious that reveals its complex nature? At first glance, Ken Kesey's book *One Flew Over the Cuckoo's Nest*\* is simply a powerful statement against institutional mistreatment of people who are mentally ill. But one student, Tim, found a more subtle, more disturbing misogynist theme. His paper first looked at the more obvious features of the novel but then focused on its less apparent antifeminist undercurrents.

## General-to-Specific or Specific-to-General

Think of general-to-specific as the "funnel" approach, inverted or not. You start with a broad look at the topic and then funnel down to some more specific aspect of it, or you begin with a narrow look and end up with some broader view. Jenny's paper on how children acquire language began with a specific anecdote about Kalinda, who is asked to read in front of her class and stumbles over a word. The paper then moved to a more general discussion of the forces that shape language acquisition. From there, it became specific again, discussing particular theorists and their ideas.

Good research writing sometimes has that quality: expansion and contraction, almost like breathing, moving in and out, again and again.

## Comparison-and-Contrast

Comparison-and-contrast is a strategy for organization you're no doubt familiar with. Depending on your purpose, it can work very well. For example, Nick wanted to understand what lessons the United States learned from the Vietnam War. The conflict with Iraq, an event that touched his life, seemed to be a useful comparison. How are the two wars different? he wondered. How are they similar? Another student, Linda, wrote a paper that compared and contrasted the creative processes involved in writing and photography. She discovered more similarities than she had expected.

Look for potentially revealing comparisons and contrasts, and organize your paper around them. You can deal with them separately—one and then the other—or you can alternate between the two, moving back and forth.

\*Ken Kesey, *One Flew Over the Cuckoo's Nest* (New York: Signet, 1962).

## Combining Approaches

Remember that each of these methods of development can be used alone, but they will more likely be used in combination. Most papers move back and forth between the general and the specific, and many involve some kind of narrative. (After all, an anecdote or case study is a kind of story.) A paper on the destruction of the Brazilian rain forest may incorporate the cause-and-effect model mentioned above, but it may also find a place for comparison-and-contrast. For instance: Which countries with rain forests have resisted economic pressures to cut trees? Would those approaches work in Brazil?

These strategies for organizing your paper are not meant to be formulas. Ignore them altogether if using them turns writing your first draft into a slow, mechanistic exercise. At best, these methods may give you a broad notion of how to organize an outline. Then you can fill in some of the detail—again, how much is up to you.

However you approach creating an outline at this stage, do so with your thesis in mind. Ask yourself, *What* do my readers need to know to understand my point, and *when* do they need to know it in my paper?

# Writing with Sources

The need for *documentation*—that is, citing sources—distinguishes the research paper from most other kinds of writing. And let's face it: Worrying about sources can cramp your style. Many students have an understandable paranoia about plagiarism and tend, as mentioned earlier, to let the voices of their sources overwhelm their own. Students are also often distracted by technical details: Am I getting the right page number? Where exactly should this citation go? Do I need to cite this or not?

As you gain control of the material by choosing your own writing voice and clarifying your purpose in the paper, you should feel less constrained by the technical demands of documentation. The following suggestions may also help you weave reference sources into your own writing without the seams showing.

## Blending Kinds of Writing and Sources

One of the wonderful things about the research essay is that it can draw on all four sources of information—reading, interviews, observation, and experience—as well as the four notetaking strategies discussed earlier—quotation, paraphrase, summary, and the writer's own analysis and commentary. Skillfully blended, these elements can make music.

Look at this paragraph from Heidi's paper on *Sesame Street:*

There is more to this show than meets the eye,
certainly. It is definitely more than just a crowd
of furry animals all living together in the middle
of New York City. Originally intended as an effort
to educate poor, less privileged youth, <u>Sesame
Street</u> is set in the very middle of an urban
development on purpose (Hellman 52). As Jon Stone,
one of the show's founders and co-producers sees
it, the program couldn't be "just another escapist
show set in a tree house or a badger den" (52).
Instead, the recognizable environment gave something to the kids they could relate to. ". . . It
had a lot more real quality to it than, say,
<u>Mister Rogers</u>. . . . Kids say the reason they
don't like <u>Mister Rogers</u> is that it's unbelievable," says Nancy Diamonti.*

The writing is lively here, not simply because the topic is interesting to those of us who know the program. Heidi has nicely
blended her own commentary with summary, paraphrase, and quotation, all in a single paragraph. She has also been able to draw on
multiple sources of information—an interview, some effective quotes
from her reading, and her own observations of *Sesame Street.* We
sense that the writer is *using* the information, not being used by it.

**Handling Quotes.**    Avoid the temptation, as Heidi did, to load up
your paragraphs with long or full quotes from your sources. I often
see what I call "hanging quotes" in research papers. Embedded in a
paragraph is a sentence or two within quotation marks. Though the
passage is cited, there's no indication of who said it. Usually, the
writer was uncertain about how to summarize or paraphrase or work
*part* of the quotation into his own prose.

Use quotations selectively. And if you can, blend them into
your own sentences, using a particularly striking or relevant part

*Used with permission of Heidi R. Dunham.

of the original source. For example, consider how quotes are used in this paragraph:

```
Black Elk often spoke of the importance of the
circle to American Indian culture. "You may have
noticed that everything an Indian does is in a
circle, and that is because the Power of the World
always works in circles, and everything tries to
be round. . . . The sky is round, and I have heard
that the earth is round like a ball, and so are
all the stars." He couldn't understand why white
people lived in square houses. "It is a bad way to
live, for there is not power in a square."
```

The quotes stand out, separate from the writer's own text. A better use of quotes is to work the same material smoothly into your own prose, doing something such as this:

```
Black Elk believed the "Power of the World always
works in circles," noting the roundness of the sun,
the earth, and the stars. He couldn't understand why
white people live in square houses: "It is a bad way
to live, for there is not power in a square."
```

Occasionally, however, it may be useful to include a long quotation from one of your sources. A quotation that is longer than four lines should be *blocked,* or set off from the rest of the text by indenting it ten spaces from the left margin. Like the rest of the paper, a blocked quotation is also typed double-spaced. For example:

```
According to Robert Karen, shame is a particularly
modern phenomenon. He notes that in medieval
times, people pretty much let loose, and by our
modern tastes, it was not a pretty sight:
     Their emotional life appears to have been
     extraordinarily spontaneous and unrestrained.
     From Joahn Huizinga's The Waning of the
```

> <u>Middle Ages</u> we learn that the average
> European town dweller was wildly erratic and
> inconsistent, murderously violent when
> enraged, easily plunged into guilt, tears,
> and pleas for forgiveness, and bursting with
> psychological eccentricities. He ate with his
> hands out of a common bowl, blew his nose on
> his sleeve, defecated openly by the side of
> the road, made love, and mourned with great
> passion, and was relatively unconcerned about
> such notions as maladjustment or what others
> might think. . . . In post-medieval centuries
> what I've called situational shame spread
> rapidly. . . . (61)

Note that the quotation marks are dropped around a blocked quotation. In this case, only part of a paragraph was borrowed, but if you quote one or more full paragraphs, indent the first line of each *three* spaces in addition to the ten the block is indented from the left margin.

We'll examine *parenthetical references* more fully in the next section, but notice how the citation in the blocked quotation above is placed *outside* the final period. That's a unique exception to the usual rule that a parenthetical citation is enclosed *within* the period of the borrowed material's final sentence.

**Handling Interview Material.**   The great quotes you glean from your interviews can be handled like quotations from texts. But there's a dimension to a quote from an interview that's lacking in a quote from a book: Namely, you participated in the quote's creation by asking a question, and in some cases, you were there to observe your subject saying it. This presents some new choices. When you're quoting an interview subject, should you enter your essay as a participant in the conversation, or should you stay out the way? That is, should you describe yourself asking the question? Should you describe the scene of the interview, your subject's manner of responding, or your immediate reaction to what she said? Or should you merely report *what* was said and *who* said it?

Christina's essay, "Crying Real Tears: The History and Psychology of Method Acting," makes good use of interviews. Notice how Christina writes about one of them in the middle of her essay:

During a phone interview, I asked my acting teacher, Ed Claudio, who studied under Stella Adler, whether or not he agreed with the ideas behind method acting. I could almost see him wrinkle his nose at the other end of the connection. He described method acting as "self-indulgent," insisting that it encourages "island acting." Because of emotional recall, acting became a far more personal art, and the actor began to move away from the script, often hiding the author's purpose and intentions under his own.*

Contrast Christina's handling of the Claudio interview with her treatment of material from an interview with Dave Pierini later in her essay:

Dave Pierini, a local Sacramento actor, pointed out, "You can be a good actor without using method, but you cannot be a good actor without at least understanding it." Actors are perhaps some of the greatest scholars of the human psyche because they devote their lives to the study and exploration of it. Aspiring artists are told to "get inside of the character's head." They are asked, "How would the character <u>feel</u>? How would the character <u>react</u>?"

Do you think Christina's entry into her report of the first interview (with Ed Claudio) is intrusive? Or do you think it adds useful information or even livens it up? What circumstances might make

*Reprinted with permission of Christina B. Kerby.

this a good move? On the other hand, what might be some advantages of the writer staying out of the way and simply letting her subject speak, as Christina chooses to do in her treatment of the second interview (with Dave Pierini)?

### Trusting Your Memory

One of the best ways to weave references seamlessly into your own writing is to avoid the compulsion to stop and study your sources as you're writing the draft. I remember that writing my research papers in college was typically done in stops and starts. I'd write a paragraph of the draft, then stop and reread a photocopy of an article, then write a few more sentences, and then stop again. Part of the problem was the meager notes I took as I collected information. I hadn't really taken possession of the material before I started writing the draft. But I also didn't trust that I'd remember what was important from my reading.

If, during the course of your research and writing so far, you've found a sense of purpose—for example, you're pretty sure your paper is going to argue for legalization of marijuana or analyze the symbolism on old gravestones on Cape Cod—then you've probably read purposefully, too. You *will* likely know what reference sources you need as you write the draft, without sputtering to a halt to remind yourself of what each says. Consult your notes and sources as you need them; otherwise, push them aside, and immerse yourself in your own writing.

# Citing Sources

## An Alternative to Colliding Footnotes

Like most people I knew back then, I took a typing class the summer between eighth grade and high school. Our instructional texts were long books with the bindings at the top, and we worked on standard Royal typewriters that were built like tanks. I got up to thirty words a minute, I think, which wasn't very good, but thanks to that class, I can still type without looking at the keyboard. The one thing I never learned, though, was how to turn the typewriter roller up a half space to type a footnote number that would neatly float above the line. In every term paper in high school, my footnotes collided with my sentences.

I'm certain that such technical difficulties were not the reason that most academic writers in the humanities and social sciences have largely abandoned the footnote method of citation for the parenthetical one, but I'm relieved, nonetheless. In the new system, borrowed material is parenthetically cited in the paper by indicating the author of the original work and the page it was taken from or the date it was published. These parenthetical citations are then explained more fully in the "Works Cited" page at the end of your paper where the sources themselves are listed.

By now, your instructor has probably told you what method of citing sources you should use: the Modern Language Association (MLA) style or the American Psychological Association (APA) style. Most English classes use MLA. A complete guide to MLA conventions is provided in Appendix A, and to APA in Appendix B.

Before you begin writing your draft, go to Appendix A and read the section "Citing Sources in Your Essay." This will describe in some detail when and where you should put parenthetical references to borrowed material in the draft of your essay. Don't worry too much about the guidelines for preparing the final manuscript, including how to do the bibliography. You can deal with that next week.

## I Hate These Theses to Pieces

Okay, here's a thesis:

```
I hate thesis statements.
```

And you wonder, What is this guy talking about now? What do you mean you hate thesis statements? *All* thesis statements? Why?

You'd be right to wonder for two reasons. First, my thesis statement about thesis statements isn't very good: It is too sweeping, it is overstated (*hate?*), and it deliberately withholds information. Its virtues, if any, are its shock value and the fact that it *is*—as any thesis must be—an assertion, or claim. Second, you're wondering why a teacher of writing would make such a claim in the first place. Doesn't most writing have a thesis, either stated or implied? Isn't writing that lacks a thesis unfocused, unclear? Doesn't a research paper, in particular, need a strong thesis?

Let me try again. Here's a thesis:

```
The thesis statement often discourages inquiry
instead of promoting it.
```

Hmmm . . . This is less overstated, and the claim is qualified in a reasonable way (*often discourages*). This thesis is also a bit more informative because it ever so briefly explains *why* I dislike thesis statements: *They often discourage inquiry.* But how do they do that? For one thing, when you arrive at a thesis statement prematurely, you risk turning the process of exploring your topic into a ritual hunt for examples that simply support what you already think. With this purpose in mind, you may suppress or ignore ideas or evidence that conflicts with the thesis—that threatens to disrupt the orderly march toward proving it is true.

Well, then, you infer, you're not saying you dislike *all* thesis statements, just those that people make up too soon and cling to compulsively.

Yes, I think so. I prefer what I would call the *found thesis,* the idea that you discover or the claim you come to *after* some exploration of a topic. This type of thesis often strikes me as more surprising (or less obvious) and more honest. It suddenly occurs to me, however, that I just discovered the term *found thesis* at this very moment, and I discovered it by starting with a conventional claim: *I hate thesis statements.* Doesn't that undermine my current thesis about thesis statements, that beginning with one can close off inquiry?

Well, yes, come to think of it.

What might we conclude from all of this discussion about the thesis that you can apply to the draft you're writing this week?

1. If you're already committed to a thesis, write it down. Then challenge yourself to write it again, making it somewhat more specific and informative and perhaps even more qualified.

2. At this stage, the most useful thesis may not be one that dictates the structure and arrangement of your draft but one that provides a focus for your thinking. Using the information you've collected, play out the truth of your idea or claim, but also invite questions about it—as I did—that may qualify or even overturn what you initially thought was true. In other words, use your draft to *test* the truthfulness of your thesis about your topic.

3. If you're still struggling to find a tentative thesis, use your draft to discover it. Then use your found thesis as the focus for the revision.

4. Your final draft *does* need to have a strong thesis, or controlling idea, around which the essay is built. The essay may ultimately attempt to *prove* the validity of the thesis, or the final essay may *explore* its implications.

## Driving through the First Draft

You have an opening, a lot of material in your notes—much of it, written in your own words—and maybe an outline. You've considered some general methods of development, looked at ways to write with sources, and completed a quick course in how to cite them. Finish the week by writing through the first draft.

Writing the draft may be difficult. All writing, but especially research writing, is a recursive process. You may find sometimes that you must circle back to a step you took before, discovering a gap in your information, a new idea for a thesis statement, or a better lead or focus. Circling back may be frustrating at times, but it's natural and even a good sign: It means you're letting go of your preconceived ideas and allowing the discoveries you make *through writing* to change your mind.

### A Draft Is Something the Wind Blows Through

Remember, too, that a *draft* is something the wind blows through. It's too early to worry about writing a research paper that's airtight, with no problems to solve. Too often, student writers think they have to write a perfect paper in the first draft. You can worry about plugging holes and tightening things up next week. For now, write a draft, and if you must, put a reminder on a piece of paper and post it on the wall next to your thesis statement. Look at this reminder every time you find yourself agonizing over the imperfections of your paper. The reminder should say, "It Doesn't Count."

Keep a few other things in mind while writing your first draft:

1. *Focus on your tentative thesis.* Use your thesis as a focus for your thinking in writing the draft. Use the information you've collected to test the validity of the claim you're making.

2. *Vary your sources.* Offer a variety of different sources as evidence to support your assertions. Beware of writing a single page that cites only one source.

3. *Remember your audience.* What do your readers want to know about your topic? What do they need to know to understand what you're trying to say?

4. *Write with your notes.* If you took thoughtful notes during the third week—carefully transforming another author's words into your own, flagging good quotes, and developing your own analysis—then you've already written at least some of your paper. You may only need to fine-tune the language in your notes and then plug them into your draft.

5. *Be open to surprises.* The act of writing is often full of surprises. In fact, it should be, since *writing* is *thinking* and the more you think about something, the more you're likely to see. You might get halfway through your draft and discover the part of your topic that *really* fascinates you. Should that happen, you may have to change your thesis or throw away your outline. You may even have to reresearch your topic, at least somewhat. It's not necessarily too late to shift the purpose or focus of your paper (though you should consult your instructor before totally abandoning your topic at this point). Let your curiosity remain the engine that drives you forward.

## CHAPTER 5

# The Fifth Week

## Revising for Purpose

My high school girlfriend, Jan, was bright, warm hearted, and fun, and I wasn't at all sure I liked her much, at least at first. Though we had a lot in common—we both loved sunrise over Lake Michigan, bird watching, and Simon and Garfunkel—I found Jan a little intimidating, a little too much in a hurry to anoint us a solid "couple." But we stuck together for three years, and as time passed, I persuaded myself—despite lingering doubts—that I couldn't live without her. There was no way I was going to break my white-knuckled hold on that relationship. After all, I'd invested all that time.

As a writer, I used to have similar relationships with my drafts. I'd work on something very hard, finally finishing the draft. I'd know there were problems, but I'd developed such a tight relationship with my draft that the problems were hard to see. And even when I recognized some problems, the thought of making major changes seemed too risky. Did I dare ruin the things I loved about the draft? These decisions were even harder if the draft took a long time to write.

Revision doesn't necessarily mean you have to sever your relationship with your draft. It's probably too late to make a complete break with the draft and abandon your topic. However, revision does demand finding some way to step back from the draft and change your relationship with it, seeing it from the reader's perspective rather than just the writer's. Revision requires that you loosen your grip. And when you do, you may decide to shift your focus or rearrange the information. At the very least, you may discover gaps in information or sections of the draft that need more development. You will certainly need to prune sentences.

The place to begin is *purpose*. You should determine whether the purpose of your paper is clear and examine how well the information is organized around that purpose.

Presumably, by now you know the purpose of your essay. If you hadn't quite figured it out before you wrote last week's draft, I hope writing the draft helped you clarify your purpose. It did? Great. Then complete the following sentence. Remember that here, you're trying to focus on the *main* purpose of your draft. There are probably quite a few things that you attempt to do in it, but what is the most central purpose?

The main purpose of my essay on _____ is to

(use the appropriate word or words) *explain, argue, explore,*

*describe*_____.

Here's how Christina filled in the blanks for her essay on method acting:

The main purpose of my essay on _____*method acting*_____ is to

(explain,) argue, explore, describe _____*the psychological aspects of*_____

*method and its impact on American theater.*

## The Thesis as a Tool for Revision

*Purpose* and *thesis* have a tight relationship. When I write an essay, I'm essentially in pursuit of a point, and not infrequently, it playfully eludes me. Just when I think I've figured out exactly what I'm trying to say, I have the nagging feeling that it's not quite right—it's too simplistic or obvious, it doesn't quite account for the evidence I've collected, or it just doesn't capture the spirit of the discoveries I've made. If a thesis is often a slippery fish, then having a strong sense of purpose helps me finally get a grip on it.

Purpose (and its sister *focus*) is a statement of intention—this is what I want to do in this piece of writing. It not only describes how I've limited the territory but what I plan to do when I'm there. That's why the words *explain, argue, explore,* and *describe* are so important. They pinpoint an *action* I'll take in the writing, and they'll move me toward particular assertions about what I see. One of these assertions will seem more important than any other, and that will be my thesis.

Maybe my tendency to see thesis statements as slippery is because I dislike encountering main points in essays that act like choolyard bullies—they overcompensate for their insecurity by idly announcing, "Hey, listen to me, bub, *I'm* the main point around here, and whaddya going to do about, huh?" Essays whose purpose is to argue something and take a broad and unqualified stand in favor of or against a whole category of people/positions/theories/ideas can be the worst offenders. Things are rarely that simple, and when they are, they usually aren't very interesting to write about.

Just as often, I encounter thesis statements that act more like the kids who get singled out by the bullies for harassment. They are meek or bland assertions that would be easy to pick apart if they weren't so uninteresting. Here's one: *Nuclear bombs are so powerful, so fast, and so deadly that they have become the weapon of today.* There *are* elements of an assertion here; the writer points out that modern nuclear weapons are *fast, powerful,* and *deadly.* But this is such an obvious claim that it probably isn't even worth stating. The phrase *weapon of today* would seem more promising if it was explained a bit. What is it about nations or warfare *today* that makes such weapons so appealing? Is the apparent passion for fast, deadly, and powerful nuclear weapons today analogous to any-thing—maybe the passion for designer labels, fax machines, and fast food?

## EXERCISE 5.1

### Dissecting the Fish

The main point in your research essay *may* be a straightfor-ward argument—*Legalization of drugs will not, as some of its sup-porters claim, reduce violent crime*—or it may be an explanation or description of some aspect of your topic—*Method acting has revolu-tionized American theater.* But in either case, *use* the main point as a launching place for thinking about what you might do in the revi-sion. Before you do anything else on your draft this week, consider doing the following:

- In a sentence or two, write down the thesis or controlling idea that emerged in your draft last week. It may have been stated or implied, or perhaps after writing the draft, you have a clearer idea of what you're trying to say. In any case, write down your thesis.

- Now generate a list of three or more questions that your thesis raises. These questions may directly challenge your assertion, or they may be questions—like those I raised earlier about the thesis about nuclear weapons—that help you further clarify or unpack what you're trying to say.

■ Next, rewrite your thesis statement at least three times. In each subsequent version, play with language or arrangement, add information, or get more specific about exactly what you're saying. For example:

1. *Method acting has had a major impact on American theater.*

2. *The method—which turned Stanislauski's original focus on external actions inward, toward the actor's own feelings—has generated controversy since the beginning.*

3. *An actor using the method may be crying tears, but whether they're real or not depends on whom you ask: the actor, who is thinking about her dead cat in the midst of a scene about a dying lover, or the writer, who didn't have a dead cat in mind when she wrote it.*

If this exercise works for you, several things will happen. Not only will you refine how you express your main point in the next draft, but you will also get guidance about how you might approach the revision—how you might reorganize it, what information you should add or cut, how you can further narrow your focus and even clarify your purpose. For example, the first version of the thesis on method acting provides the writer with little guidance about what information to *exclude* in the next draft. Aren't there lots of ways to show that method acting has had a major impact on American theater? The third version, on the other hand, is not only livelier and more interesting, it points the writer much more directly to what she should emphasize in the next draft: the conflict method acting creates over how theatrical roles are imagined, the license actors have with their material, and the ways that deception may be involved in a powerful performance using this technique.

What I'm suggesting here is this: Once you arrive at the controlling idea for your essay, it need not arrest your thinking about your topic, closing off any further discovery. A thesis is, in fact, a *tool* that will help you reopen the material you've gathered, rearrange it, and understand it in a fresh, new way.

*Revision,* as the word implies, means "re-seeing" or "reconceiving," trying to see what you failed to notice with the first look. That can be hard. Remember how stuck I was on that one picture of the lighthouse? I planted my feet in the sand, and the longer I stared through the camera lens, the harder it was to see the lighthouse from any other angle. It didn't matter that I didn't particularly like what I was seeing. I just wanted to take the picture.

You've spent more than four weeks researching your topic and the last few days composing your first draft. You may find that you've spent so much time staring through the lens—seeing your topic the way you chose to see it in your first draft—that doing a major revision is about as appealing as eating cold beets. How do you get the perspective to "re-see" the draft and rebuild it into a stronger paper?

## Using a Reader

If you wanted to save a relationship, you might ask a friend to intervene. Then you'd get the benefit of a third-party opinion, a fresh view that could help you see what you may be too close to see.

A reader can do the same thing for your research paper draft. She will come to the draft without the entanglements that encumber the writer and provide a fresh pair of eyes through which you can see the work.

### What You Need from a Reader

Your instructor may be that reader, or you might exchange drafts with someone else in class. You may already have someone whom you share your writing with—a roommate, a friend. Whomever you choose, try to find a reader who will respond honestly *and* make you want to write again.

What will be most helpful from a reader at this stage? Comments about your spelling and mechanics are not critical right now. You'll deal with those factors later. What the reader needs to point out is if the *purpose* of your paper is clear and if your thesis is convincing. Is it clear what your paper is about, what part of the topic you're focusing on? Does the information presented stay within that focus? Does the information clarify and support what you're trying to say? It would also be helpful for the reader to tell you what parts of the draft are interesting and what parts seem to drag.

## EXERCISE 5.2

### Directing the Reader's Response

Though you could ask your reader for a completely open-ended reaction to your paper, the following questions might help her focus on providing comments that will help you tackle a revision:

1. After reading the draft, what would you say is the main question the paper is trying to answer or focus on?
2. In your own words, what is the main point?

3. What do you remember from the draft that most convinces you that the ideas in the paper are true? What is least convincing?
4. Where is the paper most interesting? Where does the paper drag?

How your reader responds to the first two questions will tell you a lot about how well you've succeeded in making the purpose and thesis of your paper clear. The answer to the third question may reveal how well you've *used* the information gleaned from research. The reader's response to the fourth question will give you a preliminary reading on how well you engaged her. Did you lose her anywhere? Is the paper interesting?

A reader responding to Jeff's paper titled "The Alcoholic Family" helped him discover some problems that are typical of first drafts. His paper was inspired by his girlfriend's struggles to deal with her alcoholic father. Jeff wondered if he could do anything to help. Jeff's reader was touched by those parts of the paper where he discussed his own observations of the troubled family's behavior; however, the reader was confused about Jeff's purpose. "Your lead seems to say that your paper is going to focus on how family members deal with an alcoholic parent," the reader wrote to Jeff, "but I thought your main idea was that people outside an alcoholic family can help but must be careful about it. I wanted to know more about how you now think you can help your girlfriend. What exactly do you need to be careful about?"

This wasn't an observation Jeff could have made, given how close he is to the topic and the draft. But armed with objective and specific information about what changes were needed, Jeff was ready to attack the draft.

## Attacking the Draft

The controlling idea of your paper—that thesis you posted on an index card above your desk a week or more ago—is the heart of your paper and should, in some way, be connected to everything else in the draft.

Though a good reader can suddenly help you see things you've missed, she will likely not give much feedback on what you should do to fix these problems. Physically attacking the draft might help. If you neatly printed your first draft, then doing this may feel sacrilegious—a little like writing in books. One of the difficulties with revision is that writers respect the printed page too much. When the draft is typed up, with all those words marching neatly down the page, it is hard to mess it up again. As pages emerge from the printer, you can almost hear the sound of hardening concrete. Breaking the draft into pieces can free you to clearly see them and how they fit together.

## EXERCISE 5.3

### Cut-and-Paste Revision

Try this cut-and-paste revision exercise (a useful technique inspired by Peter Elbow and his book *Writing with Power**):

1. Make a photocopy of your first draft (one-sided pages only). Save the original; you may need it later.

2. Cut apart the photocopy of your research paper, paragraph by paragraph. (You may cut it into even smaller pieces later.) Once the draft has been completely disassembled, shuffle the paragraphs—get them wildly out of order so the original draft is just a memory.

3. Now go through the shuffled stack and find the *core paragraph,* the most important one in the whole paper. This is probably the paragraph that contains your thesis, or main point. This paragraph is the one that gets to the heart of what you're trying to say. Set it aside.

4. With your core paragraph directly in front of you, work your way through the remaining stack of paragraphs and make two new stacks: one of paragraphs that are relevant to your core and one of paragraphs that don't seem relevant, that don't seem to serve a clear purpose in developing your main idea. Be as tough as a drill sergeant as you scrutinize each scrap of paper. What you are trying to determine is whether each piece of information, each paragraph, is there for a reason. Ask yourself these questions as you examine each paragraph:
   - Does it *develop* my thesis or further the purpose of my paper, or does it seem an unnecessary tangent that could be part of another paper with a different focus?
   - Does it provide important *evidence* that supports my main point?
   - Does it *explain* something that's key to understanding what I'm trying to say?
   - Does it *illustrate* a key concept?
   - Does it help establish the *importance* of what I'm trying to say?
   - Does it raise (or answer) a *question* that I must explore, given what I'm trying to say?

*Peter Elbow, *Writing with Power* (New York: Oxford University Press, 1981).

You might find it helpful to write on the back of each relevant paragraph which of these purposes it serves. You may also discover that *some* of the information in a paragraph seems to serve your purpose, while the rest strikes you as unnecessary. Use your scissors to cut away the irrelevant material, pruning back the paragraph to include only what's essential.

5. You now have two stacks of paper scraps: those that seem to serve your purpose and those that don't. For now, set aside your "reject" pile. Put your core paragraph back into the "save" pile, and begin to reassemble a very rough draft, using what you've saved. Play with order. Try new leads, new ends, new middles. As you spread out the pieces of information before you, see if a new structure suddenly emerges. *But especially, look for gaps—places where you should add information.* Jot down ideas for material you might add on a piece of paper; then cut up the paper and splice (with tape) each idea in the appropriate place when you reassemble the draft in the next step. You may rediscover uses for information in your "reject" pile, as well. Mine that pile, if you need to.

6. As a structure begins to emerge, begin taping together the fragments of paper and splicing ideas for new information. Don't worry about transitions; you'll deal with those later. When you're done with the reconstruction, the draft should look drafty—something the wind can blow through—and may be totally unlike the version you started with.

## Examining the Wreckage

As you deal with the wreckage your scissors have wrought on your first draft, you might notice other problems with it. For example, you may discover that your draft has no real core paragraph, no part that is central to your point and purpose. Don't panic. Just make sure that you write one in the revision.

To your horror, you may find that your "reject" pile of paragraphs is bigger than your "save" pile. If that's the case, you won't have much left to work with. You may need to reresearch the topic (returning to the library this week to collect more information) or shift the focus of your paper. Perhaps both.

To your satisfaction, you may discover that your reconstructed draft looks familiar. You may have returned to the structure you started with in the first draft. If that's the case, it might mean your first draft worked pretty well; breaking it down and putting it back together simply confirmed that.

When Jeff cut up "The Alcoholic Family," he discovered immediately that his reader was right: Much of his paper did not seem clearly related to his point about the role outsiders can play in helping alcoholic families. His "reject" pile had paragraph after paragraph of information about the roles that alcoholic family members assume when there's a heavy drinker in the house. Jeff asked himself, What does that information have to do with the roles of outsiders? He considered changing his thesis, rewriting his core paragraph to say something about how each family member plays a role in dealing with the drinker. But Jeff's purpose in writing the paper was to discover what *he* could do to help.

As Jeff played with the pieces of his draft, he began to see two things. First of all, he realized that some of the ways members behave in an alcoholic family make them resistant to outside help; this insight allowed him to salvage some information from his "reject" pile by more clearly connecting the information to his main point. Second, Jeff knew he had to go back to the well: He needed to return to the library and recheck his sources to find more information on what family friends can do to help.

# Revising for Information

I know. You thought you were done digging. But as I said last week, research is a recursive process. (Remember, the word is *research,* or "look again.") You will often find yourself circling back to the earlier steps as you get a clearer sense of where you want to go.

As you stand back from your draft, looking again at how well your research paper accomplishes your purpose, you'll likely see holes in the information. They may seem more like craters. Jeff discovered he had to reresearch his topic, returning to the library to hunt for new sources to help him develop his point. Since he had enough time, he repeated some of the research steps from the third week, beginning with a first-level search (see "First-Level Searching" in Chapter 3). This time, though, he knew exactly what he needed to find.

You may find that you basically have what information you need but that your draft requires more development. Candy's draft on how child abuse affects language included material from some useful studies from the *Journal of Speech and Hearing Disorders,* which showed pretty conclusively that abuse cripples children's abilities to converse. At her reader's suggestion, Candy decided it was important to write more in her revision about what was learned from the studies, since they offered convincing evidence for her thesis. Though she could mine her notes for more information, Candy decided to recheck the journal indexes to look for any similar studies she may have missed. As you begin to see exactly what information you need, don't rule out another trip to the library, even this late in the game.

## Finding Quick Facts

The holes of information in your research paper draft may not be large at all. What's missing may be an important but discrete fact that would really help your readers understand the point you're making. For example, in Janabeth's draft on the impact of divorce on father-daughter relationships, she realized she was missing an important fact: the number of marriages that end in divorce in the United States. This single piece of information could help establish the significance of the problem she was writing about. Janabeth could search her sources for the answer, but there's a quicker way: fact books.

One of the Internet's greatest strengths is its usefulness in searching for specific facts. A few days ago, for example, my daughter Julia—who was studying China in the first grade—wanted to know the height of the Great Wall. The answer is thirty feet. We found it in minutes by consulting an online encyclopedia. As always, there are a range of statistical references on the Web. One place to start is the site that claims to be "the single best source for facts on the Net":

www.refdesk.com

I'm inclined to agree. The site has links to encyclopedias, biographical indexes, newspapers and magazines, dictionaries, and government information. Even better, refdesk.com has a convenient "Fast Facts" search engine that will return up-to-date information from a keyword search.

The standard print texts for researchers hunting down facts and statistics are still quite useful. They include the *Statistical Abstracts of the United States*, the *Information Please Alamanc, Facts on File,* and the *World Almanac Book of Facts*—all published annually—but a number of these in abbreviated versions are now available on the Web. See Figure 5.1 for an example.

Fact books and online sources can be valuable sources of information that will plug small holes in your draft. These references are especially useful during revision, when you often know exactly what fact you need. But even if you're not sure whether you can glean a useful statistic from one of these sources, they might be worth checking anyway. There's a good chance you'll find something useful.

**FIGURE 5.1** **Home Page of U.S. Census Bureau**
The U.S. Census Bureau offers a wealth of statistical information, including data from the 2000 census. The site, at www.census.gov, includes a search tool called "American Fact Finder" that will help you locate statistics about population, geography, business, housing, and industry. The results can be national statistics all the way down to data about a particular county.

# Revising for Language

Most of my students have the impression that revision begins and ends with concerns about language—about *how* they said it rather than *what* they said. Revising for language is really a tertiary concern (though an important one), to be addressed after the writer has struggled with the purpose and design of a draft.

Once you're satisfied that your paper's purpose is clear, that it provides readers with the information they need to understand what you're trying to say, and that it is organized in a logical, interesting way, *then* focus your attention on the fine points of *how* it is written. Begin with voice.

## Listening to the Voice

*Listen* to your paper by reading it aloud to yourself. You may find the experience a little unsettling. Most of us are not used to actively listening to our writing voices. But your readers will be listening.

As you read, ask yourself: Is this the voice you want readers to hear? Does it seem appropriate for this paper? Does it sound flat or wooden or ponderous in any places? Does it sound anything like you?

If revising your writing voice is necessary for any reason, begin at the beginning—the first line, the first paragraph—and rely on your ears. What sounds right?

You may discover that you begin with the right voice but lose it in places. That often happens when you move from anecdotal material to exposition, from telling a story to explaining research findings. To some extent, a shift in voice is inevitable when you move from one method of development to another, especially from personal material to factual material. But examine your word choices in those passages that seem to go flat. Do you sometimes shift to the dry language used by your sources? Can you rewrite that language in your own voice? When you do, you will find yourself cutting away unnecessary, vague, and pretentious language.

Rewriting in your own voice has another effect, too: It brings the writing to life. Readers respond to an individual writing voice. When I read David Quammen, an author whose work you've read in this text, it rises up from the page, like a hologram, and suddenly, I can see him as a distinct individual. I also become interested in how he sees the things he's writing about.

### *Avoid Sounding Glib*

Beware, though, of a voice that calls more attention to itself than the substance of what you're saying. As you've no doubt learned from reading scholarly sources, much academic writing is voiceless, partly because what's important is not *who* the writer is but *what* he has to say.

Sometimes, in an attempt to sound natural, a writer will take on a folksy or overly colloquial voice, which is much worse than sounding lifeless. What impression does the following passage give you?

```
The thing that really blew my mind was that

marijuana use among college students had actually
```

declined in the past ten years! I was psyched to
learn that.

Ugh!

As you search for the right voice in doing your revision, look for
a balance between flat, wooden prose, which sounds as if it were man-
ufactured by a machine, and forced, flowery prose, which distracts the
reader from what's most important: what you're trying to say.

## How to Control Information

One of the basic challenges of writing with sources is integrating them seamlessly. In the past, you may have practiced the "data
dump" strategy, or simply dropping factual information into your
papers in little or big clumps. Of course, this won't do. Not only does
it make the writing horribly dull, but it means that you're not *making
use* of the information you worked so hard to find. Surrounding your
sources with your own prose and purposes is an important skill you
need to learn. Let's see how it might work. Here are three facts from
the "Harper's Index," a monthly feature in *Harper's Magazine*:

**THREE FACTS**

1. Chance that an American filing for bankruptcy last year did so
   because of medical expenses: 1 in 2
2. Percentage change last year in the total profits of Fortune 500
   pharmaceutical companies: +35
3. Percentage changes in the total profits of all Fortune 500
   companies: $-54$[1]

Juxtaposed like this, these three facts tell a story which is merely
implied if they stand alone. How might they be integrated smoothly
into a paragraph that tells that story? Here's one possibility:

**VERSION 1**

According to the "Harper's Index," a monthly list
of facts gleaned from mostly government sources,
half of the people filing for bankruptcy in the
United States last year did so "because of medical
expenses." Fortune 500 drug companies, though,
increased profits by 35% while other Fortune 500

[1]"Harper's Index." *Harper's Magazine*. August 2002: 13.

```
companies lost money. This suggests that drug
companies might be making money at the expense of
their customers (13).
```

This isn't bad. Version 1 nicely uses the attribution tag, "According to . . . ," and includes information about the source of the information. The version is also careful to reword the original text. It certainly states a possible implication of the facts, so the writer offers some analysis or interpretation of the information's significance. Still, it seems lifeless and dry.

**VERSION 2**

```
There is dramatic evidence that drug companies
have fared far better than the largest American
companies in the last year. According to the
"Harper's Index," a monthly feature in Harper's
Magazine, the "total profits" of Fortune 500 com-
panies dropped by a stunning 54% while the drug
companies on the same list enjoyed a 35% gain.
What might this mean for consumers? Though I can't
claim that there's a direct correlation between
company profits and the cost of their drugs from
these statistics, it is telling that about half of
all American bankruptcies were caused by one
thing: medical expenses (13).
```

This strikes me as far more lively and interesting, and a more seamless integration of the three facts. Do you think so? It's not hard to sense the difference between versions 1 and 2 but what accounts for them might at first seem pretty subtle. Note the underlined passages in the second version, as well as how the writer seems to surround the information with his own voice and purpose. In particular, consider

■ *Active verbs that make things happen*—"fared" and "enjoyed."

■ *The careful attribution of the source and brief explanation of its origin* (A "monthly feature of *Harper's Magazine* . . ."). An explanation isn't always necessary but can be helpful if readers might be unfamiliar with the source.

■ *The moves to interpret the significance of the information both before and after the facts are mentioned:* The evidence that drug companies profit is "dramatic" and the observation that the causes of bankruptcies may be "telling", both interpret the significance of the facts. Part of controlling factual information is both characterizing its importance, commenting on its relevance or analyzing its significance.

■ *The use of a question to interrogate the information:* This is a very common analytical move that allows writers to put forth their particular interest in the information and their particular purposes in citing it. What question you ask and when you ask it is a great way to get control of information.

■ *Using hedges when necessary:* Words like "probably" or "perhaps," or in this case, "though I can't claim," open your analysis of information to speculation, theories, and possibilities. This is a quite conventional move in academic writing and frees you to mine the research sources without pretending certainty.

What else do you notice about the two versions?

## Scrutinizing Paragraphs

### How Well Do You Integrate Sources?

Go over your draft, paragraph by paragraph, and look for ways to *use* the information from your research more smoothly. Be especially alert to "hanging quotes" that appear unattached to any source. Attribution is important. To anchor quotes and ideas to people or publications in your paper, use words such as *argues, observes, says, contends, believes,* and *offers* and phrases such as *according to.* Also look for ways to use quotes selectively, lifting key words or phrases and weaving them into your own writing. What can you add that highlights what you believe is significant about the information? How does it relate to your thesis and the purpose of your paper?

### Is Each Paragraph Unified?

Each paragraph should be about one idea and organized around it. You probably know that already. But applying this notion is a particular problem in a research paper, where information abounds and paragraphs sometimes approach marathon length.

If any of your paragraphs are similar to that—that is, they seem to run nearly a page or more—look for ways to break them up into shorter paragraphs. Is more than one idea embedded in the long version? Are you explaining or examining more than one thing?

Also take a look at your shorter paragraphs. Do any present minor or tangential ideas that belong somewhere else? Are any of these ideas irrelevant? Should the paragraph be cut? The cut-and-paste exercise (Exercise 5.3) may have helped you with this already.

## Scrutinizing Sentences

### Using Active Voice

Which of these two sentences seems more passive, more lifeless?

```
Steroids have been used by many high school

athletes.
```

*or*

```
Many high school athletes use steroids.
```

The first version, written in the passive voice, is clearly the more limp of the two. It's not grammatically incorrect. In fact, you may have found texts written in the passive voice to be pervasive in the reading you've done for your research paper. Research writing is plagued by passive voice, and that's one of the reasons it can be so mind numbing to read.

*Passive voice* construction is simple: The subject of the sentence—the thing *doing the action*—becomes the thing *acted upon* by the verb. For instance:

```
Clarence kicked the dog.
```

*versus*

```
The dog was kicked by Clarence.
```

Sometimes, the subject may be missing altogether, as in:

```
The study was released.
```

*Who* or *what* released it?

*Active voice* remedies the problem by pushing the subject up front in the sentence or adding the subject if he, she, or it is missing. For example:

```
High school athletes use steroids.
```

Knowing exactly who is using the drugs makes the sentence livelier.

Another telltale sign of passive voice is that it usually requires a *to be* verb: *is, was, are, were, am, be, being, been.* For example:

```
Alcoholism among women has been extensively studied.
```

Search your draft for *be's,* and see if any sentences are written in the passive voice. (If you write on a computer, some word-processing programs will search for you.) To make a sentence active, replace the missing subject:

```
Researchers have extensively studied alcoholism

among women.
```

See the box "Active Verbs for Discussing Ideas," which was compiled by a colleague of mine, Cinthia Gannett. If you're desperate for an alternative to *says* or *argues,* this list offers 138 alternatives.

## Using Strong Verbs

Though this may seem like nit-picking, you'd be amazed how much writing in the active voice can revitalize research writing. The use of strong verbs can have the same effect.

As you know, verbs make things happen. Some verbs can make the difference between a sentence that crackles and one that merely hums. Instead of this:

```
The league gave Roger Clemens, the New York

Yankees pitcher, a $10,000 fine for arguing with

an umpire.
```

write this:

```
The league slapped Roger Clemens, the New York

Yankees pitcher, with a $10,000 fine for arguing

with an umpire.
```

## Varying Sentence Length

Some writers can sustain breathlessly long sentences, with multiple subordinate clauses, and not lose their readers. Joan Didion is one of those writers. Actually, she also knows enough not to do it

## Active Verbs for Discussing Ideas

| | | | |
|---|---|---|---|
| informs | protects | cautions | confronts |
| reviews | insists | shares | regards |
| argues | handles | convinces | toys with |
| states | confuses | declares | hypothesizes |
| synthesizes | intimates | ratifies | suggests |
| asserts | simplifies | analyzes | contradicts |
| claims | narrates | affirms | considers |
| answers | outlines | exaggerates | highlights |
| responds | allows | observes | disconfirms |
| critiques | initiates | substitutes | admires |
| explains | asserts | perceives | endorses |
| illuminates | supports | resolves | uncovers |
| determines | compares | assaults | hesitates |
| challenges | distinguishes | disputes | denies |
| experiments | describes | conflates | refutes |
| experiences | assists | retorts | assembles |
| pleads | sees | reconciles | demands |
| defends | persuades | complicates | criticizes |
| rejects | lists | urges | negates |
| reconsiders | quotes | reads | diminishes |
| verifies | exposes | parses | shows |
| announces | warns | concludes | supplements |
| provides | believes | stresses | accepts |
| formulates | categorizes | facilitates | buttresses |
| qualifies | disregards | contrasts | relinquishes |
| hints | tests | discusses | treats |
| repudiates | postulates | guides | clarifies |
| infers | acknowledges | proposes | grants |
| marshalls | defies | points out | insinuates |
| summarizes | accepts | judges | identifies |
| disagrees | emphasizes | enumerates | explains |
| rationalizes | confirms | reveals | interprets |
| shifts | praises | condemns | adds |
| maintains | supplies | implies | |
| persists | seeks | reminds | |

*Source:* Reproduced with permission of Cinthia Gannett.

too often. She carefully varies the lengths of her sentences, going from a breathless one to one that can be quickly inhaled and back again. For example, here is how her essay "Dreamers of the Golden Dream" begins. Notice the mix of sentence lengths.

> This is the story about love and death in the golden land, and begins with the country. The San Bernadino Valley lies only an hour east of Los Angeles by the San Bernadino Freeway but is in certain ways an alien place: not the coastal California of the subtropical twilights and the soft westerlies off the Pacific but a harsher California, haunted by the Mojave just beyond the mountains, devastated by the hot dry Santa Ana wind that comes down through the passes at 100 miles an hour and whines through the eucalyptus windbreaks and works on the nerves. October is a bad month for the wind, the month when breathing is difficult and the hills blaze up spontaneously. There has been no rain since April. Every voice seems a scream. It is the season of suicide and divorce and prickly dread, wherever the wind blows.*

The second sentence of Didion's lead is a whopper, but it works, especially since it's set among sentences that are more than half its length. Didion makes music here.

Examine your sentences. Are the long ones too long? You can usually tell if, when you read a sentence, there's no sense of emphasis or it seems to die out. Can you break an unnecessarily long sentence into several shorter ones? More common is a string of short, choppy sentences. For example:

```
Babies are born extrasensitive to sounds. This
unique sensitivity to all sounds does not last.
By the end of the first year, they become deaf to
speech sounds not a part of their native language.
```

This isn't horrible, but with some sentence combining, the passage will be more fluent:

```
Though babies are born extrasensitive to sounds,
this unique sensitivity lasts only through the end
```

*Joan Didion, *Slouching Toward Bethlehem* (New York: Pocket, 1968).

of the first year, when they become deaf to speech
sounds not a part of their native language.

Look for short sentences where you are repeating words or
phrases and also for sentences that begin with pronouns. Experiment with sentence combining. The result will be not only more fluent prose but a sense of emphasis, a sense of the relationship
between the information and your ideas about it.

## Editing for Simplicity

Thoreau saw simplicity as a virtue, something that's obvious not
only by the time he spent beside Walden Pond but also by the prose
he penned while living there. Thoreau writes clearly and plainly.

Somewhere, many of us got the idea that simplicity in writing
is a vice—that the long word is better than the short word, that the
complex phrase is superior to the simple one. The misconception is
that to write simply is to be simple minded. Research papers, especially, suffer from this mistaken notion. They are often filled with
what writer William Zinsser calls *clutter*.

## EXERCISE 5.4

### Cutting Clutter

The following passage is an example of cluttered writing at its
best (worst?). It contains phrases and words that often appear in college
research papers. Read the passage once. Then take a few minutes and
rewrite it, cutting as many words as you can without sacrificing the
meaning. Look for ways to substitute a shorter word for a longer one
and to say in fewer words what is currently said in many. Try to cut the
word count by half.

The implementation of the revised alcohol policy
in the university community is regrettable at the
present time due to the fact that the administra-
tion has not facilitated sufficient student input,
in spite of the fact that there have been attempts
by the people affected by this policy to make
their objections known in many instances.
*(55 words)*

If you found yourself getting a little ruthless as you edited this rather dead passage, it's all right. The passage needed some machete work. A stock phrase such as *due to the fact that,* which often appears in research papers, can be resurrected quite simply by using the word *because.* A fancy word such as *implementation* can be replaced with a simple one such as *start.* There's a lot of clutter like this in the previous passage.

I hope you will also see that simplifying the prose here does not make it more simple minded but simply more clear. Cluttered writing, which is often intended to impress readers, ends up turning them off.

Of course, it's easy to be ruthless editing someone else's work. Can you be equally ruthless with your own? Take a random page of your draft research paper, and cut *at least* seven words. Look at the kinds of clutter you cut away. Do you use long words when short ones will do just as well? Do you resort to stock phrases, such as *at the present time (now)*? Do you signal to the reader what should be obvious with phrases such as *In conclusion* or *It should be pointed out* or *It is my opinion that?*

After you study a page of your draft and see the kinds of clutter that creep into your writing, edit the rest. The rule is to simplify, simplify, making every word count.

# Preparing the Final Manuscript

I wanted to title this section "Preparing the Final Draft," but it occurred to me that *draft* doesn't suggest anything final. I always call my work a draft because until it's out of my hands, it never feels finished. You may feel that way, too. You've spent five weeks on this paper—and the last few days, disassembling it and putting it back together again. How do you know when you're finally done?

For many students, the deadline dictates that: The paper is due tomorrow. But you may find that your paper really seems to be coming together in a satisfying way. You may even like it, and you're ready to prepare the final manuscript.

## Considering "Reader-Friendly" Design

Later in this section, we'll discuss the format of your final draft. Research papers in some disciplines have prescribed forms. Some papers in the social sciences, for example, require an abstract, an introduction, a discussion of method, a presentation of results, and a discussion of those results. These sections are clearly defined using subheadings, making it easier for readers to examine those parts of the paper they're most interested in. You probably discovered that in your own reading of formal research. You'll likely learn the formats research papers should conform to in various disciplines as you take upper-level courses in those fields.

While you should document this paper properly, you may have some freedom to develop a format that best serves your purpose. As you consider the format of your rewrite, keep readers in mind. How can you make your paper more readable? How can you signal your plan for developing the topic and what's important? Some visual devices might help, including:

- Subheadings
- Graphs, illustrations, tables
- Bulleted lists (like the one you're reading now)
- Block quotes
- Underlining and paragraphing for emphasis
- White space

Long, unbroken pages of text can appear to be a gray, uninviting mass to the reader. All of the devices listed help break up the text, making it more "reader friendly." Subheadings, if not overly used, can also cue your reader to significant sections of your paper and how they relate to the whole. Long quotes, those over four lines, should be blocked, or indented ten spaces (rather than the usual five spaces customary for indenting paragraphs), separating them from the rest of the text. (See Chapter 4, "Writing with Sources," for more on blocking quotes.) Bullets—dots or asterisks preceding brief items—can be used to highlight a quick list of important information. Graphs, tables, and illustrations also break up the text, but more importantly, they can help clarify and explain information. (See "Placement of Tables, Charts, and Illustrations," in Appendix A.)

The format of the book you're reading is intended, in part, to make it accessible to readers. As you revise, consider how the look of your paper can make it more inviting and easily understood.

## Following MLA Conventions

I've already mentioned that formal research papers in various disciplines may have prescribed formats. If your instructor expects a certain format, he has probably detailed exactly what that format should be. But in all likelihood, your essay for this class doesn't need to follow a rigid form. It will, however, probably adhere to the basic

Modern Language Association (MLA) guidelines, described in detail in Appendix A. There, you'll find methods for formatting your paper and instructions for citing sources on your "Works Cited" page. You'll also find a sample paper in MLA style by Alexander M. Siegwin, "The Adonis Complex: Progressing to Failure." The American Psychological Association (APA) guidelines for research papers, the primary alternative to MLA, are described in Appendix B. Again, you'll also find a sample paper, this one by T. J. Fuller, titled "Racism in America: Still Going Strong."

## Proofreading Your Paper

You've spent weeks researching, writing, and revising your paper. You want to stop now. That's understandable, no matter how much you were driven by your curiosity. Before you sign off on your research paper, placing it in someone else's hands, take the time to proofread it.

I was often so glad to be done with a piece of writing that I was careless about proofreading it. That changed about ten years ago, after I submitted a portfolio of writing to complete my master's degree. I was pretty proud of it, especially an essay about dealing with my father's alcoholism. Unfortunately, I misspelled that word—*alcoholism*—every time I used it. It was pretty humiliating.

### Proofreading on a Computer

Proofreading used to involve gobbing on correction fluid to cover up mistakes and then trying to line up the paper and type in the changes. If you write on a computer, you're spared from that ordeal. The text can be easily manipulated on the screen.

Software programs can also help with the job. Most word-processing programs, for example, come with spelling checkers. These programs don't flag problems with sentence structure or the misuse of words, but they do catch typos and consecutive repetitions of words. A spelling checker is mighty handy. Learn how to use it.

Some programs will count the number of words in your sentences, alerting you to particularly long ones, and will even point out uses of passive voice. I find some of these programs irritating because they evaluate writing ability based on factors such as sentence length, which may not be a measure of the quality of your work at all. But for a basic review, these programs can be extremely useful, particularly for flagging passive construction.

Many writers find they need to print out their paper and proofread the hard copy. They argue that they catch more mistakes if they proofread on paper than if they proofread onscreen. It makes sense, especially if you've been staring at the screen for days. A printed copy of your paper *looks* different, and I think you see it differently, maybe with fresher eyes and attitude. You might notice things you didn't notice before. You decide for yourself how and when to proofread.

## Looking Closely

You've already edited the manuscript, pruning sentences and tightening things up. Now hunt for the little errors in grammar and mechanics that you missed. Aside from misspellings (usually typos), some pretty common mistakes appear in the papers I see. For practice, see if you can catch some of them in the following exercise.

## EXERCISE 5.5

### Picking Off the Lint

I have a colleague who compares proofreading to picking the lint off an outfit, which is often your final step before heading out the door. Examine the following excerpt from a student paper. Proofread it, catching as many mechanical errors as possible. Note punctuation mistakes, agreement problems, misspellings, and anything else that seems off.

> In an important essay, Melody Graulich notes how
> "rigid dichotomizing of sex roles" in most fron-
> tier myths have "often handicapped and confused
> male as well as female writers (187)," she
> wonders if a "universel mythology" (198) might
> emerge that is less confining for both of them.
> In Bruce Mason, Wallace Stegner seems to experi-
> ment with this idea; acknowledging the power of
> Bo's male fantasies <u>and</u> Elsa's ability to teach
> her son to feel. It is his strenth. On the other
> hand, Bruces brother chet, who dies young, lost
> and broken, seems doomed because he lacked suffi-
> cient measure of both the feminine and masculine.
> He observes that Chet had "enough of the old man

```
to spoil him, ebnough of his mother to soften him,

not enough of either to save him (Big Rock, 521)."
```

If you did this exercise in class, compare your proofreading of this passage with that of a partner. What did each of you find?

## Ten Common Mistakes

The following is a list of the ten most common errors (besides misspelled words) made in research papers that should be caught in careful proofreading. A number of these errors occurred in the previous exercise.

1. Beware of commonly confused words, such as *your* instead of *you're*. Here's a list of others:

| | |
|---|---|
| their/there/they're | advice/advise |
| know/now | lay/lie |
| accept/except | its/it's |
| all ready/already | passed/past |

2. Watch for possessives. Instead of *my fathers alcoholism,* the correct style is *my father's alcoholism.* Remember that if a noun ends in *s,* still add *'s: Tess's laughter.* If a noun is plural, just add the apostrophe: *the scientists' studies.*

3. Avoid vague pronoun references. The excerpt in Exercise 5.5 ends with the sentence *He observes that Chet . . . .* Who's *he?* The sentence should read, *Bruce observes that Chet . . . .* Whenever you use the pronouns *he, she, it, they,* and *their,* make sure each clearly refers to someone or something.

4. Subjects and verbs must agree. If the subject is singular, its verb must be, too:

```
The perils of acid rain are many.
```

What confuses writers sometimes is the appearance of a noun that is not really the subject near the verb. Exercise 5.5 begins, for example, with this sentence:

```
In an important essay, Melody Graulich notes

how "rigid dichotomizing of sex roles" in most

frontier myths have "often handicapped and

confused male as well as female writers."
```

The subject here is not *frontier myths* but *rigid dichotomizing,* a singular subject. The sentence should read:

```
In an important essay, Melody Graulich notes how

"rigid dichotomizing of sex roles" in most fron-

tier myths has "often handicapped and confused

male as well as female writers."
```

The verb *has* may sound funny, but it's correct.

5. Punctuate quotes properly. Note that commas belong inside quotation marks, not outside. Periods belong inside, too. Colons and semicolons are exceptions—they belong *outside* quotation marks. Blocked quotes don't need quotation marks at all unless there is a quote within the quote.

6. Scrutinize use of commas. Could you substitute periods or semicolons instead? If so, you may be looking at *comma splices* or *run-on sentences.* Here's an example:

```
Since 1980, the use of marijuana by college stu-

dents has steadily declined, this was something of

a surprise to me and my friends.
```

The portion after the comma, *this was . . . ,* is another sentence. The comma should be a period, and *this* should be capitalized.

7. Make sure each parenthetical citation *precedes* the period in the sentence you're citing but *follows* the quotation mark at the end of a sentence. In MLA style, there is no comma between the author's name and page number: (Marks 99).

8. Use dashes correctly. Though they can be overused, dashes are a great way to break the flow of a sentence with a related bit of information. You've probably noticed I like them. In a manuscript, type dashes as *two* hyphens (- -), not one.

9. After mentioning the full name of someone in your paper, normally use her *last name* in subsequent references. For example, this is incorrect:

```
Denise Grady argues that people are genetically pre-

disposed to obesity. Denise also believes that some

people are "programmed to convert calories to fat."
```

Unless you know Denise or for some other reason want to conceal her last name, change the second sentence to this:

```
Grady also believes that some people are

"programmed to convert calories to fat."
```

One exception to this is when writing about literature. It is often appropriate to refer to characters by their first names, particularly if characters share last names (as in Exercise 5.5).

10. Scrutinize use of colons and semicolons. A colon is usually used to call attention to what follows it: a list, quotation, or appositive. A colon should follow an independent clause. For example, this won't do:

```
The most troubling things about child abuse are: the

effects on self-esteem and language development.
```

In this case, eliminate the colon. A semicolon is often used as if it were a colon or a comma. In most cases, a semicolon should be used as a period, separating two independent clauses. The semicolon simply implies the clauses are closely related.

## Using the "Search" Function

If you're writing on a computer, use the "Search" function—a feature in most word-processing programs—to help you track down consistent problems. You simply tell the computer what word or punctuation to look for, and it will locate all occurrences in the text. For example, if you want to check for comma splices, search for commas. The cursor will stop on every comma, and you can verify if it is correct. You can also search for pronouns to locate vague references or for words (like those listed in 1 above) you commonly misuse.

## Avoiding Sexist Language

One last proofreading task is to do a *man* and *he* check. Until recently, sexism wasn't an issue in language. Use of words such as *mankind* and *chairman* was acceptable; the implication was that the terms applied to both genders. At least, that's how use of the terms was defended when challenged. Critics argued that words such as *mailman* and *businessman* reinforced ideas that only men could fill these roles. Bias in language is subtle but powerful. And it's often unintentional. To avoid sending the wrong message, it's worth making the effort to avoid sexist language.

If you need to use a word with a *man* suffix, check to see if there is an alternative. *Congressperson* sounds pretty clunky, but *representative* works fine. Instead of *mankind,* why not *humanity?* Substitute *camera operator* for *cameraman.*

Also check use of pronouns. Do you use *he* or *his* in places where you mean both genders? For example:

```
The writer who cares about his topic will bring it
to life for his readers.
```

Since a lot of writers are women, this doesn't seem right. How do you solve this problem?

1. Use *his or her, he or she,* or that mutation *s/he.* For example:

```
The writer who cares about his or her topic will
bring it to life for his or her readers.
```

This is an acceptable solution, but using *his or her* repeatedly can be awkward.

2. Change the singular subject to plural. For example:

```
Writers who care about their topics will bring
them to life for their readers.
```

This version is much better and avoids discriminatory language altogether.

3. Alternate *he* and *she, his* and *hers* whenever you encounter an indefinite person. If you have referred to a writer as *he* on one page, make the writer *she* on the next page, as long as you are not talking about the same person. Alternate throughout.

# Looking Back and Moving On

This book began with your writing, and it also will end with it. Before you close your research notebook on this project, open it one last time and fastwrite your response to the following questions. Keep your pen moving for seven minutes.

How was your experience writing this research paper different from that writing others? How was it the same?

When students share their fastwrites, this comment is typical: "It was easier to sit down and write this research paper than others I've written." One student last semester added, "I think it was easier because before writing the paper, I got to research something I wanted to know about and learn the answers to questions that mattered to me." If this research project was successful, you took charge of your own learning, as this student did.

Your research paper wasn't necessarily fun. Research takes time, and writing is work. Every week, you had new problems to solve. But if the questions you asked about your topic mattered, then you undoubtedly had moments, perhaps late at night in the library, when you encountered something that suddenly cracked your topic open and let the light come pouring out. The experience can be dazzling. It's even great when it's merely interesting.

What might you take away from this research paper that will prepare you for doing the next one? At the very least, I hope you've cultivated basic research skills: how to find information efficiently, how to document, how to avoid plagiarism, and how to take notes. But hopefully, you've learned more. Perhaps you've recovered a part of you that may have been left behind when you turned eleven or twelve—the curiosity that drove you to put bugs in mayonnaise jars, read about China, disassemble a transistor radio, and wonder about Mars. Curiosity is a handy thing in college. It gets you thinking. And that's the idea.

# Guide to MLA Style

This section contains guidelines for preparing your essay in the format recommended by the Modern Language Association, or MLA. Part One, "Citing Sources in Your Essay," will be particularly useful as you write your draft; it provides guidance on how to parenthetically cite the sources you use in the text of your essay. Part Two, "How the Essay Should Look," will help you with formatting the manuscript after you've revised it, including guidelines for margins, tables, and pagination. Part Three, "Preparing the 'Works Cited' Page," offers detailed instructions on how to prepare your bibliography at the end of your essay; this is usually one of the last steps in preparing the final manuscript. Finally, Part Four presents a sample research essay in MLA style, which will show you how it all comes together.

# Directory of MLA Style

# Part One: Citing Sources in Your Essay

## 1.1 When to Cite

Before examining the details of how to use parenthetical citations, remember when you must cite sources in your paper:

1. Whenever you quote from an original source
2. Whenever you borrow ideas from an original source, even when you express them in your own words by paraphrasing or summarizing
3. Whenever you borrow factual information from a source that is *not common knowledge*

**The Common Knowledge Exception.**    The business about *common knowledge* causes much confusion. Just what does this term mean? Basically, *common knowledge* means facts that are widely known and about which there is no controversy.

Sometimes, it's really obvious whether something is common knowledge. The fact that the Super Bowl occurs in late January and pits the winning teams from the American and National Football Conferences is common knowledge. The fact that former president Ronald Reagan was once an actor and starred in a movie with a chimpanzee is common knowledge, too. And the fact that most Americans get most of their news from television is also common knowledge, though this information is getting close to leaving the domain of common knowledge.

But what about Christine's assertion that most dreaming occurs during rapid eye movement (REM) sleep? This is an idea about which all of her sources seem to agree. Does that make it common knowledge?

It's useful to ask next, How common to whom? Experts in the topic at hand or the rest of us? As a rule, consider the knowledge of your readers. What information will not be familiar to most of your readers or may even surprise them? Which ideas might even raise skepticism? In this case, the fact about REM sleep and dreaming goes slightly beyond the knowledge of most readers, so to be safe, it should be cited. Use common sense, but when in doubt, cite.

## 1.2 The MLA Author/Page System

Starting in 1984, the Modern Language Association (MLA), a body that, among other things, decides documentation conventions for papers in the humanities, switched from footnotes to the author/page parenthetical citation system. The American Psychological Association (APA), a similar body for the social sciences, promotes use of the author/date system.

You will find it fairly easy to switch from one system to the other once you've learned both. Since MLA conventions are appropriate for English classes, we will focus on the author/page system in the following sections. APA standards are explained more fully in Appendix B, which also includes a sample paper.

**The Basics of Using Parenthetical Citation.**   The MLA method of in-text citation is fairly simple: As close as possible to the borrowed material, you indicate in parentheses the original source (usually, the author's name) and the page number in the work that material came from. For example, here's how you'd cite a book or article with a single author using the author/page system:

> From the very beginning of <u>Sesame Street</u> in 1969,
> kindergarten teachers discovered that incoming
> students who had watched the program already knew
> their ABCs (Chira 13).*

The parenthetical citation here tells readers two things: (1) This information about the success of *Sesame Street* does not originate with the writer but with someone named *Chira,* and (2) readers can consult the original source for further information by looking on page 13 of Chira's book or article, which is cited fully at the back of the paper in the "Works Cited." Here is what readers would find there:

> Works Cited
>
> Chira, Susan. "<u>Sesame Street</u> At 20: Taking Stock."
>
> <u>New York Times</u> 15 Nov. 1989: 13.

Here's another example of parenthetical author/page citation from another research paper. Note the differences from the previous example:

> "One thing is clear," writes Thomas Mallon,
> "plagiarism didn't become a truly sore point

---

*This and the following "Works Cited" example are used with permission of Heidi R. Dunham.

```
with writers until they thought of writing as
their trade. . . . Suddenly his capital and
identity were at stake" (3-4).
```

The first thing you may have noticed is that the author's last name—Mallon—was omitted from the parenthetical citation. It didn't need to be included, since it had already been mentioned in the text. *If you mention the author's name in the text of your paper, then you only need to parenthetically cite the relevant page number(s).* This citation also tells us that the quoted passage comes from two pages rather than one.

## 1.3  Placement of Citations

Place the citation as close as you can to the borrowed material, trying to avoid breaking the flow of the sentences, if possible. To avoid confusion about what's borrowed and what's not—particularly in passages longer than a sentence—mention the name of the original author *in your paper*. Note that in the next example the writer simply cites the source at the end of the paragraph, not naming the source in the text. Doing so makes it hard for the reader to figure out whether Blager is the source of the information in the entire paragraph or just part of it:

```
Though children who have been sexually abused
seem to be disadvantaged in many areas, including
the inability to forge lasting relationships,
low self-esteem, and crippling shame, they seem
advantaged in other areas. Sexually abused
children seem to be more socially mature than
other children of their same age group. It's
a distinctly mixed blessing (Blager 994).
```

In the following example, notice how the ambiguity about what's borrowed and what's not is resolved by careful placement of the author's name and parenthetical citation in the text:

```
Though children who have been sexually abused
seem to be disadvantaged in many areas, including
```

## Citations That Go with the Flow

There's no getting around it—parenthetical citations can be like stones on the sidewalk. Readers stride through a sentence in your essay and then have to step around the citation at the end before they resume their walk. Yet citations are important in academic writing because they help readers know who you read or heard that shaped your thinking.

However, you can minimize citations that trip up readers and make your essay more readable.

- Avoid lengthy parenthetical citations by mentioning the name of the author in your essay. That way, you usually only have to include a page number in the citation.
- Try to place citations where readers are likely to pause anyway—for example, the end of the sentence, or right before a comma.
- Remember you *don't* even need a citation when you're citing common knowledge, or referring to an entire work by an author.
- If you're borrowing from only one source in a paragraph of your essay, and all of the borrowed material comes from a single page of that source, don't bother repeating the citation over and over again with each new bit of information. Just put the citation at the end of the paragraph.

```
the inability to forge lasting relationships,
low self-esteem, and crippling shame, they seem
advantaged in other areas. According to Blager,
sexually abused children seem to be more socially
mature than other children of their same age group
(994). It's a distinctly mixed blessing.
```

In this latter version, it's clear that Blager is the source for one sentence in the paragraph, and the writer is responsible for the rest. Generally, use an authority's last name, rather than a formal title or first name, when mentioning her in your text. Also note that the citation is placed *inside* the period of the sentence (or last sentence) that it documents. That's almost always the case, except at the end of a blocked quotation, where the parenthetical reference is placed after the period of the last sentence. The citation can also be placed near the author's name, rather than at the end of the sentence, if it doesn't unnecessarily break the flow of the sentence. For example:

```
Blager (994) observes that sexually abused
children tend to be more socially mature than
other children of their same age group.
```

## 1.4 When You Mention the Author's Name

It's generally good practice in research writing to identify who said what. The familiar convention of using attribution tags such as "According to Fletcher . . ." or "Fletcher argues . . ." and so on helps readers attach a name with a voice, or an individual with certain claims or findings. When you do mention the author of a source, then you can drop his or her name for the parenthetical citation and just list the page number. For example,

```
Robert Harris believes that there is "widespread
uncertainty" among students about what constitutes
plagiarism (2).
```

We may also list the page number directly after the author's name.

```
Robert Harris (2) believes that there is
"widespread uncertainty" among students about what
constitutes plagiarism.
```

## 1.5 When There Is No Author

Occasionally, you may encounter a source in which the author is anonymous—the article doesn't have a byline, or for some reason the author hasn't been identified. This isn't unusual with pamphlets, editorials, government documents, some newspaper articles, online sources, and short filler articles in magazines. If you can't parenthetically name the author, what do you cite?

Most often, cite the title (or an abbreviated version, if the title is long) and the page number. If you choose to abbreviate the title, begin with the word under which it is alphabetized in the "Works Cited." For example:

```
Simply put, public relations is "doing good and
getting credit" for it (Getting Yours 3).
```

Here is how the publication cited above would be listed at the back of the paper:

```
                    Works Cited
Getting Yours: A Publicity and Funding Primer
        for Nonprofit and Voluntary Organizations.
    Lincoln: Contact Center, 1991.
```

For clarity, it's helpful to mention the original source of the borrowed material in the text of your paper. When there is no author's name, refer to the publication (or institution) you're citing or make a more general reference to the source. For example:

```
An article in Cuisine magazine argues that the
best way to kill a lobster is to plunge a knife
between its eyes ("How to Kill" 56).
```

*or*

```
According to one government report, with the
current minimum size limit, most lobsters end up
on dinner plates before they've had a chance to
reproduce ("Size at Sexual Maturity" 3-4).
```

## 1.6  Works by the Same Author

Suppose you end up using several books or articles by the same author. Obviously, a parenthetical citation that merely lists the author's name and page number won't do, since it won't be clear *which* of several works the citation refers to. In this case, include the author's name, an abbreviated title (if the original is too long), and the page number. For example:

```
The thing that distinguishes the amateur from the
experienced writer is focus; one "rides off in
all directions at once," and the other finds one
meaning around which everything revolves (Murray,
Write to Learn 92).
```

The "Works Cited" list would show multiple works by one author as follows:

```
                   Works Cited
Murray, Donald M. Write to Learn. 3rd ed. Fort
     Worth: Holt, 1990.
- - -. A Writer Teaches Writing: A Practical Method
     of Teaching Composition. Boston: Houghton,
     1968.
```

It's obvious from the parenthetical citation which of the two Murray books is the source of the information. Note that in the parenthetical reference, no punctuation separates the title and the page number, but a comma follows the author's name. If Murray had been mentioned in the text of the paper, his name could have been dropped from the citation.

How to handle the "Works Cited" page is explained more fully later in this appendix, but for now, notice that the three hyphens used in the second entry are meant to signal that the author's name in this source is the same as in the preceding entry.

## 1.7 Indirect Sources

Whenever you can, cite the original source for material you use. For example, if an article on television violence quotes the author of a book and you want to use the quote, try to hunt down the book. That way, you'll be certain of the accuracy of the quote and you may find some more usable information.

Sometimes, however, finding the original source is not possible. In those cases, use the term *qtd. in* to signal that you've quoted or paraphrased a quotation from a book or article that initially appeared elsewhere. In the following example, the citation signals that Bacon's quote was culled from an article by Guibroy, not Bacon's original work:

```
Francis Bacon also weighed in on the dangers of
imitation, observing that "it is hardly possible
at once to admire an author and to go beyond him"
(qtd. in Guibroy 113).
```

## 1.8  Personal Interviews

If you mention the name of your interview subject in your text, no parenthetical citation is necessary. On the other hand, if you don't mention the subject's name, cite it in parentheses after the quote:

```
Instead, the recognizable environment gave
something to kids they could relate to. "And
it had a lot more real quality to it than, say,
Mister Rogers . . . ," says one educator. "Kids
say the reason they don't like Mister Rogers is
that it's unbelievable" (Diamonti).
```

Regardless of whether you mention your subject's name, you should include a reference to the interview in the "Works Cited." In this case, the reference would look like this:

```
                    Works Cited
Diamonti, Nancy. Personal Interview. 5 Nov. 1999.
```

## 1.9  Several Sources in a Single Citation

Suppose two sources both contributed the same information in a paragraph of your essay? Or perhaps even more common is when you're summarizing the findings of several authors on a certain topic—a fairly common move when you're trying to establish a context for your own research question. How do you cite multiple authors in a single citation? In the usual fashion, using page name and page number, but separating each with a semicolon. For example,

```
A whole range of studies have looked closely at
the intellectual development of college students,
finding that they generally assume "stages" or
"perspectives" that differ from subject to subject
(Perry 122; Belenky et al. 12).
```

If you can, however, avoid long citations because they can be cumbersome for readers.

**Sample Parenthetical References for Other Sources.**   MLA format is pretty simple, and we've already covered some of the basic variations. You should also know five additional variations, as follow:

### 1.10  AN ENTIRE WORK

If you mention the author's name in the text, no citation is necessary. The work should, however, be listed in the "Works Cited."

```
Leon Edel's Henry James is considered by many to
be a model biography.
```

### 1.11  A VOLUME OF A MULTIVOLUME WORK

If you're working with one volume of a multivolume work, it's a good idea to mention which volume in the parenthetical reference. The citation below attributes the passage to the second volume, page 3, of a work by Baym and three or more other authors. The volume number always precedes the colon, which is followed by the page number:

```
By the turn of the century, three authors
dominated American literature: Mark Twain, Henry
James, and William Dean Howells (Baym et al. 2: 3).
```

### 1.12  SEVERAL SOURCES FOR A SINGLE PASSAGE

Occasionally, a number of sources may contribute to a single passage. List them all in one parenthetical reference, separated by semicolons:

```
American soccer may never achieve the popularity it
enjoys in the rest of the world, an unfortunate
```

```
fact that is integrally related to the nature of
the game itself (Gardner 12; "Selling Soccer" 30).*
```

### 1.13 A LITERARY WORK

Because so many literary works, particularly classics, have been reprinted in so many editions, it's useful to give readers more information about where a passage can be found in one of these editions. List the page number and then the chapter number (and any other relevant information, such as the section or volume), separated by a semicolon. Use arabic rather than roman numerals, unless your teacher instructs you otherwise:

```
Izaak Walton warns that "no direction can be given
to make a man of a dull capacity able to make a
Flie well" (130; ch. 5).
```

When citing classic poems or plays, instead of page numbers, cite line numbers and other appropriate divisions (book, section, act, scene, part, etc.). Separate the information with periods. For example, (Othello 2.3.286) indicates act 2, scene 3, line 286 of Shakespeare's work.

### 1.14 AN ONLINE SOURCE

Texts on CD-ROM and online sources frequently don't have page numbers. So how can you cite them parenthetically in your essay? You have several options.

■ Sometimes, the documents include paragraph numbers. In these cases, use the abbreviation *par.* or *pars.,* followed by the paragraph number or numbers you're borrowing material from. For example:

```
In most psychotherapeutic approaches, the
personality of the therapist can have a big impact
on the outcome of the therapy ("Psychotherapy,"
par. 1).
```

■ Sometimes, the material has an internal structure, such as sections, parts, chapters, or volumes. If so, use the abbreviation *sec., pt., ch.,* or *vol.* (respectively), followed by the appropriate number.

---

*Jason Pulsifer, University of New Hampshire, 1991. Used with permission.

■ In many cases, a parenthetical citation can be avoided entirely by simply naming the source in the text of your essay. A curious reader will then find the full citation to the article on the "Works Cited" page at the back of your paper. For example:

```
According to Charles Petit, the worldwide effort

to determine whether frogs are disappearing will

take somewhere between three and five years.
```

■ Finally, if you don't want to mention the source in text, parenthetically cite the author's last name (if any) or article title:

```
The worldwide effort to determine whether frogs

are disappearing will take somewhere between three

and five years (Petit).
```

# Part Two: Format

## 2.1 The Layout

There is, well, a certain fussiness associated with the look of academic papers. The reason for it is quite simple—academic disciplines generally aim for consistency in format so that readers of scholarship know exactly where to look to find what they want to know. It's a matter of efficiency. How closely you must follow the MLA's requirements for the layout of your essay is up to your instructor, but it's really not that complicated. A lot of what you need to know is featured in Figure A1.

### 2.11  PRINTING OR TYPING

Type your paper on white, $8\frac{1}{2}'' \times 11''$ bond paper. Avoid the erasable variety, which smudges. If you write using a computer, make sure the printer has a fresh ribbon or sufficient ink or toner. That is especially important if you have a dot-matrix printer, which can produce barely legible pages on an old ribbon.

### 2.12  MARGINS AND SPACING

The old high school trick is to have big margins. That way, you can get the length without the information. Don't try that trick with this paper. Leave one-inch margins at the top, bottom, and sides of your pages. Indent the first line of each paragraph five spaces and blocked quotes ten spaces. Double-space all of the text, including blocked quotes and "Works Cited."

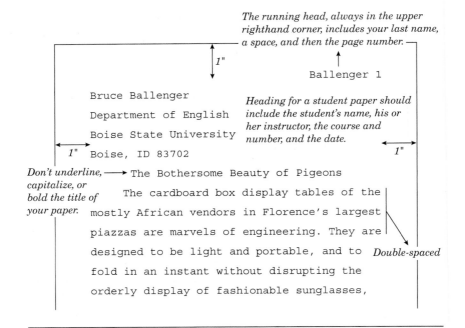

*The running head, always in the upper righthand corner, includes your last name, a space, and then the page number.*

Ballenger 1

Bruce Ballenger

Department of English

Boise State University

Boise, ID 83702

*Heading for a student paper should include the student's name, his or her instructor, the course and number, and the date.*

1"

*Don't underline, capitalize, or bold the title of your paper.* → The Bothersome Beauty of Pigeons

The cardboard box display tables of the mostly African vendors in Florence's largest piazzas are marvels of engineering. They are designed to be light and portable, and to fold in an instant without disrupting the orderly display of fashionable sunglasses,

*Double-spaced*

**FIGURE A1    The Basic Look of an MLA-Style Paper**

#### 2.13 TITLE PAGE

Your paper doesn't need a separate title page. Begin with the first page of text. One inch below the top of the page, type your name, your instructor's name, the course number, and the date (see following). Below that, type the title, centered on the page. Begin the text of the paper below the title.

Karoline Ann Fox

Professor Dethier

English 401

15 December 2002

        Metamorphosis, the Exorcist,

           and Oedipus

Ernst Pawel has said that Franz Kafka's "The Metamorphosis" . . .*

*Reprinted with permission of Karoline A. Fox.

Note that every line is double-spaced. The title is not underlined (unless it includes the name of a book or some other work that should be underlined) or boldfaced.

### 2.14 PAGINATION

Make sure that every page after the first one is numbered. That's especially important with long papers. Type your last name and the page number in the upper-righthand corner, flush with the right margin: Ballenger 3. Don't use the abbreviation *p.* or a hyphen between your name and the number.

### 2.15 PLACEMENT OF TABLES, CHARTS, AND ILLUSTRATIONS

With MLA format, papers do not have appendixes. Tables, charts, and illustrations are placed in the body of the paper, close to the text that refers to them. Number illustrations consecutively (Table 1 or Figure 3), and indicate sources below them (see Figure A2). If you use a chart or illustration from another text, give the full citation. Place any table caption above the table, flush left. Captions for illustrations or diagrams are usually placed below them.

### 2.16 HANDLING TITLES

The MLA guidelines about handling titles are, as the most recent *Handbook* observes, "strict." The general rule is that the writer should capitalize the first letters of all principal words in a title, including any that follow hyphens. The exceptions include articles (*a, an,* and *the*), prepositions (*for, of, in, to*), coordinating conjunctions (*and, or,*

**Table 1    Percentage of Students Who Self-Report Acts of Plagiarism**

| Acts of Plagiarism | Never/ Rarely | Some- times | Often/ Very Freq. |
|---|---|---|---|
| Copy text without citation | 71 | 19 | 10 |
| Copy paper without citation | 91 | 5 | 3 |
| Request paper to hand in | 90 | 5 | 2 |
| Purchase paper to hand in | 91 | 6 | 3 |

*Source:* Scanlon, Patrick M., and David R. Neumann. "Internet Plagiarism among College Students." *Journal of College Student Development* 43.3 (2002): 379.

**FIGURE A2    Example of Format for a Table**

*but, for*), and the use of *to* in infinitives. These exceptions apply *only if the words appear in the middle of a title;* capitalize them if they appear at the beginning or end.

The rules for underlining a title or putting it in quotation marks are as follows:

1. <u>Underline the Title</u> if it is a book, play, pamphlet, film, magazine, TV program, CD, audiocassette, newspaper, or work of art.
2. "Put the Title in Quotes" if it is an article in a newspaper, magazine, or encyclopedia; a short story; a poem; an episode of a TV program; a song; a lecture; or a chapter or essay in a book.

Here are some examples:

<u>The Curious Researcher</u>   (Book)

<u>English Online: The Student's Guide to the</u>
         <u>Internet</u>   (CD-ROM)

"Once More to the Lake"   (Essay)

<u>Historic Boise: An Introduction into the</u>
         <u>Architecture of Boise, Idaho</u>   (Book)

"Psychotherapy"   (Encyclopedia article)

<u>Idaho Statesman</u>   (Newspaper)

"One Percent Initiative Panned"   (Newspaper article)

### 2.17  ITALICS AND UNDERLININGS

If you are writing your paper on a computer or word processor, you can probably produce italic type, which is slanted to the right, *like this*. Many magazines and books—including this one—use italic type to distinguish certain words and phrases, such as titles of works that otherwise would be underlined. MLA style recommends the use of underlining, not italics. You should check with your instructor to see what style he or she prefers.

### 2.18  LANGUAGE AND STYLE

**Names.**   Though it may seem as if you're on familiar terms with some of the authors you cite by the end of your research project, it's not a good idea to call them by their first names. Typically, initially give the full names of people you cite, and then only their last names if you mention them again in your essay.

**Ellipsis.**   Those are the three (always three) dots that indicate you've left out a word, phrase, or even whole section of a quoted passage. It's often wise to do this since you want to emphasize only certain parts of a quotation rather than burden your reader with unnecessary information, but be careful to preserve the basic intention and idea of the author's original statement. The ellipsis can come at the beginning of a quotation, in the middle, or at the end, depending where it is you've omitted material. The accepted format for using an ellipsis is to enclose them in brackets. For example,

> "After the publication of a controversial picture
> that shows, for example, either dead or grieving
> victims [. . .], readers in telephone calls and in
> letters to the editor, often attack the
> photographer for being tasteless [. . .]."

**Quotations.**   Quotations that run more than four lines long should be blocked, or indented ten spaces from the left margin. The quotation should be double-spaced and quotation marks should be omitted. In an exception from the usual convention, the parenthetical citation is placed *outside* the period at the end of the quotation. A colon is a customary way to introduce a blocked quotation. For example,

> Chris Sherman and Gary Price, in <u>The Invisible
> Web</u>, contend that much of the Internet, possibly
> most, is beyond the reach of researchers who use
> conventional search engines:

> > The problem is that vast expanses of the Web
> > are completely invisible to general-purpose
> > search engines like AltaVista, HotBot, and
> > Google. Even worse, this "Invisible Web" is in
> > all likelihood growing significantly faster
> > than the visible Web that you're familiar
> > with. It's not that search engines and Web
> > directories are "stupid" or even badly

> engineered. Rather, they simply can't "see"
> millions of high quality resources that are
> available exclusively on the Invisible Web. So
> what is this Invisible Web and why aren't
> search engines doing anything about it to make
> it visible? (xxi)

# Part Three:
# Preparing the "Works Cited" Page

The "Works Cited" page ends the paper. (This may also be called the "References Cited" or "Sources Cited" page, depending on the nature of your sources or the preferences of your instructor.) In the old footnote system (which, by the way, is still used in some humanities disciplines), this section used to be called "Endnotes" or "Bibliography." There are also several other lists of sources that may appear at the end of a research paper. An "Annotated List of Works Cited" not only lists the sources used in the paper but also includes a brief description of each. A "Works Consulted" list includes sources that may or may not have been cited in the paper but shaped your thinking. A "Content Notes" page, keyed to superscript numbers in the text of the paper, lists short commentaries or asides that are significant but not central enough to the discussion to be included in the text of the paper.

The "Works Cited" page is the workhorse of most college papers. The other source lists are used less often. "Works Cited" is essentially an alphabetical listing of all the sources you quoted, paraphrased, or summarized in your paper. If you have used MLA format for citing sources, your paper has numerous parenthetical references to authors and page numbers. The "Works Cited" page provides complete information on each source cited in the text for the reader who wants to know. (In APA format, this page is called "References" and is only slightly different in how items are listed. See Appendix B for APA guidelines.)

If you've been careful about collecting complete bibliographic information—author, title, editor, edition, volume, place, publisher, date, page numbers—then preparing your "Works Cited" page will be easy. If you've recorded that information on notecards, all you have to do is put them in alphabetical order and then transcribe them into your paper. If you've been careless about collecting that information, you may need to take a hike back to the library.

# 3.1 Format

**Alphabetizing the List.** "Works Cited" follows the text of your paper on a separate page. After you've assembled complete information about each source you've cited, put the sources in alphabetical order by the last name of the author. If the work has multiple authors, use the last name of the first listed. If the source has no author, then alphabetize it by the first key word of the title. If you're citing more than one source by a single author, you don't need to repeat the name for each source; simply place three dashes followed by a period (- - -.) for the author's name in subsequent listings.

**Indenting and Spacing.**   Type the first line of each entry flush left, and indent subsequent lines of that entry (if any) five spaces. Double-space between each line and each entry. For example:

Hall 10

Works Cited

Biernacki, Patrick. <u>Pathways from Heroin</u>

  <u>Addiction</u>. Philadelphia: Temple UP, 1986.

Brill, Leon. <u>The De-Addiction Process</u>.

  Springfield, MA: Charles C. Thomas, 1972.

Epstein, Joan F., and Joseph C. Gfroerer. "Heroin

  Abuse in the United States." <u>OAS Working Paper</u>

  Aug. 1997. 24 Nov. 1999 <http://

  www.health.org/pubs/qdocs/depress/herpape1.htm>.

Hall, Lonny. Personal interview. 1 Mar. 1999.

Kaplan, John. <u>The Hardest Drug: Heroin and Public</u>

  <u>Policy</u>. Chicago: U of Chicago P, 1983.

"Methadone." <u>Encyclopaedia Britannica</u>. CD-ROM.

  1999 ed. 1999.

Shaffner, Nicholas. <u>Saucerful of Secrets: The Pink</u>

  <u>Floyd Odyssey</u>. New York: Dell, 1992.

Strang, John, and Michael Gossop. <u>Heroin Addiction</u>

  <u>and Drug Policy: The British System</u>. New

  York: Oxford UP, 1994.

```
Swift, Wendy, et al. "Transitions between Routes

     of Heroin Administration: A Study of

     Caucasian and Indochinese Users in South-

     Western Sydney, Australia." Addiction (1999):

     71-82.
```

## 3.2  Citing Books

You usually need three pieces of information to cite a book: the name of the author or authors, the title, and the publication information. Occasionally, other information is required. The *MLA Handbook*\* lists this additional information in the order it would appear in the citation. Remember, any single entry will include a few of these things, not all of them. Use whichever are relevant to the source you're citing.

1. Name of the author
2. Title of the book (or part of it)
3. Number of edition used
4. Number of volume used
5. Name of the series
6. Where published, by whom, and the date
7. Page numbers used
8. Any annotation you'd like to add

Each piece of information in a citation is followed by a period and one space (not two).

**Title.**    As a rule, the titles of books are underlined, with the first letters of all principal words capitalized, including those in any subtitles. Titles that are not underlined are usually those of pieces found within larger works, such as poems and short stories in anthologies. These titles are set off by quotation marks. Titles of religious works (the Bible, the Koran, etc.) are neither underlined nor enclosed within quotation marks. (See the guidelines in "Handling Titles," in Part Two.)

**Edition.**    If a book doesn't indicate any edition number, then it's probably a first edition, a fact you don't need to cite. Look on the title page. Signal an edition like this: *2nd ed., 3rd ed.,* and so on.

---

\*Joseph Gibaldi, *MLA Handbook for Writers of Research Papers,* 5th ed. (New York: MLA, 1999).

**Publication Place, Publisher, and Date.**   Look on the title page to find out who published the book. Publishers' names are usually shortened in the "Works Cited" list: for example, *St. Martin's Press, Inc.,* is shortened to *St. Martin's.*

It's sometimes confusing to know what to cite about the publication place, since several cities are often listed on the title page. Cite the first. For books published outside the United States, add the country name along with the city to avoid confusion.

The date a book is published is usually indicated on the copyright page. If several dates or several printings by the same publisher are listed, cite the original publication date. However, if the book is a revised edition, give the date of that edition. One final variation: If you're citing a book that's a reprint of an original edition, give both dates. For example:

Stegner, Wallace. <u>Recapitulation</u>. 1979. Lincoln:

U of Nebraska P, 1986.

This book was first published in 1979 and then republished in 1986 by the University of Nebraska Press.

**Page Numbers.**   Normally, you don't list page numbers of a book. The parenthetical reference in your paper specifies that. But if you use only part of a book—an introduction or an essay—list the appropriate page numbers following the publication date. Use periods to set off the page numbers. If the author or editor of the entire work is also the author of the introduction or essay you're citing, list her by last name only the second time you cite her. For example:

Lee, L. L., and Merrill Lewis. Preface. <u>Women,</u>

<u>Women Writers, and the West</u>. Ed. Lee and

Lewis. Troy: Whitston, 1980. v-ix.

## Sample Book Citations

### 3.21 A BOOK BY ONE AUTHOR

Keen, Sam. <u>Fire in the Belly</u>. New York: Bantam,

1991.

*In-Text Citation:*   (Keen 101)

**3.22  A BOOK BY TWO AUTHORS**

Ballenger, Bruce, and Barry Lane. <u>Discovering the</u>

  <u>Writer Within</u>. Cincinnati: Writer's Digest,

  1996.

*In-Text Citation:*   (Ballenger and Lane 14)

**3.23  A BOOK WITH MORE THAN THREE AUTHORS**

If a book has more than three authors, list the first and substitute the term *et al.* for the others.

Jones, Hillary, et al. <u>The Unmasking of Adam</u>.

  Highland Park: Pegasus, 1992.

*In-Text Citation:*   (Jones et al. 21-30)

**3.24  SEVERAL BOOKS BY THE SAME AUTHOR**

Baldwin, James. <u>Tell Me How Long the Train's Been</u>

  <u>Gone</u>. New York: Dell-Doubleday, 1968.

- - -. <u>Going to Meet the Man</u>. New York: Dell-

  Doubleday, 1948.

*In-Text Citation:*   (Baldwin, <u>Going</u> 34)

**3.25  A COLLECTION OR ANTHOLOGY**

Crane, R. S., ed. <u>Critics and Criticism: Ancient</u>

  <u>and Modern</u>. Chicago: U of Chicago P, 1952.

*In-Text Citation:*   (Crane xx)

**3.26  A WORK IN A COLLECTION OR ANTHOLOGY**

The title of a work that is part of a collection but was originally published as a book should be underlined. Otherwise, the title of a work in a collection should be enclosed in quotation marks.

Bahktin, Mikhail. <u>Marxism and the Philosophy</u>

  <u>of Language</u>. <u>The Rhetorical Tradition</u>.

Ed. Patricia Bizzell and Bruce Herzberg.
New York: St. Martin's, 1990. 928-44.

*In-Text Citation:* (Bahktin 929-31)

Jones, Robert F. "Welcome to Muskie Country." The
Ultimate Fishing Book. Ed. Lee Eisenberg
and DeCourcy Taylor. Boston: Houghton,
1981. 122-34.

*In-Text Citation:* (Jones 131)

### 3.27 AN INTRODUCTION, PREFACE, FOREWORD, OR PROLOGUE

Scott, Jerie Cobb. Foreword. Writing Groups:
History, Theory, and Implications. By Ann
Ruggles Gere. Carbondale, IL: Southern
Illinois UP, 1987. ix-xi.

*In-Text Citation:* (Scott x-xi)

Rich, Adrienne. Introduction. On Lies, Secrets,
and Silence. By Rich. New York: Norton,
1979. 9-18.

*In-Text Citation:* (Rich 12)

### 3.28 A BOOK WITH NO AUTHOR

American Heritage Dictionary. 3rd ed. Boston:
Houghton, 1994.

*In-Text Citation:* (American Heritage Dictionary 444)

### 3.29 AN ENCYLOPEDIA

"City of Chicago." Encyclopaedia Britannica.
1999 ed.

*In-Text Citation:* ("City of Chicago" 397)

### 3.30  A BOOK WITH AN INSTITUTIONAL AUTHOR

Hospital Corporation of America. <u>Employee Benefits</u>

   <u>Handbook</u>. Nashville: HCA, 1990.

*In-Text Citation:*   (Hospital Corporation of America 5-7)


### 3.31  A BOOK WITH MULTIPLE VOLUMES

Include the number of volumes in the work between the title and publication information.

Baym, Nina, et al., eds. <u>The Norton Anthology of</u>

   <u>American Literature</u>. 5th ed. 2 vols. New

   York: Norton, 1998.

*In-Text Citation:*   (Baym et al. 2: 3)


If you use one volume of a multivolume work, indicate which one along with the page numbers, followed by the total number of volumes in the work.

Anderson, Sherwood. "Mother." <u>The Norton Anthology</u>

   <u>of American Literature</u>. Ed. Nina Baym et al.

   5th ed. Vol 2. New York: Norton, 1998.

   1115-31. 2 vols.

*In-Text Citation:*   (Anderson 1115)


### 3.32  A BOOK THAT IS NOT A FIRST EDITION

Check the title page to determine whether the book is *not* a first edition (2nd, 3rd, 4th, etc.); if no edition number is mentioned, assume it's the first. Put the edition number right after the title.

Ballenger, Bruce. <u>The Curious Researcher</u>. 4th ed.

   Boston: Longman, 2003.

*In-Text Citation:*   (Ballenger 194)


Citing the edition is only necessary for books that are *not* first editions. This includes revised editions (*Rev. ed.*) and abridged editions (*Abr. ed.*).

### 3.33  A BOOK PUBLISHED BEFORE 1900

For a book this old, it's usually unnecessary to list the publisher.

Hitchcock, Edward. <u>Religion of Geology</u>. Glasgow,

1851.

*In-Text Citation:*   (Hitchcock 48)

### 3.34  A TRANSLATION

Montaigne, Michel de. <u>Essays</u>. Trans. J. M. Cohen.

Middlesex, England: Penguin, 1958.

*In-Text Citation:*   (Montaigne 638)

### 3.35  GOVERNMENT DOCUMENTS

Because of the enormous variety of government documents, citing them properly can be a challenge. Since most government documents do not name authors, begin an entry for such a source with the level of government (U.S. Government, State of Illinois, etc., unless it is obvious from the title), followed by the sponsoring agency, the title of the work, and the publication information. Look on the title page to determine the publisher. If it's a federal document, then the *Government Printing Office* (abbreviated *GPO*) is usually the publisher.

United States. Bureau of the Census. <u>Statistical</u>

<u>Abstract of the United States</u>. Washington:

GPO, 1990.

*In-Text Citation:*   (United States, Bureau of the
Census 79-83)

### 3.36  A BOOK THAT WAS REPUBLISHED

A fairly common occurrence, particularly in literary study, is to find a book that was republished, sometimes many years after the original publication date. In addition, some books first appear in hard cover, and then are republished in paperback. To cite, put the original date of publication immediately after the book's title, and then include the more current publication date, as usual, at the end of the citation. Do it like so:

Ballenger, Bruce, and Barry Lane. <u>Discovering the</u>

<u>Writer Within: 40 Days to More Imaginative</u>

Writing. 1989. Cincinnati, OH: Writer's

Digest, 1996.

*In-Text Citation*:   (Ballenger and Lane 31)

**3.37  AN ONLINE BOOK**

Citing a book you found online requires more information than the usual citation for a book you can hold in your hands. As usual, include the author's name (if listed), an underlined title, and publication information. What you include in publication information depends on whether the text was published exclusively online or is also based on a print version. If only a digital book, include the date of electronic publication and the group or organization that sponsored it. If the book also appeared on paper, add the usual information (if provided) about the print version (city of publication, publisher, and date). The citation ends, finally, with the date you accessed the book online and the Internet address. For example,

Badke, William. Research Strategies: Finding Your

Way through the Information Fog. Lincoln,

NE: Writers Club P, 2000. 12 July 2002

<http://www.acts.twu.ca/lbr/textbook.htm>.

*In-Text Citation:*   (Badke)

## 3.4  Citing Periodicals

**3.41  FORMAT**

Periodicals—magazines, newspapers, journals, and similar publications that appear regularly—are cited similarly to books but sometimes involve different information, such as date, volume, and page numbers. The *MLA Handbook* lists the information to include in a periodical citation in the order in which it should appear:

1. Name of the author
2. Article title
3. Periodical title
4. Series number or name
5. Volume number
6. Date
7. Page numbers

**Author's Name.**    List the author(s) as you would for a book citation.

**Article Title.**    Unlike book titles, article titles are usually enclosed in quotation marks.

**Periodical Title.**    Underline periodical titles, dropping introductory articles (*Aegis,* not *The Aegis*). If you're citing a newspaper your readers may not be familiar with, include in the title—enclosed in brackets but not underlined—the city in which it was published. For example:

```
MacDonald, Mary. "Local Hiker Freezes to Death."

    Foster's Daily Democrat [Dover, NH] 28 Jan.

    1992: 1.
```

**Volume Number.**    Most academic journals are numbered as volumes (or occasionally feature series numbers); the volume number should be included in the citation. Popular periodicals sometimes have volume numbers, too, but these are not included in the citations. Indicate the volume number immediately after the journal's name. Omit the tag *vol.* before the number.

There is one important variation: Though most journals number their pages continuously, from the first issue every year to the last, a few don't. These journals feature an issue number as well as a volume number. In that case, cite both by listing the volume number, a period, and then the issue number: for example *12.4,* or volume number *12* and issue *4.*

**Date.**    When citing popular periodicals, include the day, month, and year of the issue you're citing—in that order—following the periodical name. Academic journals are a little different. Since the volume number indicates when the journal was published within a given year, just indicate that year. Put it in parentheses following the volume number and before the page numbers (see examples following).

**Page Numbers.**    Include the page numbers of the article at the end of the citation, followed by a period. Just list the pages of the entire article, omitting abbreviations such as *p.* or *pp.* It's common for articles in newspapers and popular magazines *not* to run on consecutive pages. In that case, indicate the page on which the article begins, followed by a "+" (*12+*).

Newspaper pagination can be peculiar. Some papers wed the section (usually a letter) with the page number (*A4*); other papers simply begin numbering anew in each section. Most, however, paginate continuously. See the following sample citations for newspapers for how to deal with these peculiarities.

Online sources, which often have no pagination at all, present special problems. For guidance on how to handle them, see the section "Citing Online Sources" later in this part of the Appendix.

## Sample Periodical Citations

### 3.42  A MAGAZINE ARTICLE

Oppenheimer, Todd. "The Computer Delusion."

Atlantic Monthly July 1997: 47-60.

*In-Text Citation:*   (Oppenheimer 48)

Jones, Thom. "The Pugilist at Rest." New Yorker

12 Dec. 1991: 38-47.

*In-Text Citation:*   (Jones 40)

### 3.43  A JOURNAL ARTICLE

For a journal that is paginated continuously, from the first issue every year to the last, cite as follows:

Allen, Rebecca E., and J. M. Oliver. "The

Effects of Child Maltreatment on Language

Development." Child Abuse and Neglect 6

(1982): 299-305.

*In-Text Citation:*   (Allen and Oliver 299-300)

For an article in a journal that begins pagination with each issue, include the issue number along with the volume number.

Goody, Michelle M., and Andrew S. Levine. "Health-

Care Workers and Occupational Exposure to

AIDS." Nursing Management 23.1 (1992): 59-60.

*In-Text Citation:*   (Goody and Levine 59)

### 3.44  A NEWSPAPER ARTICLE

Some newspapers have several editions (morning edition, late edition, national edition), and each may feature different articles. If an edition is listed on the masthead, include it in the citation.

Mendels, Pamela. "Internet Access Spreads to More

    Classrooms." <u>New York Times</u> 1 Dec. 1999,

    morning ed.: C1+.

*In-Text Citation:*  (Mendels C1)

Some papers begin numbering pages anew in each section. In that case, include the section number if it's not part of pagination.

Brooks, James. "Lobsters on the Brink." <u>Portland</u>

    <u>Press</u> 29 Nov. 1999, sec. 2: 4.

*In-Text Citation:*  (Brooks 4)

Increasingly, full-text newspaper articles are available online using library databases such as *Newspaper Source* or through the newspapers themselves. Citing articles from library databases involves adding information about the specific database you used (e.g., <u>Newspaper Source</u>), the provider of that database (e.g., EBSCOhost), where (what library?) and when (date) you accessed the information online, and the Web address of the provider (e.g., www.epnet.com). You can find the addresses for most database providers in Figure A3, later in this appendix.

Here's what the citation would look like:

"Lobsterman Hunts for Perfect Bait." <u>AP Online</u>

    7 July 2002. <u>Newspaper Source</u>. EBSCOhost.

    Albertson's Lib., ID. 13 July 2002

    <www.epnet.com>.

*In-Text Citation:*  ("Lobsterman Hunts")

Here's an example of a citation for an article I found on the newspaper's own Web site:

Sterngold, James. "Lessons from '92 Keep Angry

    City Calm." <u>New York Times on the Web</u> 10 July

    2002. 12 July 2002 <http://www.nytimes.com/

    2002/07/11/national/11POLI.html?

    todaysheadlines>.

*In-Text Citation*:  (Sterngold)

### 3.45  AN ARTICLE WITH NO AUTHOR

"The Understanding." <u>New Yorker</u> 2 Dec. 1991:

34-35.

*In-Text Citation:*   ("Understanding" 35)

### 3.46  AN EDITORIAL

"Paid Leave for Parents." Editorial. <u>New York

Times</u> 1 Dec. 1999: 31.

*In-Text Citation:* ("Paid Leave" 31)

### 3.47  A LETTER TO THE EDITOR

Levinson, Evan B. "Paying Out of Pocket for

Student Supplies." Letter. <u>Boston Globe</u>

29 Jan. 1992: 10.

*In-Text Citation:*   (Levinson 10)

### 3.48  A REVIEW

Page, Barbara. Rev. of <u>Allegories of Cinema:

American Film in the Sixties</u>, by David E.

James. <u>College English</u> 54 (1992): 945-54.

*In-Text Citation:*   (Page 945-46)

### 3.49  AN ABSTRACT

It's usually better to have the full text of an article for research purposes, but sometimes all you can come up with is an abstract, or short summary of the article that highlights its findings or summarizes its argument. Online databases frequently offer abstracts when they don't feature full-text versions of an article.

To cite an abstract, begin with information about the full version, and then include the information about the source from which you got the abstract. If the title of the source fails to make it obvious that what you are citing is an abstract (i.e., it's not called something such as *Psychological Abstracts*), include the word "abstract" after the original publication information, but don't underline it or put it in quotation marks. In this example, the source of the abstract is a periodical database called MasterFILE Premier, provided by the company EBSCOhost. Since I accessed the abstract at my library, I include the library name and its location in the citation. In addition,

I include the date of access and the Web address of the database's provider is included in the citation. (For a list of URLs for these providers, see Figure 3A later in this appendix.)

> Edwards, Rob. "Air-raid Warning." <u>New Scientist</u>
>
>   14 Aug. 1999: 48–49. Abstract. <u>MasterFILE</u>
>
>   <u>Premier</u>. EBSCOhost. Albertson's Lib.,
>
>   ID. 1 May 2002 <www.epnet.com>.

*In-Text Citation:*  (Edwards)

The following citation is from another useful source of abstracts, the *Dissertation Abstracts International*. In this case, the citation is from the print version of the index.

> McDonald, James C. "Imitation of Models in the
>
>   History of Rhetoric: Classical, Belletristic,
>
>   and Current-Traditional." U of Texas, Austin.
>
>   <u>DAI</u> 48 (1988): 2613A.

*In-Text Citation:*  (McDonald 2613A)

## 3.5  Citing Nonprint and Other Sources

### 3.51  AN INTERVIEW

If you conducted the interview yourself, list your subject's name first, indicate what kind of interview it was (telephone interview, e-mail interview, or personal interview), and provide the date.

> Hall, Lonny. Personal interview. 1 Mar. 1999.

*In-Text Citation:*  (Hall)
Or avoid parenthethical reference altogether by mentioning the subject's name in the text:  According to Lonny Hall, . . .

If you're citing an interview done by someone else (perhaps from a book or article) and the title does not indicate that it was an interview, you should, after the subject's name. Always begin the citation with the subject's name.

> Stegner, Wallace. Interview. <u>Conversations with</u>
>
>   <u>Wallace Stegner</u>. By Richard Eutlain and

> Wallace Stegner. Salt Lake: U of Utah P,
>
>    1990.

*In-Text Citation:*  (Stegner 22)
Or if there are other works by Stegner on the "Works Cited"
page: (Stegner, <u>Conversations</u> 22)

As radio and TV interview programs are increasingly archived
on the Web, these can be a great source of material for a research
essay. In the example below, the interview was on a transcript I
ordered from the *Fresh Air* Web site. Note that the national network,
National Public Radio, *and* the local affiliate that produced the program, WHYY, are included in the citation along with the air date.

> Mairs, Nancy. Interview. <u>Fresh Air</u>. NPR. WHYY,
>
>    Philadelphia. 7 June 1993.

*In-Text Citation:*  (Mairs)

The following citation is for an interview published on the Web.
The second date listed is the date of access.

> Messner, Tammy Faye Bakker. Interview. <u>The Well</u>
>
>    <u>Rounded Interview</u>. Well Rounded Entertainment.
>
>    Aug. 2000. 14 July 2002 <http://www.
>
>    wellrounded.com/movies/reviews/
>
>    tammyfaye_intv.html>.

*In-Text Citation:*  (Messner)

### 3.52  SURVEYS, QUESTIONNAIRES, AND CASE STUDIES

If you conducted the survey or case study, list it under your
name and give it an appropriate title.

> Ball, Helen. "Internet Survey." Boise State
>
>    U, 1999.

*In-Text Citation:*  (Ball)

### 3.53  RECORDINGS

Generally, list a recording by the name of the performer and
underline the title. Also include the recording company, catalog number, and year. (If you don't know the year, use the abbreviation *n.d.*)

Orff, Carl. <u>Carmina Burana</u>. Cond. Seiji Ozawa.

   Boston Symphony. RCA, 6533-2-RG, n.d.

*In-Text Citation:*   (Orff)

### 3.54 TELEVISION AND RADIO PROGRAMS

List the title of the program (underlined), the station, and the date. If the episode has a title, list that first in quotation marks. You may also want to include the name of the narrator or producer after the title.

<u>All Things Considered</u>. Interview with Andre Dubus.

   NPR. WBUR, Boston. 12 Dec. 1990.

*In-Text Citation:*   (<u>All Things Considered</u>)

### 3.55 FILMS, VIDEOTAPES, AND DVD

Begin with the title (underlined), followed by the director, the distributor, and the year. You may also include names of writers, performers, or producers. End with the date and any other specifics about the characteristics of the film or videotape that may be relevant (length and size).

<u>Saving Private Ryan</u>. Dir. Steven Spielberg. Perf.

   Tom Hanks, Tom Sizemore, and Matt Damon.

   Videocassette. Paramount, 1998.

*In-Text Citation:*   (<u>Saving</u>)

You can also list a video or film by the name of a contributor you'd like to emphasize.

Capra, Frank, dir. <u>It's a Wonderful Life</u>. Perf.

   Jimmy Stewart and Donna Reed. RKO Pictures,

   1946.

*In-Text Citation:*   (Capra)

### 3.56 ARTWORK

List each work by artist. Then cite the title of the work (underlined) and where it's located (institution and city). If you've reproduced the work from a published source, include that information as well.

Homer, Winslow. <u>Casting for a Rise</u>. Hirschl and

Adler Galleries, New York. <u>Ultimate Fishing</u>

<u>Book</u>. Ed. Lee Eisenberg and DeCourcy Taylor.

Boston: Houghton, 1981.

*In-Text Citation:*    (Homer 113)

**3.57  LECTURES AND SPEECHES**

List each by the name of the speaker, followed by the title of
the address (if any) in quotation marks, the name of the sponsoring
organization, the location, and the date. Also indicate what kind of
address it was (lecture, speech, etc.).

Naynaha, Siskanna. Lecture. "Emily Dickinson's Last

Poems." Sigma Tau Delta, Boise, 15 Nov. 1999.

Avoid the need for parenthetical citation by mentioning the
speaker's name in your text.

**3.58  PAMPHLETS**

Cite a pamphlet as you would a book.

<u>New Challenges for Wilderness Conservationists</u>.

Washington, DC: Wilderness Society, 1973.

*In-Text Citation:*    (<u>New Challenges</u>)

# 3.6  Citing "Portable" Databases

Nearly every new computer these days is sold with an encyclopedia on CD-ROM. If you're doing research, I don't think they hold a
candle to the more extensive bound versions. Still, a CD-ROM encyclopedia is easy to use and, for quickly checking facts, can be quite
helpful. While the encyclopedia is the most familiar *portable*
database on CD-ROM, there are many others, including full-text versions of literary classics, journal article abstracts, indexes, and periodicals. The number of such portable databases on CD will continue
to multiply along with databases on other media, like diskettes and
tapes. Citation of these materials requires much of the usual information and in the usual order. But it will also include these three
things: the *publication medium* (for example, CD-ROM, diskette, or

tape), the *vendor* or company that distributed it (for example, Silver-Platter or UMI-Proquest), and the *date of electronic publication* (or the release date of the disk or tape).

There are two categories of portable databases: (1) those that are issued periodically, like magazines and journals, and (2) those that are not routinely updated, like books. Citing a source in each category requires some slightly different information.

### 3.61 A NONPERIODICAL DATABASE

This is cited much like a book.

- List the author. If no author is given, list the editor or translator, followed by the appropriate abbreviation (*ed., trans.*)
- Publication title (underlined) or title of the portion of the work you're using (if relevant)
- Name of editor, compiler, or translator (if relevant)
- Publication medium (for example, CD-ROM, diskette, magnetic tape)
- Edition or release or version
- City of publication
- Publisher and year of publication

For example:

Shakespeare, William. <u>Romeo and Juliet</u>. Diskette.

    Vers. 1.5. New York: CMI, 1995.

*In-Text Citation:*  (Shakespeare)

"Psychotherapy." <u>Microsoft Encarta</u>. CD-ROM.

    1994 ed. Everett, WA: Microsoft, 1993.

*In-Text Citation:*  ("Psychotherapy")

### 3.62 A PERIODICAL DATABASE

Frequently a periodical database is a computer version—or an analogue—of a printed publication. For example, the *New York Times* has a disk version, as does *Dissertation Abstracts*. Both databases refer to articles also published in print; therefore, the citation often includes two dates: the original publication date and the electronic publication date. Note the location of each in the citations below.

Haden, Catherine Ann. "Talking about the Past with

    Preschool Siblings." <u>DAI</u> 56 (1996). Emory U,

1995. <u>Dissertation Abstracts Ondisc</u>. CD-ROM.

UMI-ProQuest. Mar. 1996.

Kolata, Gina. "Research Links Writing Style to

the Risk of Alzheimer's." <u>New York Times</u>

21 Feb. 1996: 1A. <u>Newspaper Abstracts</u>.

CD-ROM. UMI-ProQuest. 1996.*

*In-Text Citation:*   (Kolata 1A)

Frequently, a periodically issued electronic source doesn't have a printed analogue. In that case, obviously, you can't include publication information about the printed version.

## 3.7  Citing Online Databases

In the first edition of *The Curious Researcher,* I barely mentioned online—or *nonportable*—databases. Since then, the amount of research information available from the Internet and commercial online services has exploded. Unfortunately, so has confusion about how to cite such material properly. Thankfully, the Modern Language Association (MLA) published the second edition of its *MLA Style Manual* in the spring of 1998. This manual clarifies and simplifies the conventions for citing online sources. The folks at MLA admit this information won't be the last word on citing online sources because electronic sources keep evolving. But the citation information in the latest *MLA Style Manual* (a book intended for graduate students and scholars) is an improvement over that in the *MLA Handbook,* fifth edition (the manual most undergraduates use to reference citing sources). You can keep up-to-date on MLA guidelines for citing online material by visiting their Web site:

http://www.mla.org

Some gaps and ambiguities in the MLA treatment of online sources remain. While some competing online citation proposals from groups such as the Alliance for Computers and Writing exist, I decided to cover the MLA conventions for citing online sources in *The Curious Researcher.*

---

*Sometimes information about an electronic source is unavailable. In that case, include what information you have. For example, in this example, I was unable to find the month of publication for the *Newspaper Abstracts* and had to omit that piece of information from the citation.

Citing most online sources is much like citing any other sources, with two crucial exceptions:

1. Electronic-source citations usually include at least two dates: the *date of electronic publication* and the *date of access* (when you visited the site and retrieved the document). There is a good reason for listing both dates: Online documents are changed and updated frequently—when you retrieve the material matters. If the online document you are using originally appeared in print, it might be necessary to include three dates: the print publication date, the online publication date, and your access date (see the McGrory citation in the following section "Is It Also in Print?").

2. The MLA now requires that you include the Internet address of the document in angle brackets at the end of your citation (for example, <http:www.cc.emory.edu/citation.formats.html>). The reason is obvious: The Internet address tells your readers where they can find the document.

**Other Recent Changes by the MLA.**   The MLA no longer requires inclusion of a number of items in a citation. For example, it's no longer necessary to include the word *online* in your citations to indicate the publication medium or mention the name of the network or service you used to retrieve the document (for example, *Internet, America Online*). Both are great improvements, I think. Another quirky thing about citing online sources is dealing with page numbers, paragraph numbers, or numbered sections. Many Internet documents simply don't have them. The MLA no longer requires inclusion of the term *n. pag.* when a document lacks pagination.

**Is It Also in Print?**   Databases from computer services or networks feature information available in printed form (like a newspaper or magazine) and online, or information available exclusively online. This distinction is important. If the online source has a printed version, include information about it in the citation. For example:

McGrory, Brian. "Hillary Clinton's Profile

Boosted." <u>Boston Globe</u> 26 June 1996: 1.

<u>Boston Globe Online</u> 27 June 1996. 8 July 1998

<http://www.boston.com/80/globe/nat/cgi-bin>.

*In-Text Citation:*   (McGrory 1)

Note that the first date lists when the print version appeared, the second date when the article was published online, and the third when the researcher accessed the document.

Material that only appeared online is somewhat simpler to cite since you'll only need to include information about the electronic version.

```
Adler, Jonathan. "Save Endangered Species, Not

    the Endangered Species Act." The Heartland

    Institute: Intellectual Ammunition Jan.-Feb.

    1996. 4 Oct. 1996 <http://www.heartland.org/

    05jnfb96.htm>.
```

*In-Text Citation:* No page or paragraph numbers were used in this document, so simply list the author's last name: (Adler). Or avoid parenthetical citation altogether by mentioning the name of the source in your essay (for example:  "According to Jonathan Adler, the ESA is . . .").

You may be missing citation information on some Internet material—like page numbers and publication dates—that are easy to find in printed texts. Use the information that you have. Keep in mind that the relevant information for a citation varies with the type of electronic source (see citation examples in the following section titled "Sample Online Citations"). To summarize, the basic format for an online citation includes the following information:

1. Author's name (if given). If there is an editor, translator, or compiler included, list that name followed by the appropriate abbreviation (*ed., trans., comp.*).
2. Publication information:
   - Title of the document, database, or Web site
   - Title of the larger work, database, or Web site (if any) of which it is a part
   - Name of editor (if any) of the project, database, or Web site (usually different from author)
   - Volume, issue, or version number (if any)
   - Date of electronic publication or latest update
   - Page or paragraph numbers (if any)
   - Publication information about print version (if any)
   - Date of access and electronic address

**Address Mistakes Are Fatal.**   When you include Internet addresses in your citations, it is crucial that you take great care in accurately recording them. Make sure you get all your slash marks going in the right direction and the right characters in the right places; also pay attention to whether the characters are upper- or lowercase. These addresses are *case sensitive,* unlike, say, the file names used to retrieve WordPerfect documents. The cut-and-paste function in your word processor is an invaluable tool in accurately transferring Internet addresses into your own documents. One last thing: If an Internet address in your citation must go beyond one line, make sure the break occurs after a slash, not in the middle of a file name, and don't include an end-of-line hyphen to mark the break.

## Sample Online Citations

### 3.71  AN ARTICLE

Notice the inclusion of the document length after the publication date in these examples. Sometimes Internet documents number paragraphs instead of page numbers. Include that information, if available, using the abbreviation *par.* or *pars.* (e.g., "53 pars."). More often, an Internet article has no page or paragraph numbers. Put the title of the article in quotation marks and underline the title of the journal, newsletter, or electronic conference.

> Haynes, Cynthia, and Jan R. Holmevik. "Enhancing Pedagogical Reality with MOOs." <u>Kairos: A Journal for Teachers of Writing in a Webbed Environment</u> 1.2 (1996): 1 p. 28 June 1996 <http://english/ttu.edu/kairos/1.2/index.html>.

*In-Text Citation:*   (Haynes and Holmevik 1)

> "Freeman Trial Delayed over Illness." <u>USA Today</u> 26 May 1998. 26 May 1998 <http://www.usatoday.com/news/nds2.htm>.

*In-Text Citation:*   ("Freeman")

> Dvorak, John C. "Worst Case Scenarios." <u>PC Magazine Online</u> 26 May 1998: 3 pp. 1 June

1998 <http://www.zdnet.com/pcmag/insites/

dvorak/jd.htm>.

*In-Text Citation:*    (Dvorak 2)

### 3.72 AN ARTICLE OR ABSTRACT IN A LIBRARY DATABASE

One of the great boons to researchers in recent years is the publication of full-text versions of articles as part of the online databases available on your campus library's Web pages. Quite a few databases, such as *MasterFILE* or *Newspaper Source,* offer this service, and more are adding it every year. Some that don't offer full-text versions of articles offer abstracts, and even these can be useful. Citing articles or abstracts from library databases requires some information beyond what is usually required for citing other online articles. Specifically, you need

- The name of the database (e.g., *Newspaper Source*)
- The name and Web address of the company or organization that provides it to your library (e.g., EBSCOHost)
- The name and location of the library (e.g., Albertson's Library, ID)
- The date you accessed the database to get the article

All of this information is pretty easy to come up with except information about the company that provides the database. You can usually find that name on the search page of the database. Figure A3 lists the Web addresses of some of the most popular of these providers, along with some of the databases each features. You can use Figure A3's address in your citation. Note in the following example that information on the print version of the article is provided first, and then information about the database and its provider.

Winbush, Raymond A. "Back to the Future: Campus

Racism in the 21$^{st}$ Century." The Black

Collegian Oct. 2001: 102–3. Expanded Academic

ASAP. Gale Group Databases. U of New Hampshire

Lib. 12 Apr. 2002 <http://www.infotrac.

galegroup.com>.

*In-Text Citation:*    (Winbush)

When citing an abstract from a library database, include the word "abstract" in the citation. For example,

Erskine, Ruth. "Exposing Racism, Exploring Race."

Journal of Family Therapy 24 (2002): 282–297.

| Database Provider | Databases | Web Address |
|---|---|---|
| Britannica Online | Encyclopaedia Britannica | http://www.britannica.com |
| EBSCOhost | Academic Search Elite, Academic Search Premier, Business Source Elite, Computer Source, Health Source, MasterFile Elite, MasterFile Premier, Newspaper Source, Nursing and Allied Health Collection, World Magazine Bank | http://www.epnet.com |
| Gale Group Databases | Contemporary Authors, Biography Index, Expanded Academic ASAP, General Business File ASAP, General Reference Center, Health Reference Center, Info Trac, Literary Index | http://www.infotrac.galegroup.com |
| LexisNexis | Academic Universe, Government Periodicals Universe, History Universe, Statistical Universe | http://www.lexisnexis.com/ |
| OCLC First Search | Art Index, Book Review, Contemporary Women's Issues, EconLit, Essay and General Literature Index, Reader's Guide Abstracts, Social Science Index, WorldCat | http://newfirstsearch.oclc.org |
| ProQuest | ABI/INFORM, Academic Research Library, Magazine Index, National Newspapers, Wall Street Journal | http://www.bellhowell.infolearning.om/proquest |

**FIGURE A3  URLs of Popular Database Providers for Use in Citations**
The table lists the Web addresses for most of the major companies that provide databases for libraries. This information is vital if you want to cite an article or abstract you found while searching your campus library's databases online. Usually a database has a specific name, such as *Expanded Academic ASAP,* as shown in the second column, and then a service that provides it, a name that you can usually find somewhere on the search page of the database. For Expanded Academic ASAP, for example, it's a provider called *Gale Group,* shown in the first column. You need both pieces of information for a citation, as well as the provider's URL.

| SilverPlatter/<br>Web SPIRS | Agricola. Biological<br>Abstracts, CINHAL,<br>EconLit, Essay and General<br>Literature Index,<br>Philosopher's Index,<br>PsychINFO | http://webspirs.<br>silverplatter.com |
|---|---|---|
| Wilson Web | Applied Science and<br>Technology Abstracts,<br>Art Index, Bibliographic<br>Index Biography Index,<br>Book Review Digest, Edu-<br>cation Index, General Science<br>Index, Reader's Guide,<br>Humanities Index, Social<br>Science Index, World Authors | http://hwwilsonweb.com/ |

**FIGURE A3**   (Continued)

> Abstract. <u>EBSCO Online Citations</u>. EBSCOHost.
>
> 3 Dec. 2002 <www.epnet.com>.

*In-Text Citation:*   (Erskine)

#### 3.73  AN ONLINE BOOK

I can't imagine why anyone would read *The Adventures of Huckleberry Finn* online, but it's available, along with thousands of other books and historical documents in electronic form. If you use an online book, remember to include publication information (if available) about the original printed version in the citation.

> Twain, Mark. <u>The Adventures of Huckleberry Finn</u>.
>
> New York: Harper, 1912. 22 July 1996
>
> <gopher://wiretap.spies.com/00/Library/
>
> Classic/huckfinn.html>.

*In-Text Citation:*   (Twain)   Or better yet, since there are no page numbers, mention the author in the text rather than citing him parenthetically:   In <u>The Adventures of Huckleberry Finn</u>, Twain re-creates southern dialect . . .

When citing part of a larger work, include the title of that smaller part in quotation marks before the title of the work. Also notice that the text cited below is part of an online scholarly project.

Include the name of the project, the editor and compiler of the work if listed, and its location.

> Service, Robert. "The Mourners." Rhymes of a
>
> Red Cross Man. 1916. Project Gutenberg.
>
> Ed. A. Light. Aug. 1995. Illinois
>
> Benedictine College. 1 July 1998 <ftp://
>
> uiarchive.cso.uiuc.edu/pub/etext/gutenberg/
>
> etext95/redcr10.txt>.

*In-Text Citation:*   (Service)

#### 3.74 A PERSONAL OR PROFESSIONAL WEB SITE

Begin with the name of the editor or creator of the site, if listed. Include the title of the site, or, if no title is given, use a descriptor such as the term *Home page*. Also include the sponsoring organization, if any, the date of access, and the electronic address.

> Sharev, Alexi. Population Ecology. Virginia Tech
>
> U. 7 Aug. 1998 <http://www.gypsymoth.
>
> ento.vt.edu/~sharov/popechome/welcome.html>.

*In-Text Citation:*   (Sharev)

> Battalio, John. Home page. 26 May 1998 <http://
>
> www.idbsu.edu/english/jbattali>.

*In-Text Citation:*   (Battalio)

You may cite a document that is part of a Web site. For example:

> Cohn, Priscilla. "Wildlife Contraception: An
>
> Introduction." Animal Rights Law Center
>
> Web Site. 1998. Rutgers U. 27 May 1998
>
> <http://www.animal-law.org/hunting/
>
> contintro.htm>.

*In-Text Citation:*   (Cohn)

#### 3.75 AN ONLINE POSTING

An online post can be a contribution to an e-mail discussion group like a listserv, a post to a bulletin board or usenet group, or a

WWW forum. The description *Online posting* is included after the title of the message (usually drawn from the subject line). List the date the material was posted, the access date, and the online address as you would for any other online citation.

> Alvoeiro, Jorge. "Neurological Effects of Music."
>> Online posting. 20 June 1996. 10 Aug. 1996
>> <news:sci.psychology.misc>.

*In-Text Citation:* (Alvoeiro)

The following example is from an e-mail discussion group. The address at the end of the citation is from the group's archives, available on the Web. If you don't have an Internet address for the post you want to cite, include the e-mail address of the group's moderator or supervisor.

> Ledgerberg, Joshua. "Re: You Shall Know Them."
>> Online posting. 2 May 1997. Darwin
>> Discussion Group. 27 May 1998 <http://
>> rjohara.uncg.edu>.

*In-Text Citation:* (Ledgerberg)

### 3.76  AN E-MAIL MESSAGE

> Tobin, Lad. "Teaching the TA Seminar." E-mail
>> to the author. 8 July 1996.

*In-Text Citation:* (Tobin)

### 3.77  A SOUND CLIP

> Gonzales, Richard. "Asian American Political
>> Strength." Natl. Public Radio. 27 May 1998.
>> 12 July 1998 <http://www.npr.org/ramfiles/
>> 980527.me.12.ram>.

*In-Text Citation:* (Gonzales)

### 3.78  AN INTERVIEW

> Boukreev, Anatoli. Interview. <u>Outside Online</u>
>> 14 Nov. 1997. 27 May 1998 <http://outside.

starwave.com/news/123097/anatolitrans.

html>.

*In-Text Citation:*   (Boukreev)

**3.79 SYNCHRONOUS COMMUNICATION (MOOS, MUDS, IRCS)**

Fanderclai, Terri. Online interview. 11 Nov. 1996.

LinguaMOO. 11 Nov. 1996 <telnet://

purple-crayon.media.mit.edu_8888>.

*In-Text Citation:*   (Fanderclai)

# Part Four:
# Student Essay in MLA Style

Thankfully, the popular press and psychological community have focused a great deal of attention on the eating disorders among American girls and women in recent years. But what about men and boys? Are they really immune to the cultural pressure to "look good"? Alex Siegwin has an answer—a resounding "no." In the following essay, Alex draws on his own experience as a weight lifter, and through additional research offers a disturbing picture of American males who suffer from the "Adonis Complex," the desire to look muscled and "manly." This can lead to a problem that psychologists call "muscle dysmorphia," an obsessive-compulsive disorder that in some ways resembles the struggles of women and girls.

One of the things I admire about Alex's essay is how deftly he uses his personal experiences with the Adonis Complex as a means of illuminating the problem, but his personal story never gets center stage. It isn't necessary. The research is compelling enough. When Alex does talk about himself, it's always relevant to the idea or claim he's developing. Alex establishes his authority on the topic because of his experience in the gym, but he gathers evidence from other sources that makes the essay even more powerful. It's clear that Alex *cares* enough to dig deeply and find out as much as he can, for himself and his readers.

Perhaps the best test of any writing is whether after having read it we see the world just a little bit differently; I know I will after reading "The Adonis Complex: Progressing to Failure." As an American male, I admit that I've been seduced by that look epitomized by the guys on "Baywatch." I wouldn't mind looking a little like that. But Alex has alerted me to the costs of making such a body, and they are high.

Siegwin 1

Alexander M. Siegwin

Professor Jill Heney

English 102-500

31 July 2002

The Adonis Complex: Progressing to Failure

    Human beings have always been vain creatures. Consider how much time we spend in front of a mirror. Traditionally, it was women who were considered mirror "maniacs." They always felt, and often were, judged by society based on their looks. Sadly, now it's men's turn. Many endure restrictive diets, endless hours of training, and a constant fear of fat in an attempt to be content with what they see in the mirror. Equality of the sexes is great, but do men really want to shoulder the weight of body scrutiny?

    Every day men become increasingly dissatisfied with their bodies, but the majority is obviously not doing anything about it because now one in four American males is overweight ("Systematic Review" 715-717). Despite this depressing statistic, worldwide men of all ages are developing an unhealthy preoccupation with how muscular, lean, or fit they appear. This unhealthy preoccupation is defined by psychiatrists as muscle dysmorphia,

*Double-space everything, including the heading that lists your name, instructor, course, and date.*

*The title should be centered but not bolded or italicized. Double-space to the first line.*

*What a great first line! Work for a strong opening like this one.*

*Cite author-less Web documents by abbreviating the title.*

Siegwin 2

an obsessive-compulsive disorder that affects
a person's perception of his body image
(Shabi). The press has dubbed this disorder
the Adonis Complex, after the half-man,
half-god of Greek mythology who was convinced
that he was the epitome of masculinity.

*This source,
like most Web
documents,
lacked page
numbers.*

Although there are many egomaniacal men
today, I think few seriously think that highly
of themselves. In fact, many men today feel a
need to improve their physiques and are
willing to do almost anything to do it. In the
gym, they are known as "bigorexics." The old
creed that men shouldn't worry about their
appearance has broken down. "I get sick of it
at times, but you gotta do it to look your
best," says fitness model John Hnatyschak,
referring to his constant trips to the gym
(qtd. in Shabi). Ironically, his words are
very much like the vocabulary women use
regarding their appearance. Just how much
damage are these men inflicting on
themselves, and given the high level
of obesity among American men, is the
hunger to look good really that bad?

*Here Alex
poses the
question that
is the focus of
his essay. We
expect him, at
some point, to
answer this
question.
Does he do it
sufficiently?*

"Hardgainers" vs. Superman

Just like an anorexic, I
always saw myself as over fat, and
endured a long period of starvation

*In MLA style,
subheadings and/or
numbers may be used to
separate sections that
have a unified focus.
Numbers are centered,
but subheadings are set
flush left. Notice that
there are no extra
spaces around it.*

Siegwin 3

just to look leaner in the mirror. Most men, however, tend to see dieting as a woman's solution to the problem. Men prefer to burn it off (Shabi). It sounds more masculine to say that you spent an hour on the treadmill than it does to admit to eating less. This is a helpful veil to throw over the problem, because exercising doesn't show the same signs as starvation, and a well-toned body doesn't appear deprived. It is not uncommon for men with muscle dysmorphia to spend more than an hour lifting, twice a day, while doing cardiovascular training daily for at least an hour.

*This is the first time Alex refers to himself. Does this disclosure change the way you read the rest of his essay?*

Yet gaining muscle is not easy. A complication for many boys and young men has to do with their metabolism. They are "ectomorphs," known as "hardgainers" in the gym, and will resist any weight gain at all. They are typically very lean, with narrow hips and shoulders (McFarling A1). Ectomorphs wish they had the genetic predisposition of mesomorphs, men who have the physiques we all envy--broad shoulders, narrow hips, and broad back: they tend to maintain a low body fat percentage and gain muscle rather easily. The comic book character Superman has a classic mesomorph

Siegwin 4

body. Finally there are the endomorphs like
me--broad, wide, and beefy men who possess
slow metabolism and can quickly gain fat and
muscle. Endomorphic men suffer from the
Adonis Complex as well, although in a
different way. They develop a fear of being
over fat, so anorexia nervosa and bulimia
often accompany or even worsen muscle
dysmorphia in endomorphic males.

Men who obsess about building up their
"chicken legs" or "puny chest" inevitably
end up dissatisfied, and they suffer from
paranoia so overwhelming that hardgainers
may never wear shorts or change in public
locker rooms. The problem increases with
each unnecessary training session because
they will find a fault in every
accomplishment. It is like running in a
gerbil wheel; a road trip to nowhere.
Simon Waterson, a distinguished British
personal trainer, says hardgainers often
feel that "there will always be someone
bigger and better than you, so you can
never be satisfied, and there's no end to
it"(qtd. in Shabi).

Just what are these men working
for? The traits they desire include wide
shoulders (by far the hardest to obtain, in

*One of the ways that writers establish their presence without simply referring to themselves is through original language. Alex's metaphor about the gerbil reminds us that there is an author here.*

my opinion), large arms, a barrel chest, and
of course, the always attractive six-pack
abs. This involves training muscle groups
that were once considered secondary, putting
themselves at risk for overtraining just to
get a broad back, flaring calves, deep
hamstrings, and huge thighs (Olivardio 1293).
The Media and Musclemania

Magazines like <u>FLEX</u> feature entire
articles dedicated to improving these
muscle groups, and the techniques are
intense. These are, of course, loaded with
pictures of professional bodybuilders (and
every bodybuilder I have met suffers from
muscle dysmorphia) that are intended to
inspire the reader. I have never heard
anyone request, "Flex your calves for me,"
but men with the Adonis Complex think that
everyone around them is as critical as a
bodybuilding judge.

But it's not just the specialty
magazines that promote the Adonis Complex.
Every year, popular magazine models become
thinner and more defined. The stars of
cinema seem to add ten pounds of muscle
for every movie they make. Arnold
Schwarzenegger's body would be considered
the norm among current actors, such as

Siegwin 6

Michael Clark Duncan. Casual lifters, bodybuilders, and even teenage athletes see these actors and become motivated to chase a near-impossible dream.

The average guy forgets that the men on the cover of GQ and FLEX magazine are paid to do nothing except look good. These guys have access to the best equipment, money for the supplements, and all the time they need to sculpt a body reminiscent of a Greek god. Bodybuilding, beyond what is done to improve health and athleticism, is pure vanity. Professional bodybuilder Scott McNicol agrees, arguing that it all boils down to "whose arms are bigger, who's tanner, who looks the best? I think a lot of that is artificial and you could tell by the way they look and the way they act aggressively" (qtd. in Shabi).

Magazines, such as Muscle Media and FLEX, may claim that their articles are innocent, that they only want to help men be healthier. Try reading one of their "inspirational" articles. They practically tell you to put your life on hold until you have reached your goals, and the cycle is unending because they also tell you to set new goals every time you make an

*See how nicely Alex weaves quoted material into his own prose? Rather than include the full quote from his source, Alex uses only that part that is relevant and striking.*

Siegwin 7

accomplishment. <u>FLEX</u> magazine routinely
interviews bodybuilders (who are muscular
beyond what any human could accomplish
naturally), inquiring about their secrets to
success. "I was always psychotic when it came
to training and eating," said King Kamali,
one of the top ten bodybuilders in the world.
"I didn't go on vacation or go out with
friends. For seven years straight, I didn't
go to family gatherings, Thanksgiving,
Christmas, nothing. That's how obsessed I
was" (Kamali 81). Just what were his secrets
to success? Nothing a steroid-free lifter
could accomplish: eating a minimum of six
thousand calories a day, lifting twice a day
for three consecutive days, often training
the same muscle group twice in one week.

    This won't be enough year-round; when
a bodybuilding competition is on the
horizon, he also suggests doing as much as
three hours on a treadmill or stationary
bicycle to "cut up" and attain single-digit
bodyfat percentage (81). Nobody clean of
steroids and with a life outside the gym
could accomplish this and still function as
a human being. Magazines present this advice
as though any regular man-on-the-street
could do it if he just had the willpower.

Siegwin 8

Such advice is potentially harmful to a
disillusioned male with muscle dysmorphia.

The Adonis Complex and Lifestyle

The media is not always to blame for
the obsession with muscularity. Most radical
changes in a person's lifestyle are brought
on by an emotional shock such as falling in
love, shame, the death of someone close, or
a traumatic event. For example, I went from
291 pounds to 192 pounds in less than a
year. What in the world could make a high
school junior lose ninety-nine pounds so
fast? A girl.

*Do you think the subheadings are helpful?*

The religious adherence to strict
workouts and diet was a part of my daily
life up until a year at college taught me
the importance of moderation and balance.
My cousin Scott also made an amazing
transformation. When he graduated from
high school, he weighed only one hundred
and forty pounds and was built like a
stork. Four years later and thirty pounds
heavier, he is built like a tank. Scott
did this because he was tired of being
small.

Some will attempt to perfect their
bodies out of jealousy or spite. In younger
boys, pressure from parents and coaches may

Siegwin 9

start them on a path that could eventually
lead to muscle dysmorphia, even though the
pressure was only meant to motivate the
child to excel. Combined with the media's
never-ending musclemania campaign, children
interpret the message this way: men are
judged on appearance, and society prefers
that appearance to be muscular. It is
certainly more prevalent in men under forty,
but that is not a rule. Older men are not
just worrying about receding hairlines and
weakened vision; articles and contests are
encouraging men over sixty to join the quest
for more muscles (Aniansson 100). Older men
should do this, but only with the guidance
of a physician and personal trainer. Many
might overestimate their capacity and decide
to go it alone because the will to improve
can be stronger than the bones and joints
(Aniansson 102).

Some men, in pursuit of near-impossible
bodies that media figures (such as
Schwarzenegger) present, may resort to
perhaps the most damaging method that a
person could: use of anabolic steroids. This
practice is not just restricted to athletes
who are tempted by promises of increased
size, strength, and performance. Because

Siegwin 10

steroids are anabolic and thermogenic,
meaning they build muscle and burn fat, the
temptation to use them is sometimes
irresistible for someone suffering from
"bigorexia" (Olivardio 1295). Bigorexics
overlook the dangers, and believe me, there
are many. They include heart disease,
dangerous cholesterol levels, impotence,
acne, depression, rage, and greatly
elevated cancer risks (Whitney 543).

Although the psychological dangers are
primarily short term (still a major risk),
the physical dangers are usually long term
and more damaging. This problem is not
confined to the ultra-vain United States; one
in ten British lifters sampled in 1993 by
their department of health admitted to using
or at least trying steroids (Shabi). Once a
man realizes what steroids will do for his
muscle mass, he is very likely to try them
and their many cousins, such as androgenics
and growth hormones. I know a professional
bodybuilder in northern Idaho who has the
biggest arms, legs, and frame I have ever
seen. Unfortunately, he has all the
undesirable traits of a pubescent teenager:
bad acne and body odor, and violent mood
swings. Even worse are the calcium deposits

that are building up on the peaks of his
biceps, where he injects the steroids.

Seeing the Signs

Can you spot someone who is suffering
from muscle dysmorphia? While the severity
of the disorder will be the determining
factor, all have similar symptoms. Not only
do victims of the problem fret over their
eating and training, they are stressed out
and anxious whenever they are not in the gym
or when they are at a place that might
derail their diet (Anderson 1947). It is a
weird feeling that I have experienced many
times; being away from home made me nervous
for no real reason, and I felt like I was no
longer in control. This constant anxiety
made me reluctant to leave the house for
anything other than lifting or grocery
shopping.

Bigorexics' social and professional
lives will become secondary to their gym
lives. This can be disastrous for someone
with a promising career or college to attend,
or who is involved in a loving relationship.
Men with muscular dysmorphia will plan their
day around meals and training. Counting the
fat, carbohydrate, and protein grams, plus
watching every single calorie, are all common

Siegwin 12

practices of men with the Adonis Complex. Can you imagine how annoying that is to family members, or even worse, a date?

After seeing my grandmother's disappointment at several Sunday dinners and noticing how eccentric it seemed when on a date at a restaurant, I finally stopped being so strict. If you want to see a sight, try detaining a bodybuilder for more than an hour after training; the post-workout meal (which I will admit is important) becomes a ritual, and pity the fool who dares to keep him from it.

Bigorexics develop a preoccupation with food, attempting to get a perfect balance of protein, fat, and carbohydrates at every meal. This is defined as the third eating disorder, orthorexia, another term that is often used at the gym. Physically, it is the least damaging eating disorder, but it is very psychologically, socially, and emotionally detrimental. Left to themselves, muscle dysmorphic men will become depressed, and if they don't see progress that suits them, can sink to a depth of misery that could have suicidal connotations (Anderson 1948).

Perhaps the most common trait is a reluctance to expose their bodies, such as at a public beach or pool. If a bigorexic does manage to remove his shirt, he will be very uncomfortable about how muscular he appears to others. In truth, bigorexics are often much more muscular than any other male present ("Adonis Complex"). They will pursue a near-superhuman workout regimen even when they know the dangers it poses to their health. Casual lifters and bodybuilders alike have come to accept that overtraining will only hinder muscular gains, but a person suffering from muscular dysmorphia doesn't care. They need the hormonal rush to feel like they have accomplished something.

I too have felt the euphoric calm that settles in after a rigorous and satisfying lifting session. But if bigorexics miss a training session due to circumstances beyond their control (I can't emphasize enough how rarely that happens), they will literally panic. Their brain starts fretting over how they will make up for the missed day: perhaps lifting chest and back on Monday to make up for missing back on Sunday? What about the amount of food they ate the day they missed? Will the lack of exercise cause them to store the calories as fat rather than use it to build muscle? Actually, for someone

Siegwin 14

subjecting their body to such an exhausting routine, a day off can do wonders ("Overtraining Syndrome"). It can boost their taxed immune system, and lower the amount of lactic acid produced by overtaxed muscles the liver must change into glucose to meet the body's energy needs (Choi 992-996).

Recovering

Men with muscle dysmorphia rarely recover on their own. And they will almost never ask for help, because for a man to be assisted, he must first come out and admit he has a problem. Eileen Murphy, the clinical director of the National Center for Eating Disorders, understood this: "I can see the agony it has taken for men to actually come and see me. It seems they have to reach a greater level of despair before they do something about it." She also stated that for every man who comes to see her, there are many more suffering alone (Shabi). It is a form of obsessive-compulsive disorder, and just like other types of obsessive-compulsive disorders, there are certain things that must and must not be done. Telling them that they have a problem will not work, because this will embarrass them and cause them to draw inward. Asking

Siegwin 15

questions, listening, and letting them know
that you are concerned are the best ways to
get them to admit they need help. Once they
do, nutritional counseling and therapy will
likely make them change their lifestyle. The
most important thing that one can do for a
man with muscle dysmorphia is wait, be
patient, and listen ("Adonis Complex").

While there is no denying that we are
falling into a pit of over fatness, males
who are tormented by muscular dysmorphia are
doing more harm than good. A man who can
recognize his own crippling disorder must
ask himself, "Is this level of muscularity I
pursue worth all the physical, emotional,
and social sacrifices I make daily?" He will
most likely agree that it is not, but he may
not be able to change his lifestyle
overnight. Some men may be able to handle it
on their own, but most will need the
comfort, support, and reassurance of friends and
loved ones; some may need to seek professional
help. This is not to say that they should stop
going to the gym, but there is a balance that a
man must maintain in order to lead a healthy
life.

*Here Alex directly answers the question he posed at the beginning of his essay. This is his thesis. In many ways, hasn't the paper been building to this idea for many pages now, making the statement almost inevitable and unsurprising? Is that a problem or a virtue of the essay?*

Works Cited

"The Adonis Complex." <u>Addictions and More</u> June
    2002. 16 July 2002 <http://www.addictions.
    net/men's_dissatisfaction.htm>.

Alpert, Jonathan E. "Harvard Med School
    Begins Study of Depression." <u>DataMonitor</u>
    <u>Healthcare Newswire</u> 26 June 2002
    <http://news.foot.com/news/697.html>.

Anderson, Arnold. "The Adonis Complex: The
    Secret Crisis of Male Body Obsession."
    <u>American Journal of Psychiatry</u> 158
    (2001): 1947-1948.

Aniansson, A., et al. "Muscle Function in 75-
    Year-Old Men and Women: A Longitudinal
    Study." <u>Scandinavian Journal of</u>
    <u>Rehabilitative Medicine</u> 9 (1983):
    92-102.

Choi, D., et al. "Effect of Passive and
    Active Recovery on the Resynthesis of
    Muscle Glycogen." <u>Medicine and Science</u>
    <u>in Sports and Exercise</u> 26 (1994):
    992-996.

Kamali, King. "King-Size Delts." <u>Muscle and</u>
    <u>Fitness</u> Nov. 2001: 79-82.

McFarling, Usha Lee. "Fidgeting Might Be Why
    Some People Stay Slim." <u>Austin American</u>
    <u>Statesman</u> 9 Jan. 1999: A18.

Olivardio, Roberto, et al. "Muscle Dysmorphia
    in Male Weightlifters: A Case-Control
    Study." <u>American Journal of Psychiatry</u>
    157 (2000): 1291-1296.

"Overtraining Syndrome." <u>SportsMed Web:</u>
    <u>Physiology & Training</u>. 3 Mar. 2001

<http://www.rice.edu/~jenky/sports/
overtraining.html>.

Shabi, Rachel. "Muscle Mania." <u>Q-Online</u>
11 Oct. 2001. 14 July 2002 <http://www.
q.co.za/2001/2001/10/11health-
bogorexia.html>.

"Systematic Review of the Interventions for
the Prevention and Treatment of Obesity,
and the Maintenance of Weight Loss."
<u>International Journal of Obesity</u> 21
(1997): 715-737.

Whitney, Eleanor Noss, and Sharon Rady
Rolfes. "Highlight 14: Supplements and
Ergogenic Aids Athletes Use."
<u>Understanding Nutrition</u>. 7th ed. New
York: West Publishing, 1996. 540-546.

# Guide to APA Style

The Modern Language Association (MLA) author/page number system for citing borrowed material, described in Appendix A, is the standard for most papers written in the humanities, though some disciplines in the fine arts as well as history and philosophy may still use the footnote system. Confirm with your instructor that the MLA system is the one to use for your paper.

Another popular documentation style is the American Psychological Association (APA) author/date system. APA style is the standard for papers in the social sciences as well as biology, earth science, education, and business. In those disciplines, the currency of the material cited is often important.

I think you'll find APA style easy to use, especially if you've had some practice with MLA. Converting from one style to the other is easy. Basically, the APA author/date style cites the author of the borrowed material and the year it appeared. A more complete citation is listed in the "References" (the APA version of MLA's "Works Cited") at the back of the paper. (See the sample APA-style paper in Part Four of this appendix.)

The *Publication Manual of the American Psychological Association*\* is the authoritative reference on APA style, and the fifth edition, published in 2001, features updates on citing electronic sources, among other things. Though the information in the section that follows should answer your questions, check the manual when in doubt. A handy "cribsheet," which provides highlights from the *Publication Manual,* is also available online at the following Web address:

http://www.psychwww.com

---

\**Publication Manual of the American Psychological Association,* 5th ed. Washington, DC: APA, 2001.

## Directory of APA Style

## Recent APA Style Changes

- Article abstracts should be no longer than 120 words.
- Use italics, rather than underlining.
- When quoting from electronic sources that lack page or paragraph numbers, use subheadings, if available, to pinpoint the location of borrowed material.
- It's okay to use boldface.
- Use the paragraph symbol (¶) or the abbreviation *para* in the citation to identify the location of borrowed material in an electronic source.
- In the references, list up to six authors. For more than six, list the first and use the abbreviation *et al*.
- Expanded list of examples to reflect a wider variety of Internet documents.
- Use serif typeface in text, and san serif in figures, tables, and illustrations.

*\*Source:* APA *Publication Manual,* 5th. ed.

# Part One: How the Essay Should Look

### 1.1 PAGE FORMAT

Papers should be double-spaced, with at least 1-inch margins on all sides. Number all pages consecutively, beginning with the title page; put the page number in the upper-righthand corner. Above or five spaces to the left of the page number, place an abbreviated title of the paper on every page, in case pages get separated. As a rule, the first line of all paragraphs of text should be indented five spaces.

### 1.2 TITLE PAGE

Unlike a paper in MLA style, an APA-style paper often has a separate title page, containing the following information: the title of the paper, the author, and the author's affiliation (e.g., what university she is from). See Figure B1. At the top of the title page, in uppercase letters, you may also include a *running head,* or an abbreviation of the title (fifty characters or less, including spaces). A page header, which uses the first two or three words of the title followed by the

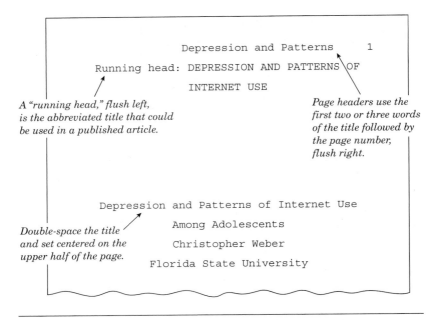

Depression and Patterns        1

Running head: DEPRESSION AND PATTERNS OF

INTERNET USE

*A "running head," flush left,*
*is the abbreviated title that could*
*be used in a published article.*

*Page headers use the*
*first two or three words*
*of the title followed by*
*the page number,*
*flush right.*

Depression and Patterns of Internet Use

Among Adolescents

Christopher Weber

Florida State University

*Double-space the title*
*and set centered on the*
*upper half of the page.*

**FIGURE B1**    **Title Page in APA Style**

page number, begins on the title page, too. This is different from the running head, which tends to be longer and appears only on the title page. Each line of information should be centered and double-spaced.

### 1.3 ABSTRACT

Though it's not always required, many APA-style papers include a short abstract (no longer than 120 words) following the title page. See Figure B2. An abstract is essentially a short summary of the paper's contents. This is a key feature, since it's usually the first thing a reader encounters. The abstract should include statements about what problem or question the paper examines and what approach it follows; the abstract should also cite the thesis and significant findings. Type the title "Abstract" at the top of the page. Type the abstract text in a single block, without indenting.

### 1.4 BODY OF THE PAPER

The body of the paper begins with the center title, followed by a double space and then the text. A page number (usually an abbreviated title and "3" if the paper has a title page and abstract) should appear in the upper-righthand corner. See Figure B3.

*An abstract usually follows the title page.*
*This is a concise (no longer than 120 words)*
*summary of the article and its thesis,*
*purpose, or findings.*

Depression and Patterns      2

Abstract

With the growth of the Internet as both a

source of information and entertainment,

researchers have turned their attention to

the psychology of Internet use, particularly

focusing on the emotional states of high

Internet users. This project focuses on the

relationship between patterns of Internet

use and depression in adolescent users,

arguing that

*Continue the*
*page header.*

**FIGURE B2**    **The Abstract Page**

Depression and Patterns      3

Depression and Patterns of Internet Use

Among Adolescents

Before Johnny Beale's family got a new

computer in August 2002, the sixteen-year-

old high school student estimated that he

spent about twenty minutes a day online,

mostly checking his e-mail. Within months,

however, Beale's time at the computer

tripled, and he admitted that he spent most

of his time playing games. At first, his

family noticed

*Center the title*
*of the paper*
*and double-space*
*to begin the body*
*of the text.*

**FIGURE B3**    **The Body of the Paper in APA Style**

You may find that you want to use headings within your paper. If your paper is fairly formal, some headings might be prescribed, such as "Introduction," "Method," "Results," and "Discussion." Or create your own heads to clarify the organization of your paper.

If you use headings, the APA recommends a hierarchy like this:

CENTERED UPPERCASE

Centered Upper- and Lowercase

Centered, Italicized, Upper- and Lowercase

Flush Left, Italicized, Upper- and Lowercase

Indented, Italicized, lowercase; ends with period.

Note that none of these headings is typed in **bold** or *italic* type; rather, underlining is used to distinguish the second-, third-, and fourth-level headings. This is the format recommended by APA style. So even if your computer or word processor can produce different kinds of type, you should stick with underlining. (This is also true for titles in your "References" section.) Check with your instructor to make sure of any preferences she may have.

### 1.5 REFERENCES PAGE

All sources cited in the body of the paper are listed alphabetically by author (or title, if anonymous) on the page titled "References." See Figure B4. This list should begin a new page. Each entry is double-spaced; begin each first line flush left, and indent subsequent lines five to seven spaces. Explanation of how to cite various sources in the references follows (see "Part Three: Preparing the 'References' List").

### 1.6 APPENDIX

This is a seldom-used feature of an APA-style paper, though you might find it helpful for presenting specific or tangential material that isn't central to the discussion in the body of your paper: a detailed description of a device described in the paper, a copy of a blank survey, or the like. Each item should begin on a separate page and be labeled "Appendix" followed by "A," "B," and so on, consecutively, if there is more than one page.

### 1.7 NOTES

Several kinds of notes might be included in a paper. The most common is *content notes,* or brief commentaries by the writer

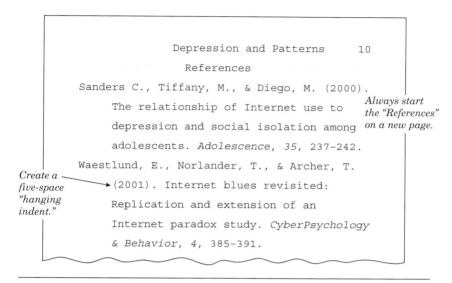

Depression and Patterns     10

References

Sanders C., Tiffany, M., & Diego, M. (2000).
The relationship of Internet use to
depression and social isolation among
adolescents. *Adolescence, 35*, 237–242.

Waestlund, E., Norlander, T., & Archer, T.
(2001). Internet blues revisited:
Replication and extension of an
Internet paradox study. *CyberPsychology
& Behavior, 4*, 385–391.

*Always start the "References" on a new page.*

*Create a five-space "hanging indent."*

**FIGURE B4     The References Page**

keyed to superscript numbers in the body of the text. These notes
are useful for discussion of key points that are relevant but might
be distracting if explored in the text of your paper. Present all
notes, numbered consecutively, on a page titled "Footnotes." Each
note should be double-spaced. Begin each note with the appropriate superscript number, keyed to the text. Indent each first line
five to seven spaces; consecutive lines run the full page measure.

### 1.8 TABLES AND FIGURES

The final section of an APA-style paper features tables and figures mentioned in the text. Tables should all be double-spaced. Type
a table number at the top of the page, flush left. Number tables
"Table 1," "Table 2," and so on, corresponding to the order they are
mentioned in the text. A table may also include a title. Each table
should begin on a separate page.

Figures (illustrations, graphs, charts, photographs, drawings)
are handled similarly to tables. Each should be titled "Figure" and
numbered consecutively. Captions may be included, but all should be
typed on a separate page, clearly labeled "Figure Captions," and
listed in order. For example:

Figure Captions

*Figure 1:* A photograph taken in the 1930s by
Dorthea Lange.

*Figure 2:* Edward Weston took a series of green pepper photographs like this. This is titled "No. 35."

#### 1.9 LANGUAGE AND STYLE

The APA is comfortable with the italics and bold functions of modern word processors, and underlining may soon be a thing of the past. The guidelines for *italicizing* call for its use when writing the following:

- The title of books, periodicals, and publications that appear on microfilm.
- When using new or specialized terms, but only the first time you use them (e.g., the authors' *paradox study* of Internet users . . .)
- When citing a phrase, letter, or word as an example (e.g., the second *a* in *separate* can be remembered by remembering the word *rat*).

The APA calls for quotation marks around the title of an article or book chapter when mentioned in your essay.

Been nagged all your life by the question of whether to spell out numbers or use numerals in APA style? Here, finally, is the answer: numbers less than 10 that aren't precise measurements should be spelled out, and numbers 10 or more should be numeric. Feel better now?

# Part Two:
# Citing Sources in Your Essay

#### 2.1 WHEN THE AUTHOR IS MENTIONED IN THE TEXT

The author/date system is pretty uncomplicated. If you mention the name of the author in text, simply place the year her work was published in parentheses immediately after her name. For example:

Herrick (1999) argued that college testing was biased against minorities.

#### 2.2 WHEN THE AUTHOR ISN'T MENTIONED IN THE TEXT

If you don't mention the author's name in the text, then include that information parenthetically. For example:

A New Hampshire political scientist (Bloom, 1992) recently studied the state's presidential primary.

Note that the author's name and the year of her work are separated by a comma.

## 2.3  WHEN TO CITE PAGE NUMBERS

If the information you're citing came from specific pages (or chapters or sections) of a source, that information may also be included in the parenthetical citation. Including page numbers is essential when quoting a source. For example:

> The first stage of language acquisition is called
> *caretaker speech* (Moskowitz, 1985, pp. 50-51), in
> which children model their parents' language.

The same passage might also be cited this way if the authority's name is mentioned in the text:

> Moskowitz (1985) observed that the first stage of
> language acquisition is called *caretaker speech*
> (pp. 50-51), in which children model their
> parents' language.

## 2.4  A SINGLE WORK BY TWO OR MORE AUTHORS

When a work has two authors, always mention them both whenever you cite their work in your paper. For example:

> Allen and Oliver (1998) observed many cases of
> child abuse and concluded that maltreatment
> inhibited language development.

If a source has more than two authors but less than six, mention them all the first time you refer to their work. However, any subsequent references can include the surname of the first author followed by the abbreviation *et al.* When citing works with six or more authors, *always* use the first author's surname and *et al.*

## 2.5  A WORK WITH NO AUTHOR

When a work has no author, cite an abbreviated title and the year. Place article or chapter titles in quotation marks, and underline book titles. For example:

> The editorial ("Sinking," 1992) concluded that the
> EPA was mired in bureaucratic muck.

**2.6  TWO OR MORE WORKS BY THE SAME AUTHOR**

Works by the same author are usually distinguished by the date; works are rarely published the same year. But if they are, distinguish among works by adding an *a* or *b* immediately following the year in the parenthetical citation. The reference list will also have these suffixes. For example:

> Douglas's studies (1986a) on the mating habits of
> lobsters revealed that the females are dominant.
> He also found that the female lobsters have the
> uncanny ability to smell a loser (1986b).

This citation alerts readers that the information came from two studies by Douglas, both published in 1986.

**2.7  AN INSTITUTIONAL AUTHOR**

When citing a corporation or agency as a source, simply list the year of the study in parentheses if you mention the institution in the text:

> The Environmental Protection Agency (2000) issued
> an alarming report on ozone pollution.

If you don't mention the institutional source in the text, spell it out in its entirety, along with the year. In subsequent parenthetical citations, abbreviate the name. For example:

> A study (Environmental Protection Agency [EPA],
> 2000) predicted dire consequences from continued
> ozone depletion.

And later:

> Continued ozone depletion may result in widespread
> skin cancers (EPA, 2000).

**2.8  MULTIPLE WORKS IN THE SAME PARENTHESES**

Occasionally, you'll want to cite several works at once that speak to a topic you're writing about in your essay. Probably the most common instance is when you refer to the findings of several relevant studies, something that is a good idea as you try to establish a context for what has already been said about your research topic. For example,

> A number of researchers have explored the
>
> connection between Internet use and depression
>
> (Sanders, Field, & Diego, 2000; Waestlund,
>
> Norlander, & Archer, 2001).

When listing multiple authors in the same parenthesis, order them as they appear in the references. Semicolons separate each entry.

### 2.9 INTERVIEWS, E-MAIL, AND LETTERS

Interviews and other personal communications are not listed in the references at the back of the paper, since they are not *recoverable data,* but they are parenthetically cited in the text. Provide the initials and surname of the subject (if not mentioned in the text), the nature of the communication, and the complete date, if possible.

> Nancy Diamonti (personal communication, November
>
> 12, 1990) disagrees with the critics of <u>Sesame
>
> Street</u>.
>
> In a recent e-mail, Michelle Payne (personal
>
> communication, January 4, 2000) complained
>
> that. . . .

### 2.10 NEW EDITIONS OF OLD WORKS

For reprints of older works, include both the year of the original publication and that of the reprint edition (or the translation).

> Pragmatism as a philosophy sought connection
>
> between scientific study and real people's lives
>
> (James, 1906/1978).

### 2.11 A WEB SITE

When referring to an *entire* Web site (see example below), cite the address parenthetically in your essay. Like e-mail, it isn't necessary to include a citation for a Web site in your references list.

```
The Northern Light search engine (http://www.
northernlight.com) is considered the best for
academic research.
```

# Part Three:
# Preparing the "References" List

All parenthetical citations in the body of the paper correspond to a complete listing of sources on the "References" page. The format for this section was described earlier in this appendix (see "References Page").

### 3.1 ORDER OF SOURCES

List the references alphabetically by author or by the first key word of the title if there is no author. The only complication may be if you have several articles or books by the same author. If the sources weren't published in the same year, list them in chronological order, the earliest first. If the sources were published in the *same* year, include a lowercase letter to distinguish them. For example:

```
Lane, B. (1991a). Verbal medicine . . .
Lane, B. (1991b). Writing . . .
```

While the alphabetical principle—listing authors according to the alphabetical placement of their last names—works in most cases, there are a few variations you should be aware of.

- If you have several entries by the same author, list them by year of publication, beginning with the earliest.
- Since scholars and writers often collaborate, you may have several references in which an author is listed with several *different* collaborators. List these alphabetically using the second author's last name. For example,

```
Brown, M., Nelson, A. (2002)
Brown, M., Payne, M. (1999)
```

- Sources with the same authors are listed chronologically.

**3.2  ORDER OF INFORMATION**

A reference to a periodical or book in APA style includes this information, in order: author, date of publication, article title, periodical title, and publication information.

**Author.**   List all authors—last name, comma, and then initials. Invert all authors' names. Use commas to separate authors' names; add an ampersand (&) before the last author's name. When citing an edited book, list the editor(s) in place of the author, and add the abbreviation Ed. or Eds. in parentheses following the last name. End the list of names with a period.

**Date.**   List the year the work was published, along with the date if it's a magazine or newspaper (see "Sample References," following), in parentheses, immediately after the last author's name. Add a period after the closing parenthesis.

**Article or Book Title.**   APA style departs from MLA, at least with respect to periodicals. In APA style, only the first word of the article title is capitalized, and it is not underlined or quoted. Book titles, on the other hand, are italicized; capitalize only the first word of the title and any subtitle. End all titles with periods.

**Periodical Title and Publication Information.**   Italicize the complete periodical title; type it using both uppercase and lowercase letters. Add the volume number (if any), also italicized. Separate the title and volume number with a comma (e.g., *Journal of Mass Communication, 10,* 138–150). If each issue of the periodical starts with page 1, then also include the issue number in parentheses immediately after the volume number (see examples following). End the entry with the page numbers of the article. Use the abbreviation *p.* or *pp.* if you are citing a newspaper. Other APA-style abbreviations include:

| | |
|---|---|
| Chap. | p. (pp.) |
| Ed. | Vol. |
| Rev. ed. | No. |
| 2nd ed. | Pt. |
| Trans. | Suppl. |

For books, list the city and state or country of publication (use postal abbreviations) and the name of the publisher; separate the city and publisher with a colon. End the citation with a period. Cities that do not require state or country abbreviations include:

| | |
|---|---|
| Baltimore | Amsterdam |
| Boston | Jerusalem |
| Chicago | London |
| Los Angeles | Milan |
| New York | Moscow |
| Philadelphia | Paris |
| San Francisco | Rome |
| | Stockholm |
| | Tokyo |
| | Vienna |

Remember that the first line of each citation should begin flush left and all subsequent lines should be indented five to seven spaces. Double-space all entries.

## 3.3 Sample References

### 3.31 A JOURNAL ARTICLE

Cite a journal article like this:

Blager, F. B. (1979). The effect of intervention
on the speech and language of children. *Child
Abuse and Neglect, 5,* 91–96.

*In-Text Citations:* (Blager, 1979)
If the author is mentioned in the text, just parenthetically cite the year: Blager (1979) stated that . . .
If the author is quoted, include the page number(s):
(Blager, 1979, p. 92)

### 3.32 A JOURNAL ARTICLE NOT PAGINATED CONTINUOUSLY

Most journals begin on page 1 with the first issue of the year and continue paginating consecutively for subsequent issues. A few journals, however, start on page 1 with each issue. For these, include the issue number in parentheses following the volume number:

Williams, J., Post, A. T., & Stunk, F. (1991). The
rhetoric of inequality. *Attwanata, 12*(3),
54–67.

*First In-Text Citation:*   (Williams, Post, & Stunk, 1991)
Subsequent citations would use *et al.:*   (Williams et al., 1991)

If quoting material, include the page number(s): (Williams et al., 1991, pp. 55-60)

### 3.33  A MAGAZINE ARTICLE

Maya, P. (1981, December). The civilizing of

   Genie. *Psychology Today*, 28-34.

*In-Text Citations:*   (Maya, 1981)
Maya (1981) observed that . . .
If quoting, include the page number(s):   (Maya, 1981, p. 28)

### 3.34  A NEWSPAPER ARTICLE

Honan, W. (1991, January 24). The war affects

   Broadway. *New York Times,* pp. C15-16.

*In-Text Citations:*   (Honan, 1991)
Honan (1991) argued that . . .
Honan (1991) said that "Broadway is a
battleground" (p. C15).

If there is no author, a common situation with newspaper articles, alphabetize using the first "significant word" in the article title. The parenthetical citation would use an abbreviation of the title in quotation marks, then the year.

### 3.35  A BOOK

Lukas, A. J. (1986). *Common ground: A turbulent*

   *decade in the lives of three American*

   *families.* New York: Random House.

*In-Text Citations:*   (Lukas, 1986)
According to Lukas (1986), . . .
If quoting, include the page number(s).

### 3.36  A BOOK OR ARTICLE WITH MORE THAN ONE AUTHOR

Rosenbaum, A., & O'Leary, D. (1978). Children: The

   unintended victims of marital violence.

*American Journal of Orthopsychiatry, 4,*

692-699.

*In-Text Citations:*    (Rosenbaum & O'Leary, 1978)
Rosenbaum and O'Leary (1978) believed that . . .
If quoting, include the page number(s).

### 3.37  A BOOK OR ARTICLE WITH AN UNKNOWN AUTHOR

New Hampshire loud and clear. (1998, February 19).

*The Boston Globe,* p. 22.

*In-Text Citations:*    ("New Hampshire," 1998)
Or mention the source in text:   In the article "New
Hampshire loud and clear" (1998), . . .
If quoting, provide the page number(s), as well.

*A manual of style* (14th ed.). (1993). Chicago:

University of Chicago Press.

*In-Text Citations:*    (*Manual of Style*, 1993)
According to the *Manual of Style* (1993), . . .
If quoting, include the page number(s).

### 3.38  A BOOK WITH AN INSTITUTIONAL AUTHOR

American Red Cross. (1999). *Advanced first aid and*

*emergency care.* New York: Doubleday.

*In-Text Citations:*    (*Advanced First Aid*, 1999)
The book *Advanced First Aid and Emergency Care*
(1999) stated that . . .
If quoting, include the page number(s).

### 3.39  A BOOK WITH AN EDITOR

Crane, R. S. (Ed.). (1952). *Critics and criticism.*

Chicago: University of Chicago Press.

*In-Text Citations:*    (Crane, 1952)
In his preface, Crane (1952) observed that . . .
If quoting, include the page number(s).

**3.40  A SELECTION IN A BOOK WITH AN EDITOR**

> McKeon, R. (1952). Rhetoric in the Middle Ages. In
>
>     R. S. Crane (Ed.), *Critics and criticism*
>
>     (pp. 260-289). Chicago: University of Chicago
>
>     Press.

*In-Text Citations:*   (McKeon, 1952)
McKeon (1952) argued that . . .
If quoting, include the page number(s).

**3.41  A REPUBLISHED WORK**

> James, W. (1978). *Pragmatism*. Cambridge, MA:
>
>     Harvard University Press. (Original work
>
>     published 1907)

*In-Text Citations:*   (James, 1907/1978)
According to William James (1907/1978), . . .
If quoting, include the page number(s).

**3.42  AN ABSTRACT**

The growth of online databases for articles has increased the availability of full-text versions or abstracts of articles. While the full article is almost always best, sometimes an abstract alone contains some useful information. To cite, use the term *Abstract* in brackets following the title and before the period. If the abstract was retrieved from a database or some other secondary source, include information about it. Aside from the name of the source, this information might involve the date, if different from the year of publication of the original article, an abstract number, or a page number. In the following example, the abstract was used from an online database, *Biological Abstracts*.

> Garcia, R. G. (2002). Evolutionary speed of species
>
>     invasions. *Evolution, 56*, 661—668. Abstract
>
>     obtained from *Biological Abstracts*.

*In-Text Citations:*   (Garcia, 2002), *or* Garcia (2002)
argues that . . .

**3.43  A SOURCE MENTIONED BY ANOTHER SOURCE**

Frequently, you'll read an article that mentions another article you haven't read. Whenever possible, track down that original article and read it in its entirety. But when that's not possible, you need to make it clear that you know of the article and its findings or arguments indirectly. The APA convention for this is to use the expression *as cited in* parenthetically, followed by the author and date of the indirect source. For example, suppose you want to use some information from Eric Weiser's piece that you read about in Charlotte Jones's book. In your essay, you would write something like:

```
Weiser argues (as cited in Jones, 2002) that. . .
```

It isn't necessary to include information about the Weiser article in your references. Just cite the indirect source; in this case, that would be the Jones book.

### 3.44  A BOOK REVIEW

```
Dentan, R. K. (1989). A new look at the brain

    [Review of the book The dreaming brain].

    Psychiatric Journal, 13, 51.
```

*In-Text Citations:*   (Dentan, 1989)
Dentan (1989) argued that . . .
If quoting, include the page number(s).

### 3.45  A GOVERNMENT DOCUMENT

```
U.S. Bureau of the Census. (1991). Statistical

    abstract of the United States (111th ed.).

    Washington, DC: U.S. Government Printing

    Office.
```

*In-Text Citations:*   (U.S. Bureau, 1991)
According to the U.S. Census Bureau (1991), . . .
If quoting, include the page number(s).

### 3.46  A LETTER TO THE EDITOR

```
Hill, A. C. (1992, February 19). A flawed history

    of blacks in Boston [Letter to the editor].

    The Boston Globe, p. 22.
```

*In-Text Citations:*   (Hill, 1992)
Hill (1992) complained that . . .
If quoting, include page number(s).

### 3.47  A PUBLISHED INTERVIEW

Personal interviews are usually not cited in an APA-style paper, unlike published interviews. Here is what such a citation might look like, however:

> Cotton, P. (1982, April). [Interview with Jake
>
>     Tule, psychic]. *Chronicles Magazine,*
>
>     pp. 24–28.

*In-Text Citations:*   (Cotton, 1982)
Cotton (1982) noted that . . .
If quoting, include the page number(s).

### 3.48  A FILM OR VIDEOTAPE

> Hitchcock, A. (Producer & Director). (1954). *Rear*
>
>     *window* [Film]. Los Angeles: MGM.

*In-Text Citations:*   (Hitchcock, 1954)
In *Rear Window,* Hitchcock (1954) . . .

### 3.49  A TELEVISION PROGRAM

> Burns, K. (Executive Producer). (1996). *The West*
>
>     [Television broadcast]. New York and
>
>     Washington, DC: Public Broadcasting Service.

*In-Text Citations:*   (Burns, 1996)
In Ken Burns's (1996) film, . . .

For an episode of a television series, use the scriptwriter as the author, and provide the director's name after the scriptwriter. List the producer's name after the episode.

> *In-Text Citations:*   (Duncan, 1996)
> In the second episode, Duncan (1996) explores . . .

### 3.50  A MUSICAL RECORDING

> Wolf, K. (1986). Muddy roads [Recorded by E.
>
>     Clapton]. On *Gold in California* [CD].
>
>     Santa Monica, CA: Rhino Records. (1990)

*In-Text Citations:*    (Wolf, 1986, track 5)
In Wolf's (1986) song, . . .

### 3.51  A COMPUTER PROGRAM

TLP.EXE (Version 1.0) [Computer software]. (1991).

Hollis, NH: Transparent Language.

*In-Text Citations:*    (TLP.EXE Version 1.0, 1991)
In TLP.EXE Version 1.0 (1991), a pop-up window . . .

## 3.6  Citing Electronic Sources

The ever-changing Internet is forcing continual change on professional organizations such as the APA. The fifth edition of the
group's *Publication Manual* significantly expanded instructions on
how to cite electronic sources, largely reflecting the growth in the
variety of documents on the Web. The APA's Web page, *www.
apastyle.org,* includes some excerpted information from the
*Publication Manual* and is a good source of news for any new
changes in documentation methods. But much of what you need to
know can be found here. The key in any citation is to help readers
find the original sources if they want to, and for Web-based documents, that means the Internet address, or URL, has to be accurate.
The copy-and-paste function of your word-processing program will be
your ally in this.

The essential information when citing an electronic source, in
order, includes the following:

- The author(s), if indicated
- The title of the document, Web page, or newsgroup
- A date of publication, update, or retrieval
- The Internet address, or URL

### 3.61  AN ELECTRONIC VERSION OF AN ARTICLE ALSO IN PRINT

Because so much scholarly information on the Web is simply an
electronic version of an article published in print, some of what you
cite will simply list the conventional bibliographic information for
any periodical article. But if you only viewed an electronic version,
you must indicate that in your citation. For example,

Codrescu, A. (March, 2002). Curious? Untouchable

porcelain meets fluttering pigeons

[Electronic version]. *Smithsonian,* 104.

*In-Text Citation:* (Codrescu, 2002), *or* Codrescu (2002) believes that . . .

If you suspect that the electronic version of an article that also appeared in print has been changed in any way, then you should include the date you retrieved the article from the Web and the URL of the document. For example,

Ballenger, B. (1999). Befriending the Internet.

*The Curious Researcher,* 59-76. Retrieved

July 18, 2002, from http://english.

boisestate.edu/bballenger

*In-Text Citation:* (Ballenger, 1999) *or* Ballenger

(1999) features an exercise . . .

### 3.62 AN ARTICLE ONLY ON THE INTERNET

Adler, J. (1996). Save endangered species, not

the Endangered Species Act. *Intellectual*

*Ammunition.* Retrieved October 12, 1999,

from http://www.heartland.org/05jnfb96.htm

*In-Text Citations:* (Adler, 1996)
According to Adler (1996) . . .
If quoting, include page number(s).

### 3.63 AN ELECTRONIC TEXT

*Encyclopedia Mythica.* (1996). Retrieved December

1, 1999, from http://www.pantheon.org/myth

*In-Text Citations:* (*Encyclopedia Mythica,* 1996)
The *Encyclopedia Mythica* (1996) presents . . .

If the text is an electronic version of a book published in print earlier, include the original publication date in parentheses following the title: (Orig. pub. 1908)

### 3.64 AN ARTICLE OR ABSTRACT FROM A LIBRARY DATABASE

As mentioned earlier, library databases, often accessed online, increasingly offer not just citations of articles, but full-text versions or abstracts, too. This wonderful service can make a trip to the library superfluous. When citing an article or abstract from a database, simply include the name of that database at the end of the citation followed by a period.

> Ullman, S., & Brecklin, L. (2002). Sexual assault
>       history and suicidal behavior in a national
>       sample of women. *Suicide and Life Threatening*
>       *Behavior, 32,* 117-130. Retrieved October 18,
>       2002, from Electronic Collections Online
>       database.

*In-Text Citations:*    (Ullman & Brecklin, 2002), *or if you like*
Ullman and Brecklin (2002) argue that . . .

An abstract from an electronic database is cited much the same way except to clarify that the source *is* an abstract. For example,

> Warm, A., & Murray, C. (2002). Who helps? Supporting
>       people who self harm. *Journal of Mental*
>       *Health, 11,* 121-130. Abstract retrieved July
>       19, 2002, from PsychINFO database.

*In-Text Citations:*    (Warm & Murray, 2002), *or*
According to Warm and Murray (2002). . .

### 3.65  A PART OF A WORK

> Hunter, J. (n.d.). Achilles. In *Encyclopedia*
>       *Mythica.* Retrieved January 4, 2000, from
>       http://www.pantheon.org/myth/achill

*In-Text Citations:*    (Hunter, n.d.)
According to Hunter (no date), Achilles was . . .
If quoting, include the page or paragraph number(s), if any.

### 3.66  AN ONLINE JOURNAL

> Schneider, M. (1998). The nowhere man and mother
>       nature's son: Collaboration and resentment

```
in the lyrical ballads of the Beatles.

Anthropoetics, 4(2), 1-11. Retrieved

November 24, 1999, from http://www.humnet.

ucla.edu/humnet/anthropoetics/ap0402/

utopia.htm
```

*In-Text Citations:* (Schneider, 1998)
Schneider (1998) recently observed that . . .
If quoting, include page or paragraph numbers, if any.

### 3.67  A NEWSPAPER ARTICLE

It's not hard anymore to find articles online from all the major American and even international newspapers. Like other nonscholarly periodicals, include more specific information about date of publication in the parenthesis following the author's name, and as usual, include the date retrieved and the URL.

```
Broad, J. W. (2002, July 18). Piece by piece a

    Civil War battleship is pulled from the sea.

    New York Times. Retrieved July 18, 2002, from

    http://www.nytimes.com
```

*In-Text Citations:* (Broad, 2002) *or* Broad (2002)

reports that . . .

### 3.68  A WEB PAGE

If you're referring to an entire Web site in the text of your essay, include the address parenthetically. However, there is no need to include it in the reference list. For example:

```
The Northern Light search engine (http://www.

    northernlight.com) is considered the best for

    academic research.
```

### 3.69  DISCUSSION LISTS

Discussion lists abound on the Internet. They range from groups of flirtatious teenagers to those with a serious academic purpose. Though virtually all of these discussion lists are based on e-mail, they do vary a bit. The most useful lists for academic research tend to be e-mail discussion lists called listservs. Newsgroups, or usenet groups, are extremely popular among more general Internet users. There are various search engines that will help you find these discussion groups on your topic. You can join or monitor the current discussion or, in some cases, search the archives for contributions that interest you. Google is a great search tool for newsgroups and includes an archive for many of them. *If there are no archives, don't include the citation in your references since the information isn't recoverable.* However, you may still cite these in your essay as a personal communication (see Part Two, Section 2.9)

The method of citation varies slightly if it's a newsgroup, an online forum, or a listserv. For example,

```
Hord, J. (2002, July 11). Why do pigeons lift one
    wing up in the air? [Msg 5]. Message posted
    to rec://pets.birds.pigeons
```

*In-Text Citations:*   (Hord), *or* Hord asks (2002) . . .

Note that the citation includes the subject line of the message as the title, and the message number of the "thread" (the particular discussion topic). The protocol for this newsgroup is *rec,* which indicates the list is hobby oriented.

Listservs, or electronic mailing lists, would be cited this way:

```
Cook, D. (2002, July 19). Grammar and the teaching
    of writing. Message posted to the CompTalk
    electronic mailing list, archived at
    http://listserv.comptalk.boisestate.edu
```

*In-Text Citations:*   (Cook, 2002), *or* According to Cook (2002) . . .

### 3.70 E-MAIL

E-mail is not cited in the list of references. But you should cite e-mail in the text of your essay. It should look like this:

*In-Text Citations:*   Michelle Payne (personal communication, January 4, 2000) believes that PDAs are silly . . .

### 3.71 CD-ROM DATABASES AND ENCYCLOPEDIAS

Cite a CD-based database like an online database, including the retrieval date. For example:

```
Drugs and Drug Interaction. (1999). Encyclopaedia
     Britannica. Retrieved from Encyclopaedia
     Britannica.
```

*In-Text Citation:*   ("Drugs and Drug Interaction," 1999)

```
Kolata, G. (1996, July 10). Research links
     writing style to the risk of Alzheimer's.
     New York Times. Retrieved from
     UMI-Proquest/Newspaper Abstracts database.
```

*In-Text Citation:*   (Kolata, 1996)

# Part Four:
# Sample Paper in APA Style

I love the courage of this student essay. With clarity and passion, T. J. Fuller goes against the current of popular thought that racism in the United States, while still somewhat of a problem, is no longer pervasive. She challenges fellow whites to closely examine their own beliefs about minorities, and confesses that she, too, might be a racist. Whites in the United States, she argues, have become so used to privilege that they no longer notice that skin color has something to do with it.

"Racism in America" is not an exploratory research essay but a more familiar argumentative research paper. T. J. Fuller makes a claim and then develops it, using evidence from her research and her own experience. It's the latter move—the resort to the first-person and evidence from personal experience—that distinguishes this essay from much conventional argumentative writing. As you read the essay, consider whether this makes the argument stronger.

Argument is a common form of research-based writing. At first blush, it seems like it's a sharp contrast to the more exploratory, open-ended method of inquiry of the researched essay. But consider how those more open-ended techniques and stances for exploring a topic—fastwriting, question-asking, and withholding judgment—can help a writer *find* arguments. Sometimes you need to first find out what you think before you decide what you want to claim.

I don't know whether T. J.'s essay began with a question, but I like to think it did. Even when you are asked to write an argumentative essay such as "Racism in America," the methods of inquiry promoted in this book can help you find your way.

*Begin pagi-
nation on the
cover page.*

Racism in America: Still Going Strong

*Center title
and your
name.*

T. J. Fuller

English 102

Professor Teresa Dewey

10 May 2002

Racism in America: Still Going Strong

America is a country that was built upon inequality and racism, and many whites continue to benefit from them. However, most whites do not see themselves as being racist or contributing to racism in any way; in fact, many are quick to say that some of their best friends are people of color. Yet whites benefit greatly from racism and while few would admit to enjoying these benefits, even fewer work to dismantle systems that perpetuate them.

*T. J. steps into the essay here and, in a sense, introduces herself. What do you think of this move? Is it effective?*

As a white person, it took me many years to understand the privileges I enjoy. Even though I am discriminated against as a woman, I am still a white woman, and my color bestows on me a multitude of benefits that most whites never even consider. How did it become so easy to take these privileges for granted, and then assume that they aren't really the benefit of skin color after all?

*The implied promise here is that the rest of the essay will answer this question.*

Most white Americans today think that we live in a meritocracy where people get ahead and achieve because of what they accomplish; the American Dream promises that if people work hard and are dedicated, they will rise  through the ranks and have job security, wealth, and happiness, no matter

Racism in America    3

what their skin color. Yet even a brief
study of today's economy proves this to be
false. This argument doesn't even hold true
for white males anymore, let alone members
of the black underclass who are either
trapped in cyclical unemployment or
extremely low-paying service sector jobs and
poverty. Experts publish study upon study
proving that there is a large disparity
between white and black Americans in
virtually all aspects of life: health,
education, housing, and employment.

The promise of the American Dream
provides a convenient explanation for this
disparity--blacks remain an underclass
because they don't work hard enough, don't
value education, and so on. "Blaming the
victim" is very common, not only in
discussions of race but also when discussing
sexual abuse against women. I think we have
all heard at some point in our lives how a
rape victim, particularly a victim of date
rape, asked for it because of the way she
dressed. This, of course, is a ridiculous
assertion. I should no more expect to be
raped if I'm out in a low-cut dress, high
heels, and makeup than I should expect to be
recruited by a professional baseball team

Racism in America    4

because I'm wearing a cap with a team logo
on it.

*T. J. argues
from analogy.
Great tech-
nique, but the
question
always is
this: are the
comparisons
relevant?*

Similarly, a black child is not to
blame if he or she is ill prepared for
college by his or her inner-city school that
has substandard buildings, books, and
equipment. According to Pinkney (1993,
p. 55), "One-third of all black people in
central city areas live below the poverty
threshold. This holds regardless of
region. Black families in central cities
are more likely than white families to
live below the poverty threshold (30
percent versus 10 percent)." You can see
by these ratios that black children are more
likely to be at an educational disadvantage
compared to white children.

*In APA style,
page num-
bers are usu-
ally omitted
in citations,
unless you're
quoting a
source like
here.*

Blaming the victim serves not to
change the social and political systems
that perpetuate the cyclical poverty and
hopelessness many find themselves in.
Instead blame-the-victim social programs
focus on ways to change the individuals to
better fit the systems. According to
William Ryan, who is quoted in Aguirre and
Baker (1995), "there is a terrifying
sameness in the programs that arise from
this kind of analysis."

Racism in America     5

In education, we have programs of
compensatory education to build up the
skills and attitudes of the ghetto
child, rather than structural changes
in the schools. In race relations we
have social engineers who think up
ways of "strengthening" the Negro
family, rather than methods of
eradicating racism. In health care, we
develop new programs to provide health
information (to correct the supposed
ignorance of the poor) and to reach out
and discover cases of untreated illness
and disability (to compensate for their
supposed unwillingness to seek
treatment). . . . The formula for
action becomes extraordinarily simple:
change the victim. (p. 126)

Ryan's argument is quite valid. Blaming
the victim not only removes culpability from
those who benefit from the creation of the
underclass, but turns the symptoms of
poverty into the reasons for poverty. Under
this model, being poor is a result of not
working hard enough or lack of desire to
achieve, alcoholism, drug abuse, or any other
symptom of hopelessness and desperation.
In reality, effects of the lack of jobs in

*Block quotations of 40 words or more. Quotation marks are not needed when you block.*

the inner city that pay livable wages should
be analyzed as causes of poverty.

I can already hear the rebuttals
from whites who buy into the
blame-the-victim ideology: "When my
great-great grandparents came to this
country, they didn't have anything.
They learned the language and worked
hard and they made it. Why should I
have to pay extra taxes to fund lazy
people who just don't want to work?"

There are so many things wrong with
this statement that I hardly know where to
begin. Primarily, the difference between my
fore-parents' stories and those of African
Americans is that they were (with the
exception of half of my paternal ancestors who
are Cherokee) white and thus much easier to
assimilate into the larger white population.
While they were surely discriminated against,
their group (German immigrants) was replaced
by another white immigrant group, which
automatically raised their social standing.

White immigrant groups formed specific
neighborhoods, social groups, and
specialized skill groups, and were able to
succeed in business in a way that African
Americans could not. In Takaki (1994),

*A key move in
many arguments
is to anticipate
the objections of
those critical of
the writer's posi-
tion. Here T. J.
literally gives
voice to one of
those objections.
Is this effective?*

Robert Blauner claims that the my-immigrant-ancestors-suffered-and-rose argument misses the point. He says that white immigrant groups had much to gain from racism:

> When blacks began to consolidate in skilled and unskilled jobs that yielded relatively decent wages and some security, Germans, Irish, and Italians came along to usurp occupation after occupation, forcing blacks out and down into the least skilled, marginal reaches of the economy. . . . Without such a combination of immigration and white racism, the Harlems and the South Chicagos might have become solid working-class and middle-class communities with the economic and social resources to absorb and aid the incoming masses of Southerners, much as European ethnic groups have been able to do for their newcomers. (p. 155)

The historic lack of economic opportunity for black Americans has far-reaching implications. Because they weren't able to amass wealth, both through income and property, African Americans were unable to pass that wealth down to their descendants. If one looks at the richest

                    Racism in America     8

people in America, most of those came upon
their wealth through inheritance, not
through creating something themselves or
their own hard work.

*Would this*          White immigrant groups also differ
*claim be*
*stronger with*  from African Americans in that the vast
*supporting*     majority of white immigrants came to the
*evidence?*
                 United States freely and could leave, while
nearly all of the ancestors of black
Americans were brought here by force.

        Aside from the differences in how
whites and blacks got their beginnings in
this country, we also differ in how we exist
in contemporary America. Alphonso Pinkney
(1993), in his book *Black Americans*,
provides a statistical picture of the U.S.
that dramatizes the large differences
between whites and blacks in most aspects of
modern life. In health care, black Americans
are at much higher risk of dying than
whites. In its 1985 report, the Task Force
on Black and Minority Health identified six
health problem areas that account for most
of the excess deaths among blacks relative
to whites: cardiovascular disease and
stroke; chemical dependency; diabetes;
homicide, suicide, and unintentional
injuries; and infant mortality.

Racism in America　　9

Another study in Pinkney (1993) found "that low income accounts for at least 54 percent of the excess mortality for blacks" (p. 112). When reviewing the six health problem areas, it is easy to see that many of these are the result of inadequate access to health care, such as pre-natal care and preventative visits, poor diet, and depression.

Health care isn't the only place that one can find the effects of ingrained racism. Self-image is another area that can have an adverse effect on the life chances of African Americans. Many black people internalize the messages they hear and see about African Americans at work, at school, and in the media. Many Euro-Americans get their only access to blacks through the media. The images of blacks that we are most likely to see on the small screen involve those who are being arrested or should be arrested, those who are lazy, illiterate, mentally ill, sexually promiscuous, or just generally sleazy.

In Solomon's (1999) book, *The Habits of Highly Deceptive Media: Decoding Spin and Lies in Mainstream News*, Dr. Michael LeNoir observes that "most of the images that one ethnic group has of another are

*APA has been won over to italics rather than underlining in titles.*

Racism in America    10

developed by the media. The incessant
portrayal of African Americans as criminals
and buffoons has been responsible for the
success of many police programs and sitcoms"
(p. 172).

It's not only the representation of
blacks on fictional TV that misleads; the
curriculum in our schools also leaves a lot to
be desired when addressing issues of blacks in
America. In Boynton (2002), when discussing
the importance of research on African
Americans being done by African Americans,
Nathaniel Norment, Jr. argues that
"ninety-five percent of the research done on
African-Americans has been done by whites, and
95 percent of it has been negative" (p. 36).

As a white person, I can only imagine
growing up with little knowledge of the
history of my people. The accomplishments of
whites are never left out of the history
books, while it wasn't until I decided to
learn on my own that I discovered that
people of color have played a major role in
American history. Perhaps having people of
color participate in the telling of history
will broaden all of our views.

Because of this type of representation,
many blacks believe that other members of

Racism in America     11

their racial group truly mirror what they
see in the media. When asking her mother why
so few blacks lived in their neighborhood,
but instead were segregated to a single
area, an African American woman recalls
being told by her mother " . . . that those
other black people hadn't worked as hard as
she had to overcome the many barriers and
boundaries that other black people were
confined to." This same woman recalls that
she found herself "hating me as a black
individual and also *my* culture" (Tatum,
1997, p. 129).

Perhaps the single most influential
thing that I have read regarding American
racism is part of an essay by Peggy McIntosh
in Richey (1998). McIntosh lists the
privileges that I currently enjoy because of
my racial status. Here is a sampling:

- I can, if I wish, arrange to be in
  the company of people of my race
  most of the time.
- I can swear, or dress in secondhand
  clothes, or not answer letters
  without having people attribute
  these choices to the bad morals,
  the poverty, or the illiteracy of
  my race.

- I can do well in a challenging situation without being called a credit to my race.
- I am never asked to speak for all the people of my racial group.
- I can easily buy posters, postcards, picture books, greeting cards, dolls, toys, and children's magazines featuring people of my race.
- Whether I use checks, credit cards, or cash, I can count on my skin color not to work against the appearance of financial reliability.
- If a cop pulls me over, or if the IRS audits my tax return, I can be sure it is not because of my race.
- No one has ever suggested that I might have dealt drugs in order to afford a certain car or house.

I have tried to share the entire list with as many people as I can because it shows how deeply racism is rooted in our society. How deeply rooted it is in our own belief system.

I have never considered myself a racist, but I am. I have those same little voices in my head that make comments about the black people on day-time talk shows or that warn me to move to the other side of the street when a black man is approaching me. These are voices that I'm ashamed of and immediately shove aside, but they are still there. I grew up with people of color, regularly have people of color to my home, and have people of color in my immediate family. I'm not supposed to have those little voices.

That is what this paper is really about--no matter how good our intentions are as white people, we are socialized and conditioned to feel that we are different and better than people of color. They look different than we do, so they must feel differently and value different things. They don't do well in school because they aren't raised to value education. They don't succeed economically because they don't value hard work or they have no ambition. These arguments are made in ignorance and help to keep the systems in place that keep people of color at the lowest rungs of the socio-economic ladder.

*How effective is it when T. J. implicates herself in the problem here?*

Racism in America     14

References

Aguirre, A., & Baker, D. V. (1995). *Sources: Notable selections in race and ethnicity.* Guilford, CT: Dushkin Publishing Group, Inc.

Boynton, R. S. (2002, April 14). Out of Africa, and back. *New York Times,* p. 36.

Pinkney, A. (1993). *Black Americans.* Englewood Cliffs, NJ: Prentice Hall.

Richey, C. M. (1998). *Images of color, images of crime: Readings.* Los Angeles: Roxbury Publishing Company.

Solomon, N. (1999). *The habits of highly deceptive media: Decoding spin and lies in mainstream news.* Monroe, MI: Common Courage Press.

Takaki, R. (1994). *From different shores: Perspectives on race and ethnicity in America.* Oxford, UK: Oxford University Press.

Tatum, B. D. (1997). *Assimilation blues. Black families in white communities: Who succeeds and why?* New York: Basic Books.

*Note that titles are italicized rather than underlined, and the letters of words that don't begin the title and aren't proper nouns are not capitalized.*

# Tips for Researching and Writing Papers on Literary Topics

Before I turned to English teaching as a profession, I had a background in science. I had written lots of research papers on science-related topics—lobsters, oak tree hybridization, environmental education—but felt totally unprepared to write a research paper on a book or a poem. What do you write *about?* I wondered. I paced back and forth all night before my first literature paper was due.

I know now—for a paper on any topic—not to waste time staring off into space and waiting for inspiration but to pick up my pen and simply start writing. I trust that I'll discover what I have to say. I also know that a paper on a literary topic isn't really so different from those papers I wrote for other classes. All good papers simply involve taking a close look at something, whether it's the mating habits of a fly or an essay by George Orwell.

## Mine the Primary Source

What distinguishes a paper on a literary topic from others is where most of information—the details—come from. When I wrote the book on lobsters, that information came largely from interviews and a variety of published sources. When I wrote about the manhood issues raised by the characters in two Wallace Stegner novels, most of that information came *from the novels.*

A research paper about a story, poem, essay, or novel will usually use that work more than any other source. Literary papers rely heavily on *primary sources.* In addition to the literary works, primary sources might also include letters or interviews by the author related to those works.

In "Breaking the 'Utter Silence,'" the remarkable personal-response essay that comes later in this appendix, Kazuko Kuramoto writes exclusively about a single primary source: an essay by George Orwell. But she also manages to weave in another text, as well: her own experiences in Manchuria during World War II. The danger in writing such autobiographical/critical responses is that the writer can easily leave the written text behind completely and concentrate on her own story. But Kazuko doesn't do that. She returns again and again to particular phrases and ideas in Orwell's essay, and then she examines how they illuminate her own experiences. If there's one general weakness in student papers on literature, it's that they don't mine the works enough. The writer should not stray too far from what's in the poem, story, novel, or essay she is writing about.

This emphasis on mining primary sources means that the research strategy for a literary paper is often a little different than that for other topics. First, remember that your most important reading will not be what you dig up in the library. It will be your reading of the work you're writing about. Be an activist reader. Mark up the book (unless it's a library copy, obviously) or the story, underlining passages that strike you in some way, perhaps because they seem to reach below the surface and hint at what you think the writer is trying to say. Use a journal. The double-entry notetaking method described in "The Third Week" (Chapter 3) is a great way to explore your reactions to your reading. Use fastwriting as a way to find out what you think after each reading of the work; explore your reaction, rather than staring off into space, trying to figure out what you want to write about.

How do you know what you think until you see what you say?

# Search Strategies

Though your close reading of the work you're writing about should be at the heart of your research, you can do other research, too. Most literary topics can be seen from several other basic angles. You can look at the *author* or what *critics* say about the author and his work. You may also discover that the author or work you're writing about fits into other recognized *categories* or *traditions*. In the most general sense, the work might be classified as British literature or American literature, but it also might fit into a subclass, such as African-American or feminist literature, or align with a particular regional school, like Southern writers. Each of these classifications is a subject by itself and will be included in reference sources.

Let's look at a few key library sources for a paper on a literary topic.

## Researching the Author

### Biographies

Frequently, research on a literary topic begins with exploration of the author. Biographical sources on authors abound. Here are a few key reference works, many of which are now available online at your campus library:

> *Authors' Biographies Index*. Detroit: Gale, 1984–present. A key source to 300,000 writers of every period.
>
> *Biography Index: A Cumulative Index to Biographical Material in Books and Magazines*. New York: Wilson, 1946–present. Remarkably extensive coverage. Includes biographies, as well as autobiographies, articles, letters, obituaries, and the like.
>
> *Contemporary Authors*. Detroit: Gale, 1962–present. Up-to-date information on authors from around the world; especially useful for obscure authors.

Other helpful sources by the Wilson company, the familiar publishers of the *Readers' Guide,* include the following: *American Authors, 1600–1900; British Authors before 1800; British Authors of the Nineteenth Century;* and *European Authors, 1000–1900.*

### Primary Bibliographies

It might be helpful to read additional works by the author you're researching. What else has he written? Biographies may tell you about other works, but they are often incomplete. For complete information, consult what's called a *primary bibliography,* or a bibliography *by* the author:

> *Bibliographic Index*. New York: Wilson, 1937–present. The "mother of all bibliographic indexes" lists works that have been published by and about the author.
>
> *Bibliography of Bibliographies in American Literature*. New York: Wilson, 1970. Works by and about American authors.
>
> *Index to British Literary Bibliography*. Oxford: Clarendon, 1969–present. Works by and about British authors.
>
> *American Fiction: A Contribution Toward a Bibliography*. San Marino: Huntington Library, 1957–present. Entries on 11,000 novels, stories, and so on, indexed by author.

## Researching the Critics

What do other people say about your author and the work you're writing about? A thorough look at criticism and reviews is an important step in most research papers on literary topics, especially after you've begun to get a sense of what *you* think. Support from critics can be important evidence to bolster your own claims, or it can further your own thinking in new ways.

Several useful reference sources have already been mentioned. For example, so-called *secondary bibliographies,* or bibliographies *about* individual authors, are listed in the *Bibliographic Index* mentioned earlier. Check that. The most important index to check for articles about your author or her work is the *MLA International Bibliography,* mentioned in "The Third Week" (Chapter 3). This source is commonly available on CD-ROM and online. Other helpful references include:

> *Contemporary Literary Criticism.* Detroit: Gale, 1973–present. Excerpts of criticism and reviews published in the last twenty-five years.
> *Magill's Bibliography of Literary Criticism.* Englewood Cliffs, NJ: Salem, 1979. Citations, not excerpts, of criticism of some 2,500 works.
> *Book Review Index.* Detroit: Gale, 1965–present. Citations for tens of thousands of book reviews, including many obscure works.
> *Current Book Review Citations.* New York: Wilson, 1976–present. Citations for reviews in about 1,200 publications.
> *New York Times Book Review Index, 1896–1970.* New York: Arno, 1973. Great for a more historical perspective on literary trends; features about 800,000 entries.

## Researching the Genre or Tradition

What type of work, or *genre,* are you researching? A novel? A poem? Might it fit into some recognized category or tradition?

Another angle on your topic is to place your work or author in the context of similar works and authors. One place to begin is with general survey books, such as *The Oxford Companion to American* or *English Literature.* Other references are surveys of period literature, such as *English Literature in the Sixteenth Century,* as well as world literature, such as *History of Spanish American Literature* and *World Literature Since 1945.*

Within each of these broad literary landscapes are some smaller ones, each with its own reference sources. For example, within the broad topic American literature, there's a growing list of references to African-American literature. For example, *Afro-American Literature:*

*The Reconstruction of Instruction* is a reference filled with essays on the place of African-American literature in literary history. Similarly, *American Indian: Language and Literature* lists 3,600 books and articles on American Indian literature and language.

Balay's *Guide to Reference Books* provides a helpful listing of sources that can help you place your topic in a larger context. But the best reference for research on a literary topic is this:

> Harner, James L. *Literary Research Guide.* 3rd ed. New York: MLA, 1998.

This amazing source reviews bibliographies, histories, indexes, surveys, and periodicals on every class and subclass of literature imaginable, from world literature to Chicano fiction. Buy the *Literary Research Guide* if you have to write a lot of papers on literature.

# Sample Essay: Personal Response

Reading imaginative literature can be a deeply personal experience. It should be. As you're reading a novel, poem, or essay, pay attention to what moves you. A character or idea that gets your attention is often the launching place for a good paper. Your emotional response is your way into the author's work.

The personal-response essay, sometimes called *personal criticism* or *autobiographical criticism,* is simply one of many ways of writing about literature. But it's often one of the most satisfying ways to explore what you think about what you've read, and it's certainly an approach that's consistent with the emphasis in this book on trying to merge the *personal* with the *scholarly.*

That's why I've chosen Kazuko Kuramoto's personal response as an inspiring model of what can be done when the writer tries to think autobiographically about what she's read. If you try this, I think you'll find it difficult to do well. You might also discover, as I suggest later, that the personal-response essay can be a draft for a more fully researched critical essay. (That might be what your instructor has in mind.) Even so, in their own right, autobiographical/critical essays can be informative and insightful responses to literature, as I think you'll see.

## "I Can Relate to It" Is Only a Start

Kazuko Kuramoto was an older woman in my Nonfiction Writing class. She was quiet, dignified, and quite lacking in confidence about her English language skills. Yet as you can see from the reading-response essay that follows, Kazuko writes elegantly about how a George Orwell essay on colonial Morocco in the 1930s challenges her to reexamine her own life as a girl in Imperial Japan during World War II. What is particularly effective about this essay is how Kazuko's autobiographical reflections are tied tightly to Orwell's text. She frequently uses phrases, quotations, and ideas from his essay as a means for understanding both her own experience *and* Orwell's. Kazuko is reading herself and Orwell's "Marrakech" simultaneously, and each illuminates the other.

The personal approach to writing about literature, then, is more than simply establishing that you can really relate to it, though that may be a start. As Kazuko demonstrates, personal criticism establishes an ongoing *conversation* with the text, interrogating it for ideas that shed light on personal experience, which then reflects back on the story or poem or essay, deepening or altering its meaning. This dialogue is not general or abstract; it is grounded in the specifics of the text and the specifics of the writer's experience.

Using the double-entry journal is one way to help get this conversation going (see Chapter 3). Another is *to read like a writer.* That means being a careful observer of your experience reading a literary text, especially those encounters with particular passages, scenes, characters, details, or ideas that make you wonder about yourself. Pay attention to things that lead you to the question, What does this say about me? In Kazuko's essay on "Marrakech," she discovers an answer to that question: Like Orwell, she once participated in the "utter silence" that is a precondition to imperialism.

"Breaking the 'Utter Silence' "* could be a draft for a more fully researched essay. Kazuko uses the primary text exclusively as a source in her response essay, though she also integrates the text of her own experience. Her essay could be further enriched in revision by using some of the biographical, bibliographic, and critical references already mentioned in this appendix. Where might further research be useful in this essay? What kinds of reference sources might Kazuko try?

(Note that Kazuko's paper follows MLA style—see Appendix A for more information.)

---

* "Breaking the 'Utter Silence': A Response to Orwell's 'Marrakech' " is reprinted with permission of Kazuko Kuramoto.

Kazuko Kuramoto

Professor Ballenger

English 201

29 February 1996

Breaking the "Utter Silence":

A Response to Orwell's "Marrakech"

In George Orwell's essay "Marrakech," which explores his experience as a British official in colonial Morocco, he does not argue his point with you. Orwell appeals to all your senses instead. As the essay opens, he takes you through the stench of a corpse that attracted the "cloud" (46) of flies from the restaurant. You follow a shabby funeral procession, breathing the smoldering air of the marketplace under the Moroccan sun--people and animals stained with sweat, souring fruits, and the dust of the traffic. You hear the wailing of a short chant "over and over again" (46). You see the mounds of a Moroccan graveyard with "no gravestone, no identifying mark of any kind, . . . like a derelict building-lot." Then you see "how easily they die," and how "they rise out of the earth, . . . sweat and starve for a few years, and . . . sink back into the nameless mounds of the graveyard" (46).

*Kazuko writes like Orwell: with rich detail. In this lead paragraph, the details come from Orwell's essay.*

Kuramoto 2

Then you understand and accept
Orwell's point quite readily that "all
colonial empires are in reality founded upon
that fact. . . . Are they really the same
flesh as you are? Do they even have names?
Or are they merely a kind of
undifferentiated brown stuff, as individual
as bees or coral insects?" (Orwell,
"Marrakech" 46). George Orwell does not argue
his point. He paints it. When the curtain
falls on this essay, you are left with
dazzling impressions.

*Here, Kazuko hints at her purpose: to face her own life as honestly as Orwell did in his essay.*

Of course, I admire George Orwell for
his skillful writing style: clear,
concrete, and without frills and
mannerisms. I dream of writing like George
Orwell someday. But more so, I admire his
honesty, his passion for truth, and his
"power of facing unpleasant facts" (qtd. in
Smart 34).

However painful or ugly it may be,
Orwell does not shy away from the truth.
In "Marrakech," he first describes an Arab
laborer, watching him feed a gazelle:
"Finally [the laborer] said shyly in French:
'I could eat some of that bread.'
I tore off a piece and he stowed it
gratefully in some secret place under his

Kuramoto 3

rags. This man is an employee of the
Municipality" (46). And then the Jews, who
live in the Jewish quarters that remind one of
medieval ghettoes; windowless houses, sore-
eyed children "in unbelievable numbers, like
clouds of flies," and the narrow street where
"there is generally running a little river of
urine" (47). Then he points out the irony of
the belief that the Jews are "the real rulers
of this country. . . . They've got all the
money. They control the banks, finance--
everything" (47). He compares this to the
burning of old women for witchcraft "when they
could not even work enough magic to get
themselves a square meal" (48). Indeed, he
does not hide behind "the utter silence that
is imposed on every Englishman in the East"
(Orwell, "Shooting" 35). He speaks up. He
shows the world the reality of imperialism.

I recognize the "utter silence." I am
a product of imperialism, a Japanese,
born and raised in Dairen, Manchuria,
when the area was one of Imperial
Japan's colonies. As the third
generation in Dairen, I was born into
the society of Japanese supremacy and
grew up believing in Japan's "divine
mission" to "save" Asia from the evil hands

*Parenthetical citations should show clearly what page(s) quoted materials come from.*

*Here, Kazuko shifts to autobiography. Does this seem awkward, or does she keep her narrative anchored to Orwell's essay?*

Kuramoto 4

of Western imperialists: British in India
and Hong Kong, French in Indo-China, and
Dutch in East Indies. Reading Orwell's essay
"Marrakech" brought back many memories that
I had long discarded, had preferred not to
remember.

The "utter silence" imposed on all
Japanese in Japanese colonies is one of
them. I did not recognize it then, but I do
now from remembering my father. My memory of
him is partly how he represented the
generation of Japanese who have kept their
"utter silence" to their graves. One
particular incident depicts the "utter
silence" clearly in my memory. It happened
one day in the spring of 1945 in a small
town at the border of the Japanese colony,
where my father was the head of the Japanese
government. My father and I visited the
town's Shinto shrine to dedicate one minute
of prayer for the war dead and also to pray
for Japan's victory, as required by
government. My father was a loyal Japanese.
On our way back, we saw a group of
Manchurian high school students. They were
marching in an orderly military column, as
required of all students at the time,
Japanese or Manchurians. As they came closer

Kuramoto 5

to us, the teacher, who was leading the column, recognized my father. Suddenly the teacher ordered his troop "Atten-tion!" followed by "Eye-e Right!" all in clear and loud Japanese. My father was astounded, to say the least. He quickly looked around to see if this formal military group salute was meant for him or someone nearby but saw no one. He straightened himself up and returned the salute, imitating military fashion as best as he could manage. I remained standing by him, dumbfounded.

"Wow, what a surprise . . ." I said, catching up to his suddenly quickened steps. I knew he was terribly embarrassed.

*Notice how dialogue speeds things up.*

"It's this uniform," he said somewhat curtly. He was wearing one of those government-ordered khaki "citizen's clothes" and the matching cap, closely resembling Japanese military uniform.

"Did that teacher take you for someone else, I wonder?" I said.

"No, he knows me."

"Oh, well, you are one of the highest-ranking people in town."

"I am only a civil servant," he cut me off short, almost angry.

Kuramoto 6

"Yeah, but . . ." I swallowed the rest of the sentence--but we are Japanese. . . .

Did I mean that Manchurians should salute all Japanese government officials just because they were Japanese? I now wonder, but I must have. The Japanese government in the Manchurian colony was the frontier symbol of Japan's international power, the power of "the Rising Sun." Why not? Salute to us. Salute to us all! Yet, on the other hand, I knew that the Japanese supremacy that my generation of Japanese in Dairen took for granted had always made my father uneasy. He had a reputation for being fair and considerate to his Manchurian subordinates and friends. He was well liked and respected among them, Japanese and Manchurians. He went out of his way to teach us children to treat local Chinese, the Manchurians, with respect, while he did not openly deny what we were taught at school: that Japanese were the almighty leaders of Asia.

We were the rulers, superior to all others--I had innocently believed it and had taken it for granted, while my father kept his "utter silence." Were we protected by the "utter silence" of the adults around us?

Kuramoto 7

Or were we deceived? Were the Manchurians simply invisible to the Japanese, as Orwell suggests was the case with the Moroccans to the Europeans?

It took Orwell several weeks before he noticed old women underneath the pile of firewood passing by, while he admits that "[he] had not been five minutes on Moroccan soil before [he] noticed the overloading of the donkeys and was infuriated by it" ("Marrakech" 49). Does he mean to say that had the old women been white, or better yet, British, he would have been infuriated? Orwell seems to blame the invisibility of the Moroccans on the color of their skin: "In a tropical landscape one's eye takes in everything except the human beings. . . . [I]t always misses the peasant hoeing at his patch. He is the same colour as the earth, and a great deal less interesting to look at." And again, ". . . But where the human beings have brown skins their poverty is simply not noticed" (48).

But this does not apply to the Japanese in colonial Dairen. Japanese and Chinese share the same skin color. Yet what Orwell says next is true of how it was with the Japanese in Dairen: "One could probably

Kuramoto 8

live here for years without noticing that
for nine-tenths of the people the reality
of life is an endless, back-breaking
struggle to wring a little food out of an
eroded soil" ("Marrakech" 48). We hardly
noticed the Chinese. We were taught to be
"nice and kind" to the native Chinese,
the Manchurians. Yet under the strict
segregation, we never had Chinese
neighbors or Chinese classmates. The native
Chinese were our domestic servants,
coolies, and peddlers, who lived in the
areas where ordinary Japanese did not even
think of going. They were invisible to us.
How did this happen among people with the
same skin color?

*Kazuko both complicates and extends the idea of invisibility in Orwell's essay.*

    When a country surrenders to another,
its people become one of the winner's
possessions, along with the land and
buildings, and they lose their individual
identity. They live in the shadow of the
ruthless oppressors. Invisible. And the rule
of the mask, "He wears a mask, and his face
grows to fit it" (Orwell, "Shooting" 38),
applies equally to both the oppressor and the
oppressed. They conspire with one another to
make imperialism possible. The oppressed
assume the role of the helpless and silent

Kuramoto 9

subjects, feeding the already dangerous hubris of the oppressor. And then, the "feeling of reverence before a white skin" (Orwell, "Marrakech" 50) existed among the colored, brown, yellow, or black, prostrating themselves before the Western power.

The white skin had represented the advancement of civilization for a long time, long enough to establish a superiority complex among the whites, an inferiority complex among the colored. Japan resisted it and became imperialist herself. She plunged into the world of "dog eats dog" when she awoke from the two hundred years of self-imposed national isolation. World War II in the Pacific stemmed from the fight among the imperialists: Western imperialists in the East against one small but refractory Eastern imperialist, Japan.

Orwell's "Marrakech" prodded me to think through my long-pending question: What is the imperialism that has toppled my life? I was possessed by Orwell's passion for truth, his power of "facing unpleasant facts," and read the essay with very personal interest. And now, perhaps, I not only recognize the "utter silence" of Orwell's imperialism but have found the courage to speak.

Kuramoto 10

Works Cited

Smart, William. <u>Eight Modern Essayists</u>.

      6th ed. New York: St. Martin's, 1995.

"George Orwell." Smart 31–34.

Orwell, George. "Marrakech." Smart 45–50.

---."Shooting an Elephant." Smart 35–41.

*To simplify the "Works Cited" when documenting*
*several selections from an anthology or reader,*
*first list the complete citation for the book; then*
*list the individual selections you've drawn from it.*
*For those selections, list the author, title, name of*
*the editor(s) of the reader, and page numbers.*

# Index

Boldface numbers indicate pages with illustrations.